D1598530

The Mediaeval Academy of America
Publication No. 86

The Friars and German Society in the Thirteenth Century

The Friars and German Society
in the Thirteenth Century

John B. Freed
Illinois State University

THE MEDIAEVAL ACADEMY OF AMERICA
Cambridge, Massachusetts   1977

0260045 .

091119

The publication of this book was made possible by grants of funds to the Mediaeval Academy from the Carnegie Corporation of New York.

Copyright © 1977
By The Mediaeval Academy of America
Library of Congress Catalog Card Number: 75–36480
ISBN 910956–60–X
Composition by Man+Tech Services, Inc., Mansfield, Massachusetts
Printed in the United States of America

For My Parents

Contents

0260045

091119

CONTENTS

Part II
SOCIAL AND POLITICAL ASPECTS
OF THE FRIARS' MINISTRY

List of Maps

List of Tables

Acknowledgments

It is only fitting that I acknowledge the assistance which I have received from various individuals and institutions. First of all, I should like to thank those individuals who have read various drafts of the manuscript of this book: Professors Brian Tierney of Cornell, Robert E. Lerner of Northwestern, Rhiman Rotz of Indiana University Northwest, and my colleagues, Lawrence Walker and David MacDonald. Their criticism was often incisive and always appreciated. I would also like to thank Professors Felix Gilbert of the Institute for Advanced Study, Gaines Post of Princeton, and Roy Austensen of Illinois State University for their suggestions and encouragement and Mr. Geoffrey Naylor, who edited several of my Latin translations. A word of thanks is also in order to Luke H. Wenger, the Deputy Executive Secretary of the Mediaeval Academy of America, for his assistance in preparing the manuscript for publication. I deeply regret that Professor Dr. Herbert Grundmann, the president of the *Monumenta Germaniae historica*, died before I was able to complete my work. He patiently answered my numerous inquiries while I was a graduate student in Munich in 1967–1968 and even placed his own office at my disposal. I am especially indebted to Professor Joseph R. Strayer, my thesis adviser, who guided my research from its earliest stages until its completion. Only those individuals who have had the good fortune to be numbered among Professor Strayer's students can fully appreciate his kindness and wisdom.

I am deeply grateful to the Woodrow Wilson Foundation and the Department of History at Princeton, whose generosity financed four years of graduate study in this country and Germany. In addition the Princeton History Department provided me during the spring of 1972 with a Shelby Cullom Davis Postdoctoral Fellowship, which enabled me to prepare my dissertation for publication. I am also indebted to Illinois State University which gave me several research grants to continue my investigations. Finally, I would like to thank the staffs of the following libraries and archives for their assistance: the Bayerische Staatsbibliothek and the *Monumenta Germaniae historica*, both in Munich; Firestone Library, Princeton; Milner Library, Illinois State University; New York Public Library; the Stadtarchiv von Köln; and the Universitätsbibliothek, Düsseldorf. Words cannot express the debt which I owe my parents.

Normal, Illinois
September 1975

Abbreviations

AbhbayAk	*Abhandlungen der historischen Classe der königlichen bayerischen Akademie der Wissenschaften*
AF	Analecta Franciscana
AFA	*Alemania Franciscana antiqua*
AFH	*Archivum Franciscanum historicum*
AFP	*Archivum fratrum Praedicatorum*
AHR	*American Historical Review*
Annales	*Annales: Economies, Sociétés, Civilisations*
AnnHVNiederrh	*Annalen des historischen Vereins für den Niederrhein*
BFA	*Bavaria Franciscana antiqua*
BGSFHK	*Beiträge zur Geschichte der sächsischen Franziskanerprovinz vom Heiligen Kreuze*
BLVSt	*Bibliothek des literarischen Vereins in Stuttgart*
DHIHFP	Dissertationes historicae Instituti historici fratrum Praedicatorum
Ergh.	Ergänzungsheft
FS	*Franziskanische Studien*
GQProvSachs	Geschichtsquellen der Provinz Sachsen
HJb	*Historisches Jahrbuch*
HZ	*Historische Zeitschrift*
MfJb	*Mainfränkisches Jahrbuch für Geschichte und Kunst*
MGH	Monumenta Germaniae historica
MGH Epis. saec. XIII	Monumenta Germaniae historicae, Epistolae saeculi XIII e regestis Pontificum Romanorum
MGH Schriften	Schriften der Monumenta Germaniae historica
MGH SRG	Monumenta Germaniae historica, Scriptores rerum Germanicarum in usum scholarum
MGH SS	Monumenta Germaniae historica, Scriptores

MIÖG	*Mitteilungen des Instituts für österreichische Geschichtsforschung*
MOPH	Monumenta ordinis fratrum Praedicatorum
MWdGFk	*Mitteilungen der westdeutschen Gesellschaft für Familienkunde*
NF	Neue Folge
PGRhGk	Publikationen der Gesellschaft für rheinische Geschichtskunde
PPrStA	Publikationen aus den k. preussischen Staatsarchiven
QDGNSachs	Quellen und Darstellungen zur Geschichte Niedersachsens
QFGDD	Quellen und Forschungen zur Geschichte des Dominikanerordens in Deutschland
RHE	*Revue d'histoire ecclésiastique*
UB	Urkundenbuch
UBHistVerNSachs	Urkundenbuch des historischen Vereins für Niedersachsen
WürttGQ	Württembergische Geschichtsquellen
WZ	*Westdeutsche Zeitschrift für Geschichte und Kunst*
Z	Zeitschrift
ZGORh	*Zeitschrift für Geschichte des Oberrheins*
ZKiG	*Zeitschrift für Kirchengeschichte*

Introduction

The troops of Christ, rearmed at such great cost,
were struggling on behind the Holy Standard,
fearful, and few, and laggard, and half lost,
When the Emperor who reigns eternally—
of His own grace and not for their own merit—
took thought of his imperiled soldiery;
and, as you have heard say, He sent His bride
two champions by whose teachings and example
the scattered companies were reunified.
    Dante, *Paradiso*, Canto XII, vv. 37–45.[1]

DURING the Investiture Conflict the church assumed the task of reshaping earthly society according to Christian ideals. Until the Gregorian era the attitude of the western church toward the world had been ambivalent. It had seemed readily apparent in the chaotic early Middle Ages that Christ's kingdom and the existing temporal world order were not identical and that the Christian was merely a pilgrim in a foreign land. The Christian ideal, as exemplified by the Benedictine abbey, had been withdrawal from the world; Christian perfection could only be attained within the seclusion of the cloister.

Christian ethics consequently had barely affected lay morality. Although the church had left in theory the management of secular affairs to the laity, many bishops and abbots, most notably in Germany, had been preoccupied with the conduct of earthly government. These warrior prelates had frequently purchased their offices and had disregarded their vows of chastity. The Gregorians wished not only to extirpate such obvious abuses as simony and Nicolaitanism, but also to alter the structure of medieval society. They were convinced that a community of professing Christians should be a replica

---

1. *The Paradiso*, trans. John Ciardi (New York, 1970).

1

of the Heavenly City; the establishment of righteousness on earth would facilitate the conversion of souls. In a properly ordered Christian society the church would be freed from lay control; the laity, including kings, subordinated to the clergy, the mediators between God and man; and the clergy in turn subjected to the authority of the pope, the successor of St. Peter. The reformers attacked lay investiture itself as the most conspicuous symbol of the unholy organization of medieval society. Henceforth the church would no longer withdraw from the world, but would labor within the world for its redemption.[2]

To arouse popular enthusiasm for its revolutionary program, the Gregorian papacy supported the agitation of ascetic reformers, whose personal austerity had gained them numerous adherents.[3] Since the beginning of the eleventh century there had been a deepening ascetic current in western Europe, which manifested itself in both orthodox and heretical forms. The half-century before the accession of St. Leo IX (1049–1054), the founder of the reform papacy, had seen the appearance of a widespread eremitical movement in Italy, associated with Sts. Romuald, John Gualbert, and Peter Damian, and the simultaneous emergence throughout Europe of isolated heretical groups whose ascetic practices, heterodox beliefs, and harsh criticism of the Catholic Church were often derived from a too literal, and sometimes naive, interpretation of the New Testament.[4] Drawing upon this ascetic ground swell, the popular reformers created with papal approval a series of mass movements directed against simoniacal and Nicolaitan clerics whose ministrations were to be shunned by the faithful: the Vallombrosan agitation in Florence, the Milanese Patarines, the Hirsau reform movement in Swabia, and the wandering preachers of western France. The ascetic reformers were so successful in diverting popular piety into channels acceptable to the Gregorian papacy that heresy virtually disappeared from western Europe in the second half of the eleventh century.

2. R.F. Bennett in the introduction to his translation of Gerd Tellenbach's *Church, State and Christian Society at the Time of the Investiture Contest* (Oxford, 1940), pp. v–xvii.
3. Ernst Werner, *Pauperes Christi: Studien zu sozial-religiösen Bewegungen im Zeitalter des Reformpapsttums* (Leipzig, 1956), pp. 89–164.
4. Jeffrey Burton Russell, *Dissent and Reform in the Early Middle Ages* (Berkeley, 1965), pp. 18–42. A good collection of sources on heresy in eleventh-century Europe may be found in Walter L. Wakefield and Austin P. Evans, *Heresies of the High Middle Ages*, Records of Civilization: Sources and Studies 81 (New York, 1969), pp. 71–93.

Nevertheless, the alliance between the Gregorian papacy and the ascetic reformers was always uneasy. St. Peter Damian, the best known of the Italian ascetics, had already opposed in the first years of the reform papacy the policies of Cardinal Humbert of Silva-Candida, the theoretician of the extreme Gregorian program, and of Hildebrand, its prime executor.[5] Although the Gregorian papacy and the ascetics were united in their desire to raise the moral standards of the clergy, their ultimate goals were divergent. The members of the curia increasingly focused their attention on the development of a carefully, legally defined papal monarchism which was capable of providing the church and Europe with effective leadership. The ascetics yearned, on the other hand, for a return to the spiritual purity of the primitive church and idealized the poor, humble monk as the true Christian. The latent hostility between the ascetics and the curia came into the open in the 1120s and brought about the double papal election of 1130.[6]

The failure of the Gregorian effort to remake the world, as well as the religious excitement generated by the reform movement, inspired a vigorous renewal of the monastic impulse among the ascetic reformers.[7] The last years of the eleventh century and the first decades of the twelfth saw the rapid proliferation of new orders: the Augustinian canons, Carthusians, Victorines, Grandmontines, Fontevrists, Savignaics, Cistercians, and Premonstratensians. Within monasteries deliberately located in remote places, the monks sought to lead the apostolic life of poverty, humility, and obedience which they had been unable to impose upon the entire church. As the heirs of the Cluniac and Gregorian reform movements, they rejected the possession of entangling feudal dues and tithes and chose instead to work with their own hands. From his monastic retreat St. Bernard, the voice of the monastic resurgence, denounced the growing papal preoccupation with judicial and administrative business and urged his protégé Eugenius III to assume his rightful place as a holy and austere leader of the contemplative saints.[8] The monks thus abandoned the Gregorian effort to remake the world and became increasingly alienated from the society in which they lived.

5. Fridolin Dressler, *Petrus Damiani: Leben und Werk*, Studia Anselmiana 34 (Rome, 1954), pp. 86–174.
6. Hayden V. White, "The Gregorian Ideal and Saint Bernard of Clairvaux," *Journal of the History of Ideas* 21 (1960), 324–335.
7. Norman F. Cantor, "The Crisis of Western Monasticism, 1050–1130," *AHR* 66 (1960), 65–67; Herbert Grundmann, *Religiöse Bewegungen im Mittelalter*, 2nd ed. (Darmstadt, 1961), pp. 488–493.
8. White, "The Gregorian Ideal," pp. 341–348.

Yet the concept of the apostolic life which the monks sought to imitate within the monasteries had itself been changed during the upheavals of the Investiture Conflict. For centuries the essence of the apostolic life had been perceived as communal living in accordance with the description in Acts 4.32 of the common possession of property in the early church. The monk sought to subject his will to the control of the community. The sons of proud warriors especially esteemed humility and obedience. The Benedictine Rule was considered to be only the precise formulation of customs which had been initiated by the apostles. The revival of the strict observance of the Benedictine Rule, which characterized the new monastic foundations of the Gregorian epoch, was thus widely viewed as a return to the standards of the primitive church.[9]

It is possible to discern in the eleventh century, however, most notably in the writings of St. Peter Damian, a new emphasis upon the humanity of Christ, which manifested itself more concretely in the adoration of the Virgin and in pilgrimages to the Holy Land which had been sanctified by His earthly presence.[10] Such journeys helped to make men aware that Jesus and the apostles had not lived in wealthy monasteries, but had been poor wandering preachers, actively engaged in propagating the Gospel. There was consequently a growing desire to imitate the life style of Jesus and the disciples, as portrayed in such passages as Luke 10.1–16. The vital essence of the apostolic life was suddenly perceived to be poverty and preaching rather than communal living and contemplation. The Gospels thus started to replace the Benedictine Rule as the yardstick for measuring the Christian life.

The new religious ideal fully emerged for the first time at the turn of the century in the activities of the French wandering preacher Robert of Arbrissel and his disciples and imitators, Bernard of Thiron, Vitalis of Savigny, and Norbert of Xanten.[11] The wandering preachers could adhere to a far more radical form of poverty than the monks. The contemplative, communal life

9. M.-D. Chenu, "Moines, clercs, laics au carrefour de la vie évangélique (XII. s.)," *RHE* 49 (1954), 59–89; Tadeusz Manteuffel, *Naissance d'une hérésie: Les Adeptes de la pauvreté volontaire au moyen âge*, trans. Anna Posner (Paris, 1970), pp. 11–38; André Vauchez, "La Pauvreté volontaire au moyen âge," *Annales* 25 (1970), 1566–1573.
10. C.N.L. Brooke, "Heresy and Religious Sentiment: 1000–1250," *Bulletin of the Institute of Historical Research* 41 (1968), 125–127.
11. For further information, see Johannes von Walter, *Die ersten Wanderprediger Frankreichs: Studien zur Geschichte des Mönchtums. Theil 1., Robert von Arbrissel*, Studien zur Geschichte der Theologie und der Kirche 9 (Leipzig, 1903); Neue Folge (Leipzig, 1906).

of the monks required that the monastery have at least a small endowment to provide for its cloistered inmates' material needs; the wandering preacher could rely solely, as Jesus had commanded, upon the charity of his listeners and upon the goodness of God.[12] In this redefinition of the apostolic life poverty often replaced humility as the highest virtue and avarice pride as the chief vice.[13] The Gregorian program for restructuring earthly society had been subtly changed into a summons to reshape men's lives in accordance with the example and commands of Christ.

While the ecclesiastical authorities could allow, though often with misgivings, a few ardent monks and clerics to undertake an active public ministry, they could not permit the numerous men and women whom the wandering preachers attracted to copy the example of their leaders.[14] The twelfth-century church firmly believed that the job of preaching had been assigned by Christ to bishops and to parish priests and perhaps to a few exceptionally qualified and licensed individuals. A large-scale apostolate undertaken by unauthorized individuals, let alone by lay men and women, entailed in the opinion of suspicious diocesan officials the complete collapse of all ecclesiastical discipline and the destruction of the divinely ordained constitution of the church. The dividing line between orthodox and heretical wandering preachers thus became their willingness to organize their followers into cloistered congregations. St. Norbert never intended, for instance, that the canons of Prémontré should imitate his own example.[15]

But the words of Jesus and the example of the disciples could not be so easily forgotten. Some of the wandering preachers rejected any attempt to substitute ecclesiastical authority or tradition for the seemingly clear dictates of the Gospels.[16] Convinced that the Gospels provided the only infallible guide for leading the Christian life, these practitioners of evangelical perfection continued their distinctive way of life in defiance of the authorities and regarded themselves as the only true Christians. Henry of Lausanne, Tanchelm, Peter of Bruys, and Arnold of Brescia, the best known of these early-twelfth-century exponents of the apostolic life, vigorously criticized the

---

12. Bernard Bligny, "Les Premiers Chartreux et la pauvreté," *Le Moyen âge* 57 (1951), 51–60, stresses this point in his discussion of the Carthusian concept of poverty.
13. Lester K. Little, "Social Changes and the Vices in Latin Christendom," *AHR* 76 (1971), 16–49.
14. Grundmann, *Religiöse Bewegungen*, pp. 38–50.
15. Charles Dereine, "Les Origines de Prémontré," *RHE* 42 (1947), 371–377.
16. Grundmann, *Religiöse Bewegungen*, pp. 513–519; Manteuffel, *Naissance*, pp. 39–56.

personal conduct of the Catholic clergy and made the moral worthiness of the bishop or priest, rather than his official legal position, the decisive factor in determining the validity of his sacramental acts. The Gregorian campaign tactic in the struggle against simoniacal and Nicolaitan clerics was thus turned against the Catholic Church. On the basis of a literal interpretation of the New Testament, these twelfth-century reformers rejected those Catholic doctrines or practices, such as the belief in purgatory, infant baptism, or the veneration of the cross, whose truth could not be readily proven from the Bible. As evangelical Christians they did not deny the basic tenets of the Christian faith, such as the doctrines of the Incarnation and Atonement.[17] The outraged ecclesiastical authorities naturally condemned these outspoken, disobedient critics as heretics. After the virtual disappearance of any trace of heterodox belief in western Europe during the second half of the eleventh century, heresy reappeared as the Gregorian reform effort slowly waned.

Although these heretics questioned many specific Catholic doctrines, their basic quarrel with the church concerned their life style rather than dogma. Their extreme asceticism provided, however, fertile ground for the reception of Balkan dualist heresies which challenged the basic metaphysical assumptions of Christianity. Bogomilism, a tenth-century Bulgarian offshoot of the ancient Gnostic tradition, taught a mitigated dualism, which claimed that Satan, the creator of the evil, material world, was the fallen son of God. The belief in two antagonistic cosmic forces, one spiritual and good and the other material and evil, logically led to the rejection of the Creator-God of the Old Testament, the denial of the humanity of Christ and his redemptive death, and the negation of the material world and all its pleasures. The Bogomil attitude toward the material world, an extreme form of the traditional Christian rejection of the world, was thus diametrically opposed to the Gregorian acceptance of earthly society as an appropriate arena for Christian endeavor.[18]

But the complex theology and cosmogony of the Bogomils had little appeal, at least initially, to western Europeans. They were attracted instead by

17. Russell, *Dissent*, pp. 54–100, provides an introduction to the various early, twelfth-century heresies. The relevant sources may be found in Wakefield and Evans, *Heresies*, pp. 95–150. For further bibliographical information, consult the notes and bibliographies in both books.

18. For further information about the Balkan dualist heresies, see Dmitri Obolensky, *The Bogomils: A Study in Balkan Neo-Manichaeism* (Cambridge, England, 1948); and Henri-Charles Puech and André Vaillant, *Le Traité contre les Bogomiles de Cosmas le Prêtre*, Travaux publiés par l'Institut d'études slaves 21 (Paris, 1945).

the puritanism of the dualists, who practiced self-denial to escape the bonds of the evil, material world. Catharism, which made its first definite appearance in western Europe in Cologne in 1143, developed from the union of the western ascetic, evangelical tradition and Balkan theology.[19] Mission activity by members of the Dragovitsan sect, who taught the complete equality and coeternity of God and Satan, resulted in the conversion of the French Cathars and many of the Italian heretics to absolute dualism in the 1160s.[20] By the end of the century the Cathars were firmly entrenched in northern Italy and above all in Languedoc.

At the same time the desire to imitate the apostles' lives, as portrayed in the Gospels, continued to attract devout individuals. The summons to evangelical perfection struck a responsive chord in the hearts of northern European women, particularly in the Low Countries.[21] James of Vitry, a sympathetic observer and patron of the new religious ideal, described the devout women of Brabant in these words:

> You have seen (and you have rejoiced) in the gardens of the Lord great crowds of holy women in diverse places who, despising fleshly charms for Christ and likewise scorning the riches of this world for the love of the heavenly kingdom, cleaving in poverty and humility to their divine husband, are seeking by the labor of their hands their meager nourishment although their relatives abound in great wealth. They, nevertheless, forgetting their people and the home of their father, preferred to endure

---

19. Russell, *Dissent*, pp. 215–217; Arno Borst, *Die Katharer*, MGH Schriften 12 (Stuttgart, 1953), pp. 88–98 and 229–230. There has been considerable controversy about the origins of the Cathar heresy in western Europe. Antoine Dondaine contended in "L'Origine de l'hérésie médiévale," *Rivista di storia della chiesa in Italia* 6 (1952), 47–78, that Bogomil teachings had already reached and infected western Europe in the first half of the eleventh century. Raffaelo Morghen in such works as "Problèmes sur l'origine de l'hérésie au moyen âge," *Revue historique* 236 (1966), 1–16, denied that the Bogomils provided any outside stimulus for the development of dualist beliefs in western Europe, which he saw as primarily moral in character and caused by far-reaching economic changes which took place in Europe in the eleventh century. After carefully examining the evidence, Henri-Charles Puech, "Catharisme médiéval et Bogomilisme," *Oriente ed occidente nel medio evo*, Accademia nazionale dei Lincei, Fondazione Alessandrio Volta 12 (Rome, 1957), pp. 56–84; Russell, *Dissent*, pp. 188–229, and "Interpretations of the Origins of Medieval Heresy," *Mediaeval Studies* 25 (1963), 26–53; and R. I. Moore, "The Origins of Medieval Heresy," *History* 55 (1970), 21–36, have concluded that while the evidence is far from clear, Bogomilism seems only to have penetrated the existing, western European, ascetic reform tradition in the mid-twelfth century.
20. Antoine Dondaine, "La Hiérarchie cathare en Italie: Le 'Tractatus de hereticis' d'Anselme d'Alexandrie, O.P.," *AFP* 20 (1950), 234–277.
21. Grundmann, *Religiöse Bewegungen*, pp. 170–198.

indigence and poverty rather than to abound in wealth wrongly acquired or to stay with danger among the proud men of this world.[22]

A similar impulse inspired the Lyonese merchant Waldes in 1176 to distribute his money to the poor. An orthodox Catholic deeply disturbed by the spread of Catharism, Waldes hoped to check its expansion by his own evangelical preaching and example. While Pope Alexander III (1159–1181) was personally moved by Waldes's piety, the Third Lateran Council and the archbishop of Lyons were unwilling to authorize his lay apostolate. Waldes's insistence upon his divinely commanded obligation to preach in defiance of all prohibitions resulted in the excommunication of his followers, the Poor of Lyons, along with other heretical sects by Pope Lucius III (1181–1185) in 1184.[23]

The spectacular growth of heresy in twelfth-century Europe was closely linked to the urbanization which accompanied the commercial revolution of the high Middle Ages. While the first exponents of the apostolic life were often, like St. Norbert, clerics of aristocratic background, and while the ideal always attracted individuals of rural origin,[24] the search for evangelical perfection was most eagerly pursued in the most economically advanced and urbanized areas: northern Italy, southern France, Flanders-Brabant, and the lower Rhine Valley.[25] As James of Vitry's description of the pious women of Brabant and the career of Waldes suggest, the beneficiaries of the rapid economic advance of the eleventh and twelfth centuries most acutely perceived the contrast between the ideal set forth in the Gospels and their own comfortable lives. The alleged words of Waldes as he distributed his wealth to the poor provide an insight into the inner anguish such sensitive individuals endured:

> No man can serve two masters, God and mammon. . . . My friends and fellow townsmen! Indeed, I am not, as you think, insane, but I have taken vengeance on my enemies who held me in bondage to them, so that I was always more anxious about money than about God and served the crea-

22. *Vita B. Mariae Ogniacensis* (Antwerp, 1717), Acta sanctorum Junii 4:636. The translation is my own.
23. Antoine Dondaine, "Aux origines du Valdéisme: Une profession de foi de Valdès," *AFP* 16 (1946), 191–235; Kurt-Victor Selge, *Die ersten Waldenser mit Edition des Liber antiheresis des Durandus von Osca*, 2 vols. (Berlin, 1967), 1:227–259.
24. See, for instance, Eva Gertrud Neumann, *Rheinisches Beginen- und Begardenwesen: Ein mainzer Beitrag zur religiösen Bewegung am Rhein*, Mainzer Abhandlungen zur mittleren und neueren Geschichte 4 (Meisenheim am Glan, 1960), pp. 60–71.
25. Grundmann, *Religiöse Bewegungen*, pp. 519–524.

ture more than the Creator. I know that a great many find fault with me
for having done this publicly. But I did it for myself and also for you: for
myself, so that they who may henceforth see me in possession of money
may think I am mad; in part also for you, so that you may learn to fix
your hope in God and to trust not in riches.[26]

This psychic tension was inevitably most strongly felt in the cities, the centers of the economic revival.

Unfortunately, the twelfth-century church neglected the cities. The prelates, who were usually recruited from the ranks of the feudal aristocracy,
were naturally suspicious of the new urban culture. They were not personally inclined either to adapt Christian theology and morality, which had largely
been formulated in opposition to the decadent, urban culture of the Roman
Empire, or to expand the parochial structure, which had been erected during
the agrarian early Middle Ages, to meet the spiritual needs of the townspeople.[27] The church's long opposition to the charging of interest, an understandable and commendable prohibition in the subsistence economy of
earlier centuries, is perhaps the best-known example of the church's attitude.
With the exception of the Augustinian canons, who made a halfhearted effort
to minister to the spiritual needs of the burghers,[28] the new orders which
arose in the twelfth century deliberately located their houses in isolated spots
and ignored the towns. The church's neglect of the cities thus provided the
wandering, evangelical preachers and dualist heretics with an appreciative
audience among the urban population. The church was destined to face a
similar problem in the nineteenth century when industrialization transformed
the structure and values of traditional western society.

Innocent III (1198–1216), under whose tutelage the medieval church
reached the height of her temporal power, took the first effective measures
to resolve the religious crisis. His predecessors had limited their actions to the
condemnation of various heretical sects and the formulation of precise legal
procedures for the detection and punishment of heretics. Most notably, in the
constitution *Ad abolendam* in 1184 Lucius III had proscribed the Cathars,
the Humiliati, the Poor of Lyons, and other heretical sects, and had promul-

26. Wakefield and Evans, *Heresies*, no. 30.
27. C.N.L. Brooke, "The Missionary at Home: The Church in the Towns, 1000–1250,"
    The Mission of the Church and the Propagation of the Faith, ed. G.J. Cuming,
    Papers Read at the Seventh Summer Meeting and the Eighth Winter Meeting of the
    Ecclesiastical History Society (Cambridge, England, 1970), pp. 65–67.
28. Richard William Southern, *Western Society and the Church in the Middle Ages*
    (Harmondsworth, England, 1970), pp. 241–250.

gated precise regulations for a systematic episcopal inquisition. Innocent continued and expanded this policy of repression. He urged his episcopal colleagues to proceed against the heretics; he sent Cistercian missions to Languedoc to root out heresy; he elaborated the anti-heretical legislation of his predecessors; he summoned the Fourth Lateran Council to deal with the problem; and he unleashed the Albigensian Crusade. These repressive measures laid the foundation for the papal inquisition.[29]

To his credit Innocent recognized that repression alone could not remove the heretical threat. He realized that the search for evangelical perfection represented a legitimate Christian aspiration which could not simply be suppressed; and he was prepared to differentiate between heretics, like the Waldenses and the Humiliati, who had quarreled with the church over discipline rather than dogma, and the Cathars, who adhered to an alien faith. He may also have perceived that fervent Christians like the Waldenses, who were conducting their own campaign against the Cathars,[30] might prove valuable allies in the struggle against the dualist heresy. Innocent tried, therefore, to incorporate the new religious ideal of evangelical perfection into the established church by approving the statutes of repentant Humiliati and Waldenses, who had submitted to Rome in exchange for a papal approbation of their distinctive life style.[31] By 1216 James of Vitry could report that the reconciled Humiliati had become the church's staunchest supporters in the heretic-ridden archdiocese of Milan.[32] But the most important result of the new papal policy was the establishment during Innocent's pontificate of the two great mendicant orders, the Dominicans and the Franciscans.

The Franciscans and Dominicans combined the wandering preachers' desire to imitate the life of Christ with the Gregorian program of reshaping earthly society. Whereas the Gregorians had concentrated upon the abolition of such abuses as simony, the liberation of the church from lay control, and

29. Grundmann, *Religiöse Bewegungen*, pp. 50–69; Jean Guiraud, *Histoire de l'Inquisition au moyen âge*, 2 vols. (Paris, 1935–1938), 1:365–419 and 2:413–434; Wakefield and Evans, *Heresies*, pp. 32–34.
30. For information about the Waldenses' struggle against the Cathars, see Antoine Dondaine, "Durand de Huesca et la polémique anti-cathare," *AFP* 29 (1959), 228–276; Selge, *Die ersten Waldenser*, 1:271–274 and vol. 2, *Der Liber antiheresis des Durandus von Osca*; Christine Thouzellier, *Catharisme et Valdéisme en Languedoc à la fin du XIIe et au début du XIIIe siècle*, 2nd ed. (Louvain, 1969).
31. Grundmann, *Religiöse Bewegungen*, pp. 70–127; Selge, *Die ersten Waldenser*, 1: 188–225.
32. R.B.C. Huygens, *Lettres de Jacques de Vitry (1160/1170–1240) évêque de Saint-Jean-d'Acre: Edition critique* (Leiden, 1960), no. 1, lines 47–61.

the establishment of an effective papal government of the church in their effort to remake the world, the friars in their first burst of enthusiasm attempted to impose the ethics of the Sermon of the Mount upon all of mankind. During the "Alleluia Year" in 1233 the friars actually succeeded, for instance, in making peace in the strife-torn cities of northern Italy. A world imbued with the spirit of the Gospel would indeed be a replica of the Heavenly City.

The friars regarded the towns as the most appropriate arena for Christian activity. It is very likely that Dominic's experiences in Languedoc and Francis's boyhood contacts with heretics in Assisi made the two saints particularly sensitive to the problems of the cities and may thus account for the original urban thrust of their orders. But while the friars initially rejected the commercial ethos of the towns, they gradually adopted many of the business tactics, oratorical skills, and values of the merchants, lawyers, and notaries in their own preaching techniques and spirituality. In the end, both through their presence in the cities and their reformulation of Christian theology and ethics in the universities and in the confessional, they sanctified medieval urban life.[33] Humbert of Romans, St. Bonaventure, and Berthold of Regensburg explained why the friars had selected cities as the sites for their convents. The Dominican master general pointed out that the prophets and apostles, as well as Christ himself, had labored most frequently in cities. He contended, furthermore, that the densely populated cities were the natural centers of civilization which exerted an enormous influence for good or evil on the surrounding countryside; any attempt to save souls had to begin in the towns.[34] St. Bonaventure argued that the city was the place where the friars could best perform their pastoral responsibilities because it provided them with the material sustenance they required to pursue their distinctive life style and because it offered greater protection than the countryside for the friars' books and valuable liturgical vessels and garments.[35] While Berthold denounced cities in his "Sermo de civitatibus" as centers of iniquity in which few burghers attained salvation, he reminded his hearers that God would have spared Sodom if he had discovered ten just men living within its walls. The Franciscan preacher counseled anxious townspeople to seek the company of

---

33. Barbara H. Rosenwein and Lester K. Little, "Social Meaning in the Monastic and Mendicant Spiritualities," *Past and Present* 63 (May 1974), 20–32.
34. Cited by Jacques le Goff, "Ordres mendiants et urbanisation dans la France médiévale: État de l'enquête," *Annales* 25 (1970), 929–930.
35. *Determinationes quaestionum circa regulam fratrum Minorum*, Opera omnia 8 (Quaracchi, 1898), 13:340–341.

such pious individuals.[36] He presumably considered the Franciscans to be the saving remnant within the medieval Sodoms.

There was, nevertheless, a distinct difference in the original mission of the two orders. St. Francis and his companions intended, as Pope Honorius III (1216–1227) explained in his 1218 bull *Cum dilecti filii*, to sow the word of God throughout the world by imitating the lives of the apostles.[37] The Franciscans were merely required, in other words, to set an example of Christian ethics in action in the midst of earthly society. Their lives were to be the fruit which proved in spite of the heretics' aspersions that the Holy Spirit still infused the Catholic Church. The Dominicans, on the other hand, were expected to take an active role in the battle against heresy. According to Honorius's 1220 bull, *Quoniam abundavit iniquitas*, the Dominicans had dedicated themselves to extirpate heresy by preaching the Gospel to the deceived masses; they had adopted voluntary poverty to give added credence to their words.[38] However, this difference in purpose gradually disappeared in the course of the thirteenth century with the transformation of the Franciscans into an order of learned clerics modeled after the Dominicans. Between them the two orders of friars did revitalize the church, and Dante's praise of Sts. Francis and Dominic, quoted at the start, is fully merited.

The success of the friars' counteroffensive against heresy unfortunately blinded historians in the nineteenth and early twentieth centuries to the basic similarity between the friars and heretics. Catholic scholars like the Capuchin Gratien[39] and the Dominican R.P. Mortier[40] stressed the friars' services to the church, while Protestant historians like Charles Henry Lea[41] and Austin P. Evans[42] emphasized the social as well as the religious causes of the here-

---

36. Anton E. Schönbach, "Studien zur Geschichte der altdeutschen Predigt. Sechstes Stück. Die Überlieferung der Werke Bertholds von Regensburg. III.," *Sitzungsberichte der kaiserlichen Akademie der Wissenschaften in Wien, Philosophisch-historische Klasse* 153 (1906), 159.
37. Ferdinand M. Delorme, "La Bonne Date de la bulle 'Cum dilecti' d'Honorius III," *AFH* 12 (1919), 591–593.
38. *Bullarium ordinis FF. Praedicatorum*, ed. Antonino Bremond (Rome, 1729), 1:11, no. 18.
39. *Histoire de la fondation et de l'évolution de l'ordre des frères Mineurs au XIII siècle* (Paris, 1928).
40. *Histoire des maîtres généraux de l'ordre des frères Prêcheurs*, 2 vols. (Paris, 1903–1905).
41. *A History of the Inquisition of the Middle Ages*, 3 vols. (New York, 1888).
42. "Social Aspects of Medieval Heresy," *Persecution and Liberty: Essays in Honor of George Lincoln Burr* (New York, 1931), pp. 93–116.

tics' opposition to the corrupt church. In such accounts the friars and the heretics only met at the inquisitor's rack. It was the great contribution of Herbert Grundmann's magisterial work, *Religiöse Bewegungen im Mittelalter* (1st ed., Berlin, 1935), to demonstrate the friars' and the heretics' common commitment to the ideal of evangelical perfection. It was this spiritual affinity which made the friars such valuable instruments in the papal response to the heretical challenge.

Grundmann's examination of the connections between the successive religious waves in the twelfth and thirteenth centuries has formed the basic analytical framework of most subsequent studies of the religious life of the high Middle Ages.[43] Nevertheless, it cannot be said that his insights have been fully utilized in more recent works about the mendicant orders. Scholarly interest in the friars has generally been confined to four basic topics: the lives and intentions of the founders, the constitutional and institutional development of the two orders, the friars' intellectual contributions, and the history of individual convents. There has been surprisingly little effort to investigate the social origins of the friars and the social and political background in which they labored.[44] The information for such a study, e.g., the location and foundation dates of the individual convents, has first to be collected; and much of the present monograph is concerned with this task. Taking as its scope the area of Germany and the early years of the friars' ministry from 1217 to 1273, this book compiles the available data about the foundation of the mendicant convents and about individual friars and their patrons, data which is then used to discuss three aspects of mendicant expansion in the context of thirteenth-century German history: the connection between urbanization and the spread of the mendicant orders, the social origins of the friars, and the effect of imperial and urban politics upon the Franciscans and Dominicans.

43. See, for instance, Ernest W. McDonnell, *The Beguines and Beghards in Medieval Culture: With Special Emphasis on the Belgian Scene* (New Brunswick, New Jersey, 1954); and Simone Roisin, "L'Efflorescence cistercienne et le courant féminin de piété au XIIIe siècle," *RHE* 39 (1943), 342–378.

44. There have of course been some exceptions, most notably, Bernhard Stüdeli's *Minoritenniederlassungen und mittelalterliche Stadt: Beiträge zur Bedeutung von Minoriten- und anderen Mendikantenanlagen im öffentlichen Leben der mittelalterlichen Stadtgemeinde, insbesondere der deutschen Schweiz*, Franziskanische Forschungen 21 (Werl/Westf., 1969), pp. 68–79. I received Williell R. Thomson's study of the social origins and careers of the Franciscan friar-bishops, *Friars in the Cathedral: The First Franciscan Bishops 1226–1261*, Pontifical Institute of Mediaeval Studies, Studies and Texts 33 (Toronto, 1975), too late for inclusion in this book.

The unsuccessful Franciscan mission to Germany in 1217 marks the logical starting point for such a study. There are several reasons for selecting 1273, the end of the Interregnum, as the terminal date. By the 1270s the friars were well established in Germany and in Europe, and a new era was beginning in mendicant history. Many of the great leaders who had guided the friars after the deaths of Sts. Francis and Dominic and who had brought the orders to the height of their prestige and influence died in the 1270s. Berthold of Regensburg, the greatest German mendicant preacher, and his lifelong companion, David of Augsburg, died in 1272; Sts. Thomas Aquinas and Bonaventure in 1274; St. Raymond of Peñafort, the third master general of the Dominicans (1238–1240), in 1275; the Bl. Humbert of Romans, the fifth general of the Dominicans (1254–1263), in 1277; and St. Albertus Magnus in 1280. Clearly a generation was passing from the scene. The 1274 decree of the Second Council of Lyons, *Religionum diversitatem*, which disbanded the mendicant orders formed after the Fourth Lateran Council, likewise marked a distinct shift in papal policy toward the friars. It heralded the end of the proliferation of new mendicant orders and left the well-entrenched Dominicans and Franciscans as the two major mendicant orders.[45] Finally, significant changes took place after the 1270s in both orders. After the death of St. Bonaventure, the Franciscans were torn asunder by the tragic dispute between the Spirituals and Conventuals. Many of the German Dominicans were increasingly attracted by mysticism toward the end of the century. Although Dominican mysticism played an important part in the development of the German language and philosophy, the mystics' emphasis on contemplation represented at least a partial denial of the friars' primary mission of living within the world. While it will be necessary to discuss various incidents which occurred after 1273, it seems appropriate to concentrate a study of the formative period in German mendicant history on the period prior to Rudolph of Habsburg's accession.

Germany, a rather amorphous entity in the thirteenth century, will be defined in the friars' own terms, i.e., as the area which was covered by the thirteenth-century Dominican province of Teutonia[46] and by the Franciscan

---

45. Richard W. Emery, "The Second Council of Lyons and the Mendicant Orders," *The Catholic Historical Review* 39 (1953), 257–271.

46. The province of Teutonia was divided in 1303, after the discovery of numerous abuses, into two new provinces, Teutonia and Saxony. *Acta capitulorum generalium ordinis Praedicatorum*, ed. Benedictus Maria Reichert, MOPH 3 (Rome, 1898), 1:298, 304, 306–309, 313–314, and 319. Unless otherwise stated, all references are to the undivided province of Teutonia.

provinces of Saxony, Cologne, Strasbourg, and Austria. These mendicant provinces included convents located in twelve modern European nations: Germany, the Netherlands, Belgium, Luxembourg, France, Switzerland, Italy, Austria, Yugoslavia, Czechoslovakia, Poland, and Russia. There are two reasons for accepting this definition of the frontiers of medieval Germany. Thirteenth-century rulers in border areas often forced the friars to assign a convent to a particular province. The boundaries of the mendicant provinces thus reveal the political allegiances and predilections of various temporal rulers in sensitive border areas. The friars were, moreover, in close contact with the populace among whom they labored; and they were consequently well-informed about cultural and linguistic differences. The friars adjusted their provincial boundaries on several occasions to conform more closely to ethnic and political changes. In a very real sense the borders of the mendicant provinces delineate thirteenth-century Germany more accurately than any other device.[47]

The amorphous character of Germany's frontiers over the centuries poses a special problem to scholars. Numerous mendicant convents were situated in towns which are known by a variety of names in different languages. It has been my general policy to use the present-day name of cities, e.g., Strasbourg and Aachen rather than Strassburg and Aix-la-Chapelle, unless the city is better known to English-speaking readers under a different name, e.g., Cologne rather than Köln. Since English-speaking medievalists are probably more familiar with the German names of cities in eastern Europe, I have used the German names of formerly German cities in Poland and Russia, e.g., Breslau rather than Wrocław. The German forms are also more appropriate in the context of a discussion about medieval German, eastward expansion. The present-day names have been placed in parentheses in the tables and in Appendix I. But there is, quite frankly, no ideal solution to this particular problem.

Part One of the book is a response to Jacques le Goff's summons to medievalists to examine the correlation between the degree and date of urbanization and the expansion of the mendicant orders.[48] An accurate and complete

---

47. John B. Freed, "The Friars and the Delineation of State Boundaries in the Thirteenth Century," *Order and Innovation in the Middle Ages: Essays in Honor of Joseph R. Strayer*, ed. William C. Jordan, Bruce McNab, and Teofilo F. Ruiz (Princeton, 1976), pp. 31–40, 425–428.
48. "Apostolat mendiant et fait urbain dans la France médiévale: l'implantation des ordres mendiants. Programme-questionnaire pour une enquête," *Annales* 23 (1968), 335–352; and "Ordres mendiants" (see above, n. 34), pp. 924–946.

Klosterverzeichnis is a *sine qua non* for such an undertaking. Unfortunately, while David Knowles[49] and Richard W. Emery[50] have prepared such lists for England and France, no such catalogue has been compiled for Germany. Appendix I contains, therefore, a list of the German Franciscan and Dominican convents and their foundation dates, where they can be determined, or the first definite reference to their existence. Once these dates have been obtained, it is possible to compare the expansion of the mendicant orders with the pattern of urbanization in the thirteenth century, the high point in medieval German town development. Chapter One is an investigation of the correlation between the spread of the mendicant orders and urbanization in western and southern Germany. The expansion of the mendicant orders east of the Elbe-Saale, the theme of Chapter Two, was complicated by the process of Germanization and Christianization. The friars' impact upon a single German city, Cologne, and the effect of its internal divisions upon them is studied in greater detail in Chapter Three.

Part Two examines some of the social and political aspects of the friars' German ministry. Chapter Four takes up the question of the social origins of the friars. There are two general theories about the social origins of the orthodox and heretical exponents of the apostolic life. Herbert Grundmann asserted that the Waldenses, Humiliati, and Franciscans were recruited from the more affluent strata of medieval society and that they had deliberately renounced their inherited wealth and social status,[51] but he was unable to provide very convincing proof for his theory. As Norman Cantor has put it: "The sociological base of his [Grundmann's] work is generally inadequate."[52] Grundmann's East German critics Ernst Werner and Martin Erbstösser have insisted, on the other hand, that the desire to imitate the life of Christ was essentially a social protest by the poor.[53] But Werner's and Erbstösser's arguments are marred by their pre-commitment to the Marxist model of class conflict. Until some hard data can be gathered about the social ori-

49. David Knowles and R. Neville Hadcock, *Medieval Religious Houses: England and Wales* (London, 1953).
50. *The Friars in Medieval France: A Catalogue of French Mendicant Convents, 1200–1500* (New York, 1962).
51. Grundmann, *Religiöse Bewegungen*, pp. 157–169.
52. "Medieval Historiography as Modern Political and Social Thought," *The Journal of Contemporary History* 3 (1968), 62.
53. Werner, *Pauperes Christi*, pp. 7–17; Werner and Erbstösser, "Sozial-religiöse Bewegungen im Mittelalter," *Wissenschaftliche Z der Karl-Marx-Universität Leipzig, Gesellschafts- und sprachwissenschaftliche Reihe* 7 (1957/58), 257–282.

gins of the followers of the apostolic life, it remains highly speculative to characterize the search for evangelical perfection as either a religious reaction by the affluent or as a social protest by the poor; and sufficient data is just not now available. In the hope of throwing some light, however obliquely, on this question, an effort is made to set forth in Appendix II the social origins of individual, identifiable German Dominicans and Franciscans in the orders' early years and to analyze in Chapter Four some of the broader implications of these findings.

Chapter Five discusses the friars' reluctant, but growing involvement in imperial politics. The friars were welcomed in the 1220s and 1230s as the best weapons in the church's counteroffensive against heresy, but by the 1240s they had become entangled in the titanic struggle between Innocent IV and Frederick II. It was a snare from which they never again escaped. By the 1270s they were active and enthusiastic participants in Rudolph of Habsburg's clash with Ottokar of Bohemia, which helped to determine the fate of Central Europe for centuries to come.

This examination of the Dominicans' and Franciscans' activities in Germany will perhaps offer some additional insights into the interaction between the friars and medieval society. There can be little doubt that the friars' impact on thirteenth-century Europe was immeasurable. They preached crusades, fought the Hohenstaufen, hunted heretics, traveled to the Far East as envoys and missionaries and upon their return wrote accounts of their journeys, advised kings, wore the miter and tiara, and inspired poets, painters, and philosophers. Above all they cared for the spiritual needs of the townspeople. But the friars' self-imposed mission to convert the world was spiritually dangerous. They were required to participate in earthly affairs without, in St. Paul's words, conforming to the standards of this world. The Franciscans and Dominicans carried the Gospel into the midst of thirteenth-century society; they soon discovered that the pressures and temptations to compromise their ideals were subtle and numerous. Were the friars indeed the salt of the earth, or were they salt which all too quickly lost its savor?

Part One

THE FRIARS AND
URBANIZATION

1

Urbanization and the Expansion
of the Mendicant Orders in Western Germany

When I consider my own lowly state and that of my companions who were sent with me to Germany and when I consider the present state and glory of our order, I am dumbfounded and praise in my heart the divine mercy.

Jordan of Giano, Prologue.

1. INTRODUCTION

JORDAN of Giano's astonishment at the phenomenal growth of the Franciscan Order, as he dictated in 1262 his recollections of the friars' arrival in Germany, is readily comprehensible.[1] In 1250, 30 years after the friars' arrival, there were already 38 Dominican and more than 100 Franciscan convents in Germany; by the end of the century there were approximately 200 Franciscan and 94 Dominican houses.[2] The expansion of the mendicant orders in Germany did not conform, however, to the general European pattern. In France, England, Belgium, and Wales the expansion of the Franciscans and Dominicans started to slow down after 1250 and virtually ceased after the Second Council of Lyons in 1274.[3] While there was a sharp decrease in the

---

1. The best edition of Jordan's chronicle is by H. Boehmer in the Collection d'études et de documents sur l'histoire religieuse et littéraire du moyen âge 6 (Paris, 1908). Hereafter cited as Jordan of Giano. For additional information about Jordan and the chronicle, see Appendix I, n. 4.
2. All statements about the location and foundation dates of individual mendicant convents in this and subsequent chapters are based on the list of Franciscan and Dominican houses in Appendix I.
3. Richard W. Emery, "The Second Council of Lyons and the Mendicant Orders," *The Catholic Historical Review* 39 (1953), 270–27; idem, *The Friars in Medieval France: A Catalogue of French Mendicant Convents 1200–1500* (New York, 1962), pp. 7–8.

number of new German foundations in mid-century, many additional houses were established between 1270 and 1300. Indeed, the Dominicans received more convents in the 1290s, 20 in all, than in any other decade in the thirteenth century.

This pattern is clearly discernable in the case of the Dominicans, where the foundation dates of the priories can be determined with a high degree of accuracy. Table I shows the number of Dominican convents which were founded in each decade of the thirteenth century.

Unfortunately, as is explained in more detail in Appendix I, it is extremely difficult to determine the foundation dates of the Franciscan houses. The foundation dates of many convents are unknown. It is necessary to rely in these cases upon the first definite, often chance, reference to the existence of a house in a medieval chronicle or document. Appendix I thus lists either the foundation date of an individual friary, where it is available, or the first definite reference in a medieval source to the existence of a house whose foundation date is unknown. Table II, which shows the number of Franciscan convents which were established in each decade of the thirteenth century, uses these two pieces of information. The figures have been obtained by com-

TABLE I

DOMINICAN CONVENTS FOUNDED PER DECADE

	Teutonia (14th-century province)	Saxony (14th-century province)	Total (13th-century province of Teutonia)
1220–1230	11	5	17[a]
1231–1240	8	8[b]	17[c]
1241–1250	1	3	4
1251–1260	1	4	5
1261–1270	5	2	7
1271–1280	8	5	13
1281–1290	6	7	13
1291–1300	7	13	20

a. This figure includes the convent in Ghent which was founded in 1228, but which was transferred to the French province in 1259. See G. Meersseman, "Les Débuts de l'ordre des frères Prêcheurs dans le comté de Flandre (1224–1280)," *AFP* 17 (1947), 9 and 29–38.
b. This figure includes the convent in Riga which was founded in 1234, but only received in 1244. See below, p. 69.
c. This figure includes the convent in Bruges which was founded in 1234, but which was transferred to the French province in 1259. See Meersseman, "Les Débuts," pp. 10–11 and 29–38.

TABLE II

FRANCISCAN CONVENTS FOUNDED PER DECADE: PRELIMINARY DATA

	Saxony	Cologne	Strasbourg	Austria	Total
1221–1230	9	2	8	0	19
1231–1240	9	9	4	2	24
1241–1250	12	8	4	6	30
1251–1260	11	6	8	4	29
1261–1270	7	9	2	1	19
1271–1280	6	3	10	3	22
1281–1290	13	5	9	2	29
1291–1300	4	2	5	1	12
Totals	71	44	50	19	184

bining the convents which are definitely known to have been founded in a particular decade with the houses whose foundation dates are unknown, but which are first mentioned in that decade.

But the figures in Table II give a misleading picture of the rapidity of the Franciscan expansion in Germany since many convents were undoubtedly founded years before they first happened to be mentioned in an extant medieval source. To compensate for these lacunae in our knowledge, I have utilized the chronicles of sixteenth-, seventeenth-, and eighteenth-century Franciscan historians, who had access to documents which are now lost and who wrote about the beginnings of individual convents, and modern local historians who have provided undocumented information, based on local tradition, about the origins of various houses. The alleged foundation dates supplied by these later historians, whenever they appear to be reasonable, have also been listed in Appendix I and have been employed in constructing Table III. These alleged foundation dates have been substituted in Table III, wherever they are available, for the first definite reference to the existence of a particular friary whose foundation date is not indicated in a medieval source. The remaining houses, whose foundation dates are not given by a medieval source or by a later historian, have been assigned in Table III to the decade in which they first happened to be mentioned. The data which has been corrected in this fashion in Table III probably provides a more accurate picture of the speed of the Franciscan advance than the preliminary data in Table II.

While Tables II and III are less accurate than Table I, they indicate that a large number of new Franciscan convents were founded in Germany between 1270 and 1300, especially in the provinces of Saxony and Strasbourg. Why

TABLE III
FRANCISCAN CONVENTS FOUNDED PER DECADE: CORRECTED DATA

	Saxony	Cologne	Strasbourg	Austria	Total
1221–1230	13	11	14	4	42
1231–1240	16	14	7	7	44
1241–1250	16	8	4	4	32
1251–1260	9	3	7	2	21
1261–1270	10	3	6	0	19
1271–1280	2	2	7	2	13
1281–1290	8	3	6	2	19
1291–1300	6	1	2	0	9
Totals	80	45	53	21	199

did Dominican and Franciscan expansion continue in Germany after it had halted in other countries?

While the political instability caused by the disintegration of the Hohenstaufen Empire probably accounts for the decline in the foundation of new convents in mid-century,[4] the resurgence in the establishment of Dominican houses and the foundation of additional Franciscan friaries after 1270 can be correlated with the pattern of German urbanization. Even by medieval standards Germany was a backward country in 1200, and there was considerable variation in the degree of urbanization in different areas. There were in 1200 approximately 200 communities which were designated *civitates*, a term which tended to be applied to every walled settlement and not just to episcopal sees as was the case in France or England. These *civitates* were concentrated in Brabant, in a belt of forest-free land stretching from Cologne to Thuringia, along the trans-Alpine trade routes, and in the valleys of the Rhine, Main, and Danube. In contrast there were few towns in the northern lowlands, in eastern Franconia, south of the Main, or east of the Elbe. These regions were only urbanized in the course of the thirteenth and fourteenth centuries. By 1400, when the medieval urban network had been completed, there were approximately 3500 *civitates* in Germany. While the overwhelming majority of these so-called cities were merely fortified farming villages, the thirteenth century saw the foundation of such relatively important towns as Colmar, Landshut, Berlin, Stettin, and Danzig.[5]

---

4. See below, pp. 160–161.
5. Robert E. Dickinson, "The Development and Distribution of the Medieval German Town," *Geography* 27 (1942), 9–21 and 47–53.

It is necessary to distinguish between the urbanization which took place in western Germany and that which occurred in the east-Elbian colonial territories. The new cities in regions such as Alsace, Bavaria, Frisia, and Swabia arose within an agrarian, but German and Christian society; the burghers who crossed the Elbe settled in what was usually Slavic and often enough pagan territory. Since the expansion of the mendicant orders east of the Elbe was also part of the Germanization and Christianization of this region, it will be treated in a separate chapter.

These differences in the degree and date of urbanization in various areas of western Germany influenced the expansion of the mendicant orders and affected the friars' subsequent role and mission. The friars settled initially in the major ecclesiastical and/or commercial centers in western and southern Germany, like Cologne or Vienna. Their expansion was particularly rapid north of the Main and in Brabant, the most urbanized regions in Germany at the beginning of the century. By 1250 there was a Dominican and/or Franciscan convent in each of the major urban centers. The expansion of the Franciscans and Dominicans in Alsace, Bavaria, Swabia, and Frisia, though retarded by the political chaos of the Interregnum, paralleled, on the other hand, the gradual urbanization of these regions in the course of the thirteenth century. The continued growth of the mendicant orders in Germany after 1270 thus reflects, as this chapter will show, the relatively later urbanization of many parts of the country.

The friars performed their most valuable services in the newer towns and in the economically underdeveloped regions. As latecomers in the older German cities, the friars were compelled to find their place in a fairly complex urban society which already possessed well-established ecclesiastical and temporal institutions, jealous of their prerogatives. There were, for instance, sixteen parish churches in Cologne in 1221.[6] The Dominican and Franciscan convents in Cologne were merely two additional ecclesiastical foundations in a city with numerous other churches. Many of the newer German cities, on the other hand, possessed only a single parish church which was often situated outside the city walls.[7] The friars' care of souls acquired in such commu-

---

6. Hermann Keussen, *Topographie der Stadt Köln im Mittelalter*, 2 vols. (Bonn, 1910), 1:147*–148*.
7. C.N.L. Brooke, "The Missionary at Home: The Church in the Towns, 1000–1250," *The Mission of the Church and the Propagation of the Faith*, ed. G.J. Cuming, Papers Read at the Seventh Summer Meeting and the Eighth Winter Meeting of the Ecclesiastical History Society (Cambridge, England, 1970), pp. 66–67.

nities a crucial significance which it lacked in places like Cologne. Although the mendicant orders had been instituted in response to the heretical threat in the most urbanized areas of western Europe, the friars' ministry was most urgently required in the thirteenth century in the less developed regions.

2. FRANCISCAN AND DOMINICAN EXPANSION PRIOR TO 1250

The 1217 general chapter decided to initiate the Franciscan apostolate in northern Europe.[8] John of Penna and sixty Italian brothers, whose German vocabulary was limited to the word *Ja*, set out for Germany. As long as they were merely asked if they wanted food and lodging for the night, their simple affirmative response proved effective. Unfortunately, the suspicious populace in one place inquired whether the brothers were heretics from Lombardy. This time the reply *Ja* nearly cost the friars their lives. The Franciscans returned to Italy convinced that only a brother seeking martyrdom would dare to labor among such savage people.[9]

St. Francis had been deeply impressed, however, by the piety of German pilgrims in Italy. Elias, speaking on Francis's behalf at the general chapter held at the Portiuncula on May 30, 1221, accordingly asked for volunteers to undertake once more the dangerous assignment. The new mission, profiting from the disastrous experiences of the earlier venture, was meticulously planned in advance. A German cleric, Caesar of Speyer, whom Elias had converted in the Holy Land and who had helped Francis draft the 1221 Rule, was appointed as provincial minister. Caesar chose from the ninety volunteers a select group of eleven clerics and fifteen laymen, several of whom were destined to achieve eminence within the order. The group included Thomas of Celano, the first official biographer of St. Francis; John of Piancarpino, the

---

8. The date of the first Franciscan missions to northern Europe has long been in dispute. Jordan, who confesses in his Prologue that his memory of dates is faulty, states in ch. 3 that the friars were sent to France, Germany, Hungary, Spain and the Italian provinces which had not yet been reached "Anno vero Domini 1219 et anno conversionis eius [Francis's] 10." As Jordan in ch. 1 also says that St. Francis's conversion occurred in 1207, the tenth year cannot have been by Jordan's own computations 1219. André Callebaut, "Autour de la rencontre à Florence de S. François et du Cardinal Hugolin (en été 1217)," *AFH* 19 (1926), 530—558, has shown that the mission to France could only have taken place in 1217. The mission to Germany was, therefore, in all probability at least planned in 1217, although it may only have been executed for some unknown reason in 1219. As John of Penna's mission was a failure, its actual date is rather immaterial as far as German Franciscan history is concerned.

9. Jordan of Giano, ch. 5.

papal envoy to the Mongols in 1245; and the chronicler, Jordan of Giano. More important, there were in addition to Caesar several other Germans: the clerics Barnabas and Conrad and the laymen Benedict of Soest and Henry of Swabia, who had presumably entered the order while on pilgrimages or business trips in Italy. They gathered in Trent on September 29 and crossed the Alps.[10]

Caesar assembled the friars in Augsburg on October 16 and put into effect his plan for evangelizing Germany as rapidly as possible by sending small groups of friars to key towns. This plan was obviously based on a first-hand knowledge of the German ecclesiastical structure. Jordan and two companions were assigned the southeastern archiepiscopal see of Salzburg. Joseph of Treviso and three others were sent to the most important bishopric and town in Bavaria, Regensburg. John of Piancarpino and the German cleric Barnabas set out for Würzburg in Franconia. From there they went to the main Rhenish cities and bishoprics of Mainz, Worms, Speyer, Strasbourg, and Cologne, preaching repentance and preparing lodgings for the friars who were to follow them. Within a year the Franciscans had settled permanently in each of the towns John and Barnabas had visited.[11]

In 1223 Albert of Pisa, the successor of Elias as minister general (1239–1240), replaced Caesar, who wished to return to Italy, as the German minister. Upon his arrival Albert assembled the leading friars for a provincial chapter in Speyer on September 8 to discuss the further expansion of the order and to appoint custodians for Franconia, Bavaria-Swabia, Alsace, and Saxony. John of Piancarpino was to begin the Franciscan mission in Saxony. He and ten companions headed for Hildesheim, where they received a cordial welcome from Bishop Conrad, who recommended the Franciscans to the clergy and people of the city and authorized the friars to preach and to hear confessions in his diocese. By the end of the year the friars had established two other houses in the bishopric, at Brunswick and Goslar, as well as convents in Magdeburg and Halberstadt. The next year the Würzburg provincial chapter decided to initiate work in Thuringia and placed Jordan in charge. Jordan and seven other friars arrived in Erfurt on November 11, 1224. Jordan sent his companions in 1225 to reconnoiter the other Thuringian towns as possible sites for additional houses. Convents were immediately founded in Eisenach, the residence of the landgrave, and in Gotha. After some initial difficulties

10. Ibid., chs. 9 and 15–22.
11. Ibid., chs. 23–28.

friaries were also established in the imperial cities of Nordhausen and Mühl-hausen.[12]

Franciscan expansion continued at so rapid a pace that the 1230 general chapter divided Germany along the Weser into two provinces, Saxony and the Rhine.[13] The 1247 general chapter probably in turn split the Rhenish province into the provinces of Cologne and Strasbourg.[14] The Moselle and Lahn Rivers formed the boundary between the two provinces. The Austrian province was mentioned for the first time in a document in 1235.[15]

Unfortunately, the chronicle of Jordan of Giano, the major source on the early history of the Franciscans in Germany, does not provide any further information about the pattern of Franciscan expansion in Germany; but the foundation dates or the first documentary references to the convents, listed in Appendix I, provide some insight into the further growth of the order. At least 73 Franciscan convents definitely had been established in Germany by 1250; another 44 houses, according to later sources, had also been founded by that date. While some of these later reports are undoubtedly erroneous, other convents which are only mentioned for the first time after 1250 probably existed by mid-century. It is safe to conclude that approximately half of the 214 friaries that existed by 1400 in the four German-speaking provinces had been founded within 30 years of the friars' arrival in the country.

A large number of these convents were situated in episcopal sees, which often were the major commercial centers as well. The Franciscans had defi-

---

12. Ibid., chs. 31–45.
13. Ibid., ch. 57. The boundary between the two provinces may have undergone some adjustments. The convent in Fulda, which subsequently belonged to the province of Cologne, was apparently received in 1237 by John of Piancarpino, the minister of Saxony. Michael Bihl, "Das Gründungsjahr der ersten Niederlassung der Franzis-kaner in Fulda," *Fuldaer Geschichtsblätter* 1 (1905), 30–32. The convent in Soest in the custody of Westphalia seems also to have been associated originally with the Saxon province. Konrad Eubel, *Geschichte der kölnischen Minoriten-Ordensprovinz*, Veröffentlichungen des historischen Vereins für den Niederrhein 1 (Cologne, 1906), p. 175.
14. While it has traditionally been believed that the division of the Rhenish province occurred in 1239, Hugolinus Lippens, "Circa divisionem Provinciae Rheni disquisito (1246–1264)," *AFH* 47 (1955), 217–224, points out that the province of the Rhine was in existence until at least 1246. Since the first definite evidence for the existence of the two provinces appears in 1249 (*Les Registres d'Innocent IV*, ed. Élie Berger, 4 vols. [Paris, 1884–1911], 2, no. 4265), it seems most probable that the 1247 general chapter of Lyons subdivided the province of the Rhine.
15. G.E. Friess, "Geschichte der oesterreichischen Minoritenprovinz," *Archiv für öster-reichische Geschichte* 64 (1882), no. 2.

nitely settled, for instance, in the archiepiscopal sees of Cologne, Magdeburg, Mainz, and Trier by 1225 and in Bremen no later than 1241. For some unknown reason no Franciscan or Dominican convent was established during the Middle Ages in the final archiepiscopal city, Salzburg.[16] Altogether, 21 of the 73 friaries which are definitely known to have been in existence by 1250 and three of the 44 houses which had allegedly been founded by that date were located in episcopal sees.

In general the distribution of the Franciscan convents in 1250 was closely related to the pattern of urbanization which had existed in Germany at the beginning of the century. The Franciscans had expanded most rapidly by mid-century in the province of Cologne, which included the most urbanized regions in the country: the lower Rhine Valley, Brabant, and the belt of forest-free land north of the Main. At least 19 of the convents in the province definitely existed by 1250 and another 14 had allegedly been founded by that date as well; altogether approximately 33 of the 48 houses which eventually existed in the province had probably been started by mid-century. There were, for instance, seven friaries in the custody of Brabant: Diest, Mechelen, Brussels, Louvain, St. Truiden, Tienen, and Maastricht. The expansion of trade along the Dyle, Meuse, Nethe, Rupel, Scheldt, and Senne Rivers in the eleventh century and the development of an east-west overland trade route between the entrepôts of Cologne and Bruges in the second half of the twelfth century had promoted the growth of these Brabantine towns.[17] It is not surprising that the Franciscan convents in these prosperous cities are either known or reputed to have been founded in the 1220s or 1230s. In any case all the Brabantine friaries definitely existed by the very latest in 1265. There were no Franciscan convents, on the other hand, in the northern lowlands between the Zuider Zee and the Weser. Franciscan expansion in the province of Cologne conformed, nevertheless, most closely to the general European pattern of a rapid spread prior to 1250 and a virtual cessation in new foundations after 1274.

In contrast to Cologne, Franciscan expansion occurred far more slowly in the province of Strasbourg, which covered Franconia, the Palatinate, Alsace, Swabia, German Switzerland, and Bavaria. On the whole, southern Germany

16. Jordan of Giano, ch. 27, states that Caesar of Speyer recalled him from Salzburg in 1222, but gives no clue why work was never resumed in Salzburg, where according to Jordan, ch. 24, he and his companions had been well received by the archbishop.

17. Paul Bonenfant, "L'Origine des villes brabançonnes et la 'route' de Bruges à Cologne," *Revue belge de philologie et d'histoire* 31 (1953), 399–447.

was a far less urbanized region at the beginning of the thirteenth century than the area north of the Main. Even an episcopal see like Strasbourg was described by a chronicler as an insignificant town in 1200.[18] By 1250 the province possessed at best 25 convents (16 definite, 9 alleged) in contrast to Cologne's 33. Twenty of these 25 houses were located in cities which had attained urban status before 1200 (see Table IV). The late foundation dates of the remaining 29 friaries in the province of Strasbourg cannot be ascribed simply to a lack of adequate information about their origins, since 13 of these houses (Bern, Breisach, Burgdorf, Fribourg, Heidelberg, Kaiserslautern, Königsfelden, Mulhouse, Offenburg, Rothenburg, Solothurn, Thann, and Villingen) are definitely known only to have been founded after 1250; only five of these towns were in existence before the accession of Frederick II (1211).

Austria, the smallest of the German provinces, included Austria, Carinthia, Carniola, Styria, and the Tyrol. The Austrian convents in 1250 were located in the Danube Valley (Linz, Stein, Tulln, Vienna, Hainburg), the valleys of the Drava and Save (Celje, Ljubljana, Maribor, Ptuj, Villach), and along the trans-Alpine trade routes (Bolzano, Bressanone, Graz, Wolfsberg). Finally, in 1250 the Franciscan houses in Saxony, a vast province which eventually stretched from the Weser in the west across the Oder into Silesia, the Neumark, Pomerania, Prussia, and the Baltic States, were concentrated to the west of the Elbe and along the Baltic Coast. The Franciscans had established a large number of convents in Thuringia, a fairly urbanized region at the beginning of the century, and in the territory between the Saale and the upper Elbe, which had been Germanized in the twelfth century. A number of friaries had also been founded in Lusatia and Silesia which still belonged to the Franciscan province of Bohemia in 1250. The Franciscans had settled first in the most important towns and in the most urbanized regions in Germany (see Map 1).

The Dominicans followed a similar policy. While we do not possess an account of the beginnings of the Dominican Order in Germany comparable to Jordan of Giano's chronicle, the list of Dominican convents in the province of Teutonia indicates that the Dominicans, like the Franciscans, deliberately settled first in the most important ecclesiastical and/or commercial centers. By 1230, ten years after the first Dominicans set foot on German territory, there were seventeen priories in the province: Bremen, Cologne, Erfurt,

18. *De rebus Alsaticis ineuntis saeculi XIII*, ed. Philipp Jaffé (Hanover, 1861), MGH SS 17:236.

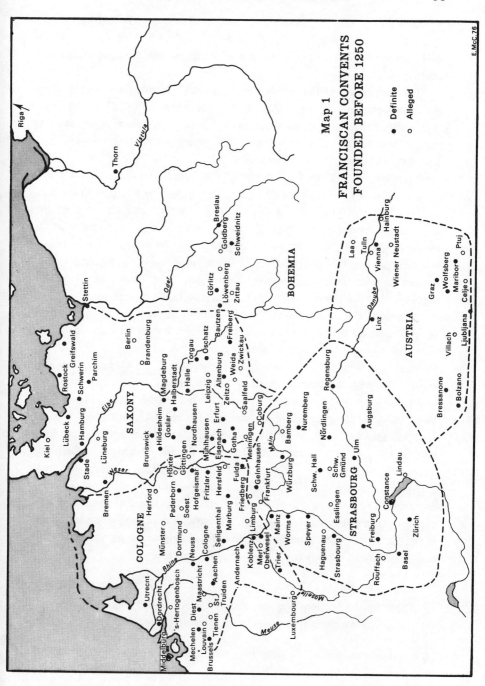

Map 1

FRANCISCAN CONVENTS
FOUNDED BEFORE 1250

● Definite
○ Alleged

Friesach, Ghent, Leipzig, Louvain, Lübeck, Magdeburg, Ptuj, Regensburg, Strasbourg, Trier, Vienna, Worms, Würzburg, and Zürich. With the exceptions of Friesach and Ptuj, all of these houses were located in major thirteenth-century cities.

The foundation of the convent in Friesach, Carinthia, the oldest German priory, appears to have been an accident. Sometime before 1221 an unknown priest from Friesach or its environs apparently joined the Dominicans in Italy and returned to his native town, where he started a house on his own volition. Unfortunately, his enthusiasm quickly waned, and he abandoned the lay brothers who had followed his example. The Danish Dominican Solomon of Aarhus, who was passing through Friesach on his way to Hungary, discovered the problem and notified the 1221 Bologna general chapter. St. Dominic accordingly instructed St. Hyacinth, the founder of the Polish province, to rescue the house before continuing his journey to Poland to initiate the Dominican ministry in eastern Europe.[19] Thus in the end it was Friesach's location on the main trade route between Venice and Vienna that explains at least the survival, if not the foundation, of this relatively obscure priory.

In general the distribution of the 38 priories in the province of Teutonia in 1250 paralleled that of the Franciscans. Since there were only 38 houses in the province in 1250, approximately the same number as in the Franciscan province of Cologne, there had been no pressing need to divide Germany into smaller, more manageable administrative units. The Dominican convents were situated in the most important cities along the major trade arteries, the Rhine, Danube, Main, Moselle, and Elbe, and in such relatively urbanized areas as Brabant, Flanders, and Thuringia. There were few houses between the Elbe and the Oder or in such regions as Alsace and Bavaria. Seventeen of the priories were located in episcopal sees. Thirty-two of the Dominican houses were situated in cities which also possessed a Franciscan convent. These 32 cities can probably be regarded as the major German urban centers in the first half of the thirteenth century (see Map 2). The expansion of the mendicant orders in Germany until 1250 thus conformed fairly closely to the pattern of urbanization which had existed at the beginning of the century.

3. The Friars' Ministry in the Major Urban Centers

The burghers' esteem was the decisive factor in the phenomenal expansion of the mendicant orders. The burghers and many members of the clergy

---

19. Raymond–J. Loenertz, "La Vie de S. Hyacinthe du lecteur Stanislas, envisagée comme source historique," *AFP* 27 (1957), 22–25 and 31.

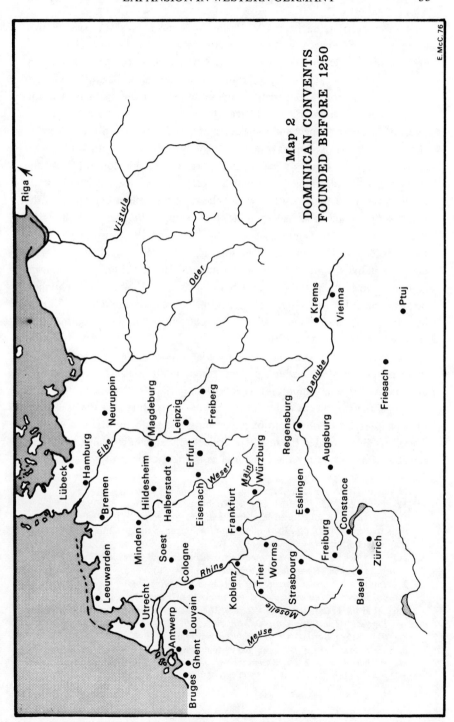

Map 2
DOMINICAN CONVENTS
FOUNDED BEFORE 1250

E. McC. 76

welcomed the friars in the 1220s. Jordan of Giano relates, for instance, that
when the friars arrived in Erfurt in November 1224, a time of the year
deemed unsuitable for construction, the burghers and the clergy of the city
housed the Franciscans in a leprosarium outside the city walls until the burghers could find more appropriate accommodations for the brothers. The following year the friars, on the advice of the burghers as well as the parish
priest of St. Bartholomew and the vidame of the city, moved into the deserted
church of the Holy Spirit, where the brothers remained until the proctor
appointed by the burghers had built the friars a suitable convent.[20] As the
friars' fame spread, municipal authorities often invited the brothers to settle
in their towns so that they and their fellow citizens might benefit from the
friars' sermons and personal example. For example, the *Rat* of Freiburg im
Breisgau, along with Count Egeno V of Urach and the parish priest of the
town, asked the Dominicans in the mid–1230s to reside in their city.[21] On
occasion individual burghers took the initiative in establishing a mendicant
convent. James of Riggisberg, a citizen of Fribourg (Freiburg im Üchtland),
bequeathed in his will of May 15, 1256, his house and garden to the Franciscans for the construction of a church and convent on the condition that they
settle within three years in Fribourg.[22]

In exchange for the burghers' material support, the friars offered the
townspeople spiritual leadership. Unfortunately, it is nearly impossible to
document this most important aspect of the friars' activity; but the rapid
spread of the mendicant orders in the thirteenth century and the popularity
of such preachers as Berthold of Regensburg testify to the friars' success.[23]
The friars also provided the burghers, collectively and individually, with more
tangible recompense for their material assistance. Lübeck offers some inter-

20. Jordan of Giano, chs. 29, 43, and 46.
21. *Freiburger UB*, ed. Friedrich Hefele (Freiburg, 1940), 1, nos. 58, 59, and 63. The
    Dominicans were summoned in a similar way to Antwerp and Bern and the Francis-
    cans to Bern, Offenburg, Rothenburg, and Villingen. See Appendix I for the docu-
    mentary citations.
22. Jean–Jacques Joho, "La Naissance de trois couvents de frères Minèurs: Berne, Fri-
    bourg, Lausanne," *Revue historique vaudoise* 67 (1959), no. 3.
23. For information about Berthold of Regensburg, see *Berthold von Regensburg: Voll-
    ständige Ausgabe seiner Predigten*, ed. Franz Pfeiffer and Joseph Strobl, 2nd ed., 2
    vols. (Berlin, 1965); Laurentius Casutt, *Die Handschriften mit lateinischen Predig-
    ten Bertholds von Regensburg O. Min. ca. 1210–1272* (Fribourg, 1961); Karl Rie-
    der, *Das Leben Bertholds von Regensburg* (Freiburg, 1901); and Anton E. Schön-
    bach, "Studien zur Geschichte der altdeutschen Predigt," *Sitzungsberichte der
    kaiserlichen Akademie der Wissenschaften in Wien, Philosophisch-historische Klasse*
    142, 147, 151, 152, 153, 154, 155 (1900–1908).

esting examples. The Dominicans, Franciscans, and the Lübeck cathedral chapter petitioned King Eric of Denmark in 1259 to confirm the commercial privileges which had been granted to the city by his predecessors, Waldemar and Christopher.[24] To cite another example, in about 1250 the Dominicans recommended to their fellow friars the Lübeck burgher Jordan, whom they described as a very special friend of their order and as a most faithful promoter of the Lübeck priory, asking them, if necessary, to counsel and to aid Jordan on his travels.[25] If Jordan was a merchant, this letter of recommendation must have been particularly valuable.

The friars' popularity with the burghers quickly aroused the resentment of the local clergy, especially of the parish priests. Papal recommendations, such as the bull *Cum dilecti filii* (1218), had cleared the friars of the suspicion of heresy which had wrecked John of Penna's mission. After the issuance of these bulls, the friars were only mistaken as heretics in Germany on one occasion in the early 1220s.[26] But the friars' care of souls infringed upon the rights and income of the parish clergy. A parish priest in Cologne was the first German cleric to express such parochial resentment. He complained to Cardinal Conrad of Porto (1219–1227) in 1225 that the friars were hearing the confessions of his parishioners.[27] The officials of the two orders tried to prevent such incidents. The Dominican general chapter repeatedly warned the friars to avoid quarrels with prelates, not to contend with the parish priests in the hearing of confessions, and to persuade the laity to honor the clergy.[28] Often when the friars settled in a town they agreed to respect the rights of the parish clergy and of various ecclesiastical institutions. John of Piancarpino, the provincial minister of Saxony (1232–1239), promised Abbot Conrad of Fulda in 1237, for instance, that the Franciscans would not preach on the special feast days of the Benedictine monastery nor bury the abbey's ministerials in the Franciscan cemetery.[29]

24. *UB der Stadt Lübeck*, Codex diplomaticus Lubecensis, lste Abtheilung (Lübeck, 1858), 2, no. 29. The texts of the privileges Eric was asked to confirm are published in *UB Lübeck*, 1 (1843), nos. 20 and 190. See also *UB Lübeck*, 2, nos. 33 and 34.
25. *UB Lübeck*, 1, no. 166.
26. Caesarius of Heisterbach, *Vita, passio et miracula S. Engelberti*, ed. Albert Poncelet (Brussels, 1910), Acta sanctorum Novembris 3:650. See below, pp. 88–89.
27. Thomas of Cantimpré, *Bonum universale de apibus*, ed. Georgius Colvenerius (Douai, 1627), 1.9.6. See below, p. 89.
28. *Acta capitulorum generalium ordinis Praedicatorum*, ed. Benedictus Maria Reichert, MOPH 3 (Rome, 1898), 1:15, 24, 63, 143, and 164.
29. Johann Friedrich Schannat, *Diocesis Fuldensis cum annexa sua hierarchia* (Frankfurt am Main, 1727), no. 54.

In spite of such warnings and reassurances, squabbles between the friars and the clergy were commonplace. A particularly bitter dispute in Strasbourg dragged on unresolved for more than a decade. The Strasbourg Dominicans, who had outgrown their accommodations outside the city walls, purchased in 1248 some land within the city.[30] As the Dominicans, who had established six nunneries in Strasbourg by 1250,[31] were extremely popular, the Strasbourg clergy clearly feared a further erosion of its position and a reduction of its income if the friars moved into the city itself and tried to block the transfer of the priory. The Dominicans were not able to begin construction of their new church and convent until 1254.[32] On August 30, 1257, the friars' opponents forged in the name of the current pope, Alexander IV, a copy of Innocent IV's bull *Etsi animarum*, which had severely restricted the friars' activities.[33] So armed, the Strasbourg clergy prohibited the Dominicans from preaching in the parish churches and from hearing confessions, impeded their mendicancy, and excommunicated burghers who had visited the Dominicans after attending mass in their own parish. The dumbfounded and furious Alexander IV (1254–1261), who had in fact revoked *Etsi animarum* immediately after his election, commanded Bishop Henry (1245–1260) and the Strasbourg clergy on February 21, 1258, to desist.[34] Not only did Henry and his clergy ignore this papal command, but they set out to harass the Franciscans.[35] This particular dispute was never resolved; it was apparently simply forgotten during Bishop Walter's battles with the burghers for control of the city in the early 1260s.

There were similar incidents prior to 1273 in the duchy of Austria (1234), Brussels (1241), Esslingen (ca. 1270), Frankfurt am Main (1270), Hamburg (1265), Linz (1231–1253), Mechelen (1233), Mühlhausen (1262), St. Truiden (1258), Worms (1265), Würzburg (1254), Zürich (1231, 1261, 1266),

---

30. *UB der Stadt Strassburg*, ed. Wilhelm Wiegand (Strasbourg, 1879), 1, nos. 321 and 324; *Elsässische Urkunden*, ed. Alfred Hessel, Schriften der wissenschaftlichen Gesellschaft in Strassburg 23 (Strasbourg, 1915), no. 13.
31. Hieronymus Wilms, *Das älteste Verzeichnis der deutschen Dominikanerinnenklöster*, QFGDD 24 (Leipzig, 1928), pp. 53–57.
32. *UB Strassburg*, 1, nos. 339, 351, 352, and 354; *Ellenhardi Argentinensis annales*, ed. Philipp Jaffé (Hanover, 1861), MGH SS 17:102.
33. *Elsässische Urkunden*, no. 24.
34. *UB Strassburg*, 1, no. 420.
35. Ibid., nos. 416, 417, 441, 442, 446, 447, 451, and 452; *Die Regesten der Erzbischöfe von Köln im Mittelalter*, ed. Richard Knipping, PGRhGk 21 (Bonn, 1909–1913), 3, nos. 1845a and 2057.

and Zwickau (1267).[36] As the dates of these disputes suggest, the problem seems to have become especially acute in the third quarter of the thirteenth century. The friars' acquisition of the right to grant indulgences to their visitors and the brothers' accumulation of additional privileges, such as the right to hear the confessions of the laity (1237), probably account for the clergy's growing resentment.[37] It is thus understandable that the masters at the University of Paris expected a sympathetic response from the secular clergy in their dispute with the friars in the 1250s. While most of these quarrels were eventually resolved, the hostility between the parish clergy and the friars smoldered within the church for centuries.

The friars also encountered considerable opposition from some bishops. During the 1220s and 1230s, it should be pointed out, many bishops, disturbed by the spread of heresy, were among the friars' most important patrons.[38] In addition the popes appointed a number of German bishops as the protectors of the friars.[39] Presumably, these prelates were favorably disposed

36. Friess, "Oesterreichische Minoritenprovinz" (see above, n. 15), no. 1; André Callebaut, "Lettres franciscaines concernant la Belgique et la France au XIIIe–XVe siècles," *AFH* 7 (1914), no. 2; *Wirtembergisches UB*, 11 vols. (Stuttgart, 1849–1913), 7, no. 2105; Heinrich Finke, *Ungedruckte Dominikanerbriefe des 13. Jahrhunderts* (Paderborn, 1891), no. 34; *Hamburgisches UB*, ed. Johann Martin Lappenberg (Hamburg, 1842), 1, nos. 685, 687, and 709; Joseph Chmel, "Das Formelbuch K. Albrechts I.," *Archiv für Kunde österreichischer Geschichtsquellen* 2 (1849), no. 24; *Diplomatum Belgicorum nova collectio sive supplementum ad opera diplomatica Auberti Miraei*, ed. Johannes Franciscus Foppens (Brussels, 1748), 4: 546–547; *UB der ehemals freien Reichsstadt Mühlhausen in Thüringen*, ed. Karl Herquet, GQProvSachs 3 (Halle, 1874), 1, no. 164; *Gesta abbatum Trudonensium*, ed. Rudolf Koepke (Hanover, 1852), MGH SS 10:401; *UB der Stadt Worms*, ed. Heinrich Boos (Berlin, 1886), 1, no. 327; *Monumenta episcopatus Wirziburgensis*, Monumenta Boica 37 (Munich, 1864), no. 326; *UB der Stadt und Landschaft Zürich*, ed. J. Escher and P. Schweizer (Zürich, 1890–1898), 1, no. 466, 3, no. 1147, and 4, nos. 1321 and 1327; *Regesta diplomatica necnon epistolaria historiae Thuringiae*, ed. Otto Dobenecker (Jena, 1939), 4, no. 39.
37. A list of the indulgences and privileges granted to the Franciscans may be found in Burkhard Mathis, *Die Privilegien des Franziskanerordens bis zum Konzil von Vienne (1311)* (Paderborn, 1928), pp. 133–135.
38. See below, pp. 138–141.
39. These episcopal conservators of the friars' privileges included: Archbishops Henry of Cologne (1225–1237) and Albert of Magdeburg (1205–1232), and Bishop Herman of Würzburg (1225–1254), *Regesten Köln* (see above, n. 35), 3, no. 736; Archbishops Conrad of Cologne (1238–1261) and Wilbrand of Magdeburg (1235–1254), ibid., no. 1211; Archbishop Gerhard of Bremen (1219–1258) and Bishops Conrad of Hildesheim (1221–1246) and Dietrich of Schwerin (1239–1247), *UB des Hochstifts Hildesheim und seiner Bischöfe*, ed. H. Hoogeweg, QDGNsachs 6 (Hanover, 1901), 2, no. 741; Bishop Albert of Regensburg (1247–1260), *UB der Stadt Halber-*

toward the friars. But a number of bishops, often for personal reasons, impeded the friars' ministry. Bishop Henry of Worms (1217–1234) had welcomed the Franciscans in 1222,[40] but he turned against the friars when the Dominicans tried to settle in Worms in 1226.[41] Gregory IX subsequently rebuked Henry for not protecting the friars from their detractors.[42] The bishop became especially incensed after the death of his nephew Count Eberhard of Leiningen, who had joined the Dominicans and who had been buried in their priory. Henry forcibly exhumed the body and reburied it in the cathedral. After the Dominicans appealed to Rome for assistance, Henry expelled them from their convent, denied them permission to exercise their apostolate, and refused to excommunicate the individuals who had beaten up a friar.[43] The dispute was finally resolved in 1231/32 when Bishop Henry permitted the Dominicans to settle within the city. They promised in return to obey the bishop in all matters not contrary to their constitutions and papal privileges. The Dominicans' right to bury burghers and to receive bequests was also carefully regulated.[44] A number of other bishops also created difficulties for the friars.[45]

The attempts by the burghers in the episcopal cities to limit or to overthrow the temporal authority of their bishops, a common occurrence in the thirteenth century, also posed a thorny problem for the friars. The brothers were torn between their desire to continue their ministry among the burghers and their dependence upon the bishops for permission to exercise their apostolate. It clearly was in the friars' best interests to prevent such disputes. Berthold of Regensburg counseled burghers not to participate in conspiracies which threatened the liberty of the church. Many burghers, he warned, had died excommunicate on account of such wicked conduct.[46] If a quarrel be-

---

stadt, ed. Gustav Schmidt, GQProvSachs 7 (Halle, 1878), 1, no. 92; Bishop Berthold of Basel (1250–1262), Regesten Köln, 3, no. 1881; and Bishop Leo of Regensburg (1262–1277), Finke, Dominikanerbriefe (see above, n. 36), no. 34.

40. Jordan of Giano, ch. 26.

41. Annales Wormatienses, ed. Georg Pertz (Hanover, 1861), MGH SS 17:38.

42. UB Worms (see above, n. 36), 1, no. 146.

43. Ibid., no. 151; Annales Wormatienses, p. 38.

44. UB Worms, 1, no. 153.

45. These bishops were: Conrad of Constance (1209–1233), Freiburger UB (see above, n. 21), 1, no. 44; Archbishop Siegfried of Mainz, Jordan of Giano, ch. 74; Bishops Otto of Brandenburg (1251–1260) and Henry of Strasbourg (1245–1260), Regesten Köln (see above, n. 35), 3, no. 2057; and Eberhard of Constance (1248–1274), Finke, Dominikanerbriefe (see above, n. 36), no. 30.

46. Anton E. Schönbach, "Studien zur Geschichte der altdeutschen Predigt. Sechstes Stück. Die Überlieferung der Werke Bertholds von Regensburg. III.," Sitzungs-

tween a bishop and his burgher subjects did break out, the friars attempted to find a peaceful solution. As mediators the friars usually tried to uphold episcopal authority and to end interdicts which endangered the salvation of souls and impeded their own work. The cities of Strasbourg, Worms, and Würzburg provide good examples of the friars' mediatorial role.

Bishop Walter of Geroldseck (1260–1263) became embroiled in a bitter conflict with the burghers of Strasbourg when he attempted to exercise what he considered to be his temporal rights and to check the growing autonomy of the city. Specifically, he claimed the right to participate in the selection of the *Bürgermeister* and the *Rat* and protested against the *Rat*'s taxation policies.[47] After Walter interdicted the city in 1261 and ordered the clergy to depart, the burghers, who hoped to avoid a conflict, sent the Dominicans and the Franciscans to the bishop to negotiate.[48] In spite of the fact that relations between the friars and the Strasbourg clergy had been strained for more than a decade, the friars left the city as Walter had ordered when they proved unable to reconcile the feuding parties.[49] The ensuing battle of Hausbergen on March 8, 1262, ended episcopal rule in Strasbourg. Bishop Henry (1263–1273), Walter's successor, lifted the interdict on June 23, 1265, at the request of the burghers, which had been conveyed to him by the prior of the Strasbourg Dominicans.[50]

The friars were more successful in helping to preserve episcopal domination in Worms and Würzburg. The *Rat* in Worms was under the control of the bishop. It was composed of nine burghers whom the bishop selected and six episcopal ministerials who were chosen by the nine burgher members. The bishop or his representative presided at sessions of the *Rat*. The bishop and the *Rat* jointly appointed four men from each of the four parishes in the city to advise them on the levying of the *Ungeld*, a tax on wine.[51] In June 1264 some prominent young burghers incited their fellow citizens against this re-

berichte der kaiserlichen Akademie der Wissenschaften in Wien, Philosophisch-historische Klasse 153 (1906), 160–161.

47. Ernst Kruse, "Verfassungsgeschichte der Stadt Strassburg besonders im 12. und 13. Jahrhundert," *WZ*, Ergh. 1 (1884), 51–52, 55–56, and 59–63.
48. *Richeri gesta Senoniensis ecclesiae*, ed. G. Waitz (Hanover, 1880), MGH SS 25: 340–341.
49. *Bellum Walterium*, ed. Philipp Jaffé (Hanover, 1861), MGH SS 17:105.
50. *UB Strassburg* (see above, n. 30), 1, no. 600.
51. Heinrich Boos, *Geschichte der rheinischen Städtekultur*, 4 vols. (Berlin, 1897–1901), 1:492–495 and 2:28–29; Carl Koehne, *Der Ursprung der Stadtverfassung in Worms, Speier und Mainz*, Untersuchungen zur deutschen Staats- und Rechtsgeschichte 31 (Breslau, 1890), pp. 325–342.

gime. They accused the *Rat* and the sixteen advisers of misappropriating the funds they received from the *Ungeld*. The rebels seized the town treasury and levied the *Ungeld* themselves. After warning them to desist, Bishop Eberhard (1257–1277) left Worms and interdicted the city. The dismayed burghers asked the Dominicans and Franciscans to arrange negotiations between them and the bishop. Through the friars' mediation a settlement was reached on November 21. The conspirators were forced to make amends and to swear obedience to the church and *Rat* of Worms. In exchange for 300 pounds Bishop Eberhard gave the *Rat* and the sixteen advisers on taxation permission to levy the *Ungeld* for a year according to the customary procedure. In accordance with the agreement, Eberhard prohibited the formation of guilds in the city and lifted the interdict.[52] The friars had played their part in keeping the episcopal regime in power in Worms.

Albertus Magnus headed a group of arbiters who settled on August 26, 1265, a lengthy dispute between Bishop Iring (1254–1266) and the burghers of Würzburg, who had been challenging episcopal authority over their city since 1254.[53] (Albert's brother was referred to in a 1278 document as the prior of the Würzburg Dominicans.)[54] The arbiters made the following decisions: the burghers were to hand over to the bishop for judgment and punishment counterfeiters and adulterators of wine; the bishop had the power to dissolve guilds; the burghers could not have a *Rat* or *Bürgermeister* without episcopal permission; the burghers were to surrender to the bishop the seal and keys of the city; the burghers were to pay the bishop 2,000 marks as reparations; the bishop could levy the *Ungeld* for the next eight years; the burghers were to compensate the Würzburg clergy for damage done to its property; all members of the episcopal household, Christian or Jew, who had supported the bishop during the dispute, were to be allowed to return to the city; and the fortifications which the burghers had built during the quarrel were to be razed.[55] The arbitral decision was in short a reassertion of episcopal authority over Würzburg.

The friars' defense of episcopal temporal authority in these disputes can best be explained by their need for episcopal permission to exercise their

52. *Annales Wormatienses* (see above, n. 41), p. 67.
53. Friedrich Stein, *Geschichte Frankens*, 2nd ed. (Aalen, 1966), 1:262–263 and 289–293.
54. Gabriel M. Löhr, *Beiträge zur Geschichte des kölner Dominikanerklosters im Mittelalter*, QFGDD 15–17 (Leipzig, 1920–1922), 2, no. 58.
55. *Monumenta Wirziburgensis* (see above, n. 36), no. 370. For further information, see Peter Joseph Jörg, "Albertus Magnus und Würzburg," *MfJb* 2 (1950), 53–77.

apostolate. Until Pope Martin IV (1281–1285) issued the bull *Ad fructus uberes* in 1281, which permitted friars who had been licensed by their superiors to preach and to hear confessions without episcopal permission, the friars required either specific papal or episcopal authorization to carry out their mission.[56] While the brothers could usually count on the support of the papacy if a bishop impeded their activities, the curia would presumably have been less inclined to aid friars harassed by a bishop for helping rebellious burghers to overthrow their episcopal overlord. The Franciscans and Dominicans thus found it generally wisest to stay in the good graces of a German prince-bishop, even if they momentarily offended some of their burgher friends. In addition the friars usually had personal ties which bound them to the episcopal as well as the burgher side in these disputes. The founders of the nunnery of the Poor Clares in Strasbourg were, for instance, the episcopal ministerials Walter, the *Schultheiss* of Strasbourg, and Eberhard, the episcopal marshal.[57] As nephews of Bishop Walter, they naturally fought on the episcopal side at Hausbergen.[58] It was these connections with both sides that made the friars ideal mediators in such quarrels.

The burghers' success in emancipating themselves from the temporal authority of their bishops did not necessarily resolve all of the friars' problems. The German municipal authorities generally tried to prevent ecclesiastical institutions from acquiring large amounts of real estate within their cities as such acquisitions often raised awkward legal problems about municipal jurisdiction, lowered tax revenue, and reduced the amount of property within the city readily available for the burghers' own use. While the municipal authorities frequently provided the friars with property and other material aid, they often added to the gift the stipulation that the friars not expand their holdings within the city. For example, at the request of the papel legate Bishop William of Modena (1222–1244), the *Rat* of Lübeck paid in 1236 a debt of thirty marks which was attached to the lot on which the Dominican priory stood and also gave the friars another lot with a house on it. In return the *Rat* required that the Dominicans repair the street next to the convent and not

---

56. Mathis, *Privilegien* (see above, n. 37), pp. 90–115. The text of the bull may be found in Luke Wadding, *Annales Minorum*, 2nd ed., 26 vols. (Rome and Quaracchi, 1731–1933), 5:479; *Bullarium ordinis FF. Praedicatorum*, ed. Antonino Bremond (Rome, 1730), 2:1–2, no. 2.

57. *UB Strassburg* (see above, n. 30), 1, no. 376.

58. *Bellum Walterium* (see above, n. 49), p. 111; Kruse, "Verfassungsgeschichte Strassburg" (see above, n. 47), p. 62.

acquire additional property within the city.[59] Since the friars had committed themselves to corporate as well as individual poverty, they could easily promise not to obtain additional real estate. The Lübeck Franciscans made a similar agreement in 1240.[60] In spite of their promises, the friars continued to enlarge their holdings. The *Rat* of Lübeck gave the Franciscans in 1256 a lot next to their church at the request of Bishop John of Lübeck (1254–1259), who had been the Franciscan John of Diest. Bishop John and the friars again assured the *Rat* that they would make no further demands on the city for property.[61] While the mendicant convents never became really wealthy ecclesiastical foundations, the friars' gradual acquisition of urban real estate eventually brought them into conflict with the town governments.

The first clear instance of such trouble occurred in the 1280s in Strasbourg, within whose walls or immediate vicinity were situated not only a Dominican and Franciscan convent, but also a house of Austin friars, one convent of Poor Clares, and seven Dominican nunneries. The *Rat*, disturbed by the friars' acquisition of large amounts of real and personal property, attempted in 1283 to curtail the friars' acquisition of new holdings and to restrict their admission of teenagers. The *Rat* demanded that the friars promise not to induce men and women upon their deathbed to bequeath all their property to the friars for the benefit of their souls and to the detriment of their heirs, not to accept any bequest without the consent of the four closest relatives of the deceased, not to sell property with the provision that it revert to the friars upon the death of the purchaser, and not to admit a boy under eighteen years of age without the consent of his parents or other relatives. The Franciscans complied, but the Dominicans repeatedly rejected the demands as prejudicial to the rights of their order. In 1286 the exasperated *Rat* prohibited the burghers from entering the Dominican church or giving the friars alms. According to the Dominicans' account, the men sent by the *Rat* to guard the doors actually entered and sacked the priory and inflicted numerous injuries on the brothers.

The confrontation between the *Rat* and the Dominicans quickly escalated. The papal legate, Cardinal John of Tusculum (1285–1309), excommunicated the Bürgermeister and the members of the *Rat* in the years 1286 and 1287 and placed the city under the interdict. The Dominicans left the city in the spring of 1287. When these measures proved ineffective, the legate

59. *UB Lübeck* (see above, n. 24), 1, no. 75.
60. Ibid., no. 86.
61. Ibid., no. 229.

threatened the city with a crusade and prohibited other cities from trading with Strasbourg. The city in turn protested against the legality of the legate's actions and appealed to the burghers of neighboring towns for support in dealing with a common problem.

The Dominicans were at a disadvantage throughout the conflict. The religious of Strasbourg, including the Dominican nuns and the Franciscans, generally ignored the interdict. The exiled Dominicans were forced to sell their books, parchments, and other valuables to pay the debts they had incurred. The conflict was finally ended by the intervention of Bishop Conrad of Strasbourg (1273–1299), whose binding arbitration was accepted by both parties on February 22, 1290. He ruled on August 11 that the Dominicans could not accept the city's demands without prejudice to their rights.[62] The Dominicans' legal arguments had been upheld, but it is difficult to avoid the conclusion that the friars' reputation must have been adversely affected.

The friars' ministry in the older German cities, especially in the episcopal sees, was thus repeatedly hampered by the demands and rivalries of powerful ecclesiastical and secular institutions, jealous of their prerogatives. While the Franciscans and Dominicans could set a personal example of moral rectitude and could minister to the spiritual needs of the burghers, the friars were constantly forced to thread their way between contending interest groups. The existing power structure within the major cities thus at times severely restricted the friars' freedom to exercise their apostolate.

4. FRANCISCAN AND DOMINICAN EXPANSION AFTER 1250

The thirteenth century was the high point in the urbanization of medieval Germany. Dozens of new towns were established not only in the east-Elbian colonial territories, but also in southern Germany. The territory south of the Main was an economically backward region in 1200 with only a handful of small, unimportant towns. A Colmar Dominican, whose long life spanned most of the century, described his native Alsace in the *De rebus Alsaticis*

---

62. C. Schmidt, "Notice sur le couvent et l'église des Dominicaines de Strasbourg," *Bulletin de la Société pour la conservation des monuments historique d'Alsace*, IIe série, 9 (1876), 177–193. The relevant sources are *UB Strassburg*, 2 (1886), nos. 92, 93, 114–123, 125, 127, 128, 130–133, 138, 140, 145, 147, 148, 150, 152–156, 161, 163–168, 170, 174, and 175; Finke, *Dominikanerbriefe* (see above, n. 36), nos. 97, 106–109, 111, 112, 120–122, and 131; *Elsässische Urkunden* (see above, n. 30), nos. 36–38; and *Annales Colmarienses maiores*, ed. Philipp Jaffé (Hanover, 1861), MGH SS 17: 214–216.

ineuntis saeculi XIII as an underdeveloped region in 1200, which had undergone enormous changes, in the chronicler's opinion for the better, during the thirteenth century. He specifically mentioned that in 1200 the two most important Alsatian cities, Basel and Strasbourg, had been small, rather insignificant towns with inadequate fortifications and unimpressive buildings, and that such towns as Colmar, Sélestat, Rouffach, and Mulhouse had not existed at all.[63] The Hohenstaufen in Alsace and Swabia, the Wittelsbachs in Bavaria, as well as lesser feudal lords, deliberately promoted the foundation of new towns in the valleys of the Rhine, Danube, Main, Neckar, Aare, Ill, and Isar between 1180 and 1250 as a means to develop their backward territories.[64]

The friars' arrival in southern Germany thus coincided with a period of rapid urbanization. Table IV[65] compares, wherever the information is available, the foundation dates of the southern German cities and of the mendicant convents located in them. Since many of these new urban sites were originally market settlements or villages situated near a castle, a monastery, or at the ford of a river, their foundation dates as cities has been defined as the year in which they were first called *civitates* or as the year in which they first received *Stadtrecht*. It is important to remember in using Table IV that the foundation dates of the cities and of the convents cannot always be determined with complete accuracy.

Table IV indicates that the expansion of the mendicant orders closely paralleled the urbanization of southern Germany. The friars settled first, as we have already seen, in the older cities, particularly the towns which had been founded before the accession of Frederick Barbarossa. It is worth noticing that these cities were far more likely to possess both a Franciscan and Dominican convent than the cities which were founded only in the course of

63. (See above, n. 18), p. 236. For additional information about the Colmar Dominican, see Karl Köster, "Die Geschichtsschreibung der kolmarer Dominikaner im 13. Jahrhundert," *Elsass-lothringisches Jahrbuch* 22 (1952), 1–100.

64. For information about the urban policies of the Hohenstaufen and Wittelsbachs, see Hella Fein, *Die staufischen Städtegründungen im Elsass*, Schriften des wissenschaftlichen Instituts der Elsass-Lothringer im Reich an der Universität Frankfurt, NF 25 (Frankfurt am Main, 1939); Karl Otto Müller, *Die oberschwäbischen Reichsstädte: Ihre Entstehung und ältere Verfassung*, Darstellungen aus der württembergischen Geschichte 8 (Stuttgart, 1912); Ludwig Rothenfelder, "Die Wittelsbacher als Städtegründer in Bayern," *Verhandlungen des historischen Vereines für Niederbayern* 47 (1911), 1–106; and Karl Weller, "Die staufische Städtegründung in Schwaben," *Württembergische Vierteljahrshefte für Landesgeschichte*, NF 36 (1930), 145–268.

65. Table IV is based on Appendix I, the monographs cited in n. 64, and Erich Keyser, *Deutsches Städtebuch: Handbuch städtischer Geschichte*, 4 vols. (Stuttgart, 1939–1964), 4.

TABLE IV
FOUNDATION DATES OF CITIES AND OF MENDICANT CONVENTS LOCATED IN SOUTHERN GERMANY

	Franciscan Foundation Date	Alleged Franciscan Foundation Date	First Definite Reference to a Franciscan Convent	Dominican Foundation Date
Cities Founded Before the Accession of Frederick Barbarossa (1152)				
Augsburg	1221			1230s
Basel		1231	1238	1233
Constance		1240	1247	1235
Freiburg im Breisgau		1226	1229	1233
Mainz	1222			1257
Nuremberg		1225	1245	ca. 1275
Regensburg	1221			1229
Speyer	1222			1260/61
Strasbourg	1221/23			1224
Worms	1222			1226
Würzburg	1222			1226/27
Zürich			1240	1230
Cities Founded During the Reign of Frederick Barbarossa (1152–1190)				
Burgdorf	1280			
Frankfurt am Main		ca. 1230	1255	1230s
Fribourg	1256			
Friedberg		1249	1293	
Gelnhausen			1248	
Haguenau		1222	1287	1288/89
Lucerne			1269	
Munich			1257	
Rothenburg	1281			
Schw. Gmünd		1221/29	1281	1293/94
Tübingen		1272	1293	
Ulm		1229	1239	ca. 1280
Wissembourg			1253	1288
Cities Founded During the Reigns of Henry VI, Philip of Swabia, and Otto IV (1190–1211)				
Bern	1255			1269
Breisach	1285			
Dieburg		1256	1291	
Eichstätt				1277/79
Landshut		1280	1292	ca. 1280
Rouffach		1250	1280	
Schw. Hall			1236	
Ueberlingen		1267	1271	

Table IV—*Continued Overleaf*

TABLE IV—*Continued*

	Franciscan Foundation Date	Alleged Franciscan Foundation Date	First Definite Reference to a Franciscan Convent	Dominican Foundation Date
Cities Founded During the Reign of Frederick II (1211–1250)				
Colmar		1230s	1278	1277/78
Esslingen		1237	1255	ca. 1230
Heidelberg	1282			
Heilbronn		1272/73	1278	
Ingolstadt		ca. 1270	1281	
Lindau		1239/40	1253	
Mulhouse	1285			
Neuenburg		1294	1320	
Nördlingen			1243	
Offenburg	1280			
Oppenheim		1290	1318	
Pforzheim		1270	1278	1277/80
Reutlingen		1259	1273	
Rottweil				1266
Schaffhausen			1253	
Sélestat		1280	1287	1288/94
Villingen	1267/68			
Wimpfen				ca. 1269
Cities Founded After 1250				
Guebwiller				1294
Kaiserslautern	1284			
Mergentheim				1289
Thann	1297			

the thirteenth century. A convent would be established in one of the newer towns when there was a sufficient number of inhabitants to support the friars' mendicancy and to require their spiritual ministry. Indeed, the presence of a mendicant house quickly became an urban status symbol, the medieval equivalent of a nineteenth-century railroad station. The *Rat* of Bern in its 1269 invitation to the Dominicans to settle in the city expressed, for example, Bern's desire to possess a priory like all other towns which gloried in the holy dwelling place of the friars.[66] The continued expansion of the Franciscans and Dominicans after 1250 in southern Germany, the region included in the Franciscan province of Strasbourg, was thus closely related to the relatively late urbanization of Alsace, Bavaria, and Swabia (see Map 3 A).

66. Finke, *Dominikanerbriefe* (see above, n. 36), no. 28.

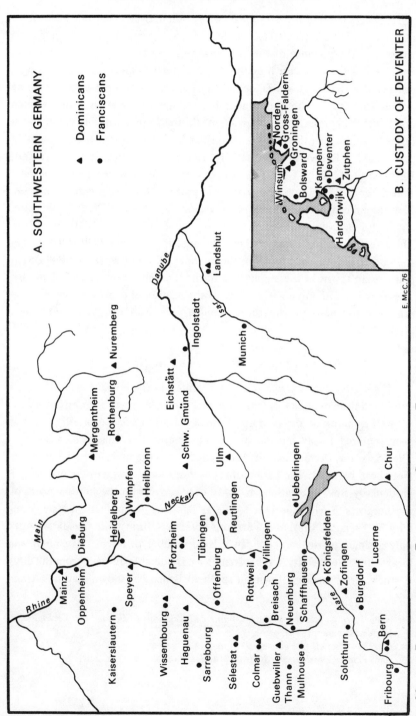

MAP 3. DOMINICAN AND FRANCISCAN CONVENTS FOUNDED AFTER 1250

It is possible to discern a similar correlation between the foundation dates of the mendicant convents and of the cities in the custody of Deventer. This custody in the province of Cologne embraced the territory between the Zuider Zee and the Ems, north of the Rhine. After 1250 merchants increasingly utilized the Ijssel and the Zuider Zee in traveling between Flanders and the Baltic. This shift in the trade routes spurred the urbanization of the extreme northwestern corner of Germany.[67] While the Franciscan convent in Groningen was first mentioned by a chronicler in 1253, the remaining houses in the custody, Bolsward (1260s/1281), Harderwijk (1290), Kampen (1300), Deventer (1311), and Gross-Faldern (Emden) (1323), were founded or mentioned for the first time in the late thirteenth or early fourteenth centuries. The Dominican priories in the same region, Leeuwarden, Norden, Winsum, and Zutphen, were received, respectively, in 1244, 1264, 1280, and 1288. The late foundation dates of these Dominican and Franciscan convents can thus be traced to the change in the commercial importance of these Dutch and Frisian towns in the second half of the thirteenth century (see Map 3 B). There can be little doubt that the late urbanization of many sections of western Germany accounts for the continued growth of the mendicant orders after 1250.

5. THE FRIARS' MINISTRY IN THE NEW TOWNS

The friars' ministry was urgently required in these new towns. The Colmar Dominican pointed out that there had been a shortage of priests in Alsace at the beginning of the century. A single, poorly educated priest had often been required to say mass in two, three, or even four villages on a Sunday. The friars, the Dominican felt, had stepped into the breach.[68] The available facts bear him out. The ecclesiastical authorities in southern Germany were particularly slow in creating new parishes to provide for the spiritual needs of the burghers. Such important towns as Bamberg, Frankfurt am Main, Freiburg im Breisgau, Ulm, and Würzburg possessed throughout the Middle Ages only a single parish church.[69] In a large number of towns this church was located outside the city walls, often at a considerable distance from the city. A study of 57 medieval towns in southern Baden has shown that in 38 cases

67. Nelly Johanna Martina Kerling, *Commercial Relations of Holland and Zeeland with England* (Leiden, 1954), pp. 2–3.
68. *De rebus Alsaticis* (see above, n. 18), p. 232.
69. Hans Planitz, *Die deutsche Stadt im Mittelalter* (Graz, 1954), p. 228.

the parish church was originally situated outside the city; in 20 of these 38 towns it was located in another village.[70] The Dominican or Franciscan convent obviously substituted for a parish church in such a town.

The friars, particularly the Dominicans, likewise assumed the task of providing for the spiritual welfare and discipline of devout women of ministerial and patrician origin in southwestern Germany who wished to lead lives of evangelical perfection. By the beginning of the fourteenth century there were 74 Dominican nunneries in Germany (65 in Teutonia, 9 in Saxony), more than the combined total in the remaining 17 Dominican provinces, and 25 houses of Poor Clares.[71] An examination of the distribution of Cistercian and mendicant nunneries has revealed that the friars' ministry was largely confined to the territory south of the Main River, most notably the dioceses of Constance and Strasbourg, while the Cistercians labored north of the Main, particularly in the bishoprics of Cologne, Liège, and Mainz. The distribution of the Cistercian and mendicant nunneries can be linked to the pattern of urbanization in western Germany. The lower Rhine Valley and the Low Countries were among the most urbanized regions in Europe by 1200, and the Cistercians assumed the *cura monialium* in this area in the first three decades of the thirteenth century. By the time the upper Rhine Valley started to experience the full impact of the economic and social changes which accompanied medieval urbanization, the Cistercian general chapter had prohibited the incorporation of additional nunneries into the Cistercian Order. While this 1228 decree was easily circumvented north of the Main by powerful individuals who wanted their favorite nunnery placed under Cistercian supervision, it was an obstacle to further Cistercian expansion south of the Main, where only nine nunneries had been established in the dioceses of Basel, Constance, Speyer, Strasbourg, and Worms prior to 1228. In spite of considerable opposition to the adoption of the *cura monialium* within both the Dominican and Franciscan Orders, the friars began to organize into nunneries women whom they found living together near chapels.[72] Within thirteen years of the Dominicans' arrival in Strasbourg in 1224, there were five

---

70. Wolfgang Müller, "Pfarrei und mittelalterliche Stadt im Bereiche Südbadens," *Neue Beiträge zur südwestdeutschen Landesgeschichte: Festschrift für Max Miller*, Veröffentlichungen der Kommission für geschichtliche Landeskunde in Baden-Württemberg, Reihe B, Forschungen 21 (Stuttgart, 1962), pp. 70–71.
71. Herbert Grundmann, *Religiöse Bewegungen im Mittelalter*, 2nd ed. (Darmstadt, 1961), pp. 313–314.
72. *De rebus Alsaticis*, p. 234; Grundmann, *Religiöse Bewegungen*, pp. 208–252.

Dominican nunneries in the city and suburbs of Strasbourg.[73] The friars' activities among pious women north of the Main were largely limited to ministering to the Beguines who usually lived in the vicinity of the mendicant houses.[74]

Strangely enough, the friars also performed, at least indirectly, a military function in many medieval towns. It has frequently been observed in architectural and topographical studies that the mendicant convents tended to be situated at strategically important positions near the walls and often became the nuclei for the development of new quarters within the city.[75] The friars may have preferred such neighborhoods for ideological reasons since recent, poorer immigrants to a medieval city usually settled at the outskirts of a town, where land was more readily and cheaply available. For their part the municipal authorities and burghers who financed the construction of the convents apparently wished simultaneously to provide the friars with a residence and to add the stone church and convent to the fortifications of the city at a vulnerable point.[76] The *Rat* and Franciscans of Prenzlau in the Uckermark agreed on July 25, 1270, to change the location of a city gate near the friary and the path to the gate because the din of traffic was disturbing the friars. The old gate was replaced by two new gates at a distance from the convent and the old roadbed was added to the convent property. The friars were required in return to leave a path through their property to the city wall for carts carrying stones in wartime for the defense of the city. The Franciscans were given custody of the keys to the new city gates, though the *Rat* retained the right to demand the surrender of the keys in a military emergency.[77]

In addition to these military functions, the mendicant convent and church, usually the biggest buildings in a medieval town, served as the meet-

73. *Les Registres de Grégoire IX*, ed. Lucien Auvray (Paris, 1907), 2, no. 3983.
74. John B. Freed, "Urban Development and the *Cura monialium* in Thirteenth-Century Germany," *Viator* 3 (1972), 311–327.
75. Richard Kurt Donin, *Die Bettelordenskirchen in Oesterreich: Zur Entwicklungsgeschichte der österreichischen Gothik* (Baden bei Wien, 1935), pp. 316–323; Richard Krautheimer, *Die Kirchen der Bettelorden in Deutschland* (Cologne, 1925), pp. 118–119; Werner Roth, *Die Dominikaner u. Franziskaner im Deutsch-Ordensland Preussen bis zum Jahre 1466* (Königsberg, 1918), p. 5; Bernhard Stüdeli, *Minoritenniederlassungen und mittelalterliche Stadt: Beiträge zur Bedeutung von Minoriten- und anderen Mendikantenanlagen im öffentlichen Leben der mittelalterlichen Stadtgemeinde, insbesondere der deutschen Schweiz*, Franziskanische Forschungen 21 (Werl/Westf., 1969), pp. 68–79.
76. Stüdeli, *Minoritenniederlassungen*, pp. 79–84.
77. *Pommersches UB*, ed. Rodgero Prümers (Stettin, 1881), 2, no. 919. See also no. 986.

ing place for the *Rat* and other municipal bodies, as the site for judicial proceedings and other public assemblies, such as the election of town officials, as the storage place for the city archives, as the reception hall for ambassadors and other important visitors, as the lodging house for distinguished guests, and as a pantheon for honoring famous citizens.[78] This utilization of the mendicant convents for secular purposes has been linked to the distinction which the Franciscans made between the ownership and the temporary use of property. While the Franciscans exercised the right to reside within the convent and to conduct services in the church, the owner, in actual practice often the town itself, retained the right to employ the buildings for other purposes as well. In exchange for financial assistance and land from the municipal authorities, the Dominicans, who could own their churches and convents outright, were forced to accept similar limitations on their rights of ownership.[79]

The foundation of a mendicant convent was an important part in the process of urbanization in thirteenth-century Germany. The friars demonstrated to newcomers from the countryside that it was possible to lead a Christian life within a city and thus helped to prevent the spread of heretical ideas among the burghers whom the church otherwise neglected. At the same time the new convent buildings could serve as a combination fortress, city hall, auditorium, and hotel as well as a religious shrine. The establishment of numerous mendicant convents in southern Germany and in the extreme northwest after 1250 was a recognition of the friars' crucial role in caring for the spiritual needs of the burghers and of the numerous extra benefits that the construction of a mendicant house provided.

6. CONCLUSION

A comparison of the distribution of the Franciscan and Dominican convents in Germany reveals that the Franciscans spread more diffusely and rapidly than the Dominicans. The Franciscans had established by 1300 nearly twice as many convents (approximately 200) as the Dominicans (111), a comparison which includes the 16 Polish and one Italian Dominican priory (Bolzano) which would have been considered German under the Franciscan provincial structure.[80] As Salimbene already observed in the thirteenth cen-

78. Stüdeli, *Minoritenniederlassungen*, pp. 84–111.
79. Ibid., pp. 21–67 and 132–134.
80. See below, pp. 69–75.

tury, the Dominicans tended to concentrate their attention on the major urban centers while the Franciscans tried to reach the smaller towns as well.[81] There is considerable truth in the medieval ditty:

> Bernard liked the valleys, Benedict the hills,
> Francis the towns, Dominic the cities of renown.[82]

Moreover, the Franciscans usually arrived in a city before the Dominicans. By 1300 there were 71 cities which possessed both Dominican and Franciscan houses. The Franciscans definitely arrived first in 43 of these cities, the Dominicans in only 25.[83] The foundation dates of the Dominican convents can usually be determined, however, with far greater accuracy than those of the Franciscan houses. If the alleged foundation dates of the Franciscan convents are substituted, where available, for the first definite reference in a document or chronicle to a Franciscan friary, the ratio tilts even further in the Franciscans' favor. In this case the Franciscans would have settled first in 52 towns, the Dominicans in only 14.

More importantly, as Jacques le Goff has suggested in the case of France,[84] the distribution of the mendicant convents provides a rough guide to the process of urbanization in medieval Germany. With the notable exceptions of Salzburg and Passau, there was no German town of any real significance which did not possess either a Dominican or Franciscan convent by the end of the thirteenth century. There were of course a few houses, such as the Dominican priory in Zofingen and the Franciscan friary in Königsfelden, built as a memorial on the site where King Albrecht I was murdered in 1308,[85] which were located in insignificant communities. But the presence of a mendicant convent in a community can generally serve as a sign that the new settlement had attained the status of a city, along with such traditional indicators as the use of the term *civitas* to describe a community, the appearance of a market, the possession of a city seal, the bestowal of a city charter or other privileges, the building of fortifications, and the presence of an autono-

---

81. Salimbene de Adam, *Cronica*, ed. Ferdinando Bernini, 2 vols. (Bari, 1942), Scrittori d'Italia 187:333.
82. William A. Hinnebusch, *The History of the Dominican Order: Origins and Growth to 1500* (Staten Island, New York, 1966), 1:260.
83. It cannot be determined who arrived first in three towns.
84. "Apostolat mendiant et fait urbain dans la France médiévale: l'implantation des ordres mendiants. Programme-questionnaire pour une enquête," *Annales* 23 (1968), 335–352; and "Ordres mendiants et urbanisation dans la France médiévale: État de l'enquête," *Annales* 25 (1970), 924–946.
85. Stüdeli, *Minoritenniederlassungen*, pp. 40–43.

mous city government. In some ways the foundation of a Franciscan or Dominican convent in a new town may in fact be the most important single indicator since the establishment of a mendicant house represented the recognition of the community's new status by an international, urban-oriented order.

At the same time the presence or absence of a mendicant house, the number of mendicant convents in a town, and their foundation dates provide a tool for ranking cities according to their relative significance. It is important to remember that the friars' peculiar life style required, as St. Bonaventure suggested in his defense of the friars' selection of cities as the sites for their convents,[86] a community large enough to satisfy the material needs of the brothers. Pope Clement IV (1265–1268) stipulated in 1268 that the two mendicant convents within the same city be separated by at least 300 yards to assure the existence of sufficient resources within a town to provide for the friars' subsistence.[87] The number of mendicant convents in a community thus gives some inkling of the approximate size of a town. Fritz Rörig pointed out that about 2800 of the approximately 3000 German communities which were designated as *civitates* in the Middle Ages had less than 1000 inhabitants and cannot really be considered cities. Another 150 communities had between 1000 and 2000 burghers and can be classified as secondary urban centers. The remaining 50 *civitates* with more than 2000 people were the major urban centers in medieval Germany.[88] Rörig's estimate of the number of major and secondary urban centers in medieval Germany conforms fairly closely to the number of mendicant convents in Germany by the end of the thirteenth century. Approximately 169 towns had either a Dominican or Franciscan convent, while 71 cities, Rörig's major urban centers, had both.[89] An analysis of the expansion of the Dominican and Franciscan Orders in Germany in the thirteenth century is in large part the history of medieval German urbanization.

86. See above, p. 11.
87. Cited by Le Goff, "Ordres mendiants," p. 932.
88. *Die europäische Stadt und die Kultur des Bürgertums im Mittelalter*, ed. Luise Rörig and Ahasver v. Brandt, 4th ed. (Göttingen, 1964), p. 76. Rörig's and Dickinson's (see above, n. 5) estimate of the number of *civitates* in medieval Germany are not identical. The discrepancy can probably be attributed to differing conceptions of the boundaries of medieval Germany.
89. The apparent discrepancy between Rörig's 50 major urban centers and the 71 cities which I have labeled as major urban centers is caused by different definitions of the borders of thirteenth-century Germany. My figure includes the convents located in formerly German areas in Poland and Russia, e.g., Breslau and Riga.

2

Germanization and the Expansion
of the Mendicant Orders in Eastern Germany

*After the Germans entered and colonized Polish territory, . . . our
rights were seriously violated. . . . And while we may remain silent a-
bout other matters, we must mention with a heavy heart that certain
German religious, deceiving others by their evil example, were the first
to ignore completely the admonitions of prelates and to weaken the
rigor of ecclesiastical discipline. Indeed, the German Franciscans, after
they expelled the Polish friars from their own country, withdrew, to
the injury of the Polish people and our own humiliation, from the
Polish province, which had been laudably and honorably governed by
their Polish brothers, and joined the province of Saxony.*
Archbishop James of Gnesen (1283–1313) to the Roman Curia.[1]

1. INTRODUCTION

AT THE beginning of the twelfth century the lower Elbe and the Saale Rivers
marked the eastern boundary of German settlement. A few pagan Slavic
tribes inhabited present-day East Germany; the Christian, but politically divided, Poles lived beyond the Oder-Neisse; and various heathen peoples
dwelled along the eastern shore of the Baltic Sea. During the next 200 years
Germans pushed steadily eastward. Although they employed force in the
Wendish Crusade in 1147 and in the conquest of Prussia and the Baltic States
in the thirteenth century, the German penetration of eastern Europe in the
high Middle Ages was generally peaceful. German and Slavic rulers invited
German burghers and peasants to settle within their sparsely populated
territories. By 1200 the Germans had colonized Nordalbingia, western Mecklenburg, and the territory between the Saale and the upper Elbe. In the thirteenth century, the highpoint in the medieval *Drang nach Osten*, the Germans

1. *Urkunden zur Geschichte des Bisthums Breslau im Mittelalter*, ed. Gustav Adolf
Stenzel (Breslau, 1845), no. 144.

settled in eastern Mecklenburg, Pomerania, Brandenburg, Lusatia, Silesia, and the Neumark, and conquered Prussia and the Baltic States.[2]

The Dominican apostolate in eastern Europe was started by Slavic brothers. The 1221 Dominican general chapter sent the Polish noble, St. Hyacinth, who had been converted in Italy, to Cracow to begin the Dominican mission among the Slavs. By 1228 the Dominican province of Poland, to which Bohemia belonged until 1301, possessed houses in Cracow, Prague, Sandomierz, Breslau, and Cammin.[3] An independent, basically Slavic Dominican province had thus been started at an early date in eastern Europe. In the meantime German Dominicans were gradually settling in the sparsely populated territory between the Elbe-Saale and the Oder-Neisse. The province of Teutonia had received by 1250, as Map 2 indicates, priories in Lübeck, Neuruppin, Leipzig, and Freiberg. The boundary between the German and Polish provinces in the Oder Valley became a major source of conflict after 1250.

The German Franciscans had also established by 1250, as Map 1 reveals, a number of convents along the Baltic coast and between the Saale and upper Elbe, the areas first occupied by German settlers. In contrast to the Dominicans, Franciscan activity in eastern Europe was initiated directly from Germany. As minister of Saxony between 1232 and 1239, John of Piancarpino sent the first Franciscans, presumably mainly Germans, to Bohemia, Hungary, and Poland.[4] The Franciscans' apostolate in eastern Europe was thus begun a decade later than the Dominicans'. In Cracow, for example, the Franciscan house was founded in 1237, fifteen years after St. Hyacinth had come to the Polish city.[5] The Franciscan province of Bohemia, which included Poland, was only organized in 1239.[6] German influence remained strong, as subsequent events showed, within the Bohemian province. The Franciscans consequently proved far more amenable to German interests in eastern Europe than the Dominicans. Like some missionaries in more recent times, the friars

2. For additional information about German expansion in eastern Europe, see the bibliography in K. Bosl, A. Gieysztor, F. Graus, M.M. Postan, and F. Seibt, *Eastern and Western Europe in the Middle Ages*, ed. Geoffrey Barraclough (London, 1970), p. 208.

3. Raymond-J. Loenertz, "La Vie de S. Hyacinthe du lecteur Stanislas, envisagée comme source historique," *AFP* 27 (1957), 31–37.

4. Jordan of Giano, *Chronica*, ed. H. Boehmer, Collection d'études et de documents sur l'histoire religieuse et littéraire du moyen âge 6 (Paris, 1908), ch. 55.

5. *Annales Cracovienses compilati*, ed. Richard Röpell and Wilhelm Arndt (Hanover, 1866), MGH SS 19:597.

6. Leonhard Lemmens, "Annales Minorum Prussicorum," *AFH* 6 (1913), 702–704.

quickly became instruments of national aggrandizement, as Archbishop James's complaint quoted above suggests.

The Franciscans and Dominicans thus played an important part in the Germanization and Christianization of the east-Elbian territories. The friars ministered to the spiritual needs of the German settlers, labored among the indigenous heathen population, raised the crusading armies which assisted the Teutonic Knights in the conquest of Prussia and Livonia, and served as bishops in the new missionary dioceses in northeastern Europe. Their ministry was particularly needed in the new German cities which arose in the formerly pagan lands between the Elbe and the Oder-Neisse and along the eastern Baltic coast. The continued expansion of the mendicant orders in Germany after 1250 can thus be attributed to the gradual Germanization of the east-Elbian territories as well as to the late urbanization of southern Germany.

2. The Friars and the East-Elbian Princes

The Dominicans and Franciscans quickly established close personal ties with several of the east-Elbian princes and their families. The German and Slavic rulers in this area welcomed the friars with an enthusiasm unmatched anywhere else in the country. Not only did the princes found numerous convents, but they and their relatives frequently picked friars as their confessors and chose to be interred in a mendicant cemetery or crypt. In an era when men and women often devoted considerable attention to the choice of a final resting place, the princes' selection of mendicant houses as their burial sites sheds considerable light on their personal religious predilections.

In 1236 John of Piancarpino, the provincial minister of Saxony, granted the widowed Countess Audacia of Schwerin and her four daughters permission to receive the sacraments in the Schwerin friary and to be buried there.[7] Audacia's son Gunzelin was married to Margaret, the sister of the Mecklenburg princes John of Mecklenburg (1227–1264) and Nicholas of Werle (1227–1277).[8] John was the founder of the Franciscan convent in Wismar, while Nicholas and his family had Dominican confessors.[9] The various Pomeranian dukes also patronized the friars. Duke Warcisław III of Pomerania-Demmin (1220–1264) gave the Cammin Dominicans in 1228 a lot next to

---

7. *Meklenburgisches UB* (Schwerin, 1863), 1, no. 450.
8. Manfred Hamann, *Mecklenburgische Geschichte von den Anfängen bis zur Landständischen Union von 1523* (Cologne, 1968), pp. 106–107.
9. *Meklenburgisches UB* (Schwerin, 1864), 2, nos. 669 and 670; Heinrich Finke, *Ungedruckte Dominikanerbriefe des 13. Jahrhunderts* (Paderborn, 1891), no. 71.

the church of St. Giles, which they had received from the family of the bur-
grave of the city.[10] The duke's cousin Dobroslawa and her husband Jaczo,
the advocate of Salzwedel, founded in 1242 the Franciscan friary in Greifswald, which had been included in her dowry.[11] Warcisław's kinsman, Duke
Świętopełk of Pomerelia (1220–1266), established in 1227 the Dominican
priory in Danzig.[12] His son Msciwoj II (1266–1294) founded the Franciscan
friary in Neuenburg (1282) and the Dominican priories in Stolp (1278) and
Dirschau (1289).[13]

The Ascanian margraves, John I (1220–1266) and Otto III (1220–1267)
of Brandenburg, were likewise closely associated with the friars. John's first
wife, Sophia, the daughter of King Waldemar II of Denmark, was buried in
1247 in the Franciscan house in Ribe, Denmark, where she had gone to
reconcile her feuding brothers; his second wife, Jutta, the daughter of Duke
Albert of Saxony, was interred in 1287 in the Franciscan convent in Sten-
dal.[14] John repeatedly, though unsuccessfully, asked the Dominicans in the
1260s to found a house in Prenzlau.[15] His brother Otto was an even more
enthusiastic benefactor of the friars. After his marriage in about 1230 to
Beatrice of Bohemia, whose dowry included Upper Lusatia, he probably
founded the Franciscan friaries in Görlitz (1234) and Bautzen (1240).[16] In
1254 Otto established the Dominican priory in Strausberg, to which he gave
land, a Bible with glosses allegedly worth 100 marks, and the money to construct a church.[17] The following year he founded the Dominican house in
Seehausen, to which he gave 120 marks for the purchase of property and 100
marks for the purchase of books.[18] Otto died on October 9, 1267, surrounded by Dominicans, in the city of Brandenburg; he was buried as he had

10. *Pommersches UB*, ed. Robert Klempin (Stettin, 1868), 1, no. 253.
11. Ibid., no. 403.
12. *Preussisches UB*, ed. R. Philippi and August Seraphim (Königsberg, 1882–1909), 1,
1. Abteilung, no. 58.
13. *Annales Minorum Prussicorum*, ed. Ernst Strehlke (Leipzig, 1874), Scriptores rerum
Prussicarum 5:648; *Pommersches UB*, ed. Rodgero Prümers (Stettin, 1881), 2, no.
1126; *Preussisches UB*, 1, 2. Abteilung, no. 537.
14. *Chronica principum Saxoniae*, ed. Oswald Holder-Egger (Hanover, 1880), MGH SS
25:479; *Chronica principum Saxoniae ampliata*, ed. Oswald Holder-Egger (Hanover,
1896), MGH SS 30:34.
15. Finke, *Dominikanerbriefe*, no. 15.
16. *Regesten der Markgrafen von Brandenburg aus askanischem Hause*, ed. Hermann
Krabbo and Georg Winter, Veröffentlichungen des Vereins für Geschichte der Mark
Brandenburg 1 (Leipzig and Berlin, 1910–1955), nos. 627 and 667.
17. Ibid., no. 773.
18. Ibid., no. 784.

wished, in the Strausberg priory.[19] Beatrice died in 1286 and was interred in the nunnery of the Breslau Poor Clares.[20] The margraves' children continued their fathers' patronage of the friars. John's sons, John II (1266–1281), Otto IV (1266–1308), and Conrad (1266–1304), repeated in 1274 their father's request, this time successfully, that the Dominicans found a priory in Prenzlau.[21] Margraves Otto V (1267–1298) and Albert III (1267–1300), the sons of Otto III, probably gave the Berlin Franciscans the land on which their convent was built.[22]

The Ascanians' patronage of the Franciscans can be explained in part by Otto III's marriage to Beatrice of Bohemia, the niece of the Bl. Agnes of Prague (d. 1282), the foundress and abbess of the Prague Poor Clares.[23] Through her influence the Premyslids and their relatives became particularly devoted to the Poor Clares and the Franciscans. Margrave Henry the Illustrious of Meissen (1221–1288) established the nunnery of the Poor Clares in Seusslitz in 1268 in memory of his wife Agnes, another niece of the Prague abbess.[24] Agnes of Prague's influence was especially strong among the Silesian Piasts. Her sister, Anna of Bohemia, founded in 1257 the nunnery of the Breslau Poor Clares, where she was subsequently buried.[25] Anna's husband, Duke Henry II of Silesia (1238–1241), who had been killed by the Mongols at Liegnitz in 1241, was interred in the convent of the Breslau Franciscans.[26] Herbord, a Breslau Franciscan, apparently served as the confessor of Henry's and Anna's sons, Bogusław II of Liegnitz (1241–1278), Henry III of Breslau (1241–1266), Conrad of Glogau (1251–1273), and Archbishop Władysław of Salzburg (1265–1270).[27] Their sister belonged to the nunnery of the Poor

19. *Chronica principum Saxoniae*, p. 480.
20. *Chronica principum Saxoniae ampliata*, p. 34.
21. Finke, *Dominikanerbriefe*, no. 63.
22. *Regesten Brandenburg*, no. 1007.
23. For additional information about Agnes, see Maria Fassbinder, *Die selige Agnes von Prag, eine königliche Klarissin* (Werl, 1957).
24. *Regesta diplomatica necnon epistolaria historiae Thuringiae*, ed. Otto Dobenecker (Jena, 1925), 3, no. 244.
25. *Chronicon Polono-Silesiacum*, ed. Wilhelm Arndt (Hanover, 1866), MGH SS 19: 568; *UB der Kustodien Goldberg und Breslau*, ed. Chrysogonus Reisch, Monumenta Germaniae Franciscana, 2. Abteilung, 1 (Düsseldorf, 1917), 1, no. 20.
26. *Chronicon Polono-Silesiacum*, p. 568.
27. Herbord appears in numerous documents issued by the Silesian dukes between 1248 and 1266: *UB Goldberg*, 1, nos. 5, 7–9, 12, 16, 20, 22, and 26–36. His office is never stated. The early sixteenth-century Franciscan historian, Nicholas Glassberger, *Chronica* (Quaracchi, 1887), AF 2:80, mentioned, however, that a friar Herbord had been the confessor of St. Hedwig, the mother of Henry II. This seems unlikely

Clares in Breslau.[28] The Piasts also patronized the Dominicans. Duke Conrad gave the Glogau Dominicans some property in 1258, while Bogusław was buried in 1278 in the Dominican priory in Liegnitz.[29] The princes clearly had considerable faith in the efficacy of the friars in this world and the next.

The east-Elbian rulers had political as well as personal motives in patronizing the friars. The princes promoted the Dominican and Franciscan Orders as a way to attract settlers to the new towns in their domains. The expansion of the mendicant orders east of the Elbe closely paralleled, as Table V indicates, the eastward advance of the German burghers. Table V compares, wherever the information is available, the foundation date of or the first reference to the existence of an east-Elbian mendicant convent with the foundation date of the city in which the house was located, the year in which the city received German *Stadtrecht*, and/or the year in which the city was first called a *civitas*.[30]

While it is often impossible to establish with precision either the foundation dates of the mendicant convents or of the cities, the evidence in Table V is sufficiently accurate to suggest that the east-Elbian princes patronized the friars as an added inducement to attract settlers to the newly founded towns in their territories. The foundation of a mendicant convent was a comparatively easy way, as was the case in southern Germany, to provide for the spiritual needs of the burghers. It is interesting to observe that in several instances the foundation of the convent and of the city nearly coincided. This was true of the Franciscan friaries in Bautzen, Greifswald, Schweidnitz, Stettin, and Thorn and of the Dominican priories in Culm, Danzig, Elbing, Greifswald, and Soldin. Like the Methodist circuit riders on the American frontier, the friars accompanied the German settlers on their eastward migration. The foundation dates of the mendicant houses can thus serve as a guide to the peaceful Germanization and urbanization of eastern Mecklenburg, Pomerania, Brandenburg, Lusatia, Silesia, and the Neumark in the thirteenth century.

---

because Hedwig died in 1243 while Herbord is first mentioned in 1248. In all probability the Franciscan was the confessor of Hedwig's grandsons. Archbishop Władysław made him bishop of Lavant: *UB Goldberg*, 1, footnote to no. 36.

28. *Chronicon Polono-Silesiacum*, p. 568.
29. *Regesten zur schlesischen Geschichte*, ed. Colmar Grünhagen, 3 vols., Codex diplomaticus Silesiae 7 (Breslau, 1875–1886), 2, no. 992; *Annales Lubenses*, ed. Wilhelm Arndt (Hanover, 1866), MGH SS 19:549.
30. Table V is based on Appendix I and Erich Keyser, *Deutsches Städtebuch: Handbuch städtischer Geschichte*, 4 vols. (Stuttgart, 1939–1964), 1 and 2.

TABLE V
FOUNDATION DATES OF CITIES AND OF MENDICANT CONVENTS LOCATED EAST OF THE ELBE

	Foundation Date of City	German Stadtrecht	Civitas	Foundation Date of Convent	Alleged Foundation Date of Convent	First Definite Reference to Convent
FRANCISCANS						
Custody of Lübeck						
Lübeck	1143 (58)				1223	1233
Schwerin	1160					1236
Riga	1201					1238
Greifswald		1250	1254			
Rostock		1218		1242		1243
Parchim	1225/26					1246
Wismar	1226		1229			
Stralsund		1234		1251/52 1254		
Custody of Stettin (Szczecin)						
Stettin (Szczecin)	1234	1243		1240		1253
Prenzlau		1251				1281
Pyritz (Pyrzyce)		1263				1285
Neubrandenburg	1248	1248	1248			1289
Greifenberg (Gryfice)	1262/64				1264	1299
Angermünde	1230/67		1284		by 1292	1338
Arnswalde (Choszczno)	1284		1291			1340
Dramburg (Drawsko)			1297			

Table V—Continued Overleaf

TABLE V—Continued

FRANCISCANS—Continued

	Foundation Date of City	German Stadtrecht	Civitas	Foundation Date of Convent	Alleged Foundation Date of Convent	First Definite Reference to Convent
Custody of Brandenburg						
Berlin	ca. 1230		1251		before 1249	1252
Salzwedel	1160/70	1207/33	1233			1261
Stendal	1170					1264
Brandenburg					before 1237	1271
Gransee	1253	1262			ca. 1270	1302
Frankfurt an der Oder					before 1270	1303
Kyritz	1237					1303
Custody of Goldberg (Złotoryja)						
Görlitz	ca. 1215				1234	1245
Bautzen		1240			1240	1248
Goldberg (Złotoryja)	1201/31	ca. 1211				1242/58
Crossen (Krosno Odrzanskie)	13th c.		1249			1272
Lauban (Luban)	before 1230					
Zittau				1273	1244	1283
Liegnitz (Legnica)	1202/38?	after 1241	1252			1284
Sagan (Żagań)		1209	1284	1284		1285
Löwenberg (Lwówek Slaski)	ca. 1221				1248	
Löbau				1336		
Sorau (Żary)		1260?	1329			1340

Custody of Breslau (Wrocław)

Breslau (Wrocław)		1261		1236	1241
Schweidnitz (Świdnica)	1241/49				1249
Neisse (Nisa)			1245	1257	1284
Brieg (Brzeg)		1248			1285
Namslau (Namysłów)	1249		1280	1296	1285
Strehlen (Strzelin)	1292				1307
Münsterberg (Ziębice)		1241/53	1291		1307
Neumarkt (Środa Śląska)	before 1214		1238		1318

Custody of Prussia

Thorn (Toruń)	1231				1239
Culm (Chełmno)	1231				1258
Neuenburg (Nowe)					1282
Braunsberg (Braniewo)		1254			1296

DOMINICANS

Province of Teutonia (after 1303 Saxony)

Lübeck	1143 (58)				1229
Riga	1201				1234
Neuruppin	before 1238		1256		1246
Stralsund	1234	1234			1251
Strausberg	1262/70	1232	1284		1254
Rostock	1200/50	1218			1256
Prenzlau	1226	1251			1275
Soldin (Myślibórz)	ca. 1230				1287
Röbel		1261	1261		1293
Wismar			1229		1297
Berlin			1251		1300
Dorpat (Tartu)	1224				

Table V—Continued Overleaf

TABLE V – *Continued*

DOMINICANS – *Continued*

	Foundation Date of City	German Stadtrecht	Civitas	Foundation Date of Convent	Alleged Foundation Date of Convent	First Definite Reference to Convent
Province of Poland[a]						
Breslau (Wrocław)		1261		1226		1285?
Brieg (Brzeg)		1248			1234	1272
Bunzlau (Bolesławiec)	after 1233					
Cammin (Kamień Pomorski)				1228		1285?
Crossen (Krosno Odrzanskie)	1201/31	1274	1249			
Culm (Chełmno)	1231		1236	1233/38		
Danzig (Gdańsk)		ca. 1224		1227		
Dirschau (Tczew)		1260		1289		
Elbing (Elbląg)	1237			1238		
Greifswald		1250	1254			
Liegnitz (Legnica)		after 1241 / 1255	1252	1254		1278
Oels (Oleśnica)						1285?
Pasewalk		ca. 1250	1276	1272		
Schweidnitz (Świdnica)	1241/49				1291	1300
Stolp (Słupsk)		1310		1278		
Thorn (Toruń)	1231			1263		

a. These Polish Dominican houses would have been considered German under the Franciscan provincial structure. See pp. 69–75.

3. PRUSSIA AND THE BALTIC STATES

The Teutonic Knights' conquest of Prussia and the Baltic States was the great exception to the generally peaceful German penetration of eastern Europe in the thirteenth century. Bishop Christian of Prussia (1215–1245), a German Cistercian, had labored as a missionary among the heathen Prussians between 1205/06 and 1220, but the Prussians' legitimate fears of Polish expansion in the guise of Christianity inspired a pagan reaction which forced Christian to abandon his efforts.[31] The Prussians' apostasy and attacks upon their Christian neighbors justified, according to medieval canon law, the use of force to protect Christians, mission activity, and new converts.[32] After an unsuccessful crusade against the Prussians by the Polish princes, the Polish duke Conrad of Mazovia asked the Teutonic Knights in the winter of 1225/26 to subdue his heathen neighbors who were raiding and devastating his duchy, the area around Warsaw. The Teutonic Knights began their conquest of Prussia in 1230 and soon became involved in the subjugation of Livonia as well. Bishop Albert of Riga (1198–1229) had founded in 1202 a military order, the Knights of the Sword, to conquer Livonia, Kurland, and Estonia. The two military orders were merged after the battle of Saule on September 22, 1236, in which the Samogitians, the inhabitants of modern Lithuania, severely defeated the Knights of the Sword. The Teutonic Knights thus assumed the major responsibility for creating sufficiently peaceful conditions in northeastern Europe so that mission activity could be undertaken safely in Prussia and the Baltic States. It took decades of fighting before German rule was firmly established along the shore of the eastern Baltic and the native population was even nominally converted to Christianity.[33]

The papacy assigned to the friars the task of raising additional troops in Germany, Poland, Bohemia, and Scandinavia to assist the Teutonic Knights. The Dominicans undertook this responsibility immediately. Gregory IX

31. Fritz Blanke, "Die Missionsmethode des Bischofs Christian von Preussen," *Heidenmission und Kreuzzugsgedanke in der deutschen Ostpolitik des Mittelalters*, ed. Helmut Beumann (Darmstadt, 1963), pp. 337–363.
32. Hans-Dietrich Kahl, "*Compellere intrare.* Die Wendenpolitik Bruns von Querfurt im Lichte hochmittelalterlichen Missions- und Völkerrechts," *Heidenmission* (see above, n. 31), pp. 177–274; and Erich Weise, *Die Amtsgewalt von Papst und Kaiser und die Ostmission besonders in der 1. Hälfte des 13. Jahrhunderts*, Marburger Ostforschungen 31 (Marburg/Lahn, 1971), pp. 85–108.
33. For additional information, see Fritz Blanke, "Die Entscheidungsjahre der Preussenmission (1206–1274)," *Heidenmission* (see above, n. 31), pp. 389–416; and Hans Patze, "Der Frieden von Christburg vom Jahre 1249," *Heidenmission*, pp. 417–485.

(1227—1241) ordered the Dominicans on September 17, 1230, eight months after he had commanded the Teutonic Knights to begin the Prussian campaign, to preach a crusade against the Prussians in the ecclesiastical provinces of Magdeburg and Bremen, and in Poland, Pomerania, Moravia, Lusatia, Holstein, and Gotland.[34] This crusading bull was the first of eighty similar mandates which were issued by various popes in the next few decades to promote the conquest of Prussia, Livonia, Kurland, Estonia, Samogitia, and Lithuania.[35] The friars who accompanied the crusading armies were instructed to urge the crusaders to help the Teutonic Knights in the building of fortifications and to obey the commands of the military order. Innocent IV instructed the Dominicans in 1253, for instance, to give indulgences to anyone who assisted in the building of fortifications along the Memel (Neman) River.[36]

Twenty-five years passed before the Franciscans received similar instructions. The Polish princes, jealous of the apparent success of the Teutonic Knights, were planning their own crusade against their eastern neighbors in 1255. In connection with this project Alexander IV ordered the Franciscan Bartholomew of Bohemia, who had been the minister of Austria in the late 1240s and who subsequently became minister of Saxony,[37] to preach a crusade in Poland, Bohemia, Moravia, and Austria against the Lithuanians and the Jadzwings, the inhabitants of southeastern Prussia.[38] The Teutonic Knights used their influence in Rome to end this rival undertaking,[39] but the Franciscans were not released from their new obligation. The Teutonic Knights needed all the assistance they could obtain from the friars and the crusading armies which they raised, particularly after the Samogitians defeated the military order at Durben on July 13, 1260. This defeat sparked a revolt which endangered all of the previous German conquests in Prussia and Livonia. The Franciscans and Dominicans received no less than twenty-two bulls to preach a crusade for the benefit of the embattled Teutonic Knights in the crisis years between 1261 and 1264.[40]

34. *Preussisches UB*, 1, 1. Abteilung, no. 81.
35. Marian Tumler, *Der Deutsche Orden im Werden, Wachsen und Wirken bis 1400* (Vienna, 1955), p. 256. The texts of most of the bulls are published in the *Preussisches UB*.
36. *Preussisches UB*, 1, 1. Abteilung, no. 275. See also nos. 99, 100, and 101.
37. G. E. Friess, "Geschichte der oesterreichischen Minoritenprovinz," *Archiv für österreichische Geschichte* 64 (1882), 183, no. 10; and Jordan of Giano, ch. 78.
38. *Preussisches UB*, 1, 1. Abteilung, no. 322.
39. Victor Gidžiunas, "De missionibus fratrum Minorum in Lituania (saec. XIII et XIV.)," *AFH* 42 (1949), 7—14.
40. Tumler, *Der Deutsche Orden*, p. 256.

It is not difficult to explain why the Dominicans became involved in the Prussian and Baltic crusades long before the Franciscans. When the Prussian campaign started in 1230, the Dominicans were already firmly established in Poland, and their Polish priories could easily serve as bases of operation. Duke Świętopełk of Pomerelia had founded the Dominican priory in Danzig in 1227 as a mission center.[41] The Franciscans for their part had not yet crossed the Elbe; their easternmost outpost in 1230 was Magdeburg. Moreover, in the 1220s and 1230s, as we will see in a subsequent chapter, the Franciscans lacked the trained personnel and contacts with the knightly class in Germany which were needed to promote such an undertaking.[42] Finally, the Dominicans had probably retained their founder's interest in the spiritual needs of northeastern Europe. Bishop Diego of Osma and St. Dominic had originally intended, it will be recalled, to go to the eastern Baltic as missionaries. It was only natural, therefore, that Gregory IX did not call on the Franciscans in 1230 to undertake the Prussian assignment. When the Franciscans were finally prepared to assume the task in the 1240s, the conflict between Frederick II and Innocent IV had overshadowed the Prussian and Baltic crusades in importance and had caused a deterioration in relations between the curia and the Teutonic Knights, who were inclined to support the Hohenstaufen.[43] The German Dominicans received, as far as I can tell, no papal order to preach a crusade on behalf of the Teutonic Knights between 1243 and 1252.[44] It was only after the Hohenstaufen danger in Germany had subsided and after Innocent IV had become increasingly conscious of the need to turn Prussia into a secure bastion against the Mongols that the papacy again felt free to direct German attention to the northeast.[45]

When an area had been sufficiently pacified by the Teutonic Knights and by the German, Polish, and Bohemian crusaders, the friars started to preach to the heathen population. As early as July 9, 1231, Gregory IX was urging the inhabitants of Pomesania, the territory on the right bank of the Vistula in East Prussia, to remain faithful to the Christian religion which they had received from the Dominicans who labored among them.[46] The appointment of friars as missionary bishops in northeastern Europe was an important step in the propagation of the Christian faith. It was customary in the Middle Ages

---

41. *Preussisches UB*, 1, 1. Abteilung, no. 58.
42. See below, p. 128.
43. Patze, "Der Frieden von Christburg" (see above, n. 33), pp. 433–434.
44. *Preussisches UB*, 1, 1. Abteilung, nos. 151 and 255.
45. Patze, "Der Frieden von Christburg," pp. 461–483.
46. *Preussisches UB*, 1, 1. Abteilung, no. 84.

to establish dioceses as quickly as possible in newly Christianized areas so that missionary activity could be undertaken under episcopal leadership.[47] Gregory IX accordingly instructed the papal legate, Bishop William of Modena, in 1236 to divide the bishopric of Prussia into three dioceses and to appoint Dominicans as bishops.[48] Bishop Christian's opposition delayed the division until 1243. The friars who filled the Prussian bishoprics before 1273 were: the Dominicans Ernest of Pomesania (1249–1260), Heidenreich of Culm (1246–1263), and Henry, bishop among the Jadzwings (1249–ca. 1262)[49]; and the Franciscans John of Diest, who briefly served as bishop of Sambia (1252–1254),[50] and Albert of Pomesania (1261–1285).[51] The Livonian mendicant bishops were: the Franciscans Henry of Luxembourg, who served as bishop of Zemgale (1247–1251) and of Kurland (1251–1263),[52] and Dietrich of Wierland (Viru) (1247–1272),[53] and the Dominican Henry of Oesel-Wiek (Sarema) (1234–1260/62).[54] Unfortunately, we know almost nothing about their actual missionary endeavors. In fact these bishops frequently served as auxiliary bishops in Germany since their dioceses were in such turmoil as to make mission activity virtually impossible. Judging by the slow Christianization of northeastern Europe, the friars seem to have had more success in preaching crusades than in converting the heathen.

Finally, as was the case in the other colonial areas, the friars ministered to the spiritual needs of the German burghers who settled in Prussia and the Baltic States. The Teutonic Knights often provided the friars with the necessary facilities to exercise their apostolate. *Landmeister* Hermann Balk of Prussia (1229–1239), under whose leadership the conquest of Prussia was started in 1230, founded the Dominican priory in Elbing in 1238 so that the friars could care for the spiritual needs of the newly established town.[55] Gerhard

47. Blanke, "Missionsmethode" (see above, n. 31), pp. 351–352.
48. *Preussisches UB*, 1, 1. Abteilung, no. 125.
49. Berthold Altaner, *Die Dominikanermissionen des 13. Jahrhunderts*, Breslauer Studien zur historischen Theologie 3 (Habelschwerdt, Silesia, 1924), pp. 167–176; Thomas Kaeppeli, "Heidenricus, Bischof von Kulm († 1263): Verfasser eines Traktates De amore S. Trinitatis," *AFP* 30 (1960), 196–205.
50. Willibrord Lampen, "Joannes van Diest, O.F.M.," *Bijdragen voor de Geschiedenis van het Bisdom van Haarlem* 44 (1926), 306–307.
51. *Preussisches UB*, 1, 2. Abteilung, no. 378.
52. Konrad Eubel, "Der Minorit Heinrich von Lützelburg, Bischof von Semgallen, Curland und Chiemsee," *HJb* 6 (1885), 92–100.
53. *Annales Egmundani*, ed. Georg Pertz (Hanover, 1859), MGH SS 16:478.
54. Altaner, *Dominikanermissionen*, pp. 191–192.
55. *Codex diplomaticus Warmiensis oder Regesten und Urkunden zur Geschichte Ermlands*, ed. Carl Peter Woelky and Johann Martin Saage, Monumenta historiae

of Hirzberg, the assistant *Landmeister* (1257–1259), likewise gave the Franciscans in 1258 their house and lot in Culm; and Anno of Sangershausen, the *Hochmeister* of the Teutonic Knights (1257–1274), granted the Thorn Dominicans in 1263 a lot, the right to use the mill stream, and permission to fish in the Culmerland.[56] Anno explained in his foundation charter that it was only proper that the Teutonic Knights repay the Dominicans for the great services which the friars had rendered the military order.

The Dominicans arrived in Riga before the Teutonic Knights. At the request of the papal legate Bishop William of Modena, Bishop Nicholas of Riga (1229–1253) gave the Dominicans in 1234 his own residence in the hope that they might be able to propagate the Christian faith in Livonia.[57] There must have been some doubt at first about the provincial assignment of this distant outpost since the priory was only received by the province of Teutonia in 1244.[58] The Franciscans had settled in Riga by 1238,[59] and the convent was assigned, rather significantly in light of the commercial and historical ties which connected Riga and Lübeck, to the distant custody of Lübeck. The Dominican province of Teutonia received in 1300 the house located in Dorpat. The Reval (Tallin) priory in northern Estonia, which was under Danish rule, belonged to the Dominican province of Dacia.[60] The friar thus played, along with the Teutonic Knight, the burgher, and the peasant, a crucial role in the history of German colonization in central and eastern Europe in the thirteenth century.

4. German-Polish Boundary Disputes

By the second half of the thirteenth century German expansion in eastern Europe aroused increasing resentment among the Polish clergy and nobility, whose position was threatened by the steady influx of German settlers.[61] As

---

Warmiensis oder Quellensammlung zur Geschichte Ermlands, 1. Abtheilung, 1 (Mainz, 1860), 1, Diplomata, no. 1.

56. *Annales Minorum Prussicorum* (see above, n. 13), p. 648; *Preussisches UB*, 1, 2. Abteilung, no. 197.

57. G. von Walter-Wittenheim, *Die Dominikaner in Livland im Mittelalter*, DHIHFP 9 (Rome, 1938), p. 135, no. 1.

58. Paulus von Loë, *Statistisches über die Ordensprovinz Saxonia*, QFGDD 4 (Leipzig, 1910), p. 12.

59. *Liv- Esth- und Curländisches UB*, ed. Friedrich Georg von Bunge (Reval, 1857), 3, Nachträge, no. 159.

60. For further information about the house in Reval, see Ernst Kühnert, "Das Dominikanerkloster zu Reval," *Beiträge zur Kunde Estlands* 12 (1926), 5–46.

61. *The Cambridge History of Poland*, ed. W.F. Reddaway, J.H. Penson, O. Halecki, and R. Dyboski (Cambridge, 1950), 1:100–101. Much of the material in this sec-

the ethnic balance slowly shifted in eastern Europe, the German friars attempted to adjust the boundaries between the Dominican provinces of Teutonia and Poland and the Franciscan provinces of Saxony and Bohemia. These efforts to change the provincial frontiers became a focal point from the 1260s in the mounting hostility between Germans and Slavs. The two orders reacted differently to their common problem. The Polish Dominicans successfully resisted the German attempts to change the provincial boundaries, but the German Franciscans, whose influence had apparently remained strong within the Bohemian province, succeeded in altering the frontiers in favor of the Saxon province.

Margrave John I of Brandenburg triggered the dispute over provincial boundaries within the Dominican Order. In the early 1260s he repeatedly asked the Dominican general chapter and the province of Teutonia to establish a convent in Prenzlau in the Uckermark, the territory to the west of the Oder sandwiched between Hither Pomerania and Brandenburg (see Map 4).[62] The Uckermark was itself a disputed territory. It had originally belonged to Pomerania, whose rulers had accepted Polish suzerainty at the beginning of the twelfth century. In 1231 Frederick II had enfeoffed Margraves John I and Otto III of Brandenburg with Pomerania, and Duke Warcisław III of Pomerania-Demmin had formally recognized the margraves in 1236 as his feudal lords. Duke Barnim I of Pomerania-Stettin (1220–1278) had finally ceded the Uckermark to the margraves in March 1250.[63] John's request thus raised once more in an altered form the thorny question whether the Uckermark was in fact German or Polish territory. The proposed priory in Prenzlau was situated, moreover, near the poorly defined boundary between the two Dominican provinces. The house in Strausberg, south of Prenzlau in eastern Brandenburg, had been received in 1254 by Teutonia, while the convent in Greifswald, northwest of Prenzlau in Hither Pomerania, had been assigned in the same year to Poland. The provincial affiliation of the new house was thus far from clear.

The Polish Dominicans in Cammin accordingly claimed the proposed foundation for their own province. Margrave John insisted in a letter written

---

tion appeared earlier in my article, "The Friars and the Delineation of State Boundaries in the Thirteenth Century," *Order and Innovation in the Middle Ages: Essays in Honor of Joseph R. Strayer*, ed. William C. Jordan, Bruce McNab, and Teofilo F. Ruiz (Princeton, 1976), pp. 31–40, 425–428, and is reprinted by permission of Princeton University Press.

62. Finke, *Dominikanerbriefe* (see above, n. 9), no. 15.

63. *Cambridge History of Poland*, 1:46–47; and Johannes Schultze, *Die Mark Brandenburg* (Berlin, 1961), 1:141–143.

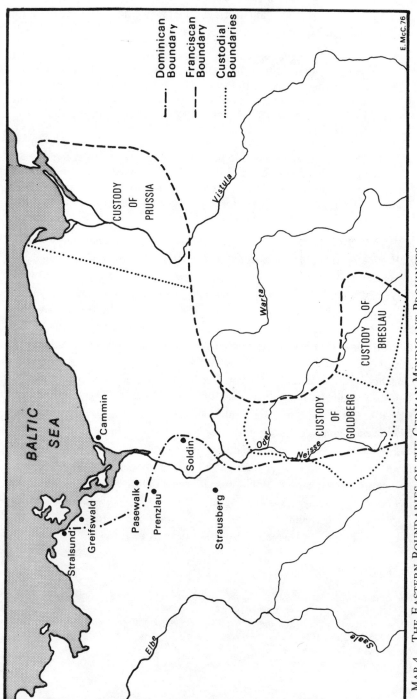

MAP 4. THE EASTERN BOUNDARIES OF THE GERMAN MENDICANT PROVINCES

to the Dominican general chapter in 1264 that he would only accept a house
which was assigned to the province of Teutonia:

> We . . . asked in our letters to your general and provincial chapters that a
> Dominican convent be founded within our domains. . . . We have learned
> that the hearing of our petition has been delayed because, among other
> reasons, the Polish brothers seek to obtain for their own province that
> part of our territory which belongs to the diocese of Cammin, where they
> already have a house and where, before your order existed, some non-
> Polish Slavs had lived. We want you to know that we are neither willing
> nor able to support them (the Polish Dominicans) within that territory if,
> God forbid, you do not grant us a house which belongs to the province of
> Teutonia. The Polish princes might otherwise use this provincial assign-
> ment as a pretext to challenge our descendants' right to this land which
> we possess by full right from the Empire.[64]

The provincial assignment of a mendicant convent had become the potential
basis for a territorial or feudal claim to the region in which it was situated.

In his reply to the margrave's request, the Dominican master general John
of Vercelli (1264–1283) promised to send some friars to the mark as quickly
as possible and expressed the pious wish that the Polish and German Dominicans could compete with one another in the service of God under the protection of a devout prince.[65] But relations between the German and Polish friars
steadily worsened. The 1267 general chapter punished the priors of the two
neighboring convents in Hither Pomerania, Stralsund in Teutonia and Greifswald in Poland, for quarreling violently over the quest for alms.[66] A decade
passed before a convent was actually founded in Prenzlau, in what appears to
have been a compromise resolution of the imbroglio. In 1272 a Dominican
convent was apparently established by Margrave John II in Pasewalk, another
town in the Uckermark, and assigned to the province of Poland.[67] In exchange the province of Teutonia was allowed to receive in 1275 the convent
in Prenzlau, as John I's sons had again requested,[68] and an additional house
in Soldin in the Neumark, the territory north of the Warta and east of the
Oder which had been acquired by the Ascanians in 1252/53.[69] It was thus

64. Finke, *Dominikanerbriefe*, no. 15.
65. Ibid., no. 16.
66. *Acta capitulorum generalium ordinis Praedicatorum*, ed. Benedictus Maria Reichert,
   MOPH 3 (Rome, 1898), 1:139–140.
67. H. Hoogeweg, *Die Stifte und Klöster der Provinz Pommern*, 2 vols. (Stettin, 1924–
   1925), 2:229–233.
68. Finke, *Dominikanerbriefe*, nos. 63–66.
69. Schultze, *Brandenburg*, 1:154–158.

impossible for either the Germans or the Poles to use the provincial assignments of the Dominican convents in the Uckermark as the basis for a territorial or feudal claim to the region.

As a result of this compromise, the boundary between the Dominican
provinces of Teutonia and Poland was highly irregular. The province of
Poland possessed two houses west of the lower Oder, Greifswald and Pasewalk, while the province of Teutonia had one house east of the Oder, Soldin.
Further south, the Neisse formed the boundary between the two provinces.
The Dominican houses in Farther Pomerania, Prussia, and Silesia, as well as
Greifswald and Pasewalk in Hither Pomerania, thus belonged to Poland. The
boundary between the two provinces bore a certain resemblance to the mod-
ern German-Polish frontier.

It is highly questionable whether this boundary accurately reflected the
ethnic composition of the Pomeranian, Prussian, and Silesian towns in the
second half of the thirteenth century. The Dominican general chapter tried,
therefore, to adjust the frontier between the German and Polish provinces.
The 1279 general chapter passed a resolution to transfer the priories of Greifswald and Pasewalk from the province of Poland to Teutonia.[70] A measure of
this type required the approval of three consecutive general chapters. After
the resolution had been approved for the second time in 1280,[71] the opponents of the proposal, presumably the Poles, used procedural means to block
the passage of the measure for the third time in 1281. The opposition succeeded in obtaining in 1281 separate votes on the transfer of the two priories.
While the transfers were again approved, the two separate resolutions were
not considered identical with the single measure which had been approved in
the previous years.[72] The transfer of the two convents thus required two
additional approbations. The 1281 general chapter also voted to transfer the
convent of Cammin from Poland to Teutonia. To compensate the Poles for
their losses, the general chapter decided to assign Soldin to Poland. The 1282
general chapter only approved the transfer of Cammin.[73] The issue either
ceased to be considered or failed to obtain an affirmative vote after 1282.
The German-Polish Dominican boundary thus remained in the end unchanged.

70. *Acta capitulorum generalium*, 1:202.
71. Ibid., 1:206.
72. Ibid., 1:212–213. The general chapter used the word *inchoamus* to indicate that a
    resolution had been approved for the first time, *approbamus* for the second time,
    and *confirmamus* for the third time. The 1281 chapter used *inchoamus* when it
    approved the transfer of the two priories.
73. Ibid., 1:216.

The firmly entrenched Polish Dominicans had kept their frontier intact. It proved to be a costly victory since it placed the Dominicans in eastern Europe at odds with German rulers and colonists. The Teutonic Knights stopped patronizing the Dominicans in the fourteenth century as relations between Prussia and Poland deteriorated.[74]

The Ascanians' territorial ambitions apparently precipitated in the 1260s a similar controversy over provincial boundaries within the Franciscan Order, which proved far more amenable to German interests than the Dominicans. In 1262 Margrave Otto III of Brandenburg, John's brother, was permanently enfeoffed with Upper Lusatia, which King Wenceslaus I of Bohemia (1230–1253) had previously mortgaged to him.[75] The next year the Pisa general chapter voted to transfer the custody of Goldberg, which included the convents in Upper Lusatia and Lower Silesia, from the province of Bohemia to the province of Saxony and also placed the custody of Moravia under the jurisdiction of the Austrian province.[76] The timing of the general chapter's decision does not appear to have been purely coincidental in view of the Ascanians' strong convictions about the boundaries of mendicant provinces. The Silesian Piasts also favored the change, while the Premyslids bitterly opposed it.[77] Bohemian counterpressure presumably made the 1266 Paris general chapter revoke the 1263 decision. But the dissension among the Polish, German and Czech friars who composed the Bohemian province persisted. The Czechs met by themselves in 1268 and elected their own provincial vicar, while the Polish and German brothers gathered in Goldberg. This internally divided province was unable to resist further German pressure. The 1269 Assisi general chapter once more transferred the custody of Goldberg to Saxony; the 1272 Lyons general chapter also assigned the custody of Breslau, which included most of the remaining Silesian houses, to the German province.[78] The custody of Prussia was likewise added to Saxony sometime between 1258 and 1284.[79] By the 1280s at the latest the Franciscan convents in Pomerania, Prussia, the Neumark, Lusatia, and most of Silesia belonged to

---

74. Werner Roth, *Die Dominikaner u. Franziskaner im Deutsch-Ordensland Preussen bis zum Jahre 1466* (Königsberg, 1918), pp. 17–18.

75. Schultze, *Brandenburg*, 1:140.

76. Jan Kazimierz Biernacki, *Speculum Minorum* (Cracow, 1688), p. 229.

77. Franz Palacky, *Ueber Formelbücher, zunächst im Bezug auf böhmische Geschichte* (Prague, 1842), pp. 287–288, no. 54.

78. Biernacki, *Speculum Minorum*, pp. 231–233; André Callebaut, "Le Chapitre général de 1272 célébré à Lyon," *AFH* 13 (1920), 313–314.

79. Lemmens, "Annales Minorum Prussicorum" (see above, n. 6), 704.

Saxony. The new eastern boundary of the Franciscan province of Saxony bore a striking resemblance to the imperial German frontier in 1914.

Two undated letters written by Queen Kunigunde, the Hungarian wife of Ottokar II of Bohemia (1253–1278), give some insight into the bitterness of this quarrel over provincial boundaries and the tactics which the German Franciscans employed. The first letter was addressed to the Cistercian abbess, Agnes of Trebnitz (1268–1278), the daughter of Duke Henry II of Silesia and Anna of Bohemia. Kunigunde rebuked Agnes for favoring the German Franciscans rather than the Polish and Bohemian brothers. It was Agnes's religious and dynastic duty as a princess of Polish and Czech blood, Kunigunde counseled, to help rather than to hurt the Slavic friars who were laboring among her own oppressed people.[80] At the same time the queen complained to an unnamed cardinal, whose aid she implored, about the persecution of the Polish Franciscans. The German friars were preventing the Polish brothers, to the detriment of the Polish realm and language, from conducting divine services for their own people. The German Franciscans, who were present in far greater numbers than was necessary, were seeking to destroy the Polish friars by filling the Polish convents with German brothers and by sending the Polish Franciscans to foreign lands where their services were not required. The Polish people suffered consequently from a lack of spiritual nourishment.[81]

The pent-up hatred between Germans and Poles finally exploded in the 1280s in a violent quarrel between Duke Henry IV of Silesia-Breslau (1266–1290), the grandson of Henry II and Anna of Bohemia, and Bishop Thomas II of Breslau (1270–1292).[82] They fought about the extent of ducal jurisdiction over the domains of the Breslau church in the Ottmachau-Neisse (Otmuchów-Nisa) area, particularly the duke's right to tax episcopal subjects. Underlying and embittering the entire conflict was the growing opposition of

80. Palacky, *Formelbücher*, pp. 287–288, no. 54.
81. Ibid., p. 288, no. 55.
82. The most detailed, though not completely accurate account of the quarrel is Gustav Adolf Stenzel's introduction in the *Urkunden zur Geschichte des Bisthums Breslau* (see above, n. 1). In addition, see: Hermann Aubin, Ludwig Petry, and Herbert Schlenger, *Geschichte Schlesiens* (Stuttgart, 1961), 1:163–174; Colmar Grünhagen, *Geschichte Schlesiens* (Gotha, 1884), 1:102–117; and Ernst Maetschke, "Der Kampf um den Grenzwald zwischen den Herzögen und Bischöfen von Breslau im 13. Jahrhundert," *Z des Vereins für Geschichte Schlesiens* 62 (1928), 65–81. Most of the relevant documents were published by Stenzel and published or summarized in the *Regesten zur schlesischen Geschichte* (see above, n. 29), 3, and in the *UB Goldberg* (see above, n. 25), 1.

the Polish clergy and nobility, led by Bishop Thomas, to German colonization, which had been zealously promoted throughout the century by the
Silesian Piasts. The dispute reveals to us the extent of the friars' entanglement
in the German-Polish confrontation in eastern Europe and the importance
which both sides attached to the provincial boundaries of the mendicant
provinces.

After Henry IV rejected a 1282 legatine arbitral decision as too favorable
to his rival, Bishop Thomas excommunicated the duke and interdicted his
domains in the spring and summer of 1284.[83] After some equivocation, the
Silesian Dominicans, who were under the jurisdiction of the Polish province,
decided to observe and to publish the episcopal sentences.[84] The duke retaliated in December 1285 by expelling the Breslau Dominicans from their convent.[85] The Franciscans, who had always been especially favored by the
Piasts and who had been affiliated since 1272 with the Saxon province, defied
the commands and censures of Bishop Thomas, Archbishop James of Gnesen,
a provincial synod, and Popes Martin IV and Honorius IV (1285–1287), and
faithfully supported the duke throughout the lengthy and bitter quarrel.[86]
Bishop Thomas in fact depicted Herman, the lector of the Breslau Franciscans, as the duke's principal adviser and confidant.[87] The grateful duke in
turn commanded his subjects in February 1285 to give alms to the Franciscans and to hear mass only in Franciscan churches; he threatened to execute
and to confiscate the property of anyone who disobeyed these orders.[88] The
Breslau Beguines, who were under the Dominicans' supervision, were expelled
from their houses for heeding the duke's excommunication, and ducal archers
were installed in the vacant buildings.[89]

Archbishop James and Bishop Thomas, who at one point referred to the
Franciscans as a pernicious disease (*morbus pestiferus*) which threatened to
infect the Polish church,[90] were convinced that the Franciscans' stubborn
disobedience was the consequence of their affiliation with the Saxon province
and of their dependence upon the German princes. The archbishop in a letter
written to several cardinals in January 1285 linked, as we have already seen,

83. *Regesten zur schlesischen Geschichte*, 3, nos. 1783 and 1832.
84. *Urkunden Breslau*, nos. 83 and 126.
85. *Regesten zur schlesischen Geschichte*, 3:77.
86. *UB Goldberg*, 1, nos. 59, 60, 62, 65–68, and 70–87.
87. Ibid., nos. 76, 77, and 86.
88. Ibid., no. 74.
89. *Regesten zur schlesischen Geschichte*, 3, no. 1884.
90. *UB Goldberg*, 1, no. 68.

the Franciscans' defiance of episcopal authority to the problem of German expansion into Polish territory. Since the German princes had conquered Polish territory and since German colonists had settled in Poland, the archbishop complained, the rights of the Polish church had been systematically disregarded and the Polish people oppressed. The German Franciscans had set a particularly bad example; to the great anger of the Poles, they had expelled the Polish friars from their convents, had separated themselves from the province of Bohemia, and had joined the Saxon province. The German Franciscans did not permit the Polish friars to reside within their houses because the Polish brothers, unlike the Germans, obeyed and revered their ecclesiastical superiors. Archbishop James requested that the cardinals protect the threatened Polish church and people by returning the Silesian Franciscan convents to the province of Bohemia since this was the only way these houses could possibly be reformed.[91] To buttress a similar request to the forthcoming Franciscan general chapter in Milan, Bishop Thomas pointed out in March 1285 that the Franciscan convents in Upper Silesia in the custody of Oppeln (Opole), which had remained under the jurisdiction of the Bohemian province, were steadfastly supporting him.[92]

The dispute was finally resolved when the childless duke on his deathbed freed the episcopal domain on June 23, 1290, from all burdens and duties, imposed by either Polish or German law, and surrendered his judicial rights in the Ottmachau-Neisse area.[93] The mounting Polish opposition to German colonization gradually halted further large-scale German expansion in eastern Europe. But the provincial boundaries of the mendicant provinces were not changed.

Few incidents reveal as clearly how much the friars had departed by the end of the thirteenth century from their original ideals than this Silesian version of Thomas à Becket's defense of ecclesiastical liberty. The friars had ceased to be independent witnesses of universal Christian truth in the midst of earthly society, but had been transformed into leading protagonists in the age-old tragic conflict between Germans and Slavs in eastern Europe.

---

91. *Urkunden Breslau*, no. 144. See the introductory quotation.
92. *UB Goldberg*, 1, no. 76.
93. *Regesten zur schlesischen Geschichte*, 3, no. 2141. See also Wilhelm Schulte, "Das Ende des Kirchenstreits zwischen dem breslauer Bishof Thomas II. und dem Herzog Heinrich IV.," *Z des Vereins für Geschichte und Altertums Schlesiens* 39 (1905), 199–225.

3

The Friars in Cologne

Cologne . . . the Holy City.
Gotfrid Hagen, vv. 7−8.[1]

1. INTRODUCTION

ALTHOUGH the fragmentary nature of the extant evidence generally makes it necessary to construct a picture of the friars' activities from scattered references throughout Germany, additional insights into the friars' involvement in urban politics can be gained from the study of a single city. Such an examination can serve as a model for the entire country. The Dominican and Franciscan convents in Cologne, the largest city in medieval Germany, have been selected for such scrutiny.

Cologne, it should be pointed out, is not an ideal choice for such an examination. It was by medieval standards a metropolis to which other German cities were invariably compared.[2] The thirteenth-century population of Cologne has been estimated as in excess of 40,000; in contrast Lübeck, the linchpin of the Hanseatic League, is said to have had 28,000 inhabitants before the Black Death, while Augsburg and Strasbourg contained approximately 25,000 people.[3] The constitution of Cologne in the thirteenth cen-

---

1. *Dit is dat boich van der stede Colne*, ed. Hermann Cardauns and K. Schröder, Die Chroniken der deutschen Städte 12 (Leipzig, 1875). This is an extremely poor edition and should only be used in conjunction with Ernst Dornfeld's *Untersuchungen zu Gottfried Hagens Reimchronik der Stadt Köln*, Germanistische Abhandlungen 40 (Breslau, 1912). For additional information about Hagen, who was the town clerk and a relative of the Overstolz family, and about the chronicle, see Heinrich Kelleter, "Gottfried Hagen und sein Buch von der Stadt Köln," *WZ* 13 (1894), 150−218.

2. See, for instance, *Codices traditionum ecclesiae Pataviensis, olim Laureacensis*, Monumenta Boica 28 (1829), pp. 274−277, no. 49.

3. Josiah Cox Russell, *Medieval Regions and their Cities* (Bloomington, Indiana, 1972), pp. 83−87, 90−96, 106−111.

79

tury was also in many ways atypical. The *Richerzeche*, a social club with governmental functions unique to Cologne, has baffled generations of legal historians, while the *Rat*, the typical institution of medieval German town government, emerged only comparatively late as the dominant communal body within the city. Finally, the Cologne convents were major intellectual centers which included among their members such famous scholars and teachers as St. Albertus Magnus, St. Thomas Aquinas, and the Bl. John Duns Scotus. The membership of the two houses was thus probably more international and better educated than in the average German convent. There can be little doubt that St. Albert, who was closely associated with the Cologne Dominicans for half a century, enormously enhanced the prestige of his priory. It would be foolish to regard either the mendicant convents in Cologne or the city itself as typical.

Cologne quite clearly is the classic example of the older German city, described in the first chapter, which possessed numerous established urban and ecclesiastical institutions. There were within the city by the time the friars arrived in 1221 a cathedral, sixteen parish churches, eleven collegiate churches, three Benedictine monasteries, two Benedictine nunneries, three Augustinian nunneries, one Cistercian nunnery, a church of the Teutonic Knights, and sixteen chapels.[4] These churches contained the relics of many famous saints, most notably the bodies of the Magi in the cathedral. The presence of these numerous ecclesiastical foundations, which gave the city a reputation for sanctity, undoubtedly restricted the scope of the friars' activities. Few Cologne patricians in the thirteenth century were inclined to exchange a comfortable living in one of the collegiate or parish churches for the austere discipline of the mendicant convents.[5] While it might have been preferable, had the sources been available, to study the friars' ministry in a less developed urban center, such as Strasbourg, or in one of the new cities south of the Main or east of the Elbe, which afforded the friars greater opportunities to exercise their apostolate and where the friars' services were more urgently needed, the absence of any simplistic pattern is in itself worth noting.

The abundance of the surviving evidence about medieval Cologne was the chief reason for its selection as the object of this study. The *Schreinsbücher*, the land registers of the city, can supply the historian with information un-

4. Hermann Keussen, *Topographie der Stadt Köln im Mittelalter*, 2 vols. (Bonn, 1910), 1:147*–148*.
5. Gabriel M. Löhr, *Beiträge zur Geschichte des kölner Dominikanerklosters im Mittelalter*, QFGDD 15–17 (Leipzig, 1920–1922), 1:36–46.

available for any other German city in the thirteenth century.[6] It is possible
to uncover the network of familial, social, political, and commercial ties
which linked many of the friars' patrons and which eventually ensnared the
brothers. Within half a century the friars were transformed from suspect out-
siders into accepted and respected members of the political and religious
establishment, closely associated with and indebted to the triumphant Overstolz faction within the patriciate. This chapter offers an example of the friars'
initial success and ultimate failure at the local level.

2. THE FOUNDATION OF THE CONVENTS

The Dominicans arrived in Cologne several months before the Franciscans.[7] The 1221 Bologna general chapter sent the Danish Dominican Solomon of Aarhus to King Waldemar II of Denmark and to Archbishop Andrew
of Lund to begin the Dominican mission in Scandinavia. Solomon passed
through Cologne on his journey and left behind as prior of the new convent
his companion Christian, a gifted preacher. But Christian was soon recognized
as a former Cistercian monk who had been excommunicated for apostasy by

6. The *Schreinsbücher*, which are located in the city archives, have not been published.
A representative sample of the approximately 150,000 entries for the thirteenth and
fourteenth centuries was published by Hans Planitz and Thea Buyken, *Die kölner
Schreinsbücher des 13. und 14. Jahrhundert*, PGRhGk 46 (Weimar, 1937). Hermann
Keussen's *Topographie der Stadt Köln* utilized much of the material contained in
the *Schreinsbücher*. The documents dealing with the Dominicans were published in
Löhr's *Beiträge zur Geschichte des kölner Dominikanerklosters*. I have used unpub-
lished entries in the *Schreinsbücher* in writing about the Franciscans. To avoid
confusion between the citations to the published and unpublished entries in the
Schreinsbücher, the documents published by Planitz and Buyken will be cited as
Planitz, *Schreinsbücher*. The other references in the notes to the *Schreinsbücher*
are to the unpublished entries.
   Scholars have been primarily interested in the origins of the Cologne commune
and of the various municipal institutions in the late eleventh and twelfth centuries
and have paid relatively little attention to the actual functioning of the patrician
regime in the thirteenth century. The emphasis has been on legal and constitutional
rather than social and economic history. The only general history of medieval
Cologne is Leonard Ennen's *Geschichte der Stadt Köln*, 5 vols. (Cologne, 1863−80),
which has been completely superseded by later research. Friedrich Lau's *Die Entwicklung der kommunalen Verfassung und Verwaltung der Stadt Köln bis zum Jahre
1396* (Bonn, 1898), still provides the best introduction to the constitutional history
and structure of the city. Other relevant literature will be cited where pertinent.
7. *Gesta Treverorum continuata*, ed. G. Waitz (Hanover, 1879), MGH SS 24:399. No
Cologne chronicler mentioned the arrival of the friars in the city. The available evidence corroborates most of the statements made by the Trier chronicler.

the abbot of Clairvaux, and he was forced to leave the city and to rejoin his own order.[8] He was quickly replaced as prior in the winter of 1221/1222 by Henry of Cologne, a former Utrecht cathedral canon and student of theology at the University of Paris. Jordan of Saxony, the second master general of the Dominicans (1222–1237), had persuaded Henry, his best friend, to enter the order with him in Paris on Ash Wednesday, 1220.[9] The new prior soon erased the bad impression which Christian's unsavory past must have created for the new order in Cologne. He had a brief, but effective, ministry until his death in 1229.[10] Under Henry's leadership the Dominicans settled on Stolkgasse in the district of Niederich in the chapel and hospital of St. Mary Magdalene, which had been built in about 1180 by a canon of St. Andrew's (see Map 5).[11] The Dominicans started immediately to build a larger church dedicated to the Holy Cross from which the convent derived its official name.[12] From their residence on Stolkgasse the Cologne Dominicans also acquired the nickname *Stolici* or *Stolicheri*.[13]

The canons of St. Andrew's formally transferred their property on Stolkgasse to the Dominicans on May 15, 1226. In the property deed the canons carefully guarded their own rights and those of the other churches in Cologne, particularly the rights of the nearby parish church of St. Paul, whose patronage the canons possessed. The canons stipulated that the Dominicans were not to use any privilege which they had received or might obtain in the future to the detriment of the various Cologne churches. If the friars accidentally violated the rights of any other church, they were to be assembled by the dean, scholastic, and custodian of St. Andrew's at the collegiate church for resolution of the difficulty. If the friars remained incorrigible, the case was to

---

8. *Historia fratrum Praedicatorum in Dania*, ed. G. Waitz (Hanover, 1892), MGH SS 29:243; Anton E. Schönbach, "Studien zur Erzählungsliteratur des Mittelalters. Vierter Theil: Ueber Caesarius von Heisterbach. I.," *Sitzungsberichte der kaiserlichen Akademie der Wissenschaften in Wien, Philosophisch-historische Klasse* 144 (1902), 83; Löhr, *Dominikanerkloster*, 1:1–2; Heribert Chr. Scheeben, *Jordan der Sachse* (Vechta in Oldenburg, 1937), pp. 119–120.

9. Jordan of Saxony, *Libellus de principiis ord. Praedicatorum*, ed. Heribert Chr. Scheeben, MOPH 16 (Rome, 1935), chs. 67–78.

10. Ibid., chs. 79–81; Berthold Altaner, *Die Briefe Jordans von Sachsen, des zweiten Dominikanergenerals (1222–37): Text und Untersuchungen*, QFGDD 20 (Leipzig, 1925), nos. 44 and 52.

11. Caesarius of Heisterbach, *Dialogus miraculorum* 2.9.56, ed. Josephus Strange, 2 vols., 2nd ed. (Ridgewood, New Jersey, 1966), pp. 209–210; Keussen, *Topographie*, 2:156, b, 13.

12. Löhr, *Dominikanerkloster*, 1:3 and 2, no. 1.

13. *Gesta Treverorum*, p. 399.

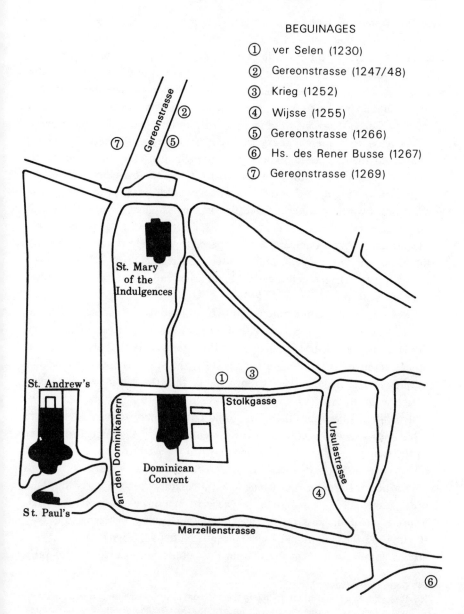

MAP 5. THE COLOGNE DOMINICANS
(Based on the maps of Niederich and St. Christopher in Hermann Keussen's *Topographie der Stadt Köln im Mittelalter*, 2:66, 227.)

be transferred to the dean of the cathedral for judgment. As a sign of their submission to the canons, the Dominicans were required to pay an annual census (*Hofzins*) of three schillings and three pennies and were to induce the lay fraternity of St. Matthias to bring its customary offering of candles to the canons and if possible to persuade the laymen to increase their donation. The friars and canons were to pray for one another and were to attend each other's funerals. The Dominicans were required in addition, unless they had a legitimate excuse, to be present at any services in St. Andrew's to which the canons summoned them. Except for members of their own order, the Dominicans were not permitted to bury anyone without the express permission of the custodian of St. Andrew's, who also was the parish priest of St. Paul's. The Dominicans were likewise obligated to give the custodian the offerings which they would receive on the feasts of Sts. John the Baptist, Mary Magdalene, Ursula, Gereon, and Cunibert, saints especially venerated in the city, and on the anniversary of the dedication of the Dominican church.[14] The terms of the agreement clearly indicate the Dominicans' subordinate position within the ecclesiastical structure of Cologne.

Several years later the canons and friars utilized the procedure outlined in the 1226 agreement to resolve a dispute about the census of two marks which the Dominicans owed St. Andrew's for three houses. The scholastic and two other canons of the collegiate church ruled that the friars were to appoint *fidejussores*. These men were to give surety that the census would be paid until the brothers could give the canons property to cover the obligation. When this had occurred, the friars would obtain complete possession of the three houses as well as of an adjacent garden and lot.[15] The friars turned over to the canons in 1232 a house which they had received from the aptly named Hartman (d. 1231) and Guderardis Gir (Avarus) to free themselves from this obligation.[16] Hartman, a parvenu, had apparently through successful land speculations raised his family to the patriciate in a single generation.[17] Beneficence to the poor friars was one way to appease a guilty conscience.

In 1232 the canons and friars renegotiated the 1226 agreement. The new accord absolved the Dominicans from their obligation to urge the fraternity

---

14. Löhr, *Dominikanerkloster*, 2, no. 2.
15. Ibid., no. 8. For information about the laws and customs governing urban landowning in medieval Germany, see Wilhelm Arnold, *Zur Geschichte des Eigentums in den deutschen Städten* (Basel, 1861), and Karl Fischer, *Die Erbleihe im Köln des 12. bis 14. Jahrhunderts* (Düsseldorf, 1939).
16. Löhr, *Dominikanerkloster*, 2, no. 9.
17. Luise v. Winterfeld, *Handel, Kapital und Patriziat in Köln bis 1400*, Pfingstblätter des hansischen Geschichtsvereins 16 (Lübeck, 1925), pp. 42–44.

of St. Matthias to give candles to the canons, to hand over their offerings on certain feast days to the custodian of St. Andrew's, or to participate, when summoned, in the services of St. Andrew's. The Dominicans received the right, furthermore, to bury whomever they wished. However, if the deceased had been a parishioner of St. Paul's or had died in that parish, the custodian of St. Andrew's was to receive half of the candles and half of the offering which were given to the Dominicans at the funeral. The other terms of the 1226 agreement remained in effect.[18]

The Franciscans John of Piancarpino and Barnabas arrived in Cologne a few months after the first Dominicans. They preached repentance and prepared lodgings for the brothers who settled in the city in 1222.[19] In 1229 a Cologne patrician, Gerhard Quartermart, gave the Franciscans a vacant lot in the district of St. Severin for the construction of an oratory.[20] The Quartermarts were wealthy merchants who had invested heavily in the lucrative trade between Cologne and England.[21] The burgher Simon of Hune, whose home bordered on the lot, assumed the responsibility of paying the annual census of eight pennies which the holder of the land owed the collegiate church of the Apostles.[22]

The Franciscans moved in 1245 from the district of St. Severin to the district of St. Columba where they built a new church (see Map 6). They obtained from Bishop Robert of Liège (1240–1246) the vacant land situated on Minoritenstrasse behind the episcopal palace of the bishops of Liège in Cologne and the land on which the episcopal kitchen and stables stood. The friars agreed in return to make a garden for the bishop, to construct a new stable and kitchen with two chimneys, to build two windows in the palace, to erect a wall, and to guard the episcopal palace. Six Cologne burghers, Gerhard Birklin, Herman of the Kornpforte, and the brothers John and Franco Leparde and Henry and Gerhard Cleingedank, served as *fidejussores* for the Fransciscans. They promised to eat and to sleep with the friars until the terms of the contract were implemented.[23] Count Henry of Sayn, whom Conrad of

18. Löhr, *Dominikanerkloster*, 2, no. 9.
19. Jordan of Giano, *Chronica*, ed. H. Boehmer, Collection d'études et de documents sur l'histoire religieuse et littéraire du moyen âge 6 (Paris, 1908), chs. 23 and 28; *Gesta Treverorum*, p. 399.
20. *Quellen zur Geschichte der Stadt Köln*, ed. Leonard Ennen und Gottfried Eckertz (Cologne, 1863), 2, no. 110.
21. Winterfeld, *Handel*, pp. 21–22.
22. *Quellen Köln*, 2, no. 110.
23. *Cartulaire de l'église Saint-Lambert de Liège*, ed. S. Bormans and E. Schoolmeesters (Brussels, 1893), 1, nos. 399 and 402.

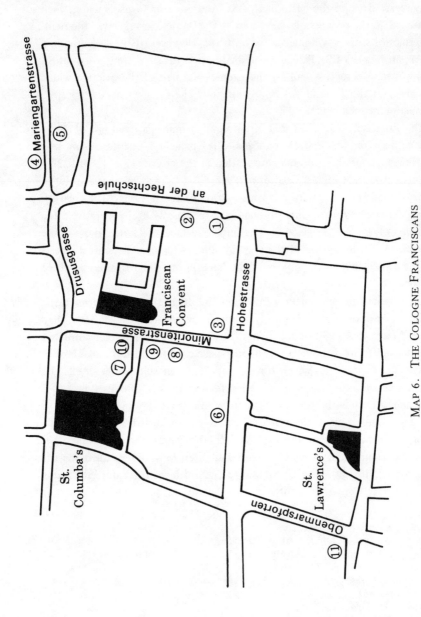

MAP 6. THE COLOGNE FRANCISCANS

(Based on the maps of St. Alban, St. Lawrence, and St. Columba in Hermann Keussen's *Topographie der Stadt Köln im Mittelalter*, 1:153, 184, 273. The numbers refer to the property owned by the *fidejussores* for the Franciscans in 1245.)

Marburg had once accused of heresy,[24] purchased in 1246 the friars' old property in St. Severin and founded in its place the Cistercian nunnery of Zion or Marienspiegel.[25]

It was not purely coincidental that these six burghers gave surety for the implementation of the agreement between the Franciscans and Bishop Robert. At least four of the six *fidejussores* owned property, as Map 6 indicates, in the immediate vicinity of the new Franciscan friary in St. Columba. Gerhard Birklin and his wife Richmudis purchased in 1244 a house and lot on the Rechtschule (Map 6, no. 1).[26] They also purchased at the same time one-third of an apartment (*mansio*) situated on the same street (2) and two-thirds of a house situated on Minoritenstrasse (3).[27] The sales' deeds stipulated that the Birklins could only dispose of these properties with the advice of two Cologne Franciscans. The Birklins were either granting the Franciscans some control over the disposition of the property surrounding the planned friary or were in fact acting on the friars' behalf. Richmudis also stipulated in 1251 that her house and lot situated on Mariengartenstrasse (4) be converted after her death into a Beguinage for fifteen women under the supervision of the Dominicans.[28] Herman of the Kornpforte was the owner, at least in about 1260, of much of the property opposite Richmudis's planned Beguinage on Mariengartenstrasse (5).[29] John Leparde purchased from the parish officials of St. Columba in 1245 two houses with their lots (6, 7).[30] A John Leparde also bought in 1280 a house situated on Minoritenstrasse (8) and was called in 1286 the owner of a house situated opposite the Franciscan convent (9).[31] John's brother Franco prohibited in 1254 the construction of a tavern on property which he owned across the street from the Franciscan convent on Minoritenstrasse (10) lest the noise disturb the brothers.[32] Henry and Gerhard Cleingedank did not possess, to my knowledge, any property in the immediate vicinity of the friary, although a Henry Cleingedank did own in 1225 a house on the nearby street of Obenmarspforten (11).[33] The Cleinge-

---

24. See below, p. 144.
25. *Quellen Köln*, 2, no. 253.
26. *Schreinsbuch* 156:6b, 4 (Keussen, *Topographie*, 1:356, a, 6).
27. *Schreinsbuch* 156:6b, nos. 5 and 6. The house on Minoritenstrasse was called *ad cervum*. Keussen, *Topographie*, 1:345, b, 1–8, refers to such a house.
28. Löhr, *Dominikanerkloster*, 2, no. 21.
29. Keussen, *Topographie*, 1:342, a, 3.
30. Ibid., 1:330, b, 7; and 333, a, 3.
31. Ibid., 1:344, a, 7; and 344, b, 13.
32. *Schreinsbuch* 156:15a, 6.
33. Keussen, *Topographie*, 1:173, a, 2.

danks had, however, familial ties to the Franciscans. A Conrad Rufus, the only Cologne patrician who is definitely known to have become a friar before 1273, is mentioned in a 1250 document.[34] The Rufi were the wealthiest branch of the Cleingedank family.[35] The six *fidejussores* apparently were either neighbors and/or relatives of the Franciscans. It seems likely that these six burghers persuaded the Franciscans to move to the district of St. Columba or that the friars had asked some of their new neighbors to serve as *fidejussores*. The church, which contains the grave of the Bl. John Duns Scotus, still stands; the Dominican church and convent were demolished in 1804.[36]

3. THE FRIARS AND THE CLERGY

While the canons of St. Andrew's had welcomed the Dominicans, many members of the Cologne clergy were at first highly suspicious of the friars' intentions. The brothers' life style clearly resembled that of several groups of heretics who had been apprehended and burned in the city in the twelfth century.[37] Shortly after the arrival of the friars, a group of clerics expressed their misgivings to Archbishop Engelbert of Berg (1216–1225), the imperial regent in the early 1220s. Engelbert, better informed than the average cleric about the friars' mission and orthodoxy, replied rather abruptly: "As long as the matter is in a good state, permit it to remain."[38] His enigmatic response quite understandably did not calm the clergy's fears. The cathedral canons, the abbots and priors of the monasteries and collegiate churches in the city, and the parish clergy returned, therefore, to the archbishop and voiced once more their doubts about the friars: "We fear that they may be the men who will afflict the clergy and endanger the city as the Holy Ghost prophesied through the mouth of St. Hildegard of Bingen."[39] She had warned the Cologne clergy in 1164 to guard against false teachers:

> Now, oh sons of God, hear and learn what the Spirit of God says to you, lest the better part of you perish. And the Spirit of God says to you: "Behold in your city and region, cast away from you evil men who are worse than Jews and like Sadducees. For as long as they will remain with

34. Planitz, *Schreinsbücher* (see above, n. 6), no. 476.
35. Winterfeld, *Handel* (see above, n. 17), p. 32.
36. Heribert Chr. Scheeben, *Albertus Magnus* (Bonn, 1932), p. 168.
37. Walter L. Wakefield and Austin P. Evans, *Heresies of the High Middle Ages*, Records of Civilization: Sources and Studies 81 (New York, 1969), nos. 15a and 39.
38. Caesarius of Heisterbach, *Vita, passio et miracula S. Engelberti*, ed. Albert Poncelet (Brussels, 1910), Acta sanctorum Novembris 3:650.
39. Ibid.

you, you will not be able to be safe. For the Church weeps and laments about their iniquity since her sons are defiled in their iniquity. Wherefore drive them out from you, lest your congregation and city perish since in Cologne long ago a banquet of a regal nuptial was prepared whence her streets until now sparkle."[40]

Engelbert replied ironically, "If it was divinely prophesied, it must be fulfilled."[41] Caesarius of Heisterbach's account of Engelbert's words suggests that the archbishop, unlike the lower clergy, recognized the friars' value in the church's counter-offensive against heresy.

But the Cologne clergy was soon uttering more familiar complaints about the friars' competition in the care of souls. After Engelbert's murder in 1225 by Count Frederick of Isenburg,[42] a Cologne parish priest protested to Cardinal Conrad of Porto, who was presiding over a provincial synod: "Behold the brothers of the Order of the Preachers, who to our damnation entered Cologne, send a sickle into another's harvest. They hear the confessions of our parishioners, and through this they gain the favor of men."[43] Conrad, who was favorably disposed toward the Dominicans, asked the priest how many parishioners he had. After learning that the priest was responsible for nine thousand souls,[44] the cardinal replied furiously:

Who are you, most miserable man, that you can alone provide the necessary spiritual guidance for so many thousands? You are ignorant, wretched man, that on that dreadful Judgment Day you will have to give account concerning all these men before the tribunal of Christ. And you complain if you have such assistants who freely lighten your burden under whose weight you ought to shake? Since this complaint indicates that you are totally unworthy of your responsibility, I deprive you of your pastoral benefice.[45]

Cardinal Conrad's angry words did not completely stifle all clerical opposition to the friars in Cologne. There is record of more trouble a generation

---

40. PL 197:253, no. 48.
41. Caesarius of Heisterbach, *Vita*, p. 650. For additional information about Engelbert's relations with the friars, see Josef Greven, "Engelbert der Heilige und die Bettelorden," *Bonner Z für Theologie und Seelsorge* 2 (1925), 32—48.
42. For information about Engelbert's murder, see Wolfgang Kleist, *Der Tod des Erzbischofs Engelbert von Köln* (Münster, 1918).
43. Thomas of Cantimpré, *Bonum universale de apibus* 1.9.6, ed. Georgius Colvenerius (Douai, 1627).
44. It is hard to see how one of the sixteen parish churches in Cologne, a city with 40,000 inhabitants, could have had 9000 parishioners.
45. Thomas of Cantimpré, *Bonum universale* 1.9.6.

later. Archbishop Conrad of Hochstaden (1238–1261), who served as the papally appointed protector of the Franciscans and Dominicans and whom Alexander IV thanked for his kindness to the Franciscans,[46] quite obviously was favorably disposed toward the mendicant orders. Nevertheless, on January 19, 1248, Conrad approved an ordinance drafted by the dean of the cathedral which outlined the privileges of the clergy of the city and diocese of Cologne. It included a provision which prohibited the Dominicans, Franciscans, and all other religious from impeding the parish clergy in exercising its rights in regard to wills, confessions, funerals, and other unspecified matters.[47] We possess no specific information why this particular provision was included in the 1248 ordinance; perhaps it was merely a formal recognition of the parish clergy's pre-eminent rights in the care of souls.

Relations between the friars and the Cologne clergy appear in fact to have been surprisingly harmonious after the initial distrust had been overcome in the 1220s. The friars received a number of gifts and bequests from individual clerics and ecclesiastical foundations. For instance, Master William, the scholastic of St. Andrew's, bequeathed both to the Franciscans and Dominicans in 1272 one-fifth of two houses he owned.[48] We can only speculate why relations between the friars and the Cologne clergy were so peaceful, but a number of possible explanations come to mind. First of all, the existence of the 1226/32 agreement between the Dominicans and the canons of St. Andrew's may have helped to prevent violent confrontations between the Dominicans and the secular and regular clergy of the city. The agreement which had been voluntarily made by both parties specified their respective rights on such sensitive issues as burials in the Dominican convent and set up a mechanism for the peaceful resolution of disputes. Second, the highly respected St. Albert,

---

46. *Die Regesten der Erzbischöfe von Köln im Mittelalter*, ed. Richard Knipping, PGRhGk 21 (Bonn, 1909–1913), 3, nos. 1211, 1217, 1668, 1845a, 1881, 1891, and 2057.

47. *Quellen Köln* (see above, n. 20), 2, no. 273.

48. Löhr, *Dominikanerkloster*, 2, no. 43. Other examples are: the Augustinian nuns of Schönstatt by Vallendar in the diocese of Trier relinquished to the Franciscans in 1251 one-third of a house and lot on Hohestrasse, *Schreinsbuch* 156:15a, 3 (Keussen, *Topographie*, 1:328, b, 3); the Cistercian monks of Heisterbach and Werner, a canon in the collegiate church of Mariengraden in Cologne, relinquished to the Franciscans in 1251 their rights to a house and lot on the Rechtschule, *Schreinsbuch* 156:15a, 5 (Keussen, 1:356, b, 14); Gerlach, the parish priest of St. Christopher's, and his sister Helewigis gave the Dominicans in 1248 a lot on Marzellenstrasse, Löhr, 2, no. 20 (Keussen, 2:124, b, c); Henry Rape, a canon in Mariengraden, bequeathed to the Dominicans in 1267 an annual census of sixteen schillings and six pennies, Löhr, 2, no. 38; and a Master Florikinus gave the Dominicans in 1272 a house and lot, Löhr, 2, no. 46 (Keussen, 2:211, a, b).

who lived in Cologne at various times between his conversion in 1229 and his death in 1280, probably exerted his influence to calm tempers on both sides in tense moments. Finally, and perhaps most important, the mendicant orders could not dominate the religious life of a city as large and as wealthy as Cologne. The Dominican and Franciscan houses were merely two convents in a city with numerous other ecclesiastical foundations which competed for the burghers' favor. In any case the example of Cologne provides a clear warning that the conventional view of constant friction between the friars and the secular clergy should not be overstated.[49]

4. THE FRIARS AND IMPERIAL POLITICS

The city of Cologne was traditionally hostile to the Hohenstaufen. Cologne's economic pre-eminence was based on her virtual monopoly of the lucrative wine and wool trade between England and the Rhine Valley. After the marriage in 1168 of Henry the Lion and Matilda, the daughter of Henry II of England, Cologne adhered to the Welfs to protect its English commercial interests. While the Welf family had abandoned its opposition to the imperial dynasty by the 1220s, the city retained a legacy of anti-Hohenstaufen feelings. It is not very surprising, therefore, that the Dominicans proclaimed in 1228 Frederick II's excommunication in Cologne, the only known instance of anti-Hohenstaufen agitation by the German friars during the emperor's first excommunication (1227–1230).[50] Frederick's marriage to Isabella of England in 1235 helped to secure the city's nominal loyalty until 1247.[51]

Although the city continued to adhere to Frederick after his second excommunication in 1239, Archbishop Conrad of Hochstaden emerged in the early 1240s as the undisputed leader of the papal party in Germany.[52] The Cologne Dominicans and Franciscans, unlike the other German friars who

---

49. It was not uncommon for individual clerics in other cities to make gifts or bequests to the friars. The parish priest of Haarlem in 1272 bequeathed five pounds to both the Dominicans and the Franciscans in Utrecht. *Oorkondenboek van Holland en Zeeland*, ed. L. Ph. C. van den Bergh (Amsterdam, 1873), 2, no. 225. Other examples are: *Mittelrheinische Regesten*, ed. Adam Goerz (Koblenz, 1879–1881), 2, no. 2233 and 3, nos. 83, 208, 859, 930, 1385, and 1822.
50. *Annales Colonienses maximi*, ed. Karl Pertz (Hanover, 1861), MGH SS 17:841. See below, pp. 140–141.
51. For further information on Cologne's relations with England, see Karl Wand, "Die Englandpolitik der Stadt Köln und ihrer Erzbischöfe im 12. und 13. Jahrhundert," *Aus Mittelalter und Neuzeit: Gerhard Kallen zum 70 Geburtstag*, ed. Josef Engel and Hans Martin Klinkenberg (Bonn, 1957), pp. 77–96.
52. Hermann Cardauns, *Konrad von Hostaden: Erzbischof von Köln* (Cologne, 1880), pp. 13–41; Manfred Stimming "Kaiser Friedrich II. und der Abfall der deutschen Fürsten," *HZ* 120 (1919), 225–235.

remained loyal to the emperor until his deposition by Innocent IV in 1245,[53] followed the example of their archbishop. Sometime between September 1241 and March 1242, Frederick complained that on Conrad's orders the Cologne Franciscans were working for his destruction.[54] The Cologne Dominicans were involved in similar machinations. On May 16, 1243, in exchange for an annual payment of fifty marks, Bishop Robert of Liège leased for six years to Werner of Bolanden, the imperial steward, a manor near Worms. The contract specifically stipulated that Werner would not be held responsible for any damages inflicted on the manor by the weather or by the imperial army. The fifty marks were to be paid in semi-annual installments in the Cologne Dominican priory either to Bishop Robert or to his representative or to the prior of the Cologne Dominicans or his vicar. Archbishops Conrad of Cologne and Siegfried of Mainz served as *fidejussores* for Werner. The manor apparently was Werner's reward for betraying the emperor.[55] The Cologne friars thus participated in the intrigues by which the Rhenish archbishops forged the anti-Hohenstaufen coalition, which eventually elected the two anti-kings, Henry Raspe and William of Holland.

William obtained the city's allegiance immediately after his election as king on October 3, 1247, by freeing the burghers from their obligations toward the *Reich*.[56] His first task as king was to capture the pro-Hohenstaufen city of Aachen so that he could be crowned there. The siege of the coronation city began in April 1248 and lasted until Aachen's capitulation on October 18. The Cologne Franciscans helped to raise the army which successfully besieged Aachen.[57] On January 2, 1249, Innocent IV also commanded the prior of the Cologne Dominicans and the Franciscan custodian of Cologne, along with other mendicant officials, to preach a crusade against Frederick and his adherents throughout Germany.[58]

The Cologne friars were amply rewarded for their political services. Bishop Henry of Liège (1247–1274), the brother of Count Otto II of Guelders and William's cousin,[59] gave the Cologne Franciscans in August 1248 the

---

53. See below, pp. 147–150.
54. *Regesten Köln* (see above, n. 46), 3, no. 1045.
55. *Cartulaire Saint-Lambert* (see above, n. 23), 1, no. 361; Otto Hintze, *Das Königtum Wilhelms von Holland* (Leipzig, 1885), p. 79.
56. Hintze, *Wilhelm von Holland*, pp. 18–20.
57. *Annales Sancti Pantaleonis Coloniensis*, ed. Hermann Cardauns (Hanover, 1872), MGH SS 22:543.
58. MGH Epis. saec. XIII, ed. Carolus Rodenberg, 3 vols. (Berlin, 1883–1894), 2, no. 630.
59. Hintze, *Wilhelm von Holland*, p. 65.

palace of the bishops of Liège, which was located next to the friars' new church in St. Columba. Henry paid the cathedral chapter of St. Lambert's in Liège 200 marks so that they could obtain a new episcopal residence in the metropolitan see.[60] Bishop Henry's valuable gift is not an example of inexplicable generosity. He had been appointed bishop in 1247 after consultations in Lyons between Innocent IV and Archbishop Conrad.[61] The pope had freed Henry from every obligation to receive Holy Orders or to be consecrated in order that he might better dedicate himself to the cause of the church, a euphemism for fighting the Hohenstaufen.[62] Henry, Innocent's most notorious political appointee, remained a layman throughout his twenty-six-year episcopal career.[63] It is difficult to avoid the conclusion that the episcopal palace was the Franciscans' reward for raising the army which was besieging Aachen in the summer of 1248. Similar circumstances may have surrounded the Dominicans' acquisition of the residence of Duke Walram IV of Limburg (1246–1279), which bordered on their property on Stolkgasse. According to an eighteenth-century chronicle which utilized documents now lost, Walram sold his residence to the Dominicans in 1250 for the comparatively low price of 150 marks. The ducal residence became the friars' new convent.[64] Like Bishop Henry, Duke Walram supported William.[65] While some friars were expelled from their convents or were even killed on account of their political agitation in the late 1240s,[66] the Cologne Dominicans and Franciscans moved into palaces. Sts. Francis and Dominic might not have approved.

5. THE FRIARS AND URBAN POLITICS

Two factions of Cologne patricians, the Weises and the Overstolzes, fought for political power in Cologne from the 1220s to the 1270s.[67] The municipal

---

60. *Cartulaire Saint-Lambert*, 1, no. 444.
61. *Annales Sancti Pantaleonis*, p. 541.
62. MGH Epis. saec. XIII, 2, no. 452.
63. Richard William Southern, *Western Society and the Church in the Middle Ages* (Harmondsworth, England, 1970), pp. 198–202.
64. *Chronica conventus S. Crucis Coloniensis*, Analecta sacri ordinis fratrum Praedicatorum 1 (Rome, 1893), p. 592.
65. Hintze, *Wilhelm von Holland*, p. 68.
66. Jordan of Giano (see above, n. 19), ch. 73. See below, pp. 159–160.
67. Hagen, *Boich* (see above, n. 1), vv. 4053–4065; Otto Oppermann, "Untersuchungen zur Geschichte des deutschen Bürgertums und der Reichspolitik vornehmlich im 13. Jahrhundert," *Hansische Geschichtsblätter* 17 (1911), 37–56 and 166–183; Winterfeld, *Handel* (see above, n. 17), pp. 65–70. Friedrich Lau, "Beiträge zur Ver-

government of the city in the thirteenth century was composed of three inter-
locking councils: the *Schöffenkollegium*, the *Richerzeche*, and the *Rat*. The
Schöffen (*scabini*) had originally been assessors familiar with the customary
law of Cologne who assisted the judges at the archiepiscopal court. While the
Schöffen had retained their judicial function, they had also assumed, as the
only legally constituted group of citizens, the leadership of the burghers in
the twelfth century. The *Schöffen* held their offices for life and filled vacan-
cies in the college by co-optation.[68] The Weise family, who were also called
von der Mühlengasse, used this electoral procedure to gain a predominant
position within the *Schöffenkollegium* in the middle of the thirteenth century.[69]

The Weises' control of the *Schöffenkollegium* also enabled them to dominate the *Richerzeche*. The *Richerzeche* was, as its name implied, a fraternity
of Cologne patricians who regulated and policed the city markets, authorized
the formation of guilds, and granted citizenship to newcomers. The two heads
of the *Richerzeche*, who held their offices for a year, were called *Bürgermeister* (*magistri civium*). The ruling body of the *Richerzeche* was composed
of the two *Bürgermeister* and the former holders of the office. One of the
two *Bürgermeister*, who were selected by the ruling body of the fraternity,
was always a *Schöffe*. At least half of the members of the ruling body of the
Richerzeche were, therefore, automatically *Schöffen*.[70] The Weises consequently had a better chance of being elected *Bürgermeister* than any other
family. The Overstolz faction was largely composed of those families who
were excluded from political power by the Weises' domination of the *Schöffenkollegium*. These patrician families used the *Rat*, the newest and least
important of the communal bodies prior to 1258, to challenge the Weises'
control of the city.[71]

fassungsgeschichte der Stadt Köln," *WZ* 14 (1895), 315−322, and *Entwicklung* (see
above, n. 6), pp. 121−125; and Paul Strait, *Cologne in the Twelfth Century* (Gainesville, Florida, 1974), pp. 74−81, discuss the criteria for including a family in the
patriciate. Both Lau and Strait define the patriciate as a political elite composed of
those families who belonged to the three municipal councils.

68. Lau, "Beiträge," pp. 172−195, and *Entwicklung*, pp. 23−29 and 72−75; Strait, *Cologne*, pp. 61−66.
69. The *Schöffenkollegium* was composed in 1235/37 of 23 *Schöffen*, five of whom
were members of the Weise family. Lau, "Beiträge," p. 193. In 1259 seven of the 18
Schöffen were Weises. *Quellen Köln* (see above, n. 20), 2, no. 394.
70. The literature on the *Richerzeche* is simply enormous. See, in particular, Lau, *Entwicklung*, pp. 76−97; and Strait, *Cologne*, pp. 70−73.
71. Winterfeld, *Handel*, p. 69. In 1259 the *Ratsherren* accused the *Schöffen* and the

There is no concrete evidence that the Weises, Cologne's most influential family, or their closest political ally, the Grins,[72] patronized the friars. Nevertheless, there may have been some contact between the Weise family and the Dominicans. Richmudis Wipperfürth, the daughter of Louis of the Mühlengasse, the Bürgermeister of Cologne in 1259, founded in 1267 a Beguinage for fifty women.[73] Since the Beguinage was situated in the vicinity of the Dominican convent (Map 5, no. 6), it is quite possible that she asked the Dominicans to provide for the spiritual welfare of the Beguines. Windrudis, the widow of John of Poylheim, whose family adhered to the Weises,[74] may have made similar arrangements for the Beguinage which she had established in 1266 (Map 5, no. 5).[75] At least two families who belonged to the Weise faction definitely assisted the friars. Gerhard of Zudendorp, who was married to a Wipperfürth,[76] relinquished to the Franciscans in 1251 two-thirds of a house he owned on Hohestrasse.[77] More important, the friars received considerable support from the Cleingedanks, who were originally allied with the Weises. Henry and Gerhard Cleingedank had been two of the six *fidejussores* for the Franciscans in 1245. Rika, the widow of Philip Cleingedank, gave the Dominicans a house and lot near Cologne between 1248 and 1252; and Agnes Cleingedank, the widow of Peter of Walde, bequeathed five marks to both the Franciscans and Dominicans in 1262.[78] But the Cleingedanks eventually abandoned the Weises and fought on the side of the Overstolzes in the decisive battles for control of the city in 1268.[79] The friars quite clearly received relatively little support from the Weise faction and virtually none from its hard core, the Weise and Grin families.

Various members of the Overstolz faction, on the other hand, were closely associated with the friars. Herman of the Kornpforte was one of the six *fidejussores* for the Franciscans in 1245. In his official capacity as *Untergraf* he demolished the Weises' houses after the *Bürgermeister*, Dietrich von der

Bürgermeister, Louis of the Mühlengasse, of numerous abuses of their authority and of corrupt practices in the selection of new *Schöffen. Quellen Köln*, 2, no. 394.
72. *UB für die Geschichte des Niederrheins*, ed. Theodor Josef Lacomblet (Düsseldorf, 1846), 2, no. 607; Hagen, *Boich*, vv. 4964–4967.
73. Keussen, *Topographie*, 2:82, a.
74. *UB des Niederrheins*, 2, no. 607; Hagen, *Boich*, vv. 5306–5313.
75. Keussen, *Topographie*, 2:253, a, 1.
76. Winterfeld, *Handel*, p. 7.
77. *Schreinsbuch* 156:15a, 3 (Keussen, *Topographie*, 1:328, b, 3).
78. Löhr, *Dominikanerkloster*, 2, nos. 25 and 37.
79. Hagen, *Boich*, vv. 4646–4667.

Mühlengasse, killed a knight and refused to heed the summons to present himself at the archiepiscopal court for judgment.[80] This incident allegedly started the bitter feud between the two patrician factions.[81] In 1260 Elizabeth Overstolz, the widow of Dietrich of the Erenporcen, bequeathed to the Dominicans a house and lot on Stolkgasse.[82] Her mother-in-law, Udelindis, had left the Franciscans in about 1250 an annual rent of one mark for the purchase of clothing.[83] Alstradis Ratze and her sons Henry and Dietrich gave the Franciscans in 1251 a house and lot on Minoritenstrasse valued at forty marks.[84] Henry was married to another Elizabeth Overstolz, while Dietrich became *Bürgermeister* in 1272 after the final triumph of the Overstolzes.[85]

The mother of Gottschalk Overstolz (d. 1205–1214), the reputed founder of his family's fortune, had been a Swartze.[86] The Swartzes, who were cloth merchants, were intimately associated with the Dominicans and Franciscans throughout the fifty-year period under consideration. Mabilia Errebolt, the wife of Pilgrim Swartze, bequeathed to the Cologne Dominicans in 1233 an annual rent of four marks and to the province of Teutonia a house situated on the Heumarkt and part of a shop among the cloth merchants. She instructed the prior of the Dominicans to sell another house with seven apartments in it and to distribute the proceeds among the poor. She also made some bequests to the Franciscans which she later revoked.[87] A Pilgrim Swartze served in the 1260s as the proctor of the Cologne Franciscans and appointed the guardian and prior of the Cologne Franciscans and Dominicans as the executors of his will.[88]

The Judes were also closely related to the Overstolzes; the two families intermarried at least five times in the thirteenth century.[89] Members of this patrician family, which probably was of ministerial rather than Jewish ances-

80. *Catalogi archiepiscoporum Coloniensium*, ed. Hermann Cardauns (Hanover, 1879), MGH SS 24:366–367.
81. Hagen,*Boich*, vv. 4053–4065.
82. Löhr,*Dominikanerkloster*, 2, no. 35.
83. Planitz, *Schreinsbücher* (see above, n. 6), no. 261.
84. *Schreinsbuch* 156:15a, 1 (Keussen, *Topographie*, 1:346, b, 15).
85. Friedrich Lau, "Das kölner Patriziat bis zum Jahre 1325," *Mitteilungen aus dem Stadtarchiv von Köln* 9–10 (1894–1895), 10:138.
86. Gerd Wunder, "Zu den Anfängen der kölner Overstolz," *MWdGFk* 18 (1957/58), 385.
87. Löhr,*Dominikanerkloster*, 2, nos. 10, 11, and 13.
88. *Schreinsbuch* 162:14a, 252–254; Planitz, *Schreinsbücher*, nos. 746 and 1090; Löhr, *Dominikanerkloster*, 2, no. 34.
89. Eberhard Quadflieg, "Erbnamensitte beim aachener und kölner Patriziat des 13. bis 15. Jahrhunderts," *MWdGFk* 18 (1957/58), 181–182.

try, served as *Schöffen*, *Ratsherren*, and *Bürgermeister* of Cologne from the twelfth to the seventeenth century. Daniel Jude, the most prominent member of the family and the *Bürgermeister* of Cologne in 1282, probably was the wealthiest burgher in the thirteenth century and was a major participant in the battles among the patricians.[90] Daniel's first wife, Ida of the Lintgasse, a granddaughter of Hartman Gir, bequeathed an annual rent of two marks and an alb to the Dominicans and one mark and an alb to the Franciscans and was buried in 1252 in the Dominican cemetery. Altogether Ida left twenty marks of annual rents, representing the sizeable capital of approximately 300 marks, to various ecclesiastical foundations.[91] St. Albert appointed Daniel as one of the two lay executors of his will in 1278.[92] Bruno Hardevust, Daniel's business partner,[93] was the other lay executor. He was a prominent member of the Overstolz faction and the proctor of the Cologne Dominicans in the 1270s.[94] Bruno was a nephew of Richmudis Birklin,[95] whose husband Gerhard had been one of the *fidejussores* for the Franciscans in 1245. The Birklins had bequeathed in their 1247 will an annual rent of one mark each to the Franciscans and Dominicans; in 1257 Richmudis left the Franciscans and Dominicans each one-sixth of her property on Hafengasse.[96]

The Quatermarts and the Scherfgins, who patronized the Franciscans, also belonged to the Overstolz faction.[97] Gerhard Quatermart had given the Franciscans in the 1220s the land on which they built their original oratory in St. Severin. Godfrey Quartermart gave the friars an apartment after they moved to St. Columba.[98] Hedwig Schalle, the widow of Gerhard Scherfgin, and her son Bruno relinquished to the Franciscans in 1264 the house and lot they owned adjacent to the choir of the friary.[99] While the Lepardes, who served as *fidejussores* for the Franciscans in 1245, were not of patrician status, they too supported the Overstolzes.[100] The political allegiance of the Girs, who

90. Strait, *Cologne* (see above, n. 67), pp. 101–103; Winterfeld, *Handel*, pp. 14–16.
91. Löhr, *Dominikanerkloster*, 2, no. 23.
92. Ibid., no. 58.
93. See, for instance, *Quellen Köln*, 2, no. 386.
94. Hagen, *Boich*, vv. 3418–3441; Löhr, *Dominikanerkloster*, 2, nos. 48 and 58.
95. Lau, "Patriziat" (see above, n. 85), 10:107.
96. Löhr, *Dominikanerkloster*, 2, nos. 17 and 32. The Birklins' position in the conflict between the Weises and the Overstolzes is unknown.
97. Hagen, *Boich*, vv. 4964–4967 and 5044–5047.
98. *Schreinsbuch* 156:15a, 4 (Keussen, *Topographie*, 1:346, b, 15).
99. *Schreinsbuch* 156:16a, 6 (Keussen, *Topographie*, 1:346, b, 15). An Albert Schalle was a member of the Dominican convent in 1256. Löhr, *Dominikanerkloster*, 2, no. 30a.
100. Hagen, *Boich*, vv. 1093–1096.

had been among the Dominicans' earliest benefactors, remains problematical. Since Gotfrid Hagen, the pro-Overstolz town chronicler, appears to make a disparaging reference to the Girs,[101] it has been suggested that the Girs belonged to the Weise faction.[102] On the other hand, the sons of Hartman and Guderardis Gir were married to Hedwig Overstolz and Ermengarde Scherfgin.[103] Since the Girs retained their political power after the downfall of the Weises, it seems likely that the Girs supported the Overstolzes in the final confrontation between the two factions in 1267/68. It is only possible to conclude that in Cologne patronage of the mendicant orders was identified with allegiance to the Overstolz faction.

While the members of the Overstolz faction certainly were the friars' most important and influential benefactors, other burghers who cannot be linked with either party also provided the friars with considerable support. Three generations of the Flemincs assisted, for instance, the Dominicans. Godfrey Fleminc gave the Dominicans in 1229 part of his courtyard so that the friars could enlarge the entrance to their church on Stolkgasse.[104] Godfrey's daughter Christiana purchased from the Dominicans in 1233 one-fifth of the three houses which her brother Arnold had given the Dominicans.[105] Albero Fleminc, who may have been Arnold's son,[106] stipulated in 1256 that if his son Gerhard, to whom he had bequeathed a census of two marks, should die before his twentieth birthday, the Dominicans and Franciscans were each to obtain a quarter of the legacy.[107] But it was the financial and moral support of the Overstolzes which was of paramount importance to the friars.

---

101. Ibid., vv. 1290–1293.
102. Winterfeld, *Handel*, p. 41.
103. Lau, "Patriziat," 9:376–377.
104. Löhr, *Dominikanerkloster*, 2, no. 4.
105. Ibid., no. 10a. Keussen, *Topographie*, 2:111, b, 8, indicates that Arnold was the son of Godfrey.
106. Albero was called *nepos Flemingi* in 1235. Keussen, *Topographie*, 2:92, b, 31.
107. Löhr, *Dominikanerkloster*, 2, no. 31. Other examples of gifts from burghers who cannot be linked with either patrician party: John, the brother of Ditmar, gave the Franciscans a house and lot on Hohestrasse in 1251, *Schreinsbuch* 156:15a, 2 (Keussen, *Topographie*, 1:329, a, 5); Henry Buclore ceded to the Dominicans in 1254 half a house and lot on Marzellenstrasse, Löhr, 2, no. 28; Albert of St. Columba left in 1254 an annual census of half a mark to the Franciscans as well as the Dominicans, Löhr, 2, no. 29; Bertradis of Drivinstorp bequeathed in 1260 an annual census of three marks to the Dominicans and six schillings to the Franciscans, Löhr, 2, no. 33; Gotstu, the widow of Dietrich, the son of Vogelo, left the Dominicans in 1261 an annual census of half a mark, Löhr, 2, no. 36; Dietrich of Limburg and his family gave the Franciscans in 1260 and 1267 a tower and a lot

There can be little doubt that the friars' close association with the Over-stolzes inclined the brothers to favor their burgher friends in their struggle with the Weises and the archbishop for control of the city. The archbishops' preoccupation with imperial affairs in the twelfth and early thirteenth centuries had permitted the prosperous city to develop into an autonomous, self-governing community, virtually independent of its nominal ruler.[108] After the collapse of the Hohenstaufen Empire, Archbishop Conrad of Hochstaden was determined to reassert archiepiscopal authority over Cologne. The city provoked Conrad's anger by signing treaties of friendship with several of the archbishop's princely opponents in 1250 and 1251.[109] Conrad retaliated at the beginning of 1252 by levying tolls on the burghers' merchandise at Neuss, downstream from Cologne, and by debasing the coinage in violation of the city's privileges. The burghers immediately protested and allied themselves with Conrad's most ruthless enemy, Count William IV of Jülich (1220–1278). On March 26, however, the archbishop and the city agreed to accept the arbitration of the papal legate, Hugh of Saint-Cher, the first Dominican cardinal (1244–1263), and of the lector of the Cologne Dominicans, Albertus Magnus.[110]

The Dominican arbiters announced their decision, which was based on Albert's preliminary determination,[111] on April 17. They ruled that Conrad had acted illegally and ordered him to desist. Hugh and Albert also upheld the burghers' contention that the archbishop was only permitted to strike a new coinage after his election and on his return from an imperial coronation in Rome.[112] These restrictions on the archbishop's right to tamper with the coinage had helped to assure the stability of the Cologne penny which circu-

---

and a house with an orchard and two apartments on the Rechtschule, *Schreinsbuch* 156:16b, 2 (Keussen, 1:356, a, 9), and *Schreinsbuch* 156:16a, 8 (Keussen, 1:356, a, 10–12); Gertrude, the widow of Henry Grove, gave the Franciscans an annual census of six schillings, *Schreinsbuch* 92:11b, 212; Gertrude, the widow of Herman Wisebolle, gave the Franciscans and the Dominicans each an annual census of nine schillings in 1270, Löhr, 2, no. 41; Vogelo, a cloth merchant, bequeathed to the Dominicans in 1272 a house and lot and his movable property, Löhr, 2, no. 42; and the Beguines Mary and Gertrude, the daughters of Baldwin Loschart, gave the Dominicans in 1272 one-third of a house on Marzellenstrasse and one-third of a house with six apartments on the Eigelstein, Löhr, 2, no. 48.
108. Strait, *Cologne* (see above, n. 67), pp. 40–43.
109. *Quellen Köln*, 2, nos. 293, 299, and 302.
110. Hagen, *Boich*, vv. 687–854; *Quellen Köln*, 2, no. 303.
111. *Quellen Köln*, 2, no. 304.
112. *Quellen Köln*, 2, no. 306.

lated widely in the thirteenth century.[113] The arbitral decision was thus highly favorable to the financial and commercial needs of the Cologne patricians, many of whom, like Daniel Jude and Bruno Hardevust, were merchants and moneylenders. St. Albert had demonstrated for the first time his understanding of the basic interests of the Cologne patricians.

Archbishop Conrad used a petty incident in 1257 as a pretext for reviving his quarrel with Cologne. After some indecisive skirmishes, the archbishop and the city reached an accord on March 20, 1258. The patricians agreed to apologize for their conduct and to renew their homage, while the archbishop promised to restore the burghers to his favor.[114] In exchange for the city's submission, Conrad consented to the arbitration of his differences with the burghers. Four Cologne prelates and St. Albert were appointed as arbiters.[115] After listening to fifty-three complaints by the archbishop and to twenty-one countercharges by the burghers, they announced their decision on June 28.[116]

The arbitral award, which was the basic constitutional document of medieval Cologne, was in reality the handiwork of St. Albert.[117] He scrupulously delineated the respective rights of the archbishop and of the city. Although the decision acknowledged that the archbishop was the supreme judge and lord of the city in temporal as well as spiritual matters, it also formally recognized for the first time the burghers' right to govern themselves. It is interesting to observe that the decision, at least indirectly, favored the Overstolzes rather than the Weises. St. Albert specifically condemned various irregular procedures in the co-optation of new *Schöffen*, such as the election of minors.[118] The Weises had presumably used such methods to gain and to maintain their predominant position within the *Schöffenkollegium*. At the same time Albert rejected Conrad's complaint that the *Rat*, the council controlled

113. Ernst Kruse, *Kölnische Geldgeschichte bis 1386*, WZ Ergh. 4 (Trier, 1888), pp. 21–25; Walter Hävernick, *Der kölner Pfennig im 12. und 13. Jahrhundert*, Vierteljahrschrift für Sozial- und Wirtschaftsgeschichte, Beiheft 18 (Stuttgart, 1930). For additional information, see Cardauns, *Konrad von Hostaden* (see above, n. 52), pp. 92–96; Scheeben, *Albertus Magnus* (see above, n. 36), pp. 72–86; and Alfred Wendehorst, "Albertus Magnus und Konrad von Hochstaden," *Rheinische Vierteljahrsblätter* 18 (1953), 32–35.
114. Hagen, *Boich*, vv. 855–1171; and *Quellen Köln*, 2, no. 382.
115. *Quellen Köln*, 2, no. 381.
116. Ibid., no. 384.
117. Hagen, *Boich*, vv. 1172–1174; Cardauns, *Konrad von Hostaden*, p. 103; Scheeben, *Albertus Magnus*, pp. 114–115; and Wendehorst, "Albertus Magnus," p. 38.
118. *Quellen Köln*, 2, no. 384, sections 4, 33, and 34.

by the Overstolzes, was an illegally constituted body.[119] The *Rat*, which had rarely been mentioned before 1258, quickly became the principal organ of municipal self-government. If the 1258 decision had been implemented, political power within Cologne would have shifted peacefully from the Weises to the Overstolzes.[120]

But Archbishop Conrad was unwilling to accept the arbitral award as the basis of Cologne's municipal government. He courted the guilds and with their support overthrew the patrician regime in 1259. The patricians were removed from their offices and replaced by burghers subservient to the archbishop's wishes. Many of the patricians were imprisoned or exiled. Conrad of Hochstaden was the undisputed ruler of Cologne until his death on September 18, 1261.[121]

The episcopate of Conrad's successor, Archbishop Engelbert of Falkenburg (1261–1274), was filled with perpetual civic strife and duplicity. His authoritarian rule quickly alienated the guildsmen. The patricians and the burghers were soon reconciled and forced the archbishop on June 16, 1262, to accept the 1258 arbitral decision.[122] Since Engelbert's consent had been extorted by force, Pope Urban IV (1261–1264) freed the archbishop from his obligation to observe the 1262 peace and ordered the patricians removed from their offices and expelled from the city.[123] At this point St. Albert, who had briefly served as bishop of Regensburg, (1260–1262),[124] again intervened in the city's affairs. He witnessed on August 25, 1263, a new accord between the city and Engelbert, similar to the 1262 agreement, and commanded that the papal bull be torn up in his presence.[125] The new civic harmony proved to be extremely short-lived. On November 27 the patricians arrested Engelbert, whom they accused of plotting with the guilds, and held him a prisoner until December 16.[126] This outrage started a new round of hostilities. Peace was finally restored in August 1266, when Pope Clement IV

---

119. *Quellen Köln*, 2, no. 384, section 43.
120. For additional information, see Hans Martin Klinkenberg, "Zur Interpretation des Grossen Schied," *Jahrbuch des kölnischen Geschichtsvereins* 25 (1950), 91–127; Cardauns, *Konrad von Hostaden*, pp. 97–104; Scheeben, *Albertus Magnus*, pp. 103–121; and Wendehorst, "Albertus Magnus," pp. 35–44.
121. Cardauns, *Konrad von Hostaden*, pp. 104–111.
122. Hagen, *Boich*, vv. 1614–3004; *Quellen Köln*, 2, no. 434.
123. Hagen, *Boich*, vv. 3005–3036; MGH Epis. saec. XIII (see above, n. 58), 3, no. 532.
124. Scheeben, *Albertus Magnus*, pp. 122–135.
125. Hagen, *Boich*, vv. 3037–3075; *Quellen Köln*, 2, no. 460.
126. Hagen, *Boich*, vv. 3076–3243; and MGH Epis. saec. XIII, 3, no. 583.

instructed Prior Conrad of the Cologne Dominicans and the dean of the cathedral to lift the interdict which had been imposed upon the rebellious city, as Engelbert and the prior had requested.[127]

In the summer of 1267 Archbishop Engelbert began once more to levy tolls on Cologne merchandise at Neuss and at other places in his duchy. His actions angered the burghers and several of the Rhenish princes who opposed the archbishop's territorial ambitions. Engelbert rebuffed the attempts by the city and its princely allies to resolve the dispute peacefully. On October 18, 1267, Count William of Jülich, the city's most important ally, captured the archbishop, who had been raiding the count's domains.[128] Engelbert was imprisoned for the next forty-three months in William's castle at Nideggen. The archbishop's supporters tried to break up the alliance between the count and the burghers by stirring up the ancient animosity between the Weises and the Overstolzes. Two clerics who were loyal to the archbishop approached the Weises, whose position in the city had been undermined by the implementation in 1262 of the 1258 arbitral award, and procured their assistance. The Weises started to wear the archbishop's colors in public. After Count William, whom the Overstolzes had asked to arbitrate their dispute with the Weises, failed to reconcile the feuding patricians, the Overstolzes defeated the Weises in a battle in the streets of Cologne on January 10, 1268. The Weises fled to the headquarters of Engelbert's adherents in Bonn.[129]

After this attempt to free the archbishop had failed, Pope Clement IV ordered his chaplain, Master Bernard of Castaneto, on March 1 to obtain Engelbert's release. On June 30 Castaneto in turn instructed four Cologne prelates, including the prior of the Cologne Dominicans and the Franciscan custodian of Cologne, to visit William and his son and to persuade them to free Engelbert. The nuncio promised to settle the count's quarrel with the archbishop after Engelbert's liberation. The next day the Dominican John of Austria publicly read Castaneto's papal mandate to the count, and the four prelates urged William to free his prisoner.[130] The count, more than familiar with Engelbert's habit of breaking agreements, insisted that his differences with the archbishop had to be resolved prior to the archbishop's release. Castaneto, who was staying in Bonn with Engelbert's supporters, including the Weises, excommunicated the two counts and interdicted their lands on

---

127. *Quellen Köln*, 2, nos. 483, 484, and 491.
128. Ibid., no. 499.
129. Hagen, *Boich*, vv. 4053–5229.
130. *UB des Niederrheins* (see above, n. 72), 2, no. 580.

August 2 in the presence of the prior of the Cologne Dominicans and of the Franciscan guardian.[131]

On the same day the nuncio threatened to excommunicate the burghers and to interdict the city if Cologne did not assist him in procuring Engelbert's freedom and if the city did not immediately overthrow its government controlled by the Overstolzes. Castaneto's demands reflected, as the city in fact protested, the Weises' influence in Bonn. When the burghers refused to obey, the nuncio carried out his threats.[132] In the meantime the Weises and Engelbert's princely allies and vassals plotted to capture the city by stealth. On the night of October 14, 1268, they entered the city through a secret passage underneath the city walls near the Ulrepforte. They were detected the following morning, and in a bloody battle the Weises were decisively defeated.[133]

Castaneto sharpened his ecclesiastical sentences against the count and the city on August 23, 1270. He ordered the secular clergy to leave Cologne and prohibited, under the threat of excommunication, the conveyance of any merchandise or food into the city.[134] In spite of their personal ties to the Overstolzes, the Dominicans and Franciscans observed the interdict.[135] The friars could not risk losing the good will of the papacy and of the archbishop by flouting an interdict which had been imposed upon rebellious burghers for complicity in the imprisonment of an archbishop. The brothers had become the unwitting allies of the Weises. Engelbert, the burghers under the leadership of the Overstolzes, and the friars thus found themselves by 1270 in untenable positions.

The impasse was finally broken at the beginning of 1271 by the return of St. Albert, who had been living for several years in Strasbourg.[136] He visited Engelbert at Nideggen and persuaded him to make peace. The weary archbishop entrusted Albert with the negotiations.[137] Engelbert announced on April 16, 1271, that he had been completely reconciled with his beloved and faithful Cologne burghers. He promised to levy no more illegal tolls, to heed no advice inimical to the city, and to banish from his territory various mem-

131. Ibid., no. 581.
132. *Quellen Köln*, 3 (1867), no. 27.
133. Hagen, *Boich*, vv. 5270–5812.
134. *UB des Niederrheins*, 2, no. 601.
135. Hagen, *Boich*, vv. 6193–6196. The Dominican provincial prior sent a letter of commiseration to the imprisoned archbishop. Heinrich Finke, *Ungedruckte Dominikanerbriefe des 13. Jahrhunderts* (Paderborn, 1891), no. 27.
136. Scheeben, *Albertus Magnus*, pp. 145–153.
137. Hagen, *Boich*, vv. 6117–6274; Scheeben, *Albertus Magnus*, pp. 153–165.

bers of the Weise faction. He revoked all ecclesiastical sentences pronounced in his name against the burghers during his imprisonment. Finally, he agreed to accept in any future dispute which might arise between him and the city the arbitration of St. Albert, Count William of Jülich, the auxiliary bishop of Cologne, and Gerhard of Landskron, an archiepiscopal vassal.[138] Albert had arranged extremely favorable terms for his burgher friends.

When the curia refused to confirm the peace, St. Albert, Prior Edmund of the Cologne Dominicans, the custodian and guardian of the Cologne Franciscans, and the brothers requested papal confirmation.[139] After Engelbert's death in 1274, his successor Siegfried of Westerburg (1275–1297) finally absolved the excommunicated burghers in the pope's name on June 2, 1275, and lifted the interdict. St. Albert and the lector of the Mainz Franciscans, Henry Knoderer, Rudolph of Habsburg's principal adviser, sealed the document.[140] Siegfried swore on June 5 to observe all the privileges which had been granted to the city in the past by emperors, kings, and archbishops.[141] After more than two decades of constant turmoil, peace had momentarily returned to Cologne.

The lengthy struggle for control of the city had ended with the victory of the burghers, the Overstolzes, and the friars. The archbishops' attempts to reassert their authority over Cologne had been checked. The burghers' right to govern themselves, which had been formally recognized for the first time in the 1258 arbitral award, had been firmly established. The Overstolzes and their patrician allies had triumphed over their hated rivals, the Weises, and were destined to rule Cologne until the guild revolution of 1396. The restoration of peace enabled the friars to resume their apostolate, which had been seriously impeded by the interdicts imposed upon the city. Significantly enough, Archbishop Siegfried gave the Dominicans on June 6, 1275, the day after he confirmed the city's privileges, the right to hear confessions in the archdiocese.[142] More important, the friars had attained a new respectability through their long association with the victorious Overstolzes. In spite of the abundance of the available evidence, it is only possible to identify positively a single Cologne patrician, Conrad Rufus, who joined the mendicant orders before 1273. In contrast, 26 or 27 patricians are known to have joined the

138. *UB des Niederrheins*, 2, no. 607.
139. *Quellen Köln*, 3, nos. 62 and 65.
140. Ibid., nos. 103 and 104.
141. *UB des Niederrheins*, 2, no. 672.
142. *Regesten Köln* (see above, n. 46), 3, no. 2611.

Dominicans between 1300 and 1360.[143] The Dominican nunnery of St. Gertrude, which was founded in 1263,[144] likewise became a favorite refuge for the daughters of the patriciate in the late thirteenth and fourteenth centuries.[145] The friars, who had once been mistaken for heretics, had become for better or worse fully accepted members of Cologne society.

While there can be little doubt that St. Albert sincerely tried to bring peace to a deeply troubled city, his well-intentioned peacemaking efforts protected the commercial and financial interests of the Cologne patriciate and helped the Overstolzes to gain the political ascendancy they maintained until 1396. Was he, therefore, a less than impartial arbiter? Conrad of Hochstaden and Engelbert of Falkenburg, even if they did not abide by his determinations, apparently trusted his fairness. But not even a saint lives in a political and social vacuum. Albert's lifelong friendship with such prominent members of the Overstolz party as Daniel Jude and Bruno Hardevust, the executors of his will, undoubtedly influenced his understanding of the Cologne constitution and of factional politics. If Albert's ideas could be shaped by his association with a particular group of burghers, it is not very surprising that less saintly and wise brothers in Cologne and elsewhere found it increasingly difficult to preserve that detachment from earthly society which their self-professed role as the disciples of Christ demanded.

143. Löhr, *Dominikanerkloster*, 1:38–39.
144. *Regesten Köln*, 3, no. 2266.
145. Gabriel M. Löhr, "Das Necrologium des Dominikanerinnenklosters St. Gertrud in Köln," *AnnHVNiederrh* 110 (1927), 87–89.

Part Two

SOCIAL AND POLITICAL ASPECTS
OF THE FRIARS' MINISTRY

4

The Social Origins of the Friars

The poor of spirit are not those who have no wealth, but those who are unwilling to possess those things which are contrary to their profession, even within the limits in which men may legitimately and honestly possess them.

David of Augsburg, *Expositio regulae.*[1]

1. THE PROBLEM

THERE are two widely held theories about the social origins of the friars which are based on different assumptions about the character of the medieval search for evangelical perfection. It was commonly believed in the nineteenth and early twentieth centuries that the friars were recruited from the lower strata of medieval society. The German Franciscan historian Patricius Schlager described the Franciscans as "close to the masses (*Volk*) out of whose ranks they had for the most part been drawn, sympathetic to popular needs, and themselves poor."[2] Eduard Winkelmann, Frederick II's nineteenth-century biographer, depicted the Dominicans as "in origin and education very frequently and in their way of life always standing on the same level as the common man."[3] More recently, the East German historians Ernst Werner and Martin Erbstösser have contended that the desire to lead the apostolic life was a medieval movement of social protest disguised in religious garb. The exploited classes in a pre-industrial and pre-Marxist world expressed their

---

1. Published by Ed. Lempp, "David von Augsburg," *ZKiG* 19 (1899), 356.
2. *Beiträge zur Geschichte der kölnischen Franziskaner-Ordensprovinz im Mittelalter* (Cologne, 1904), p. 36.
3. *Kaiser Friedrich II.*, 2 vols. (Leipzig, 1889–1897), 2:436. In addition, see Konrad Eubel, *Geschichte der oberdeutschen (strassburger) Minoriten-Provinz* (Würzburg, 1886), p. 18; and Josef Wiesehoff, *Die Stellung der Bettelorden in den deutschen freien Reichsstädten im Mittelalter* (Borna-Leipzig, 1905), p. 11.

discontent and aspirations in the words of the Gospels and for this reason followed the twelfth-century wandering preachers. St. Francis, who dressed in the clothes of a peasant or shepherd, did not deny poverty, but tried to overcome the destructive power of wealth, urban dissension, and the hostility between rich and poor by forming a brotherhood of all men united by Christian love. His egalitarian vision was rooted in the lower strata of society; and the later legends about his life, most notably the tale of how he preached to the birds, expressed the dream of the medieval proletariat for a classless society. Francis's failure proves that philanthropic love combined with personal sacrifice, no matter how noble or sincere, cannot change society and that conflicting class interests cannot be reconciled by religious idealism.[4]

In the final analysis both the nineteenth-century bourgeois and the twentieth-century Marxist historians agree that the friars, especially the Franciscans, were individuals poor by birth as well as by choice who protested against their poverty by idealizing it. No evidence has ever been presented in support of this contention. It has simply been assumed that the humble friars who ministered to the wretched poor of the medieval towns were laboring among their social peers. The advocates of this theory have forgotten that the friars also appealed to the nobly born, like St. Elizabeth and St. Louis,[5] and that socially conscious individuals from the Gracchi to the Kennedys have often belonged to the upper classes.

Herbert Grundmann stressed, on the other hand, that the desire to imitate the life of Christ in its heretical as well as orthodox variants was essentially a religious response of the well-to-do to the growing prosperity of medieval society.[6] There has been fairly general agreement since the nineteenth century, in spite of Winkelmann's comment to the contrary, that the Dominicans were educated clerics who belonged to the lower nobility and the middle classes. William A. Hinnebusch has even claimed that nearly every noble German family gave at least one of its sons to the Dominican Order in the thirteenth century.[7] Grundmann tried to demonstrate that the early Humiliati, Waldenses, and Franciscans came from a similar social milieu.

4. "Sozial-religiöse Bewegungen im Mittelalter," *Z der Karl-Marx-Universität Leipzig, Gesellschaft- und sprachwissenschaftliche Reihe* 7 (1957/58), 267–273.
5. The most balanced account of St. Elizabeth's ties to the Franciscans is presented in Wilhelm Maurer's "Zum Verständis der hl. Elisabeth von Thüringen," *ZKiG* 65 (1953/54), 16–64. On St. Louis, see Lester K. Little, "Saint Louis' Involvement with the Friars," *Church History* 33 (1964), 125–148.
6. *Religiöse Bewegungen im Mittelalter*, 2nd ed. (Darmstadt, 1961), pp. 157–169.
7. *The History of the Dominican Order: Origins and Growth to 1500* (Staten Island, New York, 1966), 1:287. See also Ralph Francis Bennett, *The Early Dominicans:*

His thesis was based on two pieces of evidence. First of all, the Humiliati, Waldenses, and Franciscans never described their poverty as a destitution imposed upon them by an unfortunate accident of birth, but always as a penury voluntarily adopted. They always referred to their poverty, as David of Augsburg did in his exposition of the Franciscan Rule, as *paupertas voluntaria*. The exponents of the apostolic life idealized, in other words, the renunciation of wealth rather than poverty itself. Furthermore, individuals like St. Francis or St. Clare who are mentioned in various literary sources as adopting the apostolic life were generally members of the upper classes. Grundmann concluded that the search for evangelical perfection was "not a reaction of the disinherited, the impoverished, the excluded against the dominant strata in church, society, and the economy of their time; but that it was rather a religious reaction within the ranks of these dominant strata themselves against the trend of social, economic, and cultural developments."[8] Specifically, he contended "that members of all estates and strata without distinction joined the [Franciscan] Order, but that the rich bourgeoisie, the nobility and the clergy were most strongly represented, rather than the poor strata of the craftsmen, let alone of the industrial proletariat."[9] The obvious fallacy in Grundmann's argument is that the social origins of the leaders are not necessarily identical with those of their followers. As Werner and Erbstösser mockingly observed, the same proof would turn Communism into a bourgeois movement since Marx, Engels, and Lenin were not exactly themselves members of the proletariat.[10]

It should be readily apparent that both these theories about the social origins of the friars are largely based on chance references to individual brothers in chronicles and on the interpretation of literary sources rather than a systematic examination of the identity of the friars mentioned in documents.[11] Until such a study is made, it remains highly speculative to describe

---

Studies in Thirteenth-Century Dominican History (Cambridge, England, 1937), pp. 71–72; Heinrich Finke, *Ungedruckte Dominikanerbriefe des 13. Jahrhunderts* (Paderborn, 1891), p. 10; and Dennis E. Showalter, "The Business of Salvation: Authority and Representation in the Thirteenth-Century Dominican Order," *The Catholic Historical Review* 57 (1973), 567–568.

8. *Religiöse Bewegungen*, p. 168.
9. Ibid., p. 167. Engelbert Grau, "Die ersten Brüder des hl. Franziskus," *FS* 40 (1958), 132–144, reached the same conclusion after examining the social origins of the first eleven companions of St. Francis.
10. "Sozial-religiöse Bewegungen," p. 267.
11. Grundmann, *Religiöse Bewegungen*, p. 164, n. 28, stated that he knew of no such study about the social origins of the thirteenth-century Franciscans.

the Franciscans as poor men protesting against social inequities or as the conscience-stricken rich abandoning their inherited wealth and social position. There is, in addition, a pressing need to analyze the membership of both the Dominican and Franciscan Orders in terms of social categories which actually existed in thirteenth-century Germany. Grundmann's "dominant strata" (*führende Schichten*) is a rather imprecise phrase. It encompasses everybody from wealthy burghers to the highest members of the feudal nobility, but an order composed of the children of wealthy burghers would have been rather different from an order in which members of the feudal nobility predominated. Likewise, while many German nobles may have become Dominicans, as Hinnebusch asserted, a wide social gulf separated the ministerials, the ancestors of the lower nobility, from the old free nobility. The identity of the German nobles who supposedly joined the Dominican Order in such large numbers thus requires closer scrutiny. In the hope of shedding some additional light on the social origins of the friars, an attempt will be made in this chapter and in Appendix II to set forth the social origins of individual, identifiable German Dominicans and Franciscans who joined the orders prior to the accession of Rudolph of Habsburg and to draw some tentative conclusions about the broader implications of these findings.

2. THE EVIDENCE

It is easier to formulate questions about the social origins of the friars than to answer them. Studies of the social origins of the religious have generally relied on two types of evidence: necrologies and documents which indicate the property possessed by an individual monk. Neither of these sources is particularly useful in ascertaining the social origins of the German friars. All of the necrologies of the Dominican and Franciscan convents which I could readily locate were begun at the earliest in the second half of the fourteenth century.[12] While these registers may have incorporated older lists, they indi-

---

12. For the Dominicans, see Laurentius Siemer, *"Liber obituum et anniversariorum* der Predigerbrüder in Osnabrück," *Archiv der deutschen Dominikaner* 1 (1937), 15−95; the Viennese necrology published by Sebastian Brunner, *Der Prediger-Orden in Wien und Oesterreich* (Vienna, 1867); and Paulus von Loë, "Das Necrologium des aachener Dominikanerklosters," *Aus Aachens Vorzeit* 17 (1904), 1−26. For the Franciscans, see Albert Haemmerle, *Das Necrologium des Ordens der Mindern Brüder zu den Barfüssern in Augsburg* (Munich, 1955); *Liber anniversariorum fratrum Minorum Ratisbonensium*, ed. Ludwig Baumann (Berlin, 1905), MGH Necrologia Germaniae 3:247−260; and *Necrologium patrum Minorum conventualium ad S. Crucem Vindobonae*, ed. Adalbert Franziskus Fuchs (Berlin, 1913), MGH Necrologia Germaniae 5:165−196.

cate in their present forms only the Christian names of the friars who died before the fifteenth century and the month and day of their death. It is thus virtually impossible to identify positively any thirteenth-century brother in a necrology.[13] Since the Dominicans and Franciscans were pledged, moreover, to corporate as well as individual poverty, they were not permitted to receive gifts from the relatives of novices, let alone to possess personal incomes. The appearance of documents telling of such gifts and private incomes, which have been used to study the social origins of the friars in the fourteenth century,[14] are a positive indication of a decline in the observance of the vow of poverty in a particular house. It is perhaps a tribute to the friars' adherence to their vows during most of the thirteenth century that it was possible to discover only a few documents of this type prior to 1273.[15]

The Cologne *Schreinsbücher*, the land registers of the city, are of some use in ascertaining the social origins of the friars. The brothers were required to divest themselves of their property before they took the habit.[16] The *Schreinsbücher* indicate what ten friars (seven Franciscans and three Dominicans) actually did with their property. Unfortunately, such letters of renunciation have only survived in one Cologne parish.[17] It must be assumed, consequently, that more than ten Cologne burghers joined the mendicant orders in a period of fifty years.[18]

It is necessary to turn to other types of evidence to obtain additional information about the social background of the Dominicans and Franciscans. The first of these is literary evidence written in the thirteenth century: the constitutions of the two orders, hagiographical writings, letters, and chronicles. There are some pitfalls, as has already been suggested in the critique of

---

13. Ch. Wittmer, "L'Obituaire des Dominicains de Strasbourg (1238–1478)," *AFP* 20 (1950), 415–423, indicates that Frederick of Haguenau (d. 1251), the provost of the Strasbourg cathedral, and Ulrich of Dellmensingen (d. 1252), the precentor and scholastic of Strasbourg, joined the Dominicans (p. 422).

14. Gabriel M. Löhr, *Beiträge zur Geschichte des kölner Dominikanerklosters im Mittelalter*, QFGDD 15–17 (Leipzig, 1920–1922), 1:36–46, discovered the names of 183 Dominicans in the Cologne *Schreinsbücher* between 1221 and 1360; 140 of these Dominicans appeared after 1300.

15. See *Kieler Stadtbuch aus den Jahren 1264–1289*, ed. Paul Hasse (Kiel, 1875), no. 91; *UB der Stadt Erfurt*, ed. Carl Beyer, GQProvSachs 23 (Halle, 1889), 1, no. 199; and *UB der Stadt und Landschaft Zürich*, ed. J. Escher and P. Schweizer (Zürich, 1892), 2, no. 796.

16. Michael Bihl, "Statuta generalia ordinis edita in capitulis generalibus celebratis Narbonae an. 1260, Assisii an. 1279, atque Parisiis an. 1292," *AFH* 34 (1941), 39.

17. Löhr, *Dominikanerkloster*, 1:xiii.

18. Four other Cologne friars who served as witnesses can also be identified.

Grundmann's argument, in using this type of material. Literary sources, particularly chronicles, like a modern newspaper were more apt to report the sensational than the ordinary. The Franciscan Albert of Stade, who had been a Benedictine abbot, recorded in the *Annales Stadenses* that Adolph IV (d. 1261), the regnant count of Holstein and the victor over the Danes at the crucial battle of Bornhövde in 1227, entered the Franciscan convent in Hamburg on August 13, 1239.[19] This was an extraordinary event and it was remembered for this reason. Adolph's and Albert's conversions prove that counts and Benedictine abbots occasionally became friars; they do not prove that all friars or even very many of them were in fact, as Grundmann was inclined to believe, former Benedictine abbots or counts.

More important, we do possess the names of a considerable number of friars who served as witnesses and arbiters in various property transactions and disputes. The usual procedure was to indicate only the friar's Christian name, his order, and his convent, since the use of a title or surname which suggested earthly status was inconsistent with the brother's renunciation of the world. It is impossible to determine the social origins of such individuals. Nevertheless, it clearly was advantageous to identify the witnesses and arbiters in such property transactions and arbitral awards, which might later be challenged, as fully as possible. In many documents, therefore, the friars were identified in some additional way. Occasionally the documents specifically indicated either the friar's former title or his relationship to one of the parties in the transaction. Count Adolph IV was sometimes called "quondam comitem Holsatie,"[20] or in charters issued by his sons Brother Adolph, "dilectus pater noster."[21] Albert of Stade was likewise referred to in a document as "quondam abbas beate Marie in Stadio."[22] The social origins of friars who are identified in this manner are readily apparent. But in most cases of this type, only the friar's surname was stated. Count Adolph was merely called in some documents Friar Adolph, "dicto de Scowenburg," a reference to the

---

19. Ed. Johann Martin Lappenberg (Hanover, 1859), MGH SS 16:365–367. Lappenberg, p. 271, surmises that Albert was of plebeian origin because he attacked knightly misconduct. Such condemnations were common, however, in clerical writings and may well reflect the prejudices of a German noble against the knights who were usually of ministerial origin. Most German Benedictine abbots in the thirteenth century belonged to the old free nobility.
20. *Hamburgisches UB*, ed. Johann Martin Lappenberg (Hamburg, 1842), 1, no. 530.
21. Ibid., no. 555.
22. Ibid., no. 557.

family's ancestral castle and county of Schaumburg.[23] The editors of the German *Urkundenbücher* have normally assigned an individual identified in this way to the prominent family which bore the same last name in the locality of the ecclesiastical foundation. For the purposes of this research, this procedure has been applied to all friars described in this fashion in property deeds and arbitral awards under the assumption that such identifications were not idly made in important documents.

Two caveats should be postulated about this methodology. First of all, while most noble or ministerial families bore the name of a castle or village, many patrician families adopted as their surnames the name of the town from which their ancestors had emigrated. It is nearly impossible to determine whether a friar who used the name of a town as his surname belonged to the patrician family with the same name who lived in the city where the convent was situated, or whether, as was more probably the case, the friar had simply come from or joined the order in the city whose name he bore. Thus the Zürich Dominican Henry of Basel, who witnessed a Kyburg charter for the Dominican nunnery of Töss,[24] may have been a native of Basel, may have joined the Dominicans in Basel, or may have belonged to the Zürich patrician family named Basel. Unless the editor of the document had reason to believe that the friar belonged to the local patrician family, a friar identified in this manner has been excluded from consideration. Second, it should not be assumed that a friar whose surname is not stated in a document necessarily belonged to an insignificant family. The Dominican Hugo Ripelin, who was the author of the *Compendium theologicae veritatis* and who was the prior of Zürich for most of the time between 1232 and 1259, belonged to a prominent Strasbourg patrician family. In no Zürich document is he called anything else but Friar Hugo.[25] Even Count Adolph occasionally was called simply Friar Adolph.[26] The social position of a friar's family apparently had to be of significance in the specific locality in which he served.

23. *UB der Stadt Lübeck*, Codex diplomaticus Lubecensis, lste Abtheilung (Lübeck, 1843), 1, no. 115.
24. *UB Zürich* (see above, n. 15), 2, no. 526. The editors, index, p. 387, believed that Henry belonged to the patrician family named Basel.
25. *De rebus Alsaticis ineuntis saeculi XIII*, ed. Philipp Jaffé (Hanover, 1861), MGH SS 17:233. For further information about Hugo, see Albert Hauck, "Hugo Ripilin," *ZKiG* 32 (1911), 378–385; and Georg Boner, "Ueber den Dominikanertheologen Hugo von Strassburg," *AFP* 24 (1954), 269–286.
26. *UB Lübeck*, 1, no. 114.

Once a friar has tentatively been identified as belonging to a particular family in the region, it often becomes clear why he specifically was selected as an arbiter or witness. If the identification is correct, he would in fact have been a relative or social peer or former dependent of one of the parties in the transaction or dispute. On December 28, 1262, a Bern Franciscan, John of Sumolswalt, witnessed a sale of property worth 140 marks by Countess Elizabeth of Kyburg, the widow of Hartmann V; on January 14, 1265, a Kyburg ministerial, Albert of Rormos, appointed the same friar as his representative on a board of arbitration. A Kyburg ministerial named John of Sumolswalt had witnessed in July 1246 the endowment of the Cistercian nunnery of Frauenbrunnen by Counts Hartmann IV and V of Kyburg.[27] It seems fairly certain that the Franciscan John of Sumolswalt belonged to the Kyburg ministerial family and that he was selected as a witness and arbiter not only because he was a member of a highly esteemed religious order, but also on account of his personal relationship to the Kyburgs and their dependents.

In two cases literary evidence corroborates identifications which can be attained in this manner. Walter of Meissenburg, the prior of the Trier Dominicans, witnessed in May 1235 the will of Alexander, the lord of Zolver; a Walter, lord of Meissenburg, granted his consent in 1246 to a gift of property by one of his vassals to the provostry of Ebernach in the diocese of Trier.[28] It would not be unreasonable to surmise that the Dominican prior was related to the noble who bore the identical name. This conjecture is confirmed by the Dominican raconteur, Thomas of Cantimpré, who wrote in the late 1250s. He related how a Dominican prior named Walter of Meseburg, a "vir nobilis" who had been the prior and lector of many houses, had renounced his prebend in the cathedral of Trier and had joined the Dominicans before he was sixteen.[29] There can be little doubt that Thomas was referring to the Trier prior, Walter of Meissenburg. In the other instance, a Bremen Dominican, Conrad of Rastede, witnessed before September 1241 the transfer of a hide by Archbishop Gerhard of Bremen (1219–1258) to the Cistercian nunnery of Liliental, which had been founded by Gerhard in memory of his brother.[30] Rastede was the name of a Benedictine monastery in the same diocese. The abbot of Rastede in the 1230s, who is last mentioned in a docu-

---

27. *Fontes rerum Bernensium* (Bern, 1877), 2, nos. 255, 527, and 575.
28. *Mittelrheinische Regesten*, ed. Adam Goerz (Koblenz, 1879–1881), 2, no. 2159, and 3, no. 461.
29. *Bonum universale de apibus* 2.29.29, ed. Georgius Colvenerius (Douai, 1627).
30. *Bremisches UB*, ed. D.R. Ehmck and W. von Bippen (Bremen, 1873), 1, no. 217.

ment of June 3, 1238, was named Conrad; by 1244 Rastede had a new abbot named Lambert.[31] While it might seem tenuous on the basis of this evidence alone to identify the Dominican named Conrad of Rastede as the former Benedictine abbot, the *Historia monasterii Rastedensis* indicates that Abbot Conrad was a relative of Archbishop Gerhard, to whom he owed his abbatial dignity, and that he changed habits sometime after 1238, when he was succeeded by Lambert.[32] Conrad's kinship to Archbishop Gerhard helps to explain of course why he in particular witnessed the archiepiscopal charter.

It has been possible to obtain from these various sources the names of 168 Germans, 102 Dominicans and 66 Franciscans, who are definitely known to have become friars before 1273. These names have been listed in Appendix II, divided into two groups: friars like Count Adolph of Holstein whose social origins are specifically stated in a document or literary source, namely, 48 Dominicans and 35 Franciscans; and those like John of Sumolswalt whose social origins could only be deduced from the available evidence, the remaining 54 Dominicans and 31 Franciscans. The friars in both groups have been classified in one of six categories: nobles, ministerials, knights, patricians, burghers, and prelates. The first five of these classifications refer to social classes, the last to an occupational grouping. Only those friars whose ancestors are definitely known to have belonged to the old free nobility, i.e., all *Freiherren*, counts, and princes, have been classified as *nobles*.[33] The designation *ministerial* has been reserved for those individuals whose families are either specifically listed among the ministerials in a document or whose families held a household office of a noble or prelate, such as the stewardship. Friars whose families occupied a municipal office in the thirteenth century or whose relatives are called both knights and burghers of a city have been labeled *patricians*. The term *burgher* has been employed for the non-patrician urban population. Finally, the term *knight*, which came into increasing vogue in the thirteenth century, has been applied to all friars whose relatives are called knights, but who cannot be classified more specifically as nobles, ministerials, or patricians, all of whom could have been and were described in thirteenth-century sources as knights. While the word *miles* clearly had occupational overtones, it increasingly meant a specific class, the lower nobility,

31. Ibid., nos. 187, 188, 192, 208, and 229.
32. Ed. G. Waitz (Hanover, 1880), MGH SS 25:505–507.
33. This definition of the nobility was used by Aloys Schulte, *Der Adel und die deutsche Kirche im Mittelalter: Studien zur Sozial-, Rechts-, und Kirchengeschichte*, 3rd ed. (Darmstadt, 1958), pp. 11–12.

within German society.[34] The final category, *prelates*, has been reserved for friars like Albert of Stade who held high ecclesiastical offices before joining the Dominicans or Franciscans, namely, cathedral and collegiate canons, provosts, abbots, and priors, but whose family background is unknown.

I do not claim that the list of friars published in Appendix II is completely accurate or that all the friars have been correctly identified. It is quite possible that some duplication of names has occurred. Thus the sons of the two German counts whom Jordan of Saxony converted in Padua in 1223 (Table XIV, nos. 1 and 2) may be identical with other noblemen listed in the appendix. Finally, it should be stressed that Appendix II is not a catalogue

TABLE VI

THE SOCIAL ORIGINS OF THE GERMAN FRIARS

Nobles	Minis-terials	Knights	Patri-cians	Burgh-ers	Prelates	Total
			DOMINICANS			
Definitely Known						
14	10	5	2	5	12	48
Possibly Known						
9	21	12	10	2	0	54
Total						
23	31	17	12	7	12	102
			FRANCISCANS			
Definitely Known						
11	2	4	3	11	4	35
Possibly Known						
5	13	10	3	0	0	31
Total						
16	15	14	6	11	4	66
Grand Total						
39	46	31	18	18	16	168

34. For further information about the concept of knighthood in medieval Germany, see Joachim Bumke, *Studien zum Ritterbegriff im 12. und 13. Jahrhundert*, Beihefte zum Euphorion: Z für Literaturgeschichte 1 (Heidelberg, 1964).

of all prominent German friars; it merely contains the names of those individuals whose social origins could be determined. David of Augsburg, whose family background remains unknown,[35] has not been listed, for instance, in the appendix.

What does this highly fragmentary data reveal about the social origins of the friars?

3. ANALYSIS

The brothers whose identity could be ascertained in this fashion quite clearly do not form a representative sample of the total number of German friars in the thirteenth century. This is particularly true of the 18 friars classified as burghers. The names of 12 of them were obtained from a single source, the Cologne *Schreinsbücher*; but their names and family backgrounds are especially valuable because such brothers were not normally identified in chronicles or charters. If we assume that there were in 1273 in Germany approximately 150 Franciscan houses with an average membership of 25 and 49 Dominican convents with an average membership of 37,[36] there would

---

35. Dagobert Stöckerl, *Bruder David von Augsburg*; *Ein deutscher Mystiker aus dem Franziskanerorden*, Veröffentlichungen aus dem kirchenhistorischen Seminar München, IV. Reihe, 4 (Munich, 1914), p. 9.
36. The number of friars in Germany in 1273 can only be estimated. The Dominican constitutions stipulated that a priory was required to have at least 12 members, including the prior and lector, before it could be received. Heribert Chr. Scheeben, *Die Konstitutionen des Predigerordens unter Jordan von Sachsen*, QFGDD 38 (Leipzig, 1939), p. 75. The Hamburg priory had 15 members in 1265. *Hamburgisches UB* (see above, n. 20), 1, no. 685. Basel had 42 friars in 1274. *Annales Basileenses*, ed. Philipp Jaffé (Hanover, 1861), MGH SS 17:196. Colmar had 30 friars in 1297. *Annales Colmarienses maiores*, ed. Philipp Jaffé (Hanover, 1861), MGH SS 17:222. The Breslau priory in the province of Poland had approximately 40 members in 1285. *Regesten zur schlesischen Geschichte*, ed. Colmar Grünhagen, 3 vols., Codex diplomaticus Silesiae 7 (Breslau, 1875—1886), 3:77. The average English priory, about which we are better informed, had 37 friars. William A. Hinnebusch, *The Early English Friars Preacher*, DHIHFP 14 (Rome, 1951), pp. 271—274. If the same average can be applied to Germany, there would have been approximately 1800 Dominicans in Germany in 1273.
    There were 36 Franciscans in Basel in 1274 (*Annales Basileenses*, p. 196), and 40 in Colmar in 1297 (*Annales Colmarienses maiores*, p. 222). Again, we are better informed about the size of the English friaries. Thomas of Eccleston, *De adventu fratrum Minorum in Angliam*, ed. Andrew G. Little, Collection d'études et de documents sur l'histoire religieuse et littéraire du moyen âge 7 (Paris, 1909), p. 14, stated that there were in England in 1256, 49 Franciscan convents with 1242 friars, i.e., approximately 25 friars per house. The English houses were considerably larger,

have been approximately 1800 Dominicans and 3750 Franciscans in the country by Rudolph's accession. The 102 Dominicans in Table VI, presuming the unlikely eventuality that each of them was still alive in 1273, would consequently have composed approximately 5.7% of the total membership of their order, while the 66 Franciscans would have formed an even smaller 1.8% of the total Franciscan membership. Moreover, twenty-one Dominicans and eleven Franciscans, a disproportionate number of the friars in Table VI, are definitely known to have held an important office within their order and/or within the universal church. Many of the remaining friars acted of course as witnesses and arbiters and presumably were also fairly important members of their convents. Finally and most fundamentally, the data in Table VI is skewed by its very nature in favor of the upper strata of medieval society. Chroniclers and other literary sources were almost exclusively interested in recording the conversions of prominent individuals, and property deeds, the most common form of extant German documentation, have primarily preserved the names of property-owning families. It is thus considerably more likely that the name of a friar of high social status, whose family can easily be identified, has survived than the name of an individual and family of more lowly origin. Table VI tends to provide, therefore, information about the leadership group within the mendicant orders rather than the rank-and-file membership.

While a comparatively large number of nobles (39) appears for this reason in Table VI, it probably was exceptional for a member of the old free nobility to become a Dominican or Franciscan. The nobility, which included the *Freiherren*, counts, and princes, had formed since the Carolingian period a virtually closed caste in Germany. While all members of the nobility were in theory free to intermarry, marriage outside the ranks of the nobility entailed an immediate loss of social status. The offspring of a mésalliance belonged to the social class of the non-noble parent.[37] Membership in numerous ecclesi-

however, by 1300. David Knowles and. R. Neville Hadcock, *Medieval Religious Houses: England and Wales* (London, 1953), 189–194. On the other hand, the average French or Italian house, at least in the fourteenth century, was considerably smaller. John Moorman, *A History of the Franciscan Order* (Oxford, 1968), pp. 350–351. If Thomas's average can be applied to Germany, there would have been approximately 3750 Franciscans in 1273.

37. For information about the old nobility, see Karl Bosl, *Frühformen der Gesellschaft im mittelalterlichen Europa* (Munich, 1964); Otto Freiherr von Dungern, *Adelherrschaft im Mittelalter* (Munich, 1927); K. Leyser, "The German Aristocracy from the Ninth to the Early Twelfth Century," *Past and Present* 41 (1968), 25–53; Gerd

astical foundations, particularly cathedral chapters, Benedictine monasteries, and collegiate churches, was restricted until at least the thirteenth century to members of the nobility. Only the orders founded during the Investiture Conflict, most notably the Premonstratensians and Cistercians, were willing to accept non-nobles from their inception.[38] Most of the friars who have been classified as prelates in Table VI probably also belonged for this reason to the nobility. But the number of noble families in Germany had been seriously reduced by the thirteenth century. Since the younger children of the nobility had embarked for centuries upon an ecclesiastical career with its mandatory vow of chastity, numerous noble families were extinguished when the oldest son failed to produce a legitimate heir. There were 222 families of noble status in Baden in 1100; only 45 survived in 1300.[39] Under the best of circumstances the old German nobility could only have provided a small percentage of the total membership of the mendicant orders.

In actuality only those nobles and prelates who were inspired by a fervent desire to lead the apostolic life joined the Franciscans and Dominicans. Albert of Stade renounced his abbatial dignity, for instance, when he was unable to reform his Benedictine monastery.[40] A noble who decided to join the mendicant orders often encountered considerable opposition from his family, who had expected that he would embark upon a more traditional and appropriate ecclesiastical career. Bishop Henry of Worms became especially incensed with the Worms Dominicans in the late 1220s when his nephew Count Eberhard of Leiningen, whom Henry presumably wished to succeed him as bishop, entered the Worms priory.[41] While hagiographical tradition may in part have dictated the relation of such tales of familial opposition, the recurrence of such incidents would be inexplicable if membership in the mendicant orders had been considered a completely acceptable religious vocation for

Tellenbach, "Vom karolingischen Reichsadel zum deutschen Reichsfürstenstand," *Adel und Bauern im deutschen Staat des Mittelalters*, ed. Theodor Mayer, 2nd ed. (Darmstadt, 1967, pp. 23–73; and idem, *Studien und Vorarbeiten zur Geschichte des grossfränkischen und frühdeutschen Adels*, Forschungen zur oberrheinischen Landesgeschichte 4 (Freiburg, 1957).

38. Schulte, *Der Adel* (see above, n. 33).
39. Ibid., pp. 49, 261–294.
40. *Annales Stadenses* (see above, n. 19), pp. 366–367.
41. *Annales Wormatienses*, ed. Georg Pertz (Hanover, 1861), MGH SS 17:38; *UB der Stadt Worms*, ed. Heinrich Boos (Berlin, 1886), 1, nos. 146, 151, 153, 162, and 167. Similar stories may also be found in Thomas of Cantimpré, *Bonum universale* (see above, n. 29), 2.28.11–13; and Gerard of Frachet, *Vitae fratrum ordinis Praedicatorum*, ed. Benedictus Maria Reichert (Louvain, 1896), MOPH 1:143–144.

a thirteenth-century German noble. Friars of noble origin inevitably had an excellent chance in the hierarchical medieval world of attaining a prominent position within their order and thus of being remembered by posterity. It is fairly safe to conclude that there were only a few friars of noble origin and that it is in fact quite possible that we possess the names of most of them.

Table VI suggests instead that the leadership group within the Dominican and Franciscan Orders was primarily recruited from the ranks of the ministerialage and patriciate. The number of ministerials in Table VI (46) actually exceeds the number of nobles (39). It is likely, moreover, that most of the friars who were classified as knights (31) also were of ministerial and patrician origin since it was upwardly mobile ministerial and patrician families who were especially anxious to conceal their non-noble ancestry under the more glamorous appellations, *miles* or *Ritter*. Indeed the term *milites* gradually replaced *ministeriales* in most witness lists in the course of the thirteenth century.[42]

A variety of evidence indicates that patricians and ministerials generally preferred to join the Dominicans rather than the Franciscans, particularly during the crucial, formative decades of the 1220s and 1230s. While most of the Franciscan officials in this period were educated clerics,[43] they were with few exceptions foreigners. Caesar of Speyer, the minister of the Franciscan province of Teutonia from 1221 to 1223, was the only known German provincial minister before 1239.[44] While the absence of Germans in top

---

42. John B. Freed, "The Origins of the European Nobility: The Problem of the Ministerials," *Viator* 7 (1976), 229.

43. Caesar of Speyer, the first provincial minister, had been a student of theology. Jordan of Giano, *Chronica*, ed. H. Boehmer, Collection d'études et de documents sur l'histoire religieuse et littéraire du moyen âge 6 (Paris, 1908), ch. 9. Nicholas of Reno, the guardian of Erfurt in 1225 and the custodian of Saxony from 1225 to 1227, and Otto of Lombardy, the minister of the Rhine (1230–?), had been lawyers (chs. 47, 49, 51, and 57); Hartmod, who eventually became custodian of Saxony, Mark of Milan, the first custodian of Franconia, and James of Treviso, the first custodian of Alsace, were called by Jordan of Giano "litterati" (chs. 25 and 32); and John of Piancarpino, the minister of Teutonia (1228–1230) and of Saxony (1232–1239), could preach in both Latin and Italian (ch. 19). Rüdiger, the guardian of Halberstadt and the spiritual teacher of St. Elizabeth, was the only layman whom Jordan mentions among the early Franciscan leaders in Germany (ch. 25).

44. The ministers of Teutonia were: Caesar of Speyer, Albert of Pisa (1223–1227), and John of Piancarpino (1228–1230). The ministers of Saxony after the division of the province of Teutonia in 1230 into the provinces of the Rhine and Saxony were: Simon of England (1230), John of Reading (1230–1232), and John of Piancarpino (1232–1239). The first minister of the Rhine was Otto of Lombardy (1230–?). Jordan of Giano likewise mentioned ten friars who served as custodians in Germany before 1239; only three were Germans.

leadership positions within the Franciscan Order can perhaps be attributed in part to the personal whims of Elias, who appointed the ministers,[45] a more probable explanation is that suitable Germans were not readily available to fill these positions. German Dominicans, on the other hand, not only administered the province of Teutonia themselves,[46] but also played a disproportionate role in the institutional and intellectual life of the entire order. Not only was a German, St. Albertus Magnus, the foremost scholar within the order in the first decades of its existence, but two Germans, Jordan of Saxony (1222–1237) and Johannes Teutonicus (1241–1252), each of whom had previously served as prior provincial of Lombardy, governed the Dominican Order for all but five of the first thirty-one years after the death of St. Dominic in 1221.[47] The tendency for upper-class Germans to become Dominicans rather than Franciscans seems to have persisted until at least the

45. The provincial ministers were appointed by the minister general until 1239, when the general chapter decreed that they were to be selected by the provincial chapters. Jordan of Giano, ch. 65. Thereafter the leadership of the German Franciscans, judging by the names of the Saxon ministers in Jordan's chronicle, was indigenous.
46. The first known Dominican provincial prior was Conrad of Höxter (ca. 1225–1234), a canonist who had joined the order in Bologna in 1220; and the prior of Cologne in the 1220s was the Utrecht cathedral canon Henry. Heribert Christian Scheeben, *Beiträge zur Geschichte Jordans von Sachsen*, QFGDD 35 (Leipzig, 1938), pp. 155–166. The Strasbourg patrician Hugo Ripelin became prior of Zürich in 1232. See above, n. 25. An Alsatian ministerial, Henry of Westhofen, served as the first prior of Basel. Johannes Meyer, *Liber de viris illustribus ordinis Praedicatorum*, ed. Paulus von Loë, QFGDD 12 (Leipzig, 1918), p. 27; Georg Boner, "Das Predigerkloster in Basel von der Gründung bis zur Klosterreform, 1233–1429," *Basler Z für Geschichte und Altertumskunde* 33 (1934), 286.
47. For further information about Jordan, see Heribert Chr. Scheeben, *Jordan der Sachse* (Vechta in Oldenburg, 1937). The scholarly apparatus for the biography is contained in Scheeben's *Beiträge* (see above, n. 46). Scheeben, *Jordan*, p. 5, and *Beiträge*, pp. 33–34, maintained that Jordan was a Saxon peasant. Theodor Rensing, "Die Herkunft des Dominikanergenerals Jordan von Sachsen," *Westfalen* 17 (1932), 174–175, argued that he was a Dassel ministerial. Since Jordan was a student of theology at the University of Paris when he joined the Dominicans, I believe that it is more probable that Jordan was of ministerial origin.

For further information about Johannes Teutonicus, see A. Rother, "Johannes Teutonicus (v. Wildeshausen)," *Römische Quartalschrift für christliche Altertumskunde und für Kirchengeschichte* 9 (1895), 139–170. We possess no definite information about John's social origins. Since Peter Ferrand, *Chronica ordinis*, ed. Benedictus Maria Reichert (Rome, 1897), MOPH 1:332, indicates that John was born in the town of Wildeshausen, he has been called a count of Wildeshausen. If John was in fact a count, it is rather strange that Peter Ferrand did not say so. John was closely associated, however, with the counts of Oldenburg-Wildeshausen in the crusade against the Stedinger. Hermann Oncken, "Studien zur Geschichte des Stedingerkreuzzuges," *Jahrbuch für die Geschichte des Herzogtums Oldenburg* 5 (1896),

fourteenth century. While the Franciscans certainly were the larger order, there were 95 Dominicans in Table VI who have been classified as nobles, ministerials, knights, patricians, or prelates, but only 55 Franciscans. Finally, studies of the social origins of the friars in Strasbourg, Cologne, and Basel in the fourteenth century, when evidence is considerably more abundant, have shown that in each town a fairly large number of patricians became Dominicans, but that only a few, if any, patricians joined the Franciscans.[48] All the available evidence suggests that while the ministerials and patricians formed the basic leadership group within both orders, there was a larger number of such individuals, both in relative and absolute terms, among the Dominicans than the Franciscans, particularly during the 1220s and 1230s.

It is still necessary to ascertain, as far as is possible, the social origins of the ordinary Dominican or Franciscan in thirteenth-century Germany. In theory any individual who was personally free could become a friar.[49] Since many German peasants had in fact acquired personal freedom by the thirteen century[50] and since it was customary in any case for a devout lord to free a serf who wished to take holy orders, this condition was not by itself a very serious restriction upon membership in either order. Both mendicant orders had, however, educational prerequisites for admission.

The Dominican Order, which needed educated men from its inception to implement its primary mission of popular preaching, always had such a requirement. The Dominican constitutions which were written in the 1220s stipulated that three suitable friars were to examine diligently the conduct and knowledge of a postulant.[51] As master general, Jordan of Saxony delib-

---

52–58. Perhaps John was a vassal or a ministerial of the counts of Oldenburg-Wildeshausen; or perhaps he just came from a Wildeshausen burgher family. The possibility still exists of course that John was a count.

48. Wilhelm Kothe, *Kirchliche Zustände Strassburgs im Vierzehnten Jahrhundert* (Freiburg im B., 1903), p. 43, discovered more patricians among the Dominicans and more sons of guildsmen among the Franciscans. Löhr, *Dominikanerkloster*, (see above, n. 14), 1:36–46, discovered in the Cologne *Schreinsbücher* between 1221 and 1360 the names of 183 Dominicans, 140 after 1300. Twenty-eight or 29 of them definitely were Cologne patricians, 26 or 27 of whom appeared after 1300. Prior to 1360, Löhr discovered the names of 65 Franciscans, 10 of whom were Cologne patricians. Boner, "Predigerkloster" (see above, n. 46), pp. 286–292, discovered many patricians and knights among the fourteenth-century Basel Dominicans, but none among the Franciscans.

49. Scheeben, *Konstitutionen* (see above, n. 36), p. 57; and Bihl, "Statuta" (see above, n. 16), 39.

50. *The Cambridge Economic History of Europe*, ed. M.M. Postan, 2nd ed. (Cambridge, England, 1966), 1:334–339, 466.

51. Scheeben, *Konstitutionen*, p. 57.

erately set out to recruit students and teachers at the new universities of France, Italy, and England.[52] He proudly informed the Bolognese Dominican nun Diana d'Andalo, for example, of the conversion of two German counts, three well-educated Germans who had been studying in Vercelli, a German regent in logic named Walter who was considered one of the greatest teachers in Paris, a German legist who had been a canon in Speyer and rector of the German school in Vercelli, and a German master named Gottschalk who had been a canon in Utrecht.[53] Altogether the Dominican biographer Gerard of Frachet, who wrote in the 1250s, estimated that Jordan won a thousand converts during his fifteen-year ministry.[54] As a German, Jordan may have been particularly successful among his compatriots studying in foreign lands. Thomas of Cantimpré related, for instance, that Count Albert of Flankenberg, who had been sent by his mother at the age of thirteen to the French court to be educated with her Capetian relatives, naturally sought the company of his fellow Germans in Paris and so came into contact with Jordan of Saxony, who won him for the order.[55] Jordan's success with his countrymen at the universities of France and Italy may explain why so few upper-class, educated German clerics joined the Franciscans in the 1220s and 1230s; Jordan had reached them first.

The German Dominicans adhered to Jordan's policy after his death. Edmund, the German prior provincial (1249–1251 and 1266–1269), instructed the German friars studying in Bologna in the late 1260s only to recruit men educated in either logic or law.[56] His successor Ulrich Engelbert (1272–1277) sharply rebuked an unnamed prior for accepting individuals who failed to meet the educational standards of the order although he made an exception for the son of the convent's leading benefactor whose educational preparation was deficient.[57] This preference for university graduates may have made the German Dominicans more socially exclusive than their brothers in other lands, since it must have been extremely difficult for a poor German boy of humble origin to attend a foreign university. In any case, regardless of their origins, the Dominicans formed an educated elite within thirteenth-century German society.

52. Berthold Altaner, *Die Briefe Jordans von Sachsen, des zweiten Dominikanergenerals (1227–37): Text und Untersuchungen*, QFGDD 20 (Leipzig, 1925), nos. 4, 8, 14, 19, 20, 21, 26, 29, 32, 34, 39, 40, 42, and 49.
53. Ibid., nos. 14, 20, and 49.
54. *Vitae* (see above, n. 41), p. 102.
55. *Bonum universale* (see above, n. 29) 2.28.11.
56. Finke, *Dominikanerbriefe* (see above, n. 7), no. 33.
57. Ibid., no. 67.

Unlike the Dominicans, the Franciscans in the 1220s and 1230s accepted large numbers of uneducated laymen. An Austin canon who recorded in his chronicle the arrival of the friars in Magdeburg in the 1220s observed that while there were many clerics among the Dominicans, the Franciscans received both clerics and laymen.[58] Indeed the majority of the early Franciscans were members of the laity. The carefully selected group which Caesar of Speyer led to Germany in 1221 was composed of fifteen laymen, but only twelve clerics[59]; and it probably included a comparatively large number of clerics. The early Franciscan mission in Germany, which suffered in Jordan of Giano's own words from a "scarcity of priests,"[60] was repeatedly hindered by a lack of clerical brothers. The situation was so critical that Jordan himself served in the summer of 1223 as the sole priest for the friaries in Worms, Mainz, and Speyer.[61] The attempts to establish Franciscan houses in the Thuringian imperial cities of Nordhausen and Mühlhausen had to be abandoned in 1225 because the new foundations were composed entirely of laymen.[62] Since the German Franciscans in 1228 still lacked a teacher of theology, the minister general, John Parenti (1227-1232), appointed an Englishman, Simon, as lector of theology in Magdeburg to remedy the deficiency.[63]

After the educated friars who governed the Franciscan Order had engineered the deposition of Elias as minister general in 1239, they consciously set out to transform the Franciscan Order from a group of laymen preaching repentance by their simple words and lives into an organization of learned clerics modeled after the Dominicans.[64] While the 1242 Bologna general chapter may already have voted to restrict lay membership within the Franciscan Order,[65] only the text of the decree as it appears in the 1260 Constitutions of Narbonne has survived:

> And because God has called us not only on account of our own salvation, but also on account of the edification of others by example, counsel, and wholesome preaching, we ordain that no one ought to be received in our

58. *Chronicon Montis Sereni*, ed. E. Ehrenfeuchter (Hanover, 1874), MGH SS 23:220.
59. Jordan of Giano, *Chronica* (see above, n. 43), ch. 19.
60. Ibid., ch. 28.
61. Ibid., ch. 30.
62. Ibid., chs. 44 and 45.
63. Ibid., ch. 54.
64. Rosalind B. Brooke, *Early Franciscan Government: Elias to Bonaventure* (Cambridge, England, 1959), pp. 181-285.
65. Ibid., pp. 243-245.

order, unless he is such a cleric who is properly instructed in either grammar or logic, or unless he is such a cleric or layman whose entry would bring exceedingly great and outstanding edification to the people and clergy.[66]

Literacy thus became, unless an individual had other exceptional qualifications to recommend him, such as nobility of birth or great wealth, a minimum prerequisite for admission into the Franciscan as well as the Dominican Order. The few lay brothers, Franciscans as well as Dominicans, who are specifically identified in the charters, were associated with convents of Dominican nuns or Poor Clares, presumably in an administrative capacity, and were of ministerial or patrician origin.[67] The evidence is clearly too fragmentary to make any conclusive judgment about the social origins of the lay brothers who continued to join the mendicant orders in Germany.[68] But the Franciscans probably never became as selective as the Dominicans, who clearly preferred not only literate individuals, but the recipients of a bachelor's degree.

Since medieval Germany obviously did not possess a system of universal compulsory education, such educational requirements inevitably severely limited membership in the mendicant orders. While the son of a peasant or a poor burgher was undoubtedly on occassion taught how to read and to write by his parish priest and thus presumably became eligible for membership in the Dominican and Franciscan Orders, such educational opportunities were probably restricted in general to at least moderately prosperous burgher families who could afford to send their sons to school rather than to work. Such boys probably attended the type of school whose teacher John of Piancarpino converted in Hildesheim in 1223.[69] The friars whose names appear in the Cologne *Schreinsbücher*, individuals who, as far as we know, did not hold an office within the order and who were thus more typical of the ordinary members, were small urban property owners, probably the sons of

66. Bihl, "Statuta" (see above, n. 16), p. 39.
67. The Dominicans were: Henry of Herten, conversus of Töss (Table XIV, no. 47); Werner Feist, conversus of Klingental (no. 66); and William Kloton, Hildebrand Merz, and William Brosma, conversi of Oetenbach (nos. 79, 80, and 81). The Franciscans Hartung and Hetzel of Zässingen were associated with the convent of the Poor Clares in Basel (Table XV, nos. 40 and 41).
68. Hinnebusch, *History* (see above, n. 7), 1:287 and 289, states that the Dominicans accepted peasants as lay brothers who performed the manual labor in the convents. I have found no evidence for this in Germany, but such brothers were hardly likely to be mentioned by name in the extant sources.
69. Jordan of Giano, *Chronica*, ch. 35.

craftsmen and shopkeepers. The Franciscan Hartmann who is mentioned in 1232 had inherited, for example, half a house and city lot.[70] Hartmann was not destitute, but he cannot be described as a member of the dominant strata of medieval society. The social background of the average German Franciscan or Dominican was, in any case, very different from that of a Benedictine. Jordan of Giano probably described the typical Franciscan best, and to a lesser extent the Dominican as well, when he adapted the words of St. Paul to the Corinthians:

> "See your vocation, brethren, that not many are wise according to the flesh," who might have built up our order by their wisdom, "not many mighty," who showed that it was to be passionately preserved, "not many noble," on account of whose favor they have undertaken to observe it. "But the foolish things of the world hath God chosen . . . and the weak things . . . and the mean things . . . and the things that are contemptible. . . ."[71]

Most German nobles would have heartily concurred with Jordan's judgment.

These differences in Franciscan and Dominican recruitment policy help to explain why the Dominicans rather than the Franciscans were assigned in the early 1230s the tasks of preaching a crusade on behalf of the Teutonic Knights in Prussia and of ferreting out heretics in Germany.[72] Educated clerics who could serve as popular preachers and inquisitors were needed to carry out such assignments. The largely lay Franciscan Order did not meet this basic requirement in the 1220s and 1230s. The successful execution of these missions was also facilitated by personal contacts between the friars and members of the ministerial and patrician classes. Those Dominicans who were themselves by birth ministerials or patricians were in a better position than most Franciscans to persuade ministerials or patricians to take the cross or to induce the local authorities to support a campaign against heretics. The difference in the social origins of the members of the two orders, which can be traced to different educational prerequisites for admission, thus profoundly affected the early development of the Franciscans and Dominicans.

4. THE BROADER IMPLICATIONS

The appearance of numerous ministerials and patricians in leadership positions within the mendicant orders can be linked to the social revolution

---

70. *Schreinsbuch* 299:7a, II, 183.
71. Prologue. The translation is taken from *The Coming of the Friars Minor to England and Germany*, tr. E. Gurney Salter (London, 1926), p. 131.
72. See above, pp. 65–67, and below, pp. 142–145.

SOCIAL ORIGINS OF THE FRIARS

SOCIAL ORIGINS OF THE FRIARS

which was taking place in Germany during the high Middle Ages. Unlike France where the Carolingian nobility and its military retainers had slowly coalesced into a single class, Germany had retained under the comparatively effective rule of the Saxon and Salian dynasties the rigid distinction between the free nobility and its servile dependents, irrespective of the military services the latter performed. Starting in the eleventh century, the lay and ecclesiastical princes, most notably the Hohenstaufen themselves, unable to rely on the loyalty of their noble vassals, increasingly used their ministerials to administer and to defend their nascent territorial states.[73] The career of the imperial ministerial, Markward of Anweiler (d. 1202), the regent of Sicily during the minority of Frederick II, is the most famous example of the political importance of the ministerial class by the end of the twelfth century.[74] By the first decades of the thirteenth century the previously servile ministerials had been accepted as a class of legally free individuals, bound to their lords by feudal rather than servile ties. The ministerials of the archbishops of Cologne had attained this status by about 1230.[75]

A few ministerial families of exceptional wealth, lineage, and political power, such as the imperial ministerials, the Bolanden and Weidas, or the Austrian Liechtensteins, eventually succeeded in intermarrying with prominent noble families. Most of the ministerials, freed from the stigma of servile birth, slowly combined with the poorer and less prestigious remnants of the old free nobility, the *Freiherren*, to form the *Ritterstand* of the fourteenth and fifteenth centuries. This new lower nobility filled the social and political vacuum which had been created by the extinction of most of the old free nobility. The early medieval dichotomy between free men and servile dependents which had survived in Germany until the twelfth century was thus gradually replaced during the high Middle Ages by the system of occupational estates (*Berufsstände*) of the later Middle Ages: the princes, knights, burghers, and peasants.[76]

Ambitious ministerials could further their own careers in a variety of

73. Freed, "Origins" (see above, n. 42), pp. 211–228.
74. For additional information about Markward, see Karl Bosl, *Die Reichsministerialität der Salier und Staufer*, MGH Schriften 10 (Stuttgart, 1950–1951), pp. 588–601; and Thomas C. Van Cleve, *Markward of Anweiler and the Sicilian Regency* (Princeton, 1937).
75. Wilhelm Pötter, *Die Ministerialität der Erzbischöfe von Köln*, Studien zur kölner Kirchengeschichte 9 (Düsseldorf, 1967), pp. 115–155.
76. Freed, "Origins," pp. 228–229.

ways in the first half of the thirteenth century. Many ministerials continued to serve the Hohenstaufen and other princes. Frederick II's Italian campaigns required a steady stream of German manpower. The emperor was accompanied by a thousand Swabian and Alsatian knights, presumably of ministerial ancestry, when he crossed the Alps in 1236 to fight the Lombards.[77] Other ministerials, like the Teutonic Knights who were largely recruited from the ranks of the ministerialage,[78] headed for the Holy Land[79] or for the eastern colonial territories, where warriors were always needed and where there was an ample supply of vacant land.[80] Many ministerials naturally became clerics.

A surprisingly large number of ministerials settled in the cities. As princely castellans, judges, toll collectors, market overseers, and minters, numerous ministerials lived within cities, invested in commerce, and even became *Ratsherren*.[81] The *Rat* of Worms was composed after 1233 of nine burghers and six episcopal ministerials; a large number of episcopal ministerials likewise belonged to the *Rat* in Strasbourg until the battle of Hausbergen in 1262.[82] Indeed the available evidence suggests that many patrician families of supposedly mercantile origin, including the burgher members of the *Rat* in Worms,[83] were themselves the descendants of ministerials who had settled at an early date in the rapidly developing German towns.[84]

77. *Annales Colonienses maximi*, ed. Karl Pertz (Hanover, 1861), MGH SS 17:845.
78. Manfred Hellmann, "Bemerkungen zur sozialgeschichtlichen Erforschung des Deutschen Ordens," *HJb* 80 (1960), 126–142.
79. Paul Kluckholm, *Die Ministerialität in Südostdeutschland*, Quellen und Studien zur Verfassungsgeschichte des Deutschen Reiches 4 (Weimar, 1910), p. 247.
80. See Harald Schieckel, *Herrschaftsbereich und Ministerialität der Markgrafen von Meissen*, Mitteldeutsche Forschungen 7 (Cologne, 1956); and Georg Winter, *Die Ministerialität in Brandenburg*, Veröffentlichungen des Vereins für Geschichte der Mark Brandenburg 19 (Munich, 1922).
81. Freed, "Origins," pp. 233–237.
82. Carl Koehne, *Der Ursprung der Stadtverfassung in Worms, Speier und Mainz*, Untersuchungen zur deutschen Staats- und Rechtsgeschichte 31 (Breslau, 1890), pp. 325–327; Ernst Kruse, "Verfassungsgeschichte der Stadt Strassburg, besonders im 12. und 13. Jahrhundert," *WZ Ergh.* 1 (1884), 49–50 and 59–63.
83. Knut Schulz, "Die Ministerialität als Problem der Stadtgeschichte. Einige allgemeine Bemerkungen, erläutert am Beispiel der Stadt Worms," *Rheinische Vierteljahrsblätter* 32 (1968), 198–205.
84. See Heinz F. Friedrichs, "Herkunft und ständische Zuordnung des Patriziats der wetterauischen Reichsstädte," *Hessisches Jahrbuch für Landesgeschichte* 9 (1959), 37–75; Hermann Nehlsen, "Cives et milites de Friburg. Ein Beitrag zur Geschichte des ältesten freiburger Patriziats," *Schau-ins-Land* 84/85 (1966–67), 79–124; Knut Schulz, *Ministerialität und Bürgertum in Trier*, Rheinisches Archiv 66 (Bonn, 1968); and Paul Strait, *Cologne in the Twelfth Century* (Gainesville, Florida, 1974), pp. 131–137.

It is important to remember that this social revolution was only at the half-way stage at the beginning of the thirteenth century. The ministerial and patrician classes had already attained by 1200 considerable political influence, wealth, and personal freedom; but they had not yet been accepted as the social peers of the old nobility. Indeed, while nobles and ministerials slowly coalesced in the course of the century in Austria and Brabant, the distinctions between the descendants of the free nobility and the servile ministerialage were rigidly preserved until the end of the Middle Ages in Guelders and Westphalia.[85] Many prestigious ecclesiastical foundations remained closed to the children of ministerials and patricians, and well-educated German clerics of ministerial and patrician origin generally had fewer chances for advancement than their social counterparts in France or England. The English or French university graduate could enter the expanding royal bureaucracies and obtain a benefice through royal patronage; the German cleric's opportunities were far more limited. There was no comparable imperial bureaucracy in Germany, and the old nobility continued to monopolize most of the lucrative positions in the church. It was highly unusual, even in the thirteenth century, for a non-noble to become a bishop. An examination of the social origins of the bishops in eighteen German dioceses has revealed, for instance, that the first known non-nobles became bishops in two dioceses in the twelfth century, in nine bishoprics in the thirteenth century, in six dioceses in the fourteenth century, and in Liège only in the fifteenth century.[86]

A noble who joined the mendicant orders probably reduced his chances of attaining the miter. Only six friars became bishops before 1273 in the forty-four dioceses of the six German ecclesiastical provinces: Bremen, Cologne, Magdeburg, Mainz, Salzburg, and Trier. Count Henry of Montfort, a Dominican, admittedly had little difficulty in becoming bishop of Chur in 1252, a diocese dominated by his family.[87] But Count Henry of Luxembourg, the nephew of Archbishop Siegfried of Mainz, had far less success in obtaining a prestigious appointment. After considerable prodding by Innocent IV, who needed the archbishop's support in the papal struggle against Frederick II, the legate procured for Henry the missionary bishopric of Zem-

---

85. Freed, "Origins," pp. 228–232.
86. Schulte, *Der Adel* (see above, n. 33), p. 65.
87. P. Aldinger, *Die Neubesetzung der deutschen Bistümer unter Papst Innocenz IV. 1243–1254* (Leipzig, 1900), pp. 99–100 and 160–161; Emil Krüger, "Die Grafen von Werdenberg-Heiligenberg und von Werdenberg-Sargans," *Mitteilungen zur vaterländischen Geschichte herausgegeben vom historischen Verein in St. Gallen* 22 (1887), 120–121.

gale (1247–1251). Henry subsequently obtained the equally insignificant dioceses of Kurland (1261–1263) and of Chiemsee (1263–1274).[88] It is hard to understand why a nephew of the German primate should have been unable to obtain a better position than Zemgale in a period when Innocent was freely distributing German bishoprics to his supporters.[89] Henry must either have been a singularly inept individual, or his membership in the Franciscan Order must have counted against him. It should be observed, however, that nobles who joined the mendicant orders may deliberately have renounced for pious reasons the ecclesiastical careers to which their births would ordinarily have entitled them. Thomas of Cantimpré related that Count Albert of Flankenberg declined to accept a bishopric from the pope.[90] The Franciscan Count Henry of Brene, Rudolph of Habsburg's chaplain and envoy to Silesia in the 1270s, probably rejected for similar reasons Martin IV's offer of the archbishopric of Gnesen in 1281.[91]

There can be little doubt, on the other hand, that membership in the Dominican and Franciscan Orders provided a few extremely capable non-nobles with the necessary opportunities and social and political contacts to further their own careers. Albertus Magnus, the most famous of the German friars, who briefly served as bishop of Regensburg (1260–1262), apparently was the son of a Hohenstaufen ministerial who lived in Lauingen.[92] Bishop Otto of Minden (1267–1270), a Dominican and a former knight, had been the chaplain of Cardinal Henry of Ostia.[93] Other friars clearly owed their preferment to the services they rendered influential princes. The Franciscan John of

---

88. *Les Registres d'Innocent IV*, ed. Élie Berger, 4 vols. (Paris, 1884–1911), 1, nos. 2326, 3198, 3502; Conrad Eubel, "Der Minorit Heinrich von Lützelburg, Bischof von Semgallen, Curland und Chiemsee," *HJb* 6 (1885), 92–103.

89. Innocent's episcopal appointments are discussed in considerable detail in Aldinger's *Neubesetzung der deutschen Bistümer*.

90. *Bonum universale* (see above, n. 29), 2.28.13.

91. *Regesten zur schlesischen Geschichte* (see above, n. 36), 3, nos. 1686 and 1754; Oswald Redlich, *Rudolf von Habsburg* (Innsbruck, 1903), pp. 269 and 293. On Henry's social origins, see *Codex diplomaticus Anhaltinus*, ed. Otto von Heinemann (Dessau, 1875), 2, no. 364.

92. Heribert Christian Scheeben, *Albert der Grosse: Zur Chronologie seines Lebens*, QFGDD 27 (Leipzig, 1931), pp. 5–7; *Albertus Magnus* (Bonn, 1932), pp. 20–21. In 1251 Albert called himself "Frater Albertus de Loginge, lector fratrum domus ordinis Praedicatorum in Colonia." *Oorkondenboek van het Sticht Utrecht tot 1301*, ed. F. Ketner (The Hague, 1949), 3, no. 1240.

93. Paulus von Loë, *Statistisches über die Ordensprovinz Saxonia*, QFGDD 4 (Leipzig, 1910), p. 49; *Les Registres de Clément IV*, ed. Edouard Jordan (Paris, 1893–1945), no. 507.

Diest, the bishop of Sambia (1251/52−1254) and of Lübeck (1254−1259), who either belonged to the Brabantine noble family named Diest or who simply was a burgher of that city, labored zealously on behalf of the anti-king, Count William of Holland.[94] Archbishop Władysław of Salzburg (1265−1270), the regent of the duchy of Silesia-Breslau (1266−1270), likewise appointed his confessor, the Breslau Franciscan Herbord, bishop of Lavant (1268−1275).[95]

But the most spectacular medieval success stories are provided by the careers of the Franciscans Henry Knoderer, the son of a baker or miller in Isny, who became bishop of Basel (1275−1286) and archbishop of Mainz (1286−1288), and Conrad Probus, the son of a blacksmith in Isny or Tübingen, who obtained the bishopric of Toul (1279−1296). Both friars had served as advisers and envoys of Rudolph of Habsburg.[96] While Henry's father was apparently sufficiently wealthy to send his son to the University of Paris to continue his education, an interesting example of medieval paternal ambition and upward social mobility, it was unprecedented, nevertheless, for a baker's or miller's son, even a rich one, to become primate of Germany. The careers of these friars, while undoubtedly exceptional, indicate that the mendicant orders could serve as an avenue for social advance for a few extremely talented individuals. But even the friar who only became the prior or

94. John may have been a relative of the Brabantine noble, Arnold of Diest, an adherent of William of Holland. Paul Bonenfant and G. Despy, "La Noblesse en Brabant aux XIIe et XIIIe siècles: Quelques sondages," *Le Moyen âge* 64 (1958), 63; and *Oorkondenboek van Holland en Zeeland*, ed. L. Ph. C. van den Bergh (Amsterdam, 1866), 1, nos. 514, 521, 587. On May 17, 1249, Innocent IV ordered that a dignity or benefice be given to Eberhard, the provost of the canons of St. George in Cologne and the brother of Arnold; on January 9, 1253, the pope ordered at Williams's request that the next vacant bishopric be given to Eberhard. *Les Registres d'Innocent IV* (see above, n. 88), 2, no. 4655, and 3, no. 6196. As far as I know, Eberhard never obtained a bishopric. It is not an unlikely suggestion, however, that John was transferred instead from Sambia to the more important bishopric of Lübeck. It is also possible of course that John was the son of a vassal or ministerial of William or of a burgher of Diest. For information about John's political activities, see below, p. 153, and Willibrord Lampen, "Joannes van Diest, O.F.M.," *Bijdragen voor de Geschiedenis van het Bisdom van Haarlem* 44 (1926), 299−312.
95. *UB der Kustodien Goldberg und Breslau*, ed. Chrysogonus Reisch, Monumenta Germaniae Franciscana, 2. Abteilung, 1 (Düsseldorf, 1917), 1, footnote to no. 36.
96. *Chronicon Colmariense*, ed. Philipp Jaffé (Hanover, 1861), MGH SS 17:256−257; *Flores temporum auctore fratre ordinis Minorum*, ed. Oswald Holder-Egger (Hanover, 1879), MGH SS 29:249. For information about their careers, see Konrad Eubel, "Die Minoriten Heinrich Knoderer u. Konrad Probus," *HJb* 9 (1888), 393−449 and 650−673.

guardian of his house could wield considerable influence in his locality and enhance the prestige of his family.

It is probably futile to seek a single motive which caused thousands of men, individuals as diverse as Albertus Magnus and Henry Knoderer, to become friars. Some may have been impelled by feelings of guilt or by youthful idealism; others may have been attracted by the example of a friend or by the prospect of a career. No study of a man's social origins can fully reveal the secrets of his heart. But it is at least worth observing that the inherent contradictions in the social position of the ministerials and patricians, who joined the mendicant orders in such large numbers in Germany, left its psychic mark upon some of them. As the courtly literature produced for the most part by ministerials reveals, they dreamed about a world in which men would be judged by their virtues and deeds rather than their birth[97]; but they also yearned, like St. Mary of Oignies or St. Francis, for liberation from the guilt they felt about the contrast between their own comfortable lives, the fruit of their fathers' labors, and the Christian ideal portrayed in the Gospels. The adoption of the apostolic life satisfied, paradoxical as it may sound, both desires. St. Francis's rejection of paternal wealth and ambition in the palace of the bishop of Assisi and his resolution of the identity crisis common to thousands of sensitive young men and women in the high Middle Ages made him the paradigm of a generation. Yet St. Francis's radical life style was expressed in the familiar imagery of the prevailing chivalric culture with its intrinsic message of equality among warriors. The friar could obtain equality and nobility not on the battlefield or in the service of a lady, but in imitation of the naked Christ. And the last could even become the first as the careers of Henry Knoderer and Conrad Probus demonstrated. It is ironic that these friars' renunciation of the world was made possible by their father's earthly success.

97. Arno Borst, "Das Rittertum im Hochmittelalter: Idee und Wirklichkeit," *Saeculum* 10 (1959), 224–228; and Herbert Moller, "The Social Causation of the Courtly Love Complex," *Comparative Studies in Society and History* 1 (1958–1959), 137–163.

5

The Friars and Imperial Politics

We have always been favorably disposed toward your order ... since we are firmly convinced that the Dominicans are the bulwark of the senescent church and of the Christian faith, which heretical depravity threatens. ... Now, however, we regret to say, the Dominicans ... are not merely content to interfere in the petty disputes of ordinary subjects, but have involved themselves in the quarrels of kings and princes. ... We are greatly distressed that the Dominicans, contrary to God and justice, everywhere attack us and our Holy Empire. ... Under the habit of their order, they are able to move about freely ... and to obtain a friendly reception from the credulous populace. ... We have boldly brought these matters to your attention, brothers ... so that you may correct them. ... If you do, we will forget these unfortunate incidents and will esteem more highly than ever the brothers, whom we desire to be fervent intercessors on our behalf to God rather than opponents of our justice.

Frederick II to the 1246 Dominican General Chapter.[1]

1. INTRODUCTION

THE previous examinations of the expansion of the mendicant orders and of the social origins of the friars have revealed that the Dominicans and Franciscans were closely associated with those elements in thirteenth-century German society—the east-Elbian princes, the ministerials, and the burghers—who profited most from the disintegration of the old imperial system. This fact immediately raises the question of the nature of the friars' relations with the chief representatives of the imperial regime, the Hohenstaufen dynasty and

---

1. J.-L.-A. Huillard-Bréholles, *Historia diplomatica Friderici Secundi* (Paris, 1857–1860), 6:479–480.

the German episcopate. Modern historians have generally agreed that the friars and Frederick II, the living embodiment of the old order, were implacable enemies. The emperor's nineteenth-century biographer, Eduard Winkelmann, called the friars "an army of willing, unquestioning agitators against whose intrigues every secular power was more or less defenseless."[2] Herbert Grundmann stressed the incompatibility between the friars and the emperor: "In the end the new religious forces which gave their stamp to the future remained alien to the Hohenstaufen emperor and turned against him. The mendicant orders ... became the shock troops of the church."[3] Indeed it is difficult to imagine two more antithetical figures than St. Francis and Frederick II.[4]

Considerable evidence can be mustered in support of such views. Jordan of Saxony had already noticed during his generalship the basic, personal antipathy between Frederick and the friars when he observed that the emperor had little respect for the religious.[5] Several chroniclers mentioned the friars' devoted service to the papacy and the emperor's mistreatment of the brothers. The Sicilian chronicler Richard of San Germano, for example, recorded that the Sicilian authorities expelled the friars, after the emperor's first and second excommunications, for agitating against him.[6] Finally, Frederick's own correspondance, such as his veiled warning to the 1246 Dominican general chapter, seemingly condemns him as an opponent and persecutor of the mendicant orders.[7] The emperor's hatred for the friars has been accepted as so axiomatic in German medieval historiography that the distin-

2. *Kaiser Friedrich II.*, 2 vols. (Leipzig, 1889–1897), 2:437.
3. "Friedrich II. und das Geistesleben seiner Zeit," *Stupor Mundi: Zur Geschichte Friedrichs II. von Hohenstaufen*, ed. Günther Wolf (Darmstadt, 1966), p. 363.
4. Ernst Kantorowicz, *Frederick the Second 1194–1250*, tr. E.O. Lorimer (New York, 1931), stressed the antithesis between Francis and Frederick. See, for instance, p. 239.
5. Berthold Altaner, *Die Briefe Jordans von Sachsen, des zweiten Dominikanergenerals 1222–37): Text und Untersuchungen*, QFGDD (Leipzig, 1925), no. 32.
6. *Ryccardi de Sancto Germano notarii chronica* (Hanover, 1866), MGH SS 19:353 and 380. See also Matthew of Paris, *Chronica maiora*, ed. F. Liebermann (Hanover, 1888), MGH SS 28:228, 295, 298, 306, and 309; and Jordan of Giano, *Chronica*, ed. H. Boehmer, Collection d'études et de documents sur l'histoire religieuse et littéraire du moyen âge 6 (Paris, 1908), ch. 73. Hereafter cited as Jordan of Giano.
7. See also Huillard-Bréholles, *Historia*, 5:844–845, 1098–1100, and 6:699–703, 710–713, 772–775; and *Acta imperii inedita saeculi XIII et XIV*, ed. Eduard Winkelmann, 2nd ed. (Aalen, 1964), 1, nos. 359, 437, and 856. Gratien, *Histoire de la fondation et de l'évolution de l'ordre des frères Mineurs au XIIIe siècle* (Paris, 1928), pp. 618–624, compiled the most complete list of Frederick's misdeeds.

guished Rhenish historian Otto Oppermann regarded the establishment of a
Dominican convent in an episcopal see in the 1220s as positive proof of the
bishop's anti-Hohenstaufen orientation.[8] Yet in 1246 the emperor reminded
the Dominicans that he had always been favorably disposed toward their
order. Was he brazenly lying or was there at least some basis for his claim?

It is important to remember that most of the evidence for Frederick's
mistreatment of the friars was written after the emperor's second excommunication in 1239 and is often propagandistic in tone and Italian in origin.[9]
It should not automatically be assumed that statements echoing imperial or
papal propaganda provide a true view of official policy toward the friars, particularly in Germany before 1239. This was after all an era of at least osten-
sibly correct relations between the papacy and empire, a period, except for
the years 1227 to 1230, in which Frederick professed his devotion to the
church and accepted the basic conventions of medieval society.[10] It hardly
seems likely that he would have openly opposed two orders favored by the
papacy. An accurate picture of the Hohenstaufen's and episcopate's attitude
toward the mendicant orders can only be gained from an examination of the
identity and political allegiances of the friars' patrons and opponents. Such an
examination reveals that there was no fundamental antagonism between the
friars and supporters of the Hohenstaufen in Germany prior to 1245 and that
imperial officials, regardless of the emperor's personal religious feelings, considered it their duty to assist the friars. It was only after Innocent IV (1243–
1254) turned the Franciscans and Dominicans into a highly effective political
weapon in his death struggle with Frederick that the friars and the emperor
became ruthless opponents.

The story of the friars' involvement in imperial politics sheds some addi-

8. "Untersuchungen zur Geschichte des deutschen Bürgertums und der Reichspolitik
   vornehmlich im 13. Jahrhundert," *Hansische Geschichtsblätter* 17 (1911), 130–133
   and 168–169. Thomas Curtis Van Cleve in his new biography of Frederick II, *The
   Emperor Frederick II of Hohenstaufen: Immutator Mundi* (Oxford, 1972), p. 357,
   also assumes that the friars received little sympathy in the 1220s from the ecclesiastical princes who were loyal to the emperor.
9. Friedrich Graefe, *Die Publizistik in der letzten Epoche Kaiser Friedrichs II.*, Heidelberger Abhandlungen zur mittleren und neueren Geschichte 24 (Heidelberg, 1909),
   discusses the role of propaganda in the imperial-papal conflict after 1239. Graefe,
   p. 26, points out that Frederick's statements, as far as they can be checked, are
   based on factually correct information.
10. James M. Powell, "Frederick II and the Church: A Revisionist View," *The Catholic
    Historical Review* 48 (1962–63), 487–497, stresses the medieval character of Fred-
    erick's reign.

tional light on a more fundamental problem than the friars' relations with an absentee and impious ruler. The great tragedy of the friars was their inability to serve Christ in the midst of earthly society without compromising their own ideals. We have already observed how the friars were slowly enmeshed in the conflict between Germans and Poles in eastern Europe and in partisan politics in Cologne. This account of the friars' entanglement in imperial politics will show the same phenomenon on an even larger scale. In half a century the friars were transformed from impartial disciples of Christ into zealous participants in the internecine political life of medieval Germany. The history of the friars' politicization is thus a case study of the failure of an ideal.

2. THE FRIARS AS THE DEFENDERS OF SOCIETY (1221–1245)

There was no open enmity between the friars and the Hohenstaufen in Germany prior to Frederick's deposition in 1245; instead the Dominicans and the Franciscans were almost universally regarded, in Frederick's words, as "the bulwark of the senescent church and of the Christian faith." Since political loyalties were not sharply defined in the 1220s and 1230s in Germany, patronage of the mendicant orders was not identified with a particular political viewpoint. Such staunch imperialists as Bishop Conrad of Hildesheim and such potential enemies of the Hohenstaufen as the counts of Urach and Kyburg supported the Franciscans and Dominicans. The friars themselves preferred to remain aloof from the quarrels among the bishops and princes, including the various clashes between Frederick II and Gregory IX. In a very real sense the friars were, as their mission demanded, impartial and apolitical witnesses of the power of the Gospel in human lives. Yet it is possible to detect in some of their activities, most notably the Dominicans' participation in the Stedinger Crusade, signs of how their fervor and influence among the princes and the masses could be twisted to secular ends.

The specter of heresy haunted the German episcopate and the imperial authorities in the 1220s and early 1230s and assured the friars a cordial reception in most dioceses and towns. Waldenses had been detected at the turn of the century in Metz and were winning numerous converts in southern Germany in the first decades of the thirteenth century.[11] The spread of the Cathars in Languedoc offered a highly visible and terrifying example of the

11. Walter L. Wakefield and Austin P. Evans, *Heresies of the High Middle Ages*, Records of Civilization: Sources and Studies 81 (New York, 1969), nos. 43B, 46; Kurt Selge, *Die ersten Waldenser mit Edition des Liber antiheresis des Durandus von Osca*, 2 vols. (Berlin, 1967), 1:288–293.

need for action. Well-informed members of the German clergy realized that the papacy had authorized the establishment of the mendicant orders to counteract the heretical threat. Burchard (d. 1230), the provost of the Premonstratensian canons of Ursberg in the diocese of Augsburg, explained in his chronicle that Innocent III had instituted the mendicant orders to combat the heretical sects which had been condemned by Lucius III in 1184.[12] Many German bishops therefore not only permitted the friars to settle in their episcopal sees in the 1220s and 1230s, as the list of mendicant convents clearly indicates, but also helped the brothers in more concrete ways. Bishop Conrad of Metz (1213–1224) and Speyer (1200–1224) founded the Dominican house in Metz in 1221; Archbishop Albert of Magdeburg (1205–1232) invited the Dominicans to settle in his archiepiscopal see on land which he gave them in 1225; and Bishop Conrad of Regensburg (1204–1226) presented the Franciscans in 1226 with a chapel, some land, and a house which he had built for their use.[13] The friars were expected in exchange to preach orthodox doctrine and to provide a good personal example.

There can be little doubt that the bishops' concern about the growth of heresy inspired them to patronize the friars. This is plainly evident in the conduct of the influential Bishop Conrad of Hildesheim (1221–1246), whom Jordan of Giano depicted as ready to aid the Franciscans at every hour of the day or night.[14] Bishop Conrad's experiences as a crusade preacher in southern France between 1204 and 1207 had apparently left an indelible impression upon him.[15] Shortly after he became bishop of Hildesheim in 1221, Conrad initiated a *cause célèbre* of the 1220s, the heresy trial of Henry Minnike, the provost of the Cistercian nunnery of Neuwerk in Goslar, who was burned after lengthy legal proceedings.[16] Like Innocent III and Gregory IX, Bishop Conrad recognized that repression alone would not resolve the problem; a wholehearted acceptance of the ideal of evangelical perfection, to which he

12. *Burchardi et Cuonradi Urspergensium chronicon*, ed. O. Abel and L. Weiland (Hanover, 1874), MGH SS 23:376–377.
13. Marie-Dominique Chapotin, *Histoire des Dominicaines de la province de France* (Rouen, 1898), pp. 31–32; *UB der Stadt Magdeburg*, ed. Gustav Hertel, GQProvSachs 26 (Halle, 1892), 1, no. 84; *Codex chronologico-diplomaticus episcopatus Ratisbonensis*, ed. Thomas Ried (Regensburg, 1816), 1, no. 364. See also Jordan of Giano (see above, n. 6), chs. 22, 24, 26, 35, and 48.
14. Jordan of Giano, ch. 48.
15. Wilhelm Maurer, "Zum Verständnis der hl. Elisabeth von Thüringen," *ZKiG* 65 (1953/54), 20.
16. Paul Braun, "Der Ketzerprozess des Propstes Minnike von Neuwerk in Goslar," *Z des Vereins für Kirchengeschichte in der Provinz Sachsen* 6 (1909), 212–218.

was personally sympathetic, offered the only truly effective antidote to the heretical contagion. While he had been cathedral scholastic in Mainz, Conrad had already protected his student, Caesar of Speyer, the future Franciscan minister, who had been accused of heresy for persuading some married women to adopt a life of humility and simplicity.[17] It is not very surprising that Conrad welcomed the Franciscans upon their arrival in Hildesheim in 1223, served as the episcopal protector of the Magdalens, a congregation of repentant prostitutes organized in 1227, and in 1233 founded the Dominican convent in his episcopal see.[18] When Conrad was forced to resign as bishop in 1246 on account of his pro-Hohenstaufen sympathies, he first took up residence in the Hildesheim priory.[19]

Conrad's forced resignation is proof by itself that patronage of the friars transcended political loyalties in the 1220s and 1230s. But Conrad was not the only pro-Hohenstaufen bishop who aided the friars. We have already seen how Archbishop Engelbert of Berg, the imperial regent during the minority of Henry (VII) (1220–1235), protected the friars in Cologne.[20] The other bishops who assisted the friars in the early 1220s also were loyal servants of Frederick. Bishop Conrad of Metz and Speyer was the imperial chancellor; Archbishop Albert of Magdeburg was the imperial legate in northern Italy during the 1220s; and Bishop Conrad of Regensburg promoted the marriage of Henry (VII) to the Babenberg princess, Margaret of Austria, in 1225.[21]

Gregory IX's excommunication of Frederick on September 21, 1227, which had little impact in Germany, did not disturb the friars' cordial relations with the bishops. While the Franciscans stirred up a rebellion against the emperor in Sicily and hindered his crusade in the Holy Land,[22] there is no evidence, except for a minor incident in the traditionally anti-Hohen-

17. Jordan of Giano, ch. 9.
18. Jordan of Giano, ch. 35; André Simon, *L'Ordre des Pénitentes de Ste. Marie-Madeleine en Allemagne au XIIIme siècle* (Fribourg, 1918), p. 52; *UB des Hochstifts Hildesheim und seiner Bischöfe*, ed. H. Hoogeweg, QDGNSachs 6 (Hanover, 1901), 2, no. 376.
19. *UB Hildesheim*, 2:395; P. Aldinger, *Die Neubesetzung der deutschen Bistümer unter Papst Innocenz IV. 1243–1254* (Leipzig, 1900), p. 55. For information about Conrad's activities on the emperor's behalf, see H. Hoogeweg, "Bischof Konrad II. von Hildesheim als Reichsfürst," *Z des historischen Vereins für Niedersachsen* (1899), 238–265.
20. See above, pp. 88–89.
21. Winkelmann, *Friedrich II.* (see above, n. 2), 1:6, n. 3; pp. 182, 462.
22. *Ryccardi de Sancto Germano notarii chronica* (see above, n. 6), p. 353; Winkelmann, *Friedrich II.*, 2:96.

staufen city of Cologne,[23] for comparable Franciscan or Dominican activity in Germany. The available evidence suggests instead that bishops loyal to the Hohenstaufen continued to patronize the friars during Frederick's first excommunication. On February 1, 1229, Bishop Siegfried of Regensburg (1227–1246) settled the Dominicans in his episcopal see on land which he had purchased for that purpose.[24] That summer Siegfried helped Henry (VII) defeat Duke Louis I of Bavaria, the only lay prince who rebelled against the emperor; the bishop was named imperial chancellor the following March.[25] Bishop Hugh of Liège (1200–1229) and his nephew and successor John (1229–1238), who received the regalia from the excommunicated Henry (VII) in 1229,[26] invited the Dominicans to come to Liège in the same year.[27] Finally, the Dominican convent in Ptuj was founded in 1230 at the petition of Archbishop Eberhard of Salzburg (1200–1246), a steadfast adherent of the Hohenstaufen.[28] It is inconceivable that Archbishop Eberhard and Bishops Siegfried and John would have invited the Dominicans to settle in their dioceses between 1227 and 1230 if the friars had been actively campaigning against the emperor and his followers. The establishment of a Dominican or Franciscan convent in an episcopal see in the 1220s cannot thus be accepted, as Oppermann assumed, as prima-facie evidence of an anti-Hohenstaufen orientation by the bishop.[29]

23. See above, p. 91.
24. *Codex Ratisbonensis* (see above, n. 13), 1, no. 374.
25. Winkelmann, *Friedrich II.*, 2:70–71 and 181.
26. Ibid., p. 73, n. 2.
27. *Corpus documentorum Inquisitionis haereticae pravitatis Neerlandicae*, ed. Paul Fredericq (Ghent, 1889), 1, nos. 74 and 75.
28. *UB des Herzogthums Steiermark*, ed. J. v. Zahn (Graz, 1879), 2, no. 271; Aldinger, *Neubesetzung*, p. 63.
29. Oppermann, "Untersuchungen" (see above, n. 8), 131–133, linked the statement in the *Annales Colonienses maximi*, ed. Karl Pertz (Hanover, 1861), MGH SS 17:841, that the Dominicans were proclaiming Frederick's excommunication in Germany to Bishop Henry's opposition to the Dominicans in Worms in the late 1220s and early 1230s. He concluded that the pro-Hohenstaufen bishop and burghers were thus resisting the machinations of the Dominicans. The Worms incident is in fact unrelated to the imperial-papal conflict. According to the *Annales Wormatienses*, ed. Georg Pertz (Hanover, 1861), MGH SS 17:38, the burghers who consistently supported Frederick II favored the Dominicans, while Bishop Henry opposed the friars because his nephew Count Eberhard of Leiningen had joined the Worms priory and because the friars had purchased some property within the city. Oppermann, 168, also regarded the establishment of the Dominican convent in Cologne in 1226 as part of the anti-Hohenstaufen policy conducted by Archbishop Siegfried of Mainz. The Dominicans settled, however, in Cologne in 1221 during the episcopate of Archbishop Engelbert of Berg, the imperial regent. See above, pp. 81–82.

After the Peace of Ceperano in 1230 had temporarily restored peaceful relations between the pope and the emperor, the German Dominicans were assigned a larger role in the combating of heresy than simply the propagation of orthodox doctrine. On June 1, 1231, Henry (VII) ordered the German princes and barons, and particularly the advocates and *Schultheissen* in the imperial cities, to assist the Regensburg Dominicans, who were laboring to extirpate heresy. This royal mandate offers the first indication that the German Dominicans had become directly involved in the pursuit of heretics. The king specifically instructed the temporal authorities to deliver heretics for judgment to the places designated by the friars. For the moment the Dominicans were merely expected to uncover heretics in accordance with the Roman statutes of February 1231.[30] In November Gregory IX expanded the Dominicans' mission. He authorized the Dominicans in Regensburg and Friesach to judge as well as to detect heretics, i.e., to serve as inquisitors in the fullest sense of the word.[31] Other friars were ordered to reform nunneries, to compel homosexuals to adopt either continence or conjugal chastity, and to suspend clerics who had committed fornication with nuns and canonesses from their offices and benefices.[32]

While these commands clearly signal the beginning of the German Dominicans' direct involvement in the apprehension and judgment of heretics and other malefactors, they do not mark the establishment of a permanent, papal inquisition exercised by the Dominicans. The bishops, assisted by individual inquisitors appointed by the pope, retained the primary responsibility for detecting and punishing heretics.[33] Nevertheless, the Dominicans' assumption of these inquisitorial functions represents a crucial diversion of the friars from their original mission. They were no longer merely required to provide an orthodox alternative for the exponents of the apostolic life, but rather to combat heretics directly. The Dominicans had become the guardians of the moral and doctrinal purity of medieval society.

30. Ludwig Förg, *Die Ketzerverfolgung in Deutschland unter Gregor IX.* (Berlin, 1932), pp. 59–61 and p. 93, no. 1.
31. Ibid., pp. 58–62 and pp. 94–96, no. 2; and *Acta imperii inedita* (see above, n. 7), 1, no. 624. The Strasbourg Dominicans received similar instructions in December 1232. *UB der Stadt Strassburg*, ed. Wilhelm Wiegand (Strasbourg, 1879), 1, no. 230.
32. *UB der Stadt Worms*, ed. Heinrich Boos (Berlin, 1886), 1, no. 150; *UB Strassburg*, 1, no. 227; MGH Epis. saec. XIII, ed. Carolus Rodenberg, 3 vols. (Berlin, 1883–1894), 1, no. 482; *Die Papsturkunden Westfalens bis zum Jahre 1378*, ed. Heinrich Finke, Westfälisches Urkunden-Buch 5 (Münster, 1888), 1, no. 386.
33. Förg, *Ketzerverfolgung*, pp. 66–70.

The princes assisted and protected the Dominicans in the execution of their new responsibilities. Gregory IX recommended the Dominicans in February 1232 to Dukes Henry I of Brabant (1183–1235) and Otto II of Bavaria (1231–1253); both dukes accordingly ordered their officials to aid the friars.[34] As the protector and advocate of the Roman Church, Frederick II codified the various ecclesiastical and temporal measures which had already been taken against heretics in Germany in his imperial constitution of March 1232, which legalized the German custom of burning obdurate heretics. The constitution placed the Dominicans who were detecting heretics under imperial protection. The temporal authorities were instructed to receive the Dominicans willingly, to protect them from attack by heretics, and to arrest and to guard all heretics whom the friars reported until the heretics had been properly condemned by the appropriate ecclesiastical authorities. The emperor thus still considered the Dominicans' chief function to be the detection rather than the judgment of heretics.[35] Frederick's personal involvement in the inquisitorial proceedings in Germany in the early 1230s was confined to the issuance of this single constitution. It was an easy way for the emperor to demonstrate his orthodoxy and his devotion to the church.[36]

The imperial authorities obeyed Frederick's instructions. Henry (VII) confirmed on June 2, 1233, the gift of a building lot to the Dominicans by the burghers of the imperial city of Esslingen.[37] The young king also provided the Franciscans in Mühlhausen and Regensburg with material assistance.[38]

34. *Bullarium ordinis FF. Praedicatorum*, ed. Antonino Bremond (Rome, 1729), 1:37–38, no. 51; Förg, *Ketzerverfolgung*, pp. 96–98, nos. 3 and 4; *Corpus documentorum Inquisitionis* (see above, n. 27), 1, no. 86.
35. Several copies of the constitution, which was sent to various priories, have survived. See *Bremisches UB*, ed. D. R. Ehmck and W. v. Bippen (Bremen, 1873), 1, no. 169; *Diplomata imperatorum authentica*, Monumenta Boica 30 (Munich, 1834), nos. 706 and 707; *Monumenta historica ducatus Carinthiae*, ed. August v. Jaksch (Klagenfurt, 1906), 4, no. 2036; and *UB Strassburg*, 1, p. 181, n. 1. See also Julius Ficker, "Die gesetzliche Einführung der Todesstrafe für Ketzerei," *MIÖG* 1 (1880), 177–226.
36. For additional information about Frederick's attitude, see Hermann Köhler, *Die Ketzerpolitik der deutschen Kaiser und Könige in den Jahren 1152–1254*, Jenaer historische Arbeiten 6 (Bonn, 1913), pp. 36–54.
37 *UB der Stadt Esslingen*, ed. Adolf Diehl and K. H. S. Pfaff, WürttGQ 4 (Stuttgart, 1899), 1, no. 33.
38. Jordan of Giano (see above, n. 6), ch. 45; *Diplomata imperatorum* (see above, n. 35), no. 718. Jordan says that the friars settled in a hospital in Mühlhausen with the permission of King Henry. Boehmer, the editor of the chronicle, p. 40, n. 2, identified King Henry as Henry Raspe, the landgrave of Thuringia, who was elected king on May 22, 1246. Boehmer gave no reason for his identification, but he probably assumed that the Hohenstaufen did not patronize the Franciscans. As the text

The campaign to eradicate heresy in Germany in the early 1230s marks the high point in imperial support for the mendicant orders.

The inquisitorial proceedings in Germany in the early 1230s were dominated by Conrad of Marburg, the Premonstratensian confessor of St. Elizabeth of Hungary. The story of Conrad's relentless and merciless pursuit of heretics in the archdiocese of Mainz is too well known to warrant repetition.[39] The frenzy persisted until Conrad made the fatal mistake of accusing the influential and apparently innocent Count Henry of Sayn (1208–1247) of heresy. When Conrad refused to drop the charges against the count at a provincial synod and imperial diet in Mainz on July 25, 1233, the assembled prelates advised and assisted Henry in appealing to Rome. Five days later, on July 30, Conrad and his longtime companion and relative, the Franciscan Gerhard Lutzelkolb,[40] were murdered on the road to Marburg.

The news of these murders infuriated Gregory IX. On October 21, he commanded Archbishop Siegfried of Mainz, Bishop Conrad of Hildesheim, and the Dominican provincial prior Conrad of Höxter (ca. 1225–1234) to proceed against the heretics in Germany.[41] But the imperial diet which convened at Frankfurt on February 2, 1234, under the presidency of Henry (VII) was bitterly opposed to a continuation of the Inquisition. The king personally rebuked Bishop Conrad for preaching a crusade against heretics in Saxony and Thuringia; and one prelate even proposed that the body of Conrad of

---

shows, Henry (VII) aided two other mendicant convents, Esslingen and Regensburg, between 1231 and 1233. In addition Henry Raspe was rather hostile to the new religious currents during the lifetime of his sister-in-law, St. Elizabeth (d. 1231). Maurer, "Verständnis" (see above, n. 15), pp. 41–42. It seems more probable, therefore, that Jordan's King Henry was the monarch who was ruling Germany in 1231 and not the anti-king who was elected fifteen years later and who ruled for less than a year.

39. Paul Braun's "Der Beichtvater der heiligen Elisabeth und deutsche Inquisitor Konrad von Marburg," *Beiträge zur hessischen Kirchengeschichte*, Ergh. 4 (1911), 248–300, 331–364, remains the standard account of Conrad's inquisitorial career. Maurer, "Verständis" (see above, n. 15), has re-examined Conrad's relationship with St. Elizabeth. Karl Hermann May, "Zur Geschichte Konrads von Marburg," *Hessisches Jahrbuch für Landesgeschichte* 1 (1951), 87–109, identified Conrad as a Premonstratensian.

40. Gerhard is mentioned in the *Annales Wormatienses* (see above, n. 29), p. 40. A knight named Henry Lutzelkolb witnessed several charters of the hospital of St. Francis in Marburg, which St. Elizabeth had founded with Conrad's guidance. *UB der Deutschordens-Ballei Hessen*, ed. Arthur Wyss, PPrStA 3 (Leipzig, 1879), 1, nos. 37, 56, 84, and 101. It seems very likely that Henry and Gerhard Lutzelkolb and Conrad of Marburg were kinsmen.

41. MGH Epis. saec. XIII (see above, n. 32), 1, no. 558.

Marburg, who had been buried next to St. Elizabeth, be exhumed and burned. Only Bishop Conrad of Hildesheim and a Dominican named Otto dared to defend the dead inquisitor. Four days later twelve Franciscan guardians and three Dominican priors, along with eight bishops and twelve Cistercian abbots, took an oath of compurgation on behalf of Count Henry of Sayn.[42] The Dominicans and Franciscans, sensitive to the change in public opinion, had joined the general German reaction against the Inquisition.

Conrad's unfounded accusations discredited the Inquisition for decades in Germany. The fear of heresy subsided noticeably after Conrad's murder. The German friars received only isolated orders after 1233 to ferret out heretics. Innocent IV instructed the Freiburg Dominicans in 1247 to proceed against certain wandering preachers in the diocese of Constance who denied the perpetual virginity of Mary.[43] More important, the Dominicans and the Franciscans, most notably David of Augsburg, fought the Waldenses in Austria and Bavaria in the 1250s and 1260s.[44] Finally, the friars appear to have uncovered around 1270 in the Swabian Ries in the diocese of Augsburg some early adherents of the Free-Spirit heresy.[45] But the heretical threat cannot have been perceived as especially acute after 1233. The well-informed Bishop Bruno of Olomouc (Olmütz) (1245–1281), who was the Bohemian regent in Styria in the 1260s, reported to Gregory X in 1273 that he was unaware of the existence of any heretics in Germany.[46] The experiences of the early 1230s had considerably dampened German enthusiasm for forceful action against heretics for the remainder of the century.

The imperial authorities remained, nevertheless, favorably disposed toward the friars. Frederick II demonstrated his official regard for the mendicant orders during his brief sojourns in Germany between 1235 and 1237, his only visits to his ancestral home during the last thirty years of his reign. For instance, he placed the Dominican nunnery of Altenhohenau under imperial

---

42. Braun, "Beichtvater," pp. 354–357.
43. *Freiburger UB*, ed. Friedrich Hefele (Freiburg, 1940), 1, no. 100.
44. For additional information, see Alexander Patschovsky, *Der Passauer Anonymus: Ein Sammelwerk über Ketzer, Juden, Antichrist aus der Mitte des 13. Jahrhunderts*, MGH Schriften 22 (Stuttgart, 1968).
45. Herbert Grundmann, *Religiöse Bewegungen im Mittelalter*, 2nd ed. (Darmstadt, 1961), pp. 402–438; Robert E. Lerner, *The Heresy of the Free Spirit in the Later Middle Ages* (Berkeley, 1972), pp. 13–19.
46. Constantin Höfler, "Analecten zur Geschichte Deutschlands und Italiens," *Abhbay-Ak* 4 (Munich, 1846), 28; Ottokar Lorenz, *Geschichte König Ottokars II. von Böhmen und seiner Zeit* (Vienna, 1866), p. 256.

protection in 1235.[47] After he attended the translation of St. Elizabeth's body, Frederick dutifully informed Elias and the Franciscans of her miracles, one of which he had personally witnessed, and asked for the friars' prayers.[48] The Dominicans and Franciscans had become accepted members of German society.

The crusade against the Stedinger in the archbishopric of Bremen, though superficially connected with the general concern about heresy in Germany in the early 1230s, provides the first intimation of how the Dominicans' influence among the princes and burghers could be utilized to achieve secular rather than ecclesiastical goals.[49] The Stedinger were free Saxon, Frisian, and Dutch peasants who had drained and cultivated the marshes to the west of the lower Weser in the twelfth century. During the protracted conflicts between the Danes, Welfs, and Hohenstaufen for control of northwestern Germany in the first quarter of the thirteenth century, the Stedinger had become virtually independent of their nominal territorial lords, the archbishop of Bremen and the count of Oldenburg. Archbishop Gerhard (1219–1258), who wished to increase the temporal power of the archbishopric and to restore the decimated archiepiscopal finances, was determined to collect rents and tithes from the peasants. The Stedinger resisted and managed to defeat the archiepiscopal forces led by Gerhard's brother, Herman of the Lippe, who was killed in a battle on Christmas Day in 1229. The archbishop, inspired by a desire for revenge as well as earthly gain, summoned a provincial synod for March 17, 1230. The assembled clerics had no difficulty in finding heterodox beliefs and customs among the illiterate peasants, who were duly proscribed as heretics.

Gregory IX, preoccupied with the resolution of his conflict with Frederick, reacted slowly and with untypical caution to these charges. On July 26, 1231, more than a year after the Stedinger had been condemned as heretics, he ordered Bishop John of Lübeck (1231–1247), the prior of the Bremen Dominicans, and the Dominican papal penitentiary John to investigate the complaints of the clergy, nobles, and burghers of Bremen against the Stedinger and to take all steps which they deemed expedient, if the accusations

47. *Monumenta parthenii Altenhohenau*, Monumenta Boica 17 (Munich 1806), no. 2.
48. *Acta imperii inedita* (see above, n. 7), 1, no. 338.
49. For additional information about the crusade, see H. A. Schumacher, *Die Stedinger* (Bremen, 1865); Hermann Oncken, "Studien zur Geschichte des Stedingerkreuzzuges," *Jahrbuch für die Geschichte des Herzogtums Oldenburg* 5 (1896), 27–58; and Dietrich Schomburg, *Die Dominikaner im Erzbistum Bremen während des dreizehnten Jahrhunderts* (Brunswick, 1910), pp. 14–19.

were true, to coerce the Stedinger to return to the faith.[50] The papal penitentiary was in all probability the future master general, Johannes Teutonicus,
a native of the town of Wildeshausen and a subject of the counts of Oldenburg.[51] Archbishop Gerhard also turned for aid to Frederick, who sent to
Bremen in March 1232 a copy of his imperial constitution for the combating
of heresy.[52] The archbishop's quarrel with the Stedinger over rents and tithes
had been officially, though erroneously, linked with the hunt for heretics in
the rest of Germany.

The pope finally commanded the bishops of Minden, Lübeck, and Ratzeburg on October 29, 1232, to preach with the Dominicans' help a crusade in
northwestern Germany against the Stedinger; participants were promised a
twenty-day indulgence.[53] The success of the crusade hinged in large part
upon the attitude of the burghers of Bremen, who, it was feared, might prefer
the Stedinger rather than their archiepiscopal overlord to control the mouth
of the Weser. But the Dominicans managed to arrange an alliance between the
archbishop and the city which was highly favorable to the burghers.[54] In
spite of the burghers' aid, the archiepiscopal forces were unable to defeat the
stubborn peasants in their marshy homeland. To obtain additional men and
to arouse greater enthusiasm for the crusade, Gregory conceded to the crusaders on June 17, 1233, the same indulgence which was bestowed on those
who fought for the liberation of the Holy Land.[55] This proved to be the correct formula. The Dominicans preached the crusade with remarkable success
in the Rhineland, Westphalia, Frisia, Holland, Brabant, and Flanders. In the
words of one chronicler, "They flew like clouds and incited the princes and
people against the Stedinger."[56] The Stedinger were unable to resist the overwhelming forces which the Dominicans raised, and the peasants were decisively defeated on May 27, 1234. The Stedinger Crusade offers the first clear
example in German history of how the Dominicans could be utilized to arouse
princely and popular support for an essentially secular goal, in this case the
re-establishment of a prince's temporal authority over rebellious peasants.

Gregory IX proved unable, however, to enlist the German friars' potential

---

50. *Bremisches UB* (see above, n. 35), 1, no. 166.
51. Oncken, "Studien," pp. 52–58. See above pp. 123–124, n. 47.
52. *Bremisches UB*, 1, no. 169.
53. MGH Epis saec. XIII (see above, n. 32), 1, no. 489.
54. *Bremisches UB*, 1, nos. 172 and 174.
55. Ibid., no. 176.
56. *Emonis et Menkonis Werumensium chronica*, ed. L. Weiland (Hanover, 1874), MGH
    SS 23:516.

talents as agitators in his renewed struggle against the Hohenstaufen, following Frederick's second excommunication on March 20, 1239. While the Dominicans and Franciscans were ordered to announce the sentence on May 22,[57] few, if any, German friars obeyed. The excommunication was in fact generally ignored in Germany. Gregory pinned his chief hopes on an anti-Hohenstaufen alliance between Austria, Bavaria, and Bohemia, which had been formed in Passau at the beginning of the year. But Frederick managed without much difficulty to outmaneuver the pope, and the alliance quickly disintegrated.

Gregory's diplomatic failure can in large part be attributed to his singularly inept legate, the Passau archdeacon Albert Behaim, whose excessive zeal and tactlessness only further alienated the German princes and bishops. Behaim used the Friesach Dominicans in his unsuccessful attempts to preserve the Passau alliance. To retain the support of Otto II of Bavaria, Behaim tried to settle the duke's long quarrel with Bishop Conrad of Freising, a Hohenstaufen partisan, over the borders of their respective territories. At the duke's and archdeacon's request, the pope on April 15, 1239, commanded Bishop Henry of Seckau, a Cistercian abbot, and the prior of the Friesach Dominicans to resolve the dispute.[58] Behaim likewise sent the Dominican Otto of Friesach to Duke Frederick the Quarrelsome of Austria (1230–1246) on December 22 to warn him to carry out the planned marriage between his niece Gertrude and Vladislav, the son of King Wenceslaus I of Bohemia (1230–1253), a key provision in the Austro-Bohemian alliance.[59] But Behaim's efforts proved fruitless. The extent of Gregory's and Behaim's failure can best be gauged by the fact that in May 1240 the archdeacon actually excommunicated the Vienna and Brno Dominicans, along with the archbishops of Salzburg and Magdeburg and the bishops of Regensburg and Freising, for failure to comply with his orders.[60] There is no other evidence, except from Cologne,[61] that the German friars engaged in anti-Hohenstaufen activities prior to Frederick's deposition.

---

57. MGH Epis. saec. XIII, 1, no. 747.
58. Ibid., no. 743.
59 *Regesta imperii*, ed. Julius Ficker and Eduard Winkelmann (Innsbruck, 1881–1892), 5, no. 11242.
60. *Codex diplomaticus et epistolaris regni Bohemiae*, ed. Gustav Friedrich and Zdeněk Kristen (Prague, 1962), 3, Part 2, no. 229. For additional information about Behaim's diplomacy, see G. Ratzinger, *Forschungen zur bayrischen Geschichte* (Kempten, 1898), pp. 80–159.
61. See above, pp. 91–92.

Most of the German friars, like the Viennese Dominicans, continued in fact to cooperate with and to enjoy the support of the imperial authorities and Hohenstaufen partisans in the early 1240s. For example, Archbishop Eberhard of Salzburg, one of Behaim's principal opponents, granted an indulgence in 1244 to the new Dominican nunnery in Lienz,[62] which was allegedly founded by the pro-Hohenstaufen courts of Gorizia.[63] More important, Frederick's son, King Conrad IV (1237–1254), repeatedly patronized the friars after the emperor's second excommunication. At the request of the Franciscan Albert of Ulm, the king placed the new nunnery of the Poor Clares at Ulm under imperial protection in November 1239.[64] Indeed as late as February 20, 1245, nearly six years after Frederick's excommunication, Conrad appointed a Nuremberg burgher, Conrad Roth, as proctor of the Nuremberg Franciscans, whose poverty the king wished to alleviate.[65] These facts hardly suggest that the friars agitated openly against the Hohenstaufen in Germany in the early 1240s.

The Dominican Order seems in fact to have deliberately pursued a policy of benevolent neutrality in the early 1240s. On February 27, 1241, the emperor warned the forthcoming Dominican general chapter to keep out of his personal quarrel with the pope and not to perform missions hostile to the empire. As in his 1246 warning, Frederick stressed his devotion to the Dominicans, whose prayers he requested.[66] The 1241 general chapter heeded the imperial admonition. It elected as the new master general Johannes Teutonicus, whom Frederick personally knew and highly esteemed.[67] The Dominicans thus tacitly accepted Frederick's contention that he was quarreling with Gregory as an individual rather than with the church and disassociated themselves from the conflict.

---

62. *Salzburger UB*, ed. Willibald Hauthaler and Franz Martin (Salzburg, 1918), 3, no. 1057.
63. Hieronymus Wilms, *Das älteste Verzeichnis der deutschen Dominikanerinnenklöster*, QFGDD 24 (Leipzig, 1928), p. 21; Lorenz, *Ottokar II.* (see above, n. 46), p. 69.
64. *Ulmisches UB*, ed. Friedrich Pressel (Stuttgart, 1873), 1, no. 45.
65. *Nürnberger UB*, Quellen und Forschungen zur Geschichte der Stadt Nürnberg 1 (Nuremberg, 1959), no. 322. See also *UB Esslingen* (see above, n. 37), 1, nos. 42 and 47; and *UB der Stadt und Landschaft Zürich*, ed. J. Escher and P. Schweizer (Zürich, 1892), 2, no. 538. Some Italian friars were also favorably disposed toward the Hohenstaufen. See Huillard-Bréholles, *Historia* (see above, n. 1), 5:1146–1148; and *Regesta imperii* (see above, n. 59), 5, no. 13440.
66. Huillard-Bréholles, *Historia*, 5:1098–1100.
67. Thomas of Cantimpré, *Bonum universale de apibus*, ed. Georgius Colvenerius (Douai, 1627) 2.30.43.

It would of course be erroneous to suggest that Frederick was either personally sympathetic to the ideal of evangelical perfection or that he was an
enthusiastic patron of the mendicant orders. The emperor and his sons did
not found a single German mendicant convent or nunnery; their patronage of
the friars was confined to the issuance of imperial letters of protection, the
bestowal of small pieces of property, the confirmation of charters, and *pro
forma* requests for prayer. The Hohenstaufen merely provided the friars with
the minimal support and assistance which any order might ordinarily expect
in the thirteenth century from Christian princes. But it is equally important
to recognize that the Hohenstaufen did not impede the friars' ministry or prevent their political allies from helping the Franciscans and Dominicans. Frederick II could thus with some justification claim in 1246 that he had always
been favorably disposed toward the friars.

3. THE FRIARS AS OPPONENTS OF THE HOHENSTAUFEN (1245–1256)

Innocent IV's deposition of Frederick II at the Council of Lyons on
July 17, 1245, was the watershed in the friars' relations with the Hohenstaufen and with earthly society. Although Gregory IX had employed the
Dominicans extensively as papal agents, their services had been confined to
the promotion of ecclesiastical goals, such as the detection of heresy or the
preaching of crusades. Gregory had only rarely asked the German Franciscans to carry out such assignments. He had used them primarily to preach a
crusade in 1241 against the Mongols.[68] But Innocent, who became pope in
1243, engaged the Franciscans as well as the Dominicans in an essentially
secular undertaking, the destruction of the Hohenstaufen Empire. He counted
on the friars' ability, which had already been amply demonstrated by such
incidents as the Stedinger Crusade, to arouse princely and popular fury. The
Dominicans and Franciscans served after Lyons as crusade preachers against
the Hohenstaufen, collected papal funds to finance the war, persuaded vacil-
lating imperial adherents to change allegiances, and sought recognition for the
anti-kings. Their religious habit and reputation allowed the friars, as Frederick
feared, considerable freedom of movement and gave added credence to their
inflammatory words. But the friars' agitation undermined their status as

---

68. *Annales Sancti Pantaleonis Coloniensis*, ed. Hermann Cardauns (Hanover, 1872),
    MGH SS 22:535; MGH Epis. saec. XIII (see above, n. 32), 1, no. 822; *Regesta epis-
    coporum Constantiensum*, ed. Paul Ladewig and Theodor Müller (Innsbruck, 1895),
    1, nos. 1536 and 1538.

holy men detached from transient, temporal concerns. The Franciscans and Dominicans were in fact irrevocably caught up in the maelstrom of German politics after 1245. Innocent's decision to employ the friars in the battle against the Hohenstaufen was thus a decisive step in the politicization and even secularization, if that word can be used, of the mendicant orders.

Frederick's warning to the 1246 Dominican general chapter, though clearly motivated by his own political interests, was a final plea that the friars not embark upon the new course charted by the pope. Unlike the 1241 general chapter, the 1246 assembly did not heed the imperial admonition. It decreed instead:

> The brothers are most diligently warned not to speak unfavorably in any way either among themselves or in the presence of seculars about the actions of the lord pope or to show favor to Frederick in either word or deed. If any friar does contrary to this, we wish that he be severely punished by his priors or visitors.[69]

The words of the decree are a tacit admission that many friars had previously supported the emperor. The 1247 and 1248 general chapters repeated the warning and commanded the friars to aid the church in word and deed; the friars were strictly enjoined from helping the Hohenstaufen.[70] A few friars undoubtedly ignored these commands. A Swabian Dominican named Arnold, inspired by Joachimist prophecies, maintained in 1248 that Innocent IV was the Antichrist and Frederick II the divinely selected reformer of the church at the end of the sixth age.[71] But most of the German Franciscans and Dominicans were faithful servants of the papacy after 1245.

While Gregory IX had concentrated on fighting Frederick in Italy, where the expansion of Hohenstaufen power directly threatened the independence of the papacy, Innocent IV successfully transferred the battle to Germany, the major source of imperial manpower. To foment dissension in Germany, Innocent encouraged the selection of anti-kings, who might serve as the nominal leaders of the papal party. Innocent's nominees, Landgrave Henry Raspe of Thuringia (1227–1247) and Count William of Holland (1247–

---

69. *Acta capitulorum generalium ordinis Praedicatorum*, ed. Benedictus Maria Reichert, MOPH 3 (Rome, 1898), 1:37.
70. Ibid., pp. 39 and 42.
71. Eduard Winkelmann, *Fratris Arnoldi ord. Praed. De correctione ecclesiae epistola* (Berlin, 1865); Marjorie Reeves, *The Influence of Prophecy in the Later Middle Ages* (Oxford, 1969), pp. 170 and 310–311.

1256), were figureheads who required considerable papal assistance merely to keep their cause afloat.[72]

There is no evidence that either Henry or William had been particularly devoted to the mendicant orders prior to their election. Henry had shown in fact little sympathy for the new religious currents during the lifetime of his sister-in-law, St. Elizabeth, whom he had forced to leave the Wartburg.[73] Her canonization apparently changed his mind. In 1239, at Henry's request, Gregory IX commanded the minister of Saxony, John of Piancarpino, to appoint a Franciscan as Henry's confessor.[74] As Henry was wavering in his loyalties to the Hohenstaufen in 1239,[75] the pope may have hoped that a Franciscan confessor would strengthen the landgrave's resolution. But Henry remained loyal to Frederick for the time being and was duly appointed imperial regent in 1242. Henry had clearly switched sides by May 5, 1246, when at his request Innocent asked Archbishop Albert of Prussia to appoint the landgrave's confidant, the Dominican Werner, as bishop of Kurland or Pomesania.[76] At the pope's prodding a handful of bishops elected the landgrave king on May 22, 1246; no lay prince participated in the election. The size and composition of the electoral body are indicative of the extent of Henry's support; he clearly required any assistance the friars might offer. Innocent had already instructed the German Dominicans and Franciscans in April to exhort the faithful to aid and to obey the new king who was about to be chosen, and he subsequently empowered individual friars to absolve excommunicated supporters of the Hohenstaufen who switched to the papal side.[77] The friars zealously carried out these orders.[78] Henry Raspe died in February 1247.

The friars also provided considerable assistance to Henry's successor, the twenty-year-old Count William of Holland, who was elected on October 3,

---

72. For information about the history of Germany between 1245 and 1256, see Otto Hintze, *Das Königtum Wilhelms von Holland* (Leipzig, 1885); Johann Kempf, *Geschichte des Deutschen Reiches während des grossen Interregnums* (Würzburg, 1893); and Manfred Stimming, "Kaiser Friedrich II. und der Abfall der deutschen Fürsten," *HZ* 120 (1919), 210–249.
73. Maurer, "Verständnis" (see above, n. 15), pp. 41–42.
74. *Regesta diplomatica necnon epistolaria historiae Thuringiae*, ed. Otto Dobenecker (Jena, 1925), 3, no. 808.
75. Ratzinger, *Forschungen* (see above, n. 60), p. 96.
76. MGH Epis. saec. XIII (see above, n. 32), 2, no. 181.
77. Ibid., no. 162; *Regesta imperii* (see above, n. 59), 5, nos. 7685, 7699, and 7737; *Freiburger UB* (see above, n. 43), 1, no. 96.
78. *UB Strassburg* (see above, n. 31), 1, no. 306.

1247. After his election William cultivated the friendship of the friars, aiding the Dordrecht and Middelburg Franciscans in 1248.[79] William's first task as king was to capture the pro-Hohenstaufen city of Aachen in order to be crowned there. The siege of the city began in April 1248 and lasted until Aachen's capitulation on October 18. Aroused by the preaching of the Franciscans and Dominicans, crusaders came from the Rhineland, the Moselle Valley, Holland, and in particular from Frisia to besiege the town.[80] During the siege the pope ordered the Dominican priors of Antwerp and Louvain to collect and to hold at his pleasure all the money obtained from the physically incapacitated for the redemption of crusading vows against the Hohenstaufen or for the liberation of the Holy Land. The two priors were also instructed to collect all legacies which had been made for these purposes in northwestern Germany, as well as the five-percent tax which had been levied on the German church.[81] These funds presumably reached William's empty coffers.

After the count's coronation in Aachen, the friars labored zealously on William's behalf. Innocent commanded the German Franciscans and Dominicans on January 2, 1249, to preach a crusade against Frederick and his adherents throughout Germany. Special emphasis was placed on the dioceses of Cambrai, Cologne, Liège, and Utrecht, where William enjoyed the greatest support.[82] William's chaplains, the Franciscan John of Diest, who subsequently was rewarded with the bishoprics of Sambia and Lübeck, and the Dominican William of Maaseik distinguished themselves in William's service. Between 1249 and 1254 the two friars received numerous papal commands to preach a crusade against Frederick II and Conrad IV; to compel princes and ministerials to pay homage to William; to collect the money raised on William's behalf from the redemption of crusading vows, legacies, and the five-percent tax on the German church; to supply William with funds; and to provide marriage dispensations to William's supporters.[83] William of Holland owed his crown, at least in part, to the friars' successful agitation.

79. *Regesta imperii*, 5, no. 4899; *Oorkondenboek van Holland en Zeeland*, ed. L. Ph. C. van den Bergh (Amsterdam, 1866), 1, no. 454.

80. *Annales Sancti Pantaleonis Coloniensis* (see above, n. 68), p. 543; and Matthew of Paris, *Chronica maiora* (see above, n. 6), pp. 295 and 298.

81. MGH Epis. saec. XIII (see above, n. 32), 2, no. 589.

82. Ibid., no. 630. See also no. 720.

83. Ibid., nos. 669, 718, 719, 721; and 3, nos. 48, 54, 187, 188, 199, 209, 225, 241, 265, 274, 296. John's activities are described in greater detail by Willibrord Lampen, "Joannes van Diest, O.F.M.," *Bijdragen voor de Geschiedenis van het Bisdom van Haarlem* 44 (1926), 299–312.

Until Frederick's death in December 1250, William's authority was largely confined to northwestern Germany. The political situation in the late 1240s in Swabia, the hereditary duchy of the Hohenstaufen, was chaotic; political allegiances were constantly realigned as the balance of power momentarily shifted. The Dominican papal penitentiary, Count Henry of Montfort, who could rely on a network of family connections, labored on Innocent's and William's behalf in the southwest. The pope ordered Henry on October 13, 1248, to make Abbot Berthold of Saint Gall, who was to be provided with the necessary dispensation so that he could retain his abbatial dignity, bishop of Chur in place of the undependable Bishop Volcard. In fact it was Henry who eventually succeeded Volcard as bishop.[84] On February 20, 1251, Innocent instructed Henry to proceed with spiritual and temporal weapons against all Swabian cities and castles which did not acknowledge William as king.[85] After a delegation of Swabian nobles headed by Count Ulrich of Württemberg arrived in Lyons in March 1251 to assure the pope of their loyalty, Innocent commanded Henry to preach a crusade against Conrad IV in conjunction with a contemplated advance by William into the duchy.[86] But the burghers of the imperial and episcopal cities, the Hohenstaufen's most faithful allies in the southwest, only recognized William as king in 1254.

Southeastern Germany, where Gregory IX had hoped to gain his greatest support in 1239, rather than Swabia was the major center of Hohenstaufen power north of the Alps after 1245. Duke Otto II of Bavaria in the early 1240s had gradually abandoned the pro-papal policy advocated by Albert Behaim; the marriage of Otto's daughter Elizabeth to Conrad IV in September 1246 sealed the Wittelsbach-Hohenstaufen alliance. Otto's most important Bavarian enemy was Count Conrad of Wasserburg, the founder of the Dominican nunnery of Altenhohenau,[87] who had protected Behaim after Otto had expelled the troublesome archdeacon from Bavaria in 1241. After Otto's son Louis besieged the Wasserburg in 1247, the count and Behaim secretly fled to the papal court in Lyons, where the archdeacon had already resided from December 1244 until the spring of 1247. Innocent ordered the Franciscans Henry of Angersberg and Herman of Pottenbrunn on May 5, 1248, to threaten the Wittelsbachs with excommunication and the interdict if

---

84. MGH Epis. saec. XIII, 2, no. 597; Aldinger, *Neubesetzung* (see above, n. 19), pp. 99–100 and 160–161.
85. MGH Epis. saec. XIII, 3, no. 78.
86. Ibid., no. 101; Hintze, *Wilhelm von Holland* (see above, n. 72), pp. 43–46.
87. *Monumenta Altenhohenau* (see above, n. 47), no. 1.

they did not immediately return Conrad's domains.[88] The friars also became involved in the affairs of Behaim's personal enemy, Bishop Rüdiger of Passau (1233–1250), a staunch imperialist who was the only German bishop who actually was deposed for adhering to the Hohenstaufen. Rüdiger sent two Krems Dominicans, Henry and Walter, to Lyons in 1246 to try to settle his quarrel with Behaim. Although the two Dominicans reached an accord with the Passau archdeacon, Rüdiger rejected it.[89] On May 11, 1248, the pope commanded the same Franciscans who were working on Count Conrad's behalf to stop the bishop from alienating the property of the Passau church, an assignment which they were unable to carry out on account of other business.[90] Innocent also ordered a Viennese Dominican on February 4, 1249, to cite Bishop Rüdiger for reading mass while excommunicated.[91]

In the southeast political attention focused on the vacant Babenberg territories of Austria, Styria, and Carniola, whose last ruler, the childless Duke Frederick the Quarrelsome, died in June 1246. While the emperor claimed the duchies as vacant imperial fiefs, the pope initially backed the niece of the last duke, Gertrude, who was supported by an Austrian noble party led by Count Conrad of Hardeck. Innocent commanded the Friar Minor Francis on January 23, 1248, to hear the confessions of Gertrude and the count; and on December 13, 1249, the pope ordered the Franciscan provincial of Austria, Bartholomew, to appoint four friars as the confessors of the duchess and her papally selected husband, Margrave Herman of Baden.[92] Like William of Holland's chaplains, John of Diest and William of Maaseik, they probably did more than merely hear confessions. But the balance of power in the southeast only shifted in favor of the papacy in 1251 after Ottokar II of Bohemia occupied Austria. The Franciscan Velascus, a papal penitentiary, granted Ottokar in 1253 a dispensation to legalize his consanguineous marriage the preceding year to the elderly Margaret of Austria, the sister of Duke Fred-

88. MGH Epis. saec. XIII, 2, nos. 550 and 552; Ratzinger, *Forschungen* (see above, n. 60), pp. 160–174, 201–203.
89. Constantin Höfler, "Albert von Beham und Regesten Papst Innocenz IV.," *BLVSt* 16 (1847), nos. 14, 15, and 16; Aldinger, *Neubesetzung*, pp. 89–92, 119–124, 133–138; Ratzinger, *Forschungen*, pp. 175–185 and 201–215.
90. G.E. Friess, "Geschichte der oesterreichischen Minoritenprovinz," *Archiv für österreichische Geschichte* 64 (1882), no. 13; MGH Epis. saec. XIII, 2, no. 657.
91. MGH Epis. saec. XIII, 2, no. 652.
92. Friess, "Geschichte," nos. 11, 12, and 14. For additional information, see Lorenz, *Ottokar II.* (see above, n. 46), pp. 53–98; Hermann Meier, "Gertrud Herzogin von Oesterreich und Steiermark," *Z des historischen Vereins für Steiermark* 23 (1927), 5–38.

erick and the widow of Henry (VII). In exchange Ottokar swore to assist the papal cause and to pay homage to and receive the regalia from William.[93]

The friars who executed these papal orders in the late 1240s and early 1250s undoubtedly utilized the personal contacts they had previously formed with various prominent noble families. The friars had established particularly close ties in the 1220s and 1230s with an important group of interrelated, potentially rebellious Swabian nobles, the counts of Urach, Kyburg, and Dillingen.[94] Cardinal Conrad of Porto (1219–1227), the papal legate in Germany in the 1220s, probably introduced the Dominicans and Franciscans to his relatives. The Cistercian cardinal, who had protected the friars in Cologne after the murder of Archbishop Engelbert of Berg,[95] was especially fond of the Dominicans. He allegedly said to the Bolognese Dominicans: "Indeed although I display outwardly the habit of another profession, I bear your mind, nevertheless, within. Do not doubt that I am completely yours and that I am of your order; I commit myself to you with all love."[96] It is not very surprising under these circumstances that Count Egeno V of Urach (d. 1236) and his son Conrad of Freiburg (d. 1271), the brother and nephew of the cardinal, invited the Dominicans to reside in Freiburg im Breisgau in the early 1230s.[97] Countess Adelaide, Egeno's wife, likewise asked Bishop Henry of Constance in 1234 to take the newly founded Dominican nunnery of Adelhausen near Freiburg under his protection.[98] Count Hartmann IV of Kyburg (d. 1264), Conrad's first cousin, founded the Dominican nunneries of Töss (1233) and Diessenhofen (1242) and in 1253 moved the convent of Paradise, a house of Poor Clares, from Constance to Schaffhausen.[99] Finally, Count Hartmann IV of Dillingen (d. 1258), a member of a collateral line of the Dillingen-Kyburg house, founded the Dominican nunnery of Medingen (1238)

---

93. *Codex diplomaticus et epistolaris Moraviae*, ed. Anton Boczek (Olmütz, 1841), 3, nos. 194, 195, and 199.
94. The genealogical tree on p. 157 will help to clarify the familial relationship between the various Swabian patrons of the friars. It is based on Oswald Redlich, *Rudolf von Habsburg: Das Deutsche Reich nach dem Untergange des alten Kaisertums* (Innsbruck, 1903), p. 769, Stammtafeln 5 and 6; and F.E. Pipitz, *Die Grafen von Kyburg* (Leipzig, 1839), appendix. An asterisk denotes a patron of the friars.
95. See above, p. 89.
96. Peter Ferrand, *Legenda Sancti Dominici*, ed. M.-H. Laurent (Rome, 1935), MOPH 16:242.
97. *Freiburger UB* (see above, n. 43), 1, no. 63.
98. Ibid., no. 55.
99. *UB Zürich* (see above, n. 65), 1 (1890), nos. 484 and 496, and 2, nos. 567 and 876.

Swabian Patrons of the Friars—*See p. 156, n. 94*

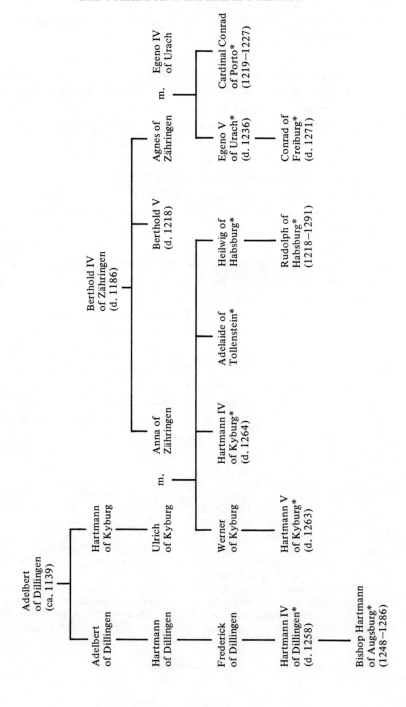

and in 1258 provided the Ulm Poor Clares with the land which enabled them to move to Söfflingen.[100]

The counts of Urach, Kyburg, and Dillingen had been bitterly resentful of the Hohenstaufen *Hausmacht* in Swabia since the death of the childless Duke Berthold V of Zähringen in 1218. Berthold's heirs had been his two sisters, Agnes, the mother of Count Egeno V of Urach and Cardinal Conrad, and Anna, the mother of Count Hartmann IV of Kyburg and Heilwig of Habsburg, Rudolph's mother. When the Zähringen inheritance had been divided, Frederick II had retained Berthold's fiefs and advocacies; while the Zähringen allods had been split between the Urachs and Kyburgs. This division never satisfied the two comital families. They and their kinsman Count Hartmann IV of Dillingen had participated, for instance, in Henry (VII)'s abortive revolt against his father in 1234. The friars presumably had little difficulty in persuading their friends the Urachs, the Kyburgs, and the Dillingens, who formed the nucleus of the papal party in Swabia, to acknowledge Henry Raspe or William of Holland as king.[101] The pope rewarded the counts for their loyalty by incorporating between 1245 and 1250 their favorite nunneries, Adelhausen, Diessenhofen, Medingen, and Töss, into the Dominican Order.[102]

After Frederick's death in 1250, the papal-Hohenstaufen conflict slowly petered out in Germany. Innocent and the friars tried to persuade the remaining Hohenstaufen partisans to abandon the faltering imperial cause. In 1253 the Dominicans and Franciscans induced the pro-Hohenstaufen burghers of Worms to permit their pro-papal bishop, Richard of Daun (1247–1257), to enter the city.[103] The pope and the friars exerted considerable pressure,

---

100. Placidus Braun, "Geschichte der Grafen von Dillingen und Kiburg," *AbhbayAk* 5 (1823), pp. 471–472, no. 4; *Ulmisches UB* (see above, n. 64), 1, no. 80. The count's son Bishop Hartmann of Augsburg (1248–1286), the last member of the family, also aided the friars. See Anton Michael Seitz, "Die Grafen von Dillingen und ihre Klosterstiftungen," *Jahrbuch des historischen Vereins Dillingen an der Donau* 64–65 (1962–1963), 48–50.

101. For additional information, see Winkelmann, *Friedrich II.* (see above, n. 2), 1: 3–5, 8–11, 27–28; Sigmund Riezler, *Geschichte des fürstlichen Hauses Fürstenberg und seiner Ahnen bis zum Jahre 1509* (Tübingen, 1883), pp. 36–68, 99–108; and Hintze, *Wilhelm von Holland* (see above, n. 72), pp. 81–83.

102. Wilms, *Verzeichnis* (see above, n. 63), pp. 33, 36, 38, 48. The six Dominican nunneries in Strasbourg, one of the few German cities which was loyal to Rome throughout the conflict, were also incorporated in the late 1240s. On the other hand, the nunneries of Lienz and Steinach, which were associated with the pro-Hohenstaufen counts of the Tyrol and Gorizia, were not granted this privilege at this time.

103. *Annales Wormatienses* (see above, n. 29), p. 54.

moreover, on Duke Otto of Bavaria, who became the head of the imperial party in Germany after Conrad IV's departure for Italy in 1251. Henry of Montfort was sent to Otto and his son Louis in February 1251 to urge them to recognize William; but they refused.[104] Berthold of Regensburg was equally unsuccessful in 1253, and Otto died excommunicate on November 29, 1253.[105]

After Otto's death the Wittelsbachs were reconciled with the church and with the friars. Otto's daughter Elizabeth, the widow of Conrad IV, presented to the Dominican nunnery of Altenhohenau in 1259 the patronage of the parish church in Moeringen.[106] In the 1270s her brother, Duke Louis II of Upper Bavaria (1253–1294), established the Dominican nunnery of Pettendorf; and her sister Countess Sophia of Hirschberg founded the Dominican priory in Eichstätt.[107] Lesser members of the Hohenstaufen party, like the Hohenlohes, also made peace with the friars. In his 1275 will Conrad of Hohenlohe, who had a Dominican confessor, bequeathed fifty pounds to the Würzburg Dominicans; ten pounds each to the Wimpfen Dominicans, the Franciscans in Schwäbisch Hall, and the Dominican nuns in Nuremberg and Würzburg; and unspecified amounts to the Würzburg Franciscans and the Poor Clares in Schaffhausen.[108] Friendly relations between the friars and former members of the Hohenstaufen party were thus quickly restored.

Nevertheless, the friars paid a high price for their political involvement. Jordan of Giano observed:

From that time (1245), moreover, the friars were greatly troubled by Frederick, who had been legally deposed by the Council of Lyons, and were with great confusion expelled from their convents in many provinces, and many were imprisoned, some were even killed because, obedient to the commands of the church, they as pious sons manfully stood by their mother. No other religious order did more than the Friars Minor.[109]

104. MGH Epis. saec. XIII (see above, n. 32), 3, nos. 59, 69, and 78.
105. *Hermanni Altahensis annales*, ed. Philipp Jaffé (Hanover, 1861), MGH SS 17:396.
106. *Monumenta Altenhohenau* (see above, n. 47), no. 17.
107. *Die Regesten der Bischöfe von Eichstätt*, ed. Franz Heidingsfelder, Veröffentlichungen der Gesellschaft für fränkische Geschichte, VI. Reihe (Erlangen, 1938), nos. 889 and 919. The Colmar Dominican in the *Annales Colmarienses maiores*, ed. Philipp Jaffé (Hanover, 1861), MGH SS 17:217, called Elizabeth's other brother, Duke Henry of Lower Bavaria (1253–1290), a great friend of his order.
108. *Wirtembergisches UB* (Stuttgart, 1900), 7, no. 2542. For information about Conrad's political activities on Frederick's behalf, see Karl Weller, "Gottfried und Konrad von Hohenlohe im Dienste Kaiser Friedrichs II.," *Württembergische Vierteljahrshefte für Landesgeschichte*, NF 5 (1896), 209–233.
109. Jordan of Giano (see above, n. 6), ch. 73.

While the tone of Jordan's comment perhaps suggests that the German friars did not bear the brunt of Frederick's wrath, a few German convents and friars were directly affected. The Franciscan convent in Nuremberg, which changed allegiances several times, was severely damaged during the fighting.[110] The burghers of Zürich were reluctant to allow the Dominicans to return to their city after the friars left the interdicted town in 1247.[111] Some Hohenstaufen partisans in Strasbourg beat up several Dominicans, hurled one friar from a bridge into the Ill River, and hanged another.[112] The friars' political entanglement undoubtedly impaired at least momentarily the brothers' ministry among the German burghers, most of whom were Hohenstaufen adherents.

This change in the hitherto cordial relations between the friars and the burghers, as well as the general political instability during the last years of Frederick's reign and during the Interregnum, helps to explain why the expansion of the mendicant orders in Germany slowed in mid-century. Table I gives a clear picture of the impact of the conflict between Innocent IV and Frederick II upon the growth of the Dominican Order.[113] While the Dominicans had established thirty-four priories between 1220 and 1240 in the province of Teutonia, only sixteen additional houses were founded between 1240 and 1270 in Germany. The situation was particularly bad during the crisis years between 1245 and 1260 when only six convents were started. Significantly enough, five of these six houses, Neuruppin, Stralsund, Strausberg, Seehausen, and Rostock, were located in the Altmark, Brandenburg, Mecklenburg, or Pomerania, territories which were affected least by the prolonged conflict.

The difficulties in determining the foundation dates of the Franciscan houses obscures the effects of the political instability upon the growth of the Franciscan Order. Table III suggests, however, that the Franciscan rate of expansion at least slowed after 1240.[114] This decline can be attributed in part to the Franciscans' political activities after 1245. Bishop Rüdiger of Passau apparently thwarted, for instance, the Franciscans' plan to found a convent in his episcopal see in 1247.[115] Toward the end of Frederick's reign the Franciscans were also forced to abandon a house in Heidelberg, which was only refounded in 1282.[116] It is probably safe to conclude that those Fran-

110. *Nürnberger UB* (see above, n. 65), nos. 334, 337, 342, 368, 370.
111. *UB Zürich* (see above, n. 65), 2, nos. 768, 771, 776.
112. *UB Strassburg* (see above, n. 31), 1, nos. 346, 401, 405.
113. See above, p. 22.
114. See above, p. 24.
115. Friess, "Geschichte" (see above, n. 90), no. 10.
116. Leonhard Lemmens, "Chronicon provinciae Argentinensis," *AFH* 4 (1911), 678.

ciscan convents in the provinces of Cologne, Strasbourg, and Austria (such as Louvain, Frankfurt, and Vienna) which happen to be mentioned for the first time in a surviving document between 1245 and 1260 actually existed before Frederick's deposition. The revival in the foundation of mendicant convents in Germany in the last three decades of the thirteenth century can be attributed to the continued need for the friars' ministry in the new German cities and to a return of more stable political conditions after Rudolph's accession.

4. THE FRIARS AS KINGMAKERS (1257–1278)

The Dominicans' and Franciscans' success in arousing public opinion against the Hohenstaufen after 1245 had demonstrated that the mendicant orders had become a potent force within German political life. It was impossible for even the most pious ruler to regard the establishment of a mendicant convent within his territory as a purely religious matter. After the downfall of the Hohenstaufen dynasty, ambitious princes like Margraves John I and Otto III of Brandenburg sought to assure themselves of the friars' good will and to employ the brothers in the fulfillment of their own political designs. The friars' political activities on behalf of individual princes, like Rudolph of Habsburg, represent the final stage in the politicization of the mendicant orders and in the brothers' failure to maintain their independent status within medieval society. Although the friars had labored after Frederick's deposition for the realization of a basically secular goal, the destruction of the Hohenstaufen Empire, they had acted at the behest of the highest religious authority in Christendom; but the services which the friars rendered to the princes often lacked even this religious justification.

William of Holland's death on January 28, 1256, left Germany in a political void. The double election of 1257 only compounded the problem. King Alfonso X of Castile (1252–1284) never set foot on German soil, while Earl Richard of Cornwall (1209–1272), the brother of Henry III, was preoccupied with English affairs. The two contenders courted the friars in their feeble efforts to gain the German throne. Alfonso assured the German Dominicans of his affection and requested their prayers.[117] A Dominican named Bar-

---

117. Heinrich Finke, *Ungedruckte Dominikanerbriefe des 13. Jahrhunderts* (Paderborn, 1891), no. 7. For information about the history of Germany between 1257 and 1278, see Charles C. Bayley, *The Formation of the German College of Electors in the Mid-Thirteenth Century* (Toronto, 1949); Noël Denholm-Young, *Richard of Cornwall* (Oxford, 1947); Karl Hampe, *Geschichte Konradins von Hohenstaufen* (Innsbruck, 1894); Lorenz, *Ottokar II.* (see above, n. 46); and Redlich, *Rudolf von Habsburg* (see above, n. 94).

tholomew traveled around Germany in 1257 trying to persuade the burghers to recognize Richard as their king.[118] In return for such favors the earl gave the Frankfurt Dominicans permission in 1262 to cut timber in the imperial forests for building and heating and bequeathed 500 marks to the German Dominicans.[119] But not even the prayers and the persuasive power of the friars could perform the miracle of turning Alfonso or Richard into a real German king. Frederick II's grandson Conradin (1252–1268), the son of Conrad IV and Elizabeth of Bavaria, likewise sought to obtain the friars' good will before he left on his ill-fated expedition in the autumn of 1267 to claim the Sicilian crown. For example, he recommended the newly founded Dominican convent of Rottweil to the burghers of the city on January 6.[120]

The confrontation between King Ottokar II of Bohemia (1253–1278) and Rudolph of Habsburg (1273–1291), which determined the destiny of central Europe, offers the best illustration of the friars' new role in German politics. Grillparzer's tragic hero was the real ruler of Germany during the Interregnum. Ottokar utilized the political turmoil to unite by force and luck a conglomerate of territories—his hereditary domains of Bohemia and Moravia, the duchies of Austria, Styria, and Carinthia, and the margraviate of Carniola—which foreshadowed the later Danubian Monarchy. Since Ottokar lacked a firm legal basis for his acquisitions, his own interests were best served by a perpetuation of the political uncertainty.

The Bohemian court, thanks to the influence of Ottokar's paternal aunt, the Bl. Agnes of Prague (1206–1282), the founder and abbess of the Prague Poor Clares, had always been favorably disposed toward the friars, particularly the Franciscans. Agnes naturally encouraged her relatives to patronize the Franciscans and the Poor Clares. As we have already seen, various Bohemian princesses and their husbands, like Duchess Anna of Silesia and Margrave Otto III of Brandenburg, founded a number of Franciscan convents and nunneries in Brandenburg, Meissen, and Silesia.[121] Ottokar, whom Salimbene

---

118. *Regesten der Reichsstadt Aachen*, ed. Wilhelm Mummenhoff, PGRhGk 47 (Bonn, 1961), 1, no. 107.

119. *UB der Reichsstadt Frankfurt*: *Codex diplomaticus Moenofrancofurtanus*, ed. Johann Friedrich Boehmer and Friedrich Lau (Frankfurt, 1901), 1, no. 242; and *Registrum epistolarum fratris Johannis Peckham archiepiscopi Cantuariensis*, ed. Charles Trice Martin, Rerum Britannicarum medii aevi scriptores 77 (London, 1885), 3:1027.

120. *UB der Stadt Rottweil*, ed. Heinrich Günter, WürttGQ 3 (Stuttgart, 1896), 1, no. 29. See also *Wirtembergisches UB* (Stuttgart, 1894), 6, nos. 1911, 1912, 1925.

121. See above, pp. 58–60.

described as a great friend of the Franciscan Order,[122] also patronized the Dominicans. Like the east-Elbian princes, Ottokar founded Dominican priories in Bohemia and Moravia to provide for the spiritual needs of the German burghers whom he hoped to attract to the new cities in his domains.[123] Ottokar might normally have obtained the friars' complete support in the fulfillment of his political ambitions.

But relations between the Bohemian court and the German friars had noticeably soured by the 1260s. Gerhard, the parish priest of Vienna, assured Ottokar in the late 1260s that the Austrian and Styrian Franciscans would obey royal commands in the future.[124] About the same time Edmund, the German Dominican provincial prior, tried to placate Ottokar's anger with the German Dominicans, who had been accused, in Edmund's opinion wrongly, of sending to the curia letters hostile to the Bohemian king.[125] Unfortunately, the precise cause of Ottokar's displeasure is not stated in these letters.

The *Relatio* of Bishop Bruno of Olomouc, Ottokar's chief adviser and personal representative at the second ecumenical council in Lyons in 1274, contains additional evidence of the tension between the friars and the Bohemian court. This report on the state of the church and on the political situation in central Europe was prepared in December 1273 for the consideration of Pope Gregory X and of the forthcoming council. It is best known for its views on the German political crisis—Bruno expressed in the *Relatio* Ottokar's opposition to Rudolph's election as king the preceding October and implied that Ottokar might be a more suitable candidate for the German crown.[126] About a quarter of the report, however, was devoted to complaints about the friars' infringement of episcopal and parochial rights. Since it was

122. Salimbene de Adam, *Cronica*, ed. Ferdinando Bernini, 2 vols. (Bari, 1942), Scrittori d'Italia 188:200.
123. Vladimir Koudelka, "Zur Geschichte der böhmischen Dominikanerprovinz im Mittelalter," *AFP* 26 (1956), 143, 148—151.
124. *Quellen zur Geschichte der Stadt Wien*, ed. Anton Mayer, I. Abtheilung (Vienna, 1895), 1, no. 207.
125. Finke, *Dominikanerbriefe*, no. 20.
126. Höfler, "Analecten" (see above, n. 46), 18—22; Lorenz, *Ottokar II.*, pp. 256—259, 483. Jaroslav Goll, "Zu Brunos von Olmütz Bericht an Papst Gregor X (1273)," *MIÖG* 23 (1902), 487—490, argued that Bruno advocated the papal and conciliar recognition of Alfonso as German king and future Roman emperor. Bruno stressed in the *Relatio*, however, that Ottokar had been the only central European prince who had defended Christendom from its heathen enemies in the east. The defense of the church from such enemies had for centuries been the primary responsibility of the emperor. Otto I's victories over the Hungarians and Slavs had been in fact a

necessary in Bruno's opinion to sustain the good work of the friars as well as to preserve the authority of prelates and priests, he proposed for the council's consideration what he called a middle way between Innocent IV's *Etsi animarum* and Alexander IV's *Nec insolitum*. Bruno advocated, among other things, that each bishop be empowered to select the friars who would serve as confessors and preachers in his diocese, to restrain any friars who presumed to exercise these pastoral responsibilities without authorization, and to silence permanently any friar who dared to make derogatory comments about the secular clergy.[127] While Bruno undoubtedly voiced in the *Relatio* the feelings of many bishops and parish priests about the friars, it is rather surprising, nevertheless, that Bishop Bruno, the brother of the Franciscan Count Adolph IV of Holstein,[128] should have emerged at Lyons as the leading spokesman of the episcopal opposition to the mendicant orders. Twenty years earlier he had indignantly dismissed similar complaints from his clergy at a diocesan synod.[129]

The key to Bruno's and Ottokar's initial displeasure with the friars is probably contained in the two letters which were written sometime between 1268 and 1278 by Queen Kunigunde, Ottokar's second wife, to Abbess Agnes of Trebnitz and an unnamed cardinal. Kunigunde had objected in the strongest terms, it will be recalled, to the transfer of the Silesian Franciscan convents from the province of Bohemia to the province of Saxony.[130] Ottokar presumably perceived the transfer of these convents as a blow to his influence in Silesia, where he repeatedly intervened among his perpetually squabbling Piast cousins.[131] More important, he had valid reasons to fear that some of the mendicant houses within his own hereditary domains, where numerous

major justification for his imperial coronation. See Hans Hirsch, "Der mittelalterliche Kaisergedanke in den liturgischen Gebeten," *Heidenmission und Kreuzzugsgedanke in der deutschen Ostpolitik des Mittelalters*, ed. Helmut Beumann (Darmstadt, 1963), pp. 22–46; and Carl Erdmann, "Der Heidenkrieg in der Liturgie und die Kaiserkrönung Ottos I.," *Heidenmission*, pp. 47–64. Bruno's emphasis on Ottokar's campaigns against the heathens suggests that he was proposing Ottokar's own candidacy for the imperial dignity. For additional information about the reform proposal, see Josef Auer, *Studien zu den Reformschriften für das zweite lyoner Konzil* (Freiburg, 1910).

127. Höfler, "Analecten," pp. 22–26.
128. *Codex diplomaticus historiae comitum Schauenburgensium*, ed. F.A. von Aspern (Hamburg, 1850), 2, no. 47, and the genealogical table following p. 409.
129. *Codex Moraviae* (see above, n. 93), 3, no. 200.
130. Franz Palacky, *Ueber Formelbücher, zunächst in Bezug auf böhmische Geschichte* (Prague, 1842), pp. 287–288, no. 54, and p. 288, no. 55. See above, p. 75.
131. Colmar Grünhagen, *Geschichte Schlesiens* (Gotha, 1884), 1:94–98.

Germans were settling in the towns, might also be assigned to a German province. The 1263 Pisa general chapter, which had transferred the custody of Goldberg to Saxony, had also assigned the custody of Moravia to Austria. Both decisions had been revoked in 1266, in the case of the Moravian custody, as it turned out, permanently.[132] The transfer of the Moravian friaries from the Bohemian to the Austrian province was contrary to Ottokar's and Bruno's policy of loosening rather than strengthening the ties which bound the Premyslid kingdom to the *Reich*. The king and bishop were hoping in the 1260s, for instance, to obtain papal consent for their plan to elevate Olomouc, a suffragan bishopric of the ecclesiastical province of Mainz, into the archiepiscopal center for the expanded Bohemian monarchy.[133] The attempts by the German friars in the 1260s and 1270s to adjust the provincial boundaries in central and eastern Europe were thus diametrically opposed to Ottokar's own dream of a Danubian kingdom under Bohemian control. Ottokar's anger at the German Dominicans and Franciscans, particularly with the Austrian and Styrian Franciscans, was probably caused by their advocacy of such provincial realignments. Bruno's reform proposal may have been intended, at least in part, as a device to thwart such schemes. It would have been extremely easy, if Bruno's proposal had been enacted, for a bishop of Olomouc to silence any friar who dared to propose the transfer of the Moravian custody.

Bruno's complaints about the friars in December 1273 may also have been directly linked to Ottokar's opposition to Rudolph's election as king. The Bohemian court had ample reason to fear that Rudolph might exploit Ottokar's troubled relations with the German friars, particularly in Austria and Styria, in furthering his own interests. As the nephew and heir of Count Hartmann IV of Kyburg, the founder of the Dominican nunneries of Töss and Diessenhofen and of the convent of the Poor Clares in Schaffhausen, Rudolph (b. 1218) had undoubtedly been personally acquainted with the friars since adolescence. Rudolph had confirmed in 1243, for instance, a gift of his mother, Heilwig of Kyburg, to Töss.[134] Shortly after his election on October 1,

132. Jan Kazimierz Biernacki, *Speculum Minorum* (Cracow, 1688), pp. 229 and 231. See above, pp. 74–75.
133. Lorenz, *Ottokar II.*, pp. 262–270. See my article, "The Friars and the Delineation of State Boundaries in the Thirteenth Century," *Order and Innovation in the Middle Ages: Essays in Honor of Joseph R. Strayer*, ed. William C. Jordan, Bruce McNab, and Teofilo F. Ruiz (Princeton, 1976), pp. 31–40, 425–428, for further evidence that thirteenth-century rulers placed great importance on the provincial assignments of mendicant convents in trying to define the boundaries of their nascent states.
134. *UB Zürich* (see above, n. 65), 2, no. 587. See above, n. 94.

Rudolph had met in Frankfurt with the Dominican master general, John of Vercelli, and with the German provincial prior, Ulrich Engelbert. Ulrich subsequently informed the German Dominicans that Rudolph had listened most attentively to John's and Ulrich's exhortations and had promised to obey the church, to preserve peace and justice, and to promote Gregory X's proposed crusade to the Holy Land. Ulrich heartily recommended the newly elected king to his German brothers as a ruler who had previously demonstrated his devotion to the Dominicans and, more significantly, expressed the hope that the Dominicans might be able to guide and to assist Rudolph on his path to the imperial dignity.[135]

In actuality the Franciscans appear to have been of more assistance than the Dominicans in Rudolph's quest for the elusive imperial crown. Rudolph employed two Franciscans, Henry Knoderer, the lector in Mainz, and Conrad Probus, the minister of Strasbourg, in the complex diplomatic negotiations which ended, in spite of Ottokar's protests, in Gregory X's formal recognition of Rudolph's election on September 20, 1274. After Henry arranged a meeting between the pope and king in Lausanne in October 1275, Gregory X personally consecrated the Franciscan lector as bishop of Basel. Conrad Probus eventually became bishop of Toul. Their further diplomatic missions on the king's behalf, however, never secured Rudolph's imperial coronation.[136]

The Franciscans and Dominicans performed their most valuable and permanent service for the Habsburgs in Austria, which the king claimed as a usurped fief. Rudolph zealously cultivated the friars' friendship before he invaded Austria in the autumn of 1276. On March 6, for example, he granted the Nuremberg Dominicans the use of part of the tax revenue from the city for six years to finance their building program.[137] The Franciscans and Dominicans for their part labored secretly on Rudolph's behalf in Austria.[138] When Rudolph's army actually entered Austria at the beginning of October, the Dominicans and Franciscans persuaded the Austrian ministerials, whom they released in the pope's name from their oaths of fealty to Ottokar, to

135. Finke, *Dominikanerbriefe* (see above, n. 117), no. 59; Redlich, *Rudolf von Habsburg* (see above n. 94), pp. 206–207.
136. See Konrad Eubel, "Die Minoriten Heinrich Knoderer u. Konrad Probus," *HJb* 9 (1888), 393–449, 650–673. This material has been incorporated in Redlich's biography of Rudolph.
137. *Nürnberger UB* (see above, n. 65), 1, no. 538. See also Finke, *Dominikanerbriefe*, no. 80; and *Regesta imperii*, ed. Oswald Redlich (Innsbruck, 1898), 6, no. 553.
138. Finke, *Dominikanerbriefe*, nos. 75–79; Redlich, *Rudolf von Habsburg*, pp. 260–261 and Appendix 2, no. 5.

adhere to Rudolph. The friars' influence may also be seen in the decision of the Austrian towns, except for Vienna, to open their gates to the German king.[139] On November 26 Ottokar was forced to surrender most of his German acquisitions to Rudolph. The friars' secret agitation had prepared the way for the quick collapse of Bohemian rule in Austria.

Ottokar was determined to regain his lost empire. On August 26, 1278, Rudolph's and Ottokar's forces met for the last time at Dürnkrut, northeast of Vienna. Bishop Henry Knoderer of Basel, who had brought with him a contingent of 100 Alsatian knights,[140] rode before the Habsburg forces encouraging the troops and promising a "dwelling place in the angelic choir" to all who died in the ensuing battle. Other friars encouraged the Bohemian army.[141] Ottokar was killed and buried in a Franciscan convent; the grateful Rudolph founded the Dominican nunnery in Tulln; and Henry Knoderer became regent of southern Moravia.[142]

The career of the baker's son who became the primate of Germany and the confidant of popes and kings is one of the great Horatio Alger tales in medieval history. Henry Knoderer was an excellent imperial bishop, a worthy companion of a Rainald of Dassel or an Engelbert of Berg. But was he a Franciscan? What resemblance was there between the bishop mounted on his charger and the Poverello of Assisi? Henry's career is a graphic illustration of the failure of the mendicant ideal in the whirlpool of daily life. The lure of earthly glory had proven stronger than the promise of eternal life. Frederick II had been a better friend than either he or the friars had realized when he had warned the brothers not to meddle in the quarrels of kings and princes.

139. *Continuatio Vindobonense*, ed. Wilhelm Wattenbach (Hanover, 1851), MGH SS 9: 708.
140. *Chronicon Colmariense*, ed. Philipp Jaffé (Hanover, 1861), MGH SS 17:250.
141. *Ottokars österreichische Reimchronik*, ed. Joseph Seemüller, MGH, Scriptorum qui vernacula lingua usi sunt, Deutsche Chroniken, 5, Part 1 (Hanover, 1890), lines 16077–16111.
142. *Chronicon Colmariense*, p. 251; *Regesta imperii*, 6 nos. 1220 and 1221; Redlich, *Rudolf von Habsburg*, pp. 328–329.

Conclusion

But his flock has grown so greedy for the taste
of new food that it cannot help but be
far scattered as it wanders through the waste.
The more his vagabond and distant sheep
wander from him, the less milk they bring back
when they return to the fold. A few do keep
close to the shepherd, knowing what wolf howls
in the dark around them, but they are so few
it would take little cloth to make their cowls.
Dante, *Paradiso*, Canto XI, vv. 124–132.[1]

THE friars started their German ministry in a period of far-reaching political and social changes: the disintegration of the Hohenstaufen Empire, the urbanization of western Germany, the struggle for communal independence in the episcopal cities, the Germanization of the east-Elbian territories, and the transformation of the ministerialage into the new lower nobility. Germany developed during these years the basic institutional and societal structure which it retained until the end of the Holy Roman Empire. The desire to imitate the life style of the poor Jesus was an essentially negative response to this transformation in the traditional order of early medieval society. Many ministerials and burghers, who were the prime beneficiaries of the commercial and social revolutions of the twelfth and thirteenth centuries, were deeply disturbed by their new wealth and by the ambiguities in their social status. The church's condemnation of avarice made them keenly conscious of the contrast between their own affluence and the spiritual and ethical ideals set forth in the Gospels. While many of them, like Hartman Gir in Cologne, soothed

1. *The Paradiso*, trans. John Ciardi (New York, 1970).

169

their guilty conscience by patronizing the friars, more sensitive individuals could only relieve their inner anxieties by adopting the apostolic life. In an increasingly prosperous age, the friars and their benefactors idealized poverty.

Nevertheless, though the personal and subconscious decision to become a friar often stemmed from a negative reaction to the changes in German society, collectively and consciously the friars came to admire and ultimately to promote the transformation of the traditional social and political order. The Colmar Dominican was extremely impressed, for instance, with the improvements in living standards, agriculture, trade, knowledge, morality, and religion which he had witnessed in his native Alsace during his lifetime. He sincerely believed that the friars, who had prepared compendiums of sacred and secular knowledge and who had offered spiritual nourishment and ethical instruction to thousands, had exerted a positive influence upon medieval society.[2] The phenomenal expansion of the mendicant orders can be attributed in large part to the friars' close association with the beneficiaries of these changes: the Habsburgs, the east-Elbian princes, the Swabian dynasts, the ministerials, the burghers, and the Overstolzes. The friars supplied their friends with assistance in worldly matters as well as with spiritual consolation. They agitated against the Hohenstaufen; they raised the crusading armies which conquered Prussia and the Baltic States; they stirred up rebellion against Ottokar of Bohemia on Rudolph's behalf; they accompanied the German settlers on their eastward migration; and they aided the Overstolzes in their rise to pre-eminence in Cologne. The friars' actions thus hastened the social and political reorganization of German society in the thirteenth century. They had indeed gone into the world.

But as Dante's harsh criticism of the Dominicans indicates, there was a widespread feeling by 1300 that the friars had compromised their principles. Examples of the spiritual decline within the mendicant order come readily to mind: the Strasbourg Dominicans' stubborn defense of their right to acquire property, the Silesian Franciscans' partisan intervention in the dispute between Duke Henry and Bishop Thomas, and the Austrian friars' agitation against Ottokar of Bohemia. The friars' close association with their powerful patrons was a major factor in this tragedy. If St. Albert's arbitral decisions were influenced by his friendship with such prominent members of the Overstolz party as Daniel Jude and Bruno Hardevust, it is not surprising that less

---

2. *De rebus Alsaticis ineuntis saeculi XIII*, ed. Philipp Jaffé (Hanover, 1861), MGH SS 17:232–238.

perceptive and saintly brothers, like Henry Knoderer and Herman, the lector
of the Breslau Franciscans, openly championed their patrons' interests.

The friars might have avoided such fatal entanglements in temporal affairs
if they had strictly adhered to their vows of poverty. As Malcolm D. Lambert
has astutely pointed out, St. Francis did not so much condemn the possession
of property as the dependence upon earthly society which such ownership
implied.[3] Absolute poverty also meant absolute freedom. In reality, however,
the success of the mendicant orders, measured at least in human terms, de-
pended upon the existence of familial, feudal, and personal ties between the
friars and potential patrons. The Dominicans were the more influential order
in the 1220s and 1230s precisely because they had a greater number of such
personal contacts than the Franciscans. The price which the friars paid for
such material and moral support was a partial loss of their independence. It
was impossible for the friars to ignore completely the temporal interests of
their benefactors. As the disparity between the friars' professed spiritual aims
and actual practices became increasingly more obvious, criticism of the mendicant orders mounted. The hypocritical friar, like Chaucer's Huberd, was in
fact a familiar object of ridicule after 1250.[4]

But it would be unfair to stress unduly the friars' failures. The rapid
spread of the Franciscans and Dominicans marks in fact a key stage in the
Christianization of western Europe. Until the twelfth century the ideal Christian had been the monk. The ordinary layman could only attend incompre-
hensible religious services and hope that the monks' intercessory prayers
would benefit his soul. The friars demonstrated, in spite of their personal and
institutional shortcomings, that it was possible for a Christian to live in the
midst of society. More important, the friars' sermons and personal example
familiarized the laity of Europe with the basic doctrines and ethical code of
Christianity. The friars' ministry thus turned Christianity for the first time
into a living faith which infused the daily lives of ordinary men and women.

3. *Franciscan Poverty: The Doctrine of the Absolute Poverty of Christ and the Apostles
   in the Franciscan Order 1210–1323* (London, 1961), p. 51.
4. Ernest W. McDonnell, *The Beguines and Beghards in Medieval Culture: With Special
   Emphasis on the Belgian Scene* (New Brunswick, New Jersey, 1954), pp. 456–473.
   Paul L. Nyhus in his recently published monograph, *The Franciscans in South Germany, 1400–1530: Reform and Revolution*, Transactions of the American Philosophical Society NS 65, Pt. 8 (Philadelphia, 1975), deals with the question of how
   the Franciscans, the great heroes of the thirteenth century, became the villains of the
   sixteenth. His answer in large part is that the friars' too great entanglement in earthly
   affairs made it impossible for them to live up to the ideals which they professed
   (p. 10).

Appendix I

Franciscan and Dominican Convents

A basic prerequisite for any study of the mendicant orders in the thirteenth century is a determination of the locations and foundation dates of the individual Dominican and Franciscan convents. While David Knowles's and R. Neville Hadcock's *Medieval Religious Houses: England and Wales* (London, 1953) and Richard W. Emery's *The Friars in Medieval France* (New York, 1962) contain accurate lists of the English and French convents, there is no comparable catalogue of German mendicant houses. The gaps in the extant German documentation make the preparation of such a list a difficult task, but it is impossible to relate the development of the Franciscan and Dominican Orders to overall German social and political conditions without this information.

Fortunately, it is easy to determine the locations of the German Franciscan convents. Accurate lists of the houses situated in the province of Saxony in 1340 and of the convents located in the provinces of Cologne, Strasbourg and Austria in 1400 have survived.[1] Documentary or literary evidence confirms the existence by the end of the fourteenth century of all but four of the 214 convents which appear on these lists.[2] I have found only one definite reference to a convent, Bruck an der Leitha in the province of Austria, which was not named on these lists; in all probability it no longer existed in 1400.[3]

1. Patricius Schlager, "Verzeichnis der Klöster der sächsischen Franziskaner-Provinzen," *FS* 1 (1914), 230–240; and Bartholomew of Pisa, *De conformitate vitae b. Francisci ad vitam Domini Iesu*, AF 4 (Quaracchi, 1906), pp. 548–553.
2. I have been unable to find conclusive evidence for the existence of the convents in Grein, Sorau, Zeitz, and Zistersdorf.
3. The convent in Bruck is mentioned in the 1324 will of Countess Gutta of Oettingen, the daughter of King Albrecht I, who apparently left bequests to each of the mendicant convents in the Habsburg domains. Marquard Herrgott, *Taphographia principum Austriae*, Monumenta aug. domus Austriacae 4 (Vienna, 1772), 2, no. 12. There is no other evidence for the existence of the house. G.E. Friess, "Geschichte der oesterreichischen Minoritenprovinz," *Archiv für österreichische Geschichte* 64 (1882), pp. 101–102.

These lists thus provide a terminal date for the existence of the German Franciscan houses. The real problem is to ascertain the foundation dates of these convents or, where this is impossible, the earliest definite reference in a document or chronicle to the existence of a friary. This information can only be obtained through a careful scrutiny of medieval literary and documentary sources and the monographs of modern local historians.

The *Chronica* of Jordan of Giano, who came to Germany in 1221 and who held several offices within the Franciscan Order, is the most important single source for the early history of the Friars Minor in Germany. Jo.dan dictated his recollections of the beginning of the Franciscan Order in Germany to Baldwin of Brunswick in 1262 at the behest of Bartholomew, the minister of Saxony. As Jordan recounted his memoirs, his attention increasingly focused on the province of Saxony and the custody of Thuringia, where he had spent most of his career. After 1239 his account, at least in the extant form of the text, becomes merely a list of Saxon provincial chapters. Jordan and the friars who listened to his tales were probably primarily interested in the heroic early days of their order.[4]

4. Only one incomplete manuscript of the text survives. The *Chronica* was first published by Georg Voigt, "Die Denkwürdigkeiten (1207–1238) des Minoriten Jordanus von Giano," *Abhandlungen der philologisch-historischen Classe der königlich sächsischen Gesellschaft der Wissenschaften* 5 (1870), 421–545. Voigt's edition was based on a transcript made for his father, the archivist in Königsberg. The text ended abruptly with ch. 63 in 1238. Voigt was unable to find the original manuscript. The fourteenth-century manuscript, a hasty and inaccurate copy, was subsequently discovered in the royal library in Berlin and published by the Quaracchi Fathers in the Analecta Franciscana 1 (1885), pp. 1–19. The abrupt ending of the chronicle in 1238, its composition in 1262, and a citation by Nicholas Glassberger of Jordan for the year 1240 raised the suspicion that the original version had in fact extended to the year 1262. H. Boehmer discovered in the *Landesbibliothek* in Karlsruhe a fifteenth-century fragment of the chronicle, which consisted of chapters 57–62 as well as a continuation of the *Chronica* beyond 1238. With the aid of the Karlsruhe fragment, the sixteenth-century Franciscan historians Nicholas Glassberger and John Komerowski, who had used Jordan, and the *Epitome Lipsiensis*, a fifteenth-century précis of various chapters of Jordan's *Chronica*, Boehmer published a new edition in the Collection d'études et de documents sur l'histoire religieuse et littéraire du moyen âge 6 (Paris, 1908). The Karlsruhe manuscript was published by Leonhard Lemmens, "Continuatio et finis Chronicae Fratris Iordani de Yano O.F.M.," *AFH* 3 (1910), 47–54. Edwin J. Auweiler, without using the manuscript, made a few critical textual corrections in *The "Chronica Fratris Jordani a Giano"* (Washington, 1917). Nevertheless, Boehmer's edition remains the standard text.

Jordan was a member of the 1221 mission to Germany (ch. 19), guardian of Speyer in 1223 (ch. 32) and of Mainz in 1223–1224 (ch. 38), custodian of Thurin-

After Jordan's death the list of Saxon ministers and provincial chapters was kept up in the *Continuatio Saxonica.*[5] The *Epitome Lipsiensis* is a fifteenth-century précis of Jordan's *Chronica* and of the *Continuatio Saxonica.*[6] One other important narrative source should be singled out. In approximately 1325 an unknown Basel friar wrote the *Chronicon provinciae Argentinensis,*[7] a history of the province of Strasbourg. Since his prime source for the early history of the German Franciscans was Jordan's *Chronica,* he offers no new information on the formative years of the order. He does offer, however, some valuable information about the province of Strasbourg in the last decades of the thirteenth century and in the first years of the fourteenth century which cannot be found in other sources. Most contemporary non-mendicant chroniclers ignored the friars. Franciscan and other chroniclers thus provide the foundation dates of only a few of the convents.

Therefore the major source for early German Franciscan history must be documentary references to the friars. Regrettably, such references are far from abundant. The archives of many houses were destroyed during the Reformation or during the secularization of the convents at the end of the *ancien régime.* War, fire, and other man-made disasters also took their inevitable toll. More important, it is highly unlikely that the individual houses ever possessed extensive records dating from the thirteenth century. Since the early Franciscans were pledged not only to individual poverty, but also to the strictest corporate poverty, they probably never possessed many property deeds, by far the commonest form of thirteenth-century German

gia from 1224 until at least 1231 (chs. 38, 60), the envoy of the Saxon province to John Parenti in 1230 to request a new minister after the sudden death of Simon of England (ch. 58), the bearer of the complaints of the Saxon friars against Elias's misrule to Gregory IX in 1238 (ch. 63), most likely a member of the commission of twenty friars who met in 1239 to reform the order and of the 1239 general chapter (Boehmer, Introduction, p. lxi), most probably vicar of the province of Bohemia during the Mongol invasion of 1241 (Boehmer, Introduction, pp. lxi–lxii), and vicar of Saxony in 1242–1243 (ch. 71).

5. Boehmer published the *Continuatio Saxonica* as an appendix to Jordan's *Chronica* in the Collection d'études (See above, n. 4), pp. 63–67. See also Boehmer's introduction, pp. xliii–xliv. Lemmens, "Continuatio" (See above, n. 4) provides a more complete text.

6. Boehmer published the *Epitome Lipsiensis* as an appendix to Jordan's *Chronica* in the Collection d'études (See above, n. 4), pp. 76–80. See also Boehmer's introduction, pp. xlix–li.

7. Published by Leonhard Lemmens as "Chronicon provinciae Argentinensis O.F.M. circa an. 1310–27 a quondam Fratre Minore Basileae conscriptum (1206–1325)," *AFH* 4 (1911), 671–687. Hereafter cited as Lemmens, "Chronicon."

documentation. The first proof for the existence of many friaries is thus frequently only a chance reference to the house or one of its members in the records of another ecclesiastical institution. The inadequacy of such evidence can be demonstrated by the following example. Jordan of Giano, ch. 36, clearly states that the Franciscans settled in Brunswick, Goslar, Halberstadt, and Magdeburg in 1223. The first documentary proof for the friars' presence in Goslar occurs in 1232, in Brunswick in 1249, in Magdeburg in 1259, and in Halberstadt in 1275, that is, between nine and fifty-two years after their known date of arrival in these four cities.[8] Quite obviously, silence does not necessarily prove the non-existence of a convent. Such documentary references can thus only provide at best a *terminus ad quem* for a friary's existence.

The historiographical tradition of the Franciscan Order further complicates the task of determining the foundation dates of the individual houses. In the sixteenth, seventeenth, and eighteenth centuries several Franciscans wrote often-cited accounts of the origins of various convents. These histories include: Nicholas Glassberger's *Chronica* (1508)[9]; Francesco Gonzaga's *De origine seraphicae religionis Franciscanae eiusque progressibus de regularis observanciae institutione, forma administrationis ac legibus, admirabilique eius propagatione* (Rome 1587); Luke Wadding's *Annales Minorum*[10]; Adam Bürvenich's *Annales seu chronicon almae provinciae Coloniae fratrum Minorum strictae observantiae regularis seu recollectorum* (1665)[11]; Berard Müller's and Victor Tschan's *Chronica de ortu et progressu almae provinciae Argentinensis* (1703–1720)[12]; and Vigilius Greiderer's *Germania Franciscana.*[13] These historians present considerable information about the origins of various convents, much of it undoubtedly based on documents which they

8. *UB der Stadt Goslar*, ed. George Bode, GQProvSachs 29 (Halle, 1893), 1, no. 518; *UB des Hochstifts Hildesheim und seiner Bischöfe*, ed. H. Hoogeweg, QDGNSachs 6 (Hanover, 1901), 2, no. 814; *UB der Stadt Magdeburg*, ed. Gustav Hertel, GQProvSachs 26 (Halle, 1892), 1, no. 123; and *Les Registres de Grégoire X*, ed. Jean Guiraud and E. Cadier (Paris, 1892–1960), no. 638.
9. Published in the Analecta Franciscana 2 (Quaracchi, 1887). Hereafter cited as Glassberger.
10. 2nd ed., 26 vols. (Rome and Quaracchi, 1731–1933). Hereafter cited as Wadding.
11. The unpublished manuscript may be found in the Universitätsbibliothek in Düsseldorf. Hereafter cited as Bürvenich.
12. Ed. Meinrad Sehi (Ulm, 1964), *AFA* 12. Hereafter cited as Müller.
13. Vols. 1 and 2 were published in Innsbruck in 1777 and 1781. Vol. 3 was edited by Gerold Fussenegger in the *Alemania Franciscana antiqua* 11 (Ulm, 1964). Hereafter cited as Greiderer.

discovered in the now lost convent archives or on the traditions of a friary which was still in existence when they wrote.

This information must be carefully scrutinized in the light of existing documentary evidence or more reliable, earlier literary sources. Often such evidence conclusively proves that a friary existed within a few years of the date provided by a later Franciscan author. Gonzaga (p. 998) states that the friary in Diest, which happens to be first mentioned in a 1232 document,[14] was started in 1228. Such foundation dates are probably accurate. In a few cases documentary evidence suggests that a friary actually existed before the foundation date given by the later historians. Müller (p. 63) states that the convent in Frankfurt am Main was founded in 1271. It is in fact first mentioned in a 1255 document.[15] But the later Franciscan authors usually tended to assign too early a date to the establishment of a friary since an early foundation date and/or famous founder added to the prestige of a house. Occasionally such dates and stories are clearly preposterous and can easily be rejected. Müller (pp. 69–70) states that the friary in Schwäbisch Gmünd was founded by David, a Swabian friar, and his seven companions, whom St. Francis had sent back to their native land in 1208, that is, before St. Francis had even received permission from Innocent III to begin his apostolate. The story and date are clearly erroneous.

The real problem is posed of course by those convents where there is a sizeable gap between the foundation date supplied by a later Franciscan author and the first definite proof for the house's existence, but no obvious inherent reason for simply rejecting the information provided by the later historian as a fabrication. The convent in Haguenau offers a good, though extreme, example of the problem. Müller (p. 78) relates that the convent was founded by two nobles, Casper and Melchior of Fleckenstein, and by the Haguenau patrician, Balthasar Bechtel, whom Caesar of Speyer converted in 1222 and in whose honor the Haguenau convent was dedicated to the Magi. The friary is specifically mentioned for the first time in a 1287 document.[16] We have already seen that documentary silence does not necessarily preclude the existence of a convent.

14. Ch. Stallaert, "Inventaire analytique des chartes concernant les seigneurs et la ville de Diest," *Compte rendu des séances de la Commission royale d'histoire*, 4th series 3 (1876), p. 173.
15. *UB der Reichsstadt Frankfurt: Codex diplomaticus Moenofrancofurtanus*, ed. Johann Friedrich Boehmer and Friedrich Lau (Frankfurt, 1901), 1, no. 201.
16. *Regesten der Bischöfe von Strassburg*, ed. Alfred Hessel and Manfred Krebs (Innsbruck, 1928), 2, no. 2226.

An analysis of the available evidence offers no simple resolution of the problem. The names Casper, Melchior, and Balthasar, which were hardly common in thirteenth-century Germany, sound contrived, a clumsy attempt to explain the convent's dedication to the Magi. On the other hand, the story, or at least the early foundation date, is not as preposterous as it first seems. The Fleckensteins were in fact a family of imperial ministerials, whose castle was located near Haguenau.[17] More important, Jordan of Giano, ch. 32, mentioned the appointment in 1223 of a custodian of Alsace. This appointment would appear to indicate that there was more than one house in Alsace by 1223. Since Strasbourg and Haguenau were the most important towns in Alsace at the beginning of the thirteenth century,[18] it seems likely that the first Franciscan convents in Alsace would have been located in these two cities. It is thus quite plausible, though not provable, that the Haguenau convent was also founded, as Müller maintained, in the 1220s. In any case the Franciscans had almost certainly settled in Haguenau long before 1287. But there is clearly no way to know for sure, given the present state of the evidence, when the Haguenau friary was actually established.

To handle this problem, I have distinguished in the list of convents which appear in this appendix between the alleged foundation date of a convent, which is based on unverifiable but not inherently wrong information supplied by a later Franciscan or local historian, and the first definite reference to the existence of a convent in a document or other trustworthy source. In the case of the Haguenau house, these dates are 1222 and 1287.

The foundation dates of the German Dominican priories can be ascertained with far greater accuracy and ease than those of the Franciscan friaries. The Dominican Order had precise regulations about the founding of new convents. The provincial prior or diffinitors were required to ask the annual general chapter for permission to establish a new house within their province. When the new foundation, which was called a *locus*, had at least twelve members, including a prior and lector, it achieved full status as a priory. The new priory was then formally received by the order and entitled to send its prior and another friar to the annual provincial chapters.[19] The representatives of

---

17. Karl Bosl, *Die Reichsministerialität der Salier und Staufer*, MGH Scriften 10 (Stuttgart, 1950–1951), pp. 202–204.
18. Hella Fein, *Die staufischen Städtegründungen im Elsass*, Schriften des wissenschaftlichen Instituts der Elsass-Lothringer im Reich an der Universität Frankfurt, NF 25 (Frankfurt, 1939), pp. 13–18 and 53.
19. Heribert Chr. Scheeben, *Die Konstitutionen des Predigerordens unter Jordan von Sachsen*, QFGDD 38 (Leipzig, 1939), p. 75.

the various houses normally sat in the order in which their convents had been received. A house was usually received shortly after its foundation. The Dominicans arrived in Erfurt in 1228; and the priory was formally received in 1229.[20] The seating arrangements in the fourteenth century at the provincial chapters of the two German Dominican provinces, Teutonia and Saxony, which were created in 1303, have survived.

No further investigation is required for the province of Saxony. A list, written in approximately 1380 and published as Table XI, indicates not only the seating arrangement at the Saxon provincial chapters, but also the year when each priory was received.[21] Documentary or other evidence confirms the accuracy of the dates on the list.[22] The fourteenth-century province of Teutonia poses more of a problem. Only the seating arrangement in 1301, when the division of the original province was being planned, is known.[23] The foundation and/or reception dates of these priories must be obtained in the same way as the foundation dates of the Franciscan friaries.

The Dominican historiographical tradition is of little use in determining

20. *Monumenta Erphesfurtensia saec. XII. XIII. XIV.*, ed. Oswald Holder-Egger (Hanover, 1899) MGH SRG 41:81. The reception date is taken from Table XI.

21. Paulus von Loë, *Statistisches über die Ordensprovinz Saxonia*, QFGDD 4 (Leipzig, 1910), pp. 11–12.

22. Three examples will be cited to demonstrate the accuracy of the list. The 1380 seating arrangement indicates that the convents in Magdeburg, Halberstadt, and Cheb were received, respectively, in 1224, 1232, and 1296. The *Chronicon Montis Sereni*, ed. E. Ehrenfeuchter (Hanover, 1874), MGH SS 23:220–221, indicates that the Dominicans arrived in Magdeburg in 1224. Bishop Frederick of Halberstadt gave the Halberstadt Dominicans in 1231 a courtyard which he had purchased for their use. *UB der Stadt Halberstadt*, ed. Gustav Schmidt, GQProvSachs 7 (Halle, 1878), 1, no. 27. Finally, Adolph of Nassau gave the Dominicans permission on July 29, 1294, to settle in Cheb. *Regesta imperii*, ed. Oswald Redlich (Innsbruck, 1898), 6, no. 418.

I could only find two cases which cast doubt on the accuracy of the list. On February 17, 1252, Cardinal Hugh of Saint-Cher allegedly issued a document (content unspecified) on behalf of the Warburg Dominicans. *Regesta imperii*, ed. Julius Ficker and Eduard Winkelmann (Innsbruck, 1881–1892), 5, no. 10308. The editors cite as a source R. Wilmans, "Ergänzungen zu den *Regesta Pontificum Romanorum* von Jaffé und Potthast," *Archivalische Z* 3 (1878), 52. As far as I can tell, the reference only indicates that a document issued on behalf of the Dominican nuns in Soest is located in the Warburg Dominican archives. The document in question thus does not prove that the Warburg priory existed in 1252. The convent was in fact founded in 1281 and received in 1282 as the 1380 list indicates. For further information, see Adolf Gottlob, "Die Gründung des Dominikanerklosters Warburg," *Z für vaterländische Geschichte und Altertumskunde* 60 (1902), 109–175. The other case is Riga, discussed on p. 69.

23. Paulus von Loë, *Statistisches über die Ordensprovinz Teutonia*, QFGDD 1 (Leipzig, 1907), p. 7.

these dates. The medieval Dominicans lacked the historical self-consciousness of the Franciscans. There was no Dominican Jordan of Giano to record the early history of his order in Germany. Thirteenth-century German Dominican chroniclers, like the Colmar Dominican, tended to write about the region in which they lived rather than about their own order. Some information about the origins of various Dominican priories can be obtained, however, from Johannes Meyer's *Chronica brevis*,[24] which was written in the fifteenth century, and from Bernaert de Jonghe's *Desolata Batavia Dominicana* (Ghent, 1717) and *Belgium Dominicanum* (Brussels, 1719), which contain histories of the Dominican houses located in the Low Countries.

For a variety of reasons, however, there are many more documentary references in the thirteenth century to the Dominicans than the Franciscans. First of all, while the Dominicans were also pledged to corporate as well as individual poverty, they owned their own churches and convents and thus kept at least some property deeds in their archives. Second, the Dominicans were, as we have seen, the more influential order in Germany and consequently were mentioned more frequently in the records of other ecclesiastical institutions than the Franciscans. Finally, the Dominicans often served as witnesses in the property transactions of the numerous Dominican nunneries. From these documentary references and the information supplied by the Dominican historians, the foundation and/or reception dates of most priories in the fourteenth-century province of Teutonia can readily be obtained.

The reception date of the remaining Dominican convents in Teutonia can be interpolated from the seating arrangement at the provincial chapter. The priory in Vienna provides a good example. The earliest clear reference to the Viennese house only occurs in 1239,[25] but the representatives of the convent were seated between the friars from Trier, where the Dominicans had settled by 1225,[26] and the representatives from Würzburg and Worms, the latter of which was founded in 1226 and allegedly received in 1227.[27] The Viennese house was thus almost certainly founded and received sometime between 1225 and 1227.

Table XII lists the convents in the fourteenth-century province of Teu-

---

24. Ed. Heribert Chr. Scheeben (Leipzig, 1933), QFGDD 29.
25. *Quellen zur Geschichte der Stadt Wien*, ed. Karl Uhlirz, II. Abtheilung (Vienna, 1898), 1, no. 2.
26. *Gesta Treverorum*, ed. G. Waitz (Hanover, 1879), MGH SS 24:399–400.
27. *Annales Wormatienses*, ed. Georg Pertz (Hanover, 1861), MGH SS 17:38; and Meyer, *Chronica brevis*, p. 29.

tonia in the order in which their representatives were seated, that is the approximate order in which the convents had been received and presumedly founded. In those cases where the foundation and/or reception date is definitely known, it is indicated in the table along with the source of the information. Table XII also gives the date and source for the first definite reference to the remaining priories and the date of reception, as far as it can be interpolated from the convent's position at the provincial chapter. A question mark after a date indicates that the date is based on somewhat questionable later evidence.

I have also included as Table XIII a list of the sixteen Polish Dominican houses which would have been considered German under the Franciscan provincial structure. Unfortunately I was unable to find a list of the Polish houses which indicated the seating arrangement, i.e., the order of reception, at the Polish provincial chapters. I have tried to discover, therefore, either the foundation date of the convent or the earliest documentary or literary reference to the existence of the priory.

It should be obvious from what has been said that no list of convents and dates can be completely accurate. In using the tables which appear in this appendix, it would be wise to remember the late David Knowles's warning in his introduction to *The Religious Houses of Medieval England*:

> No catalogue of this kind can hope as yet to be complete or final. Even apart from the errors which may be detected in it, many of the dates must necessarily depend upon a personal judgment with which others may disagree, and in such a wide field, it would be vain to hope that notice has been taken of all the possible sources of information already existing. Moreover, many of these dates are only approximate, and every year sees the publication of new matter which may give precision to the history of this house or the other. These lists are, therefore, capable of improvement to an indefinite degree. It is at least hoped that, once printed, they may attract criticisms and suggestions from those acquainted with the history of particular houses.[28]

I can only concur.

28. (London, 1940), pp. 9–10.

TABLE VII[a]
FRANCISCANS
PROVINCE OF SAXONY

Convent	Foundation Date	Alleged Foundation Date	First Definite Reference	Source
Custody of Thuringia				
Erfurt	1224			Jordan of Giano (see above, n. 4), ch. 39.
Eisenach	1225			Ibid., ch. 41.
Gotha[b]	1225			Ibid., ch. 42.
Nordhausen	1230			Ibid., ch. 44.
Mühlhausen	1231			Ibid., ch. 45.
Arnstadt[b]	1250			*Monumenta Erphesfurtensia* (see above, n. 20), p. 766.
Meiningen		1239	1252	Pusch, "Das meininger Franziskanerkloster," *BGSFHK* 3 (1910), 58; *Regesta diplomatica necnon epistolaria historiae Thuringiae*, ed. Otto Dobenecker (Jena, 1925), 3, no. 2077.
Saalfeld		mid-13th	1276	H. Schwesinger, "Das Franziskanerkloster in Saalfeld a. S.," *FS* 10 (1923), 246; and *Regesta Thuringiae*, 4 (1939), no. 1373.
Coburg		1250	1307	Walter Heins, "Das ehemalige Franziskanerkloster in Coburg," *BFA* 1 (1954), 124 and 126.
Custody of Halberstadt				
Halberstadt	1223			Jordan of Giano, ch. 36.
Brunswick	1223			Ibid., ch. 36.
Hildesheim	1223			Ibid., chs. 35 and 36.
Goslar	1223			Ibid., ch. 36.
Quedlinburg			1253	*Epitome Lipsiensis* (see above, n. 6), p. 77.

Table VII—*Continued*

Convent	Foundation Date	Alleged Foundation Date	First Definite Reference	Source
Custody of Halberstadt				
Hanover	1291			*UB der Stadt Hannover*, ed. C.L. Grotefend and G.F. Fiedeler, UBHistVerNSachs 5 (Hanover, 1860), 1, no. 54.
Custody of Bremen				
Hamburg[c]		1227	1239	Albert of Stade, *Annales Stadenses*, ed. Johann M. Lappenberg (Hanover, 1859), MGH SS 16:365.
Stade			1240	Ibid., p. 367.
Bremen		1225	1241	Patricius Schlager, "Geschichte des Franziskaner-kloster in Bremen," *BGSFHK* 4 and 5 (1911–1912), 3; *Bremisches UB*, ed. D.R. Ehmck, W. von Bippen (Bremen, 1873), 1, no. 217.
Lüneburg		1235	1258	*UB der Stadt Lüneburg*, ed. W.F. Volger, UBHist-VerNSachs 8 (Hanover, 1872), no. 46; and *Epitome Lipsiensis*, p. 77.
Kiel[d]		before 1239	1261	*Chronicon Holtzatiae auctore presbytero Bremensis dioecesis a. 1172–1428*, ed. Johann Martin Lappenberg (Hanover, 1869), MGH SS 21:266.
Custody of Lübeck				
Lübeck		1223	1233	Otto Grote, *Lexicon deutscher Stifter, Klöster und Ordenshäuser* (Osterwieck a. Harz, 1881), 1:314; *UB der Stadt Lübeck*, Codex diplomaticus Lubecensis, 1. Abtheilung (Lübeck, 1843), 1, no. 54.

Table VII–*Continued*

Convent	Foundation Date	Alleged Foundation Date	First Definite Reference	Source
Custody of Lübeck				
Schwerin			1236	*Meklenburgisches UB* (Schwerin, 1863), 1, no. 450.
Riga			1238	*Liv- Esth- und Curländisches UB*, ed. Friedrich Georg von Bunge (Reval, 1857), 3, Nachträge, no. 159.
Greifswald	1242			*Pommersches UB*, ed. Robert Klempin (Stettin, 1868), 1, no. 403; H. Hoogeweg, *Die Stifte und Klöster der Provinz Pommern*, 2 vols. (Stettin, 1924–1925), 1: 608–609.
Rostock			1243	*Meklenburgisches UB*, 1, no. 550.
Parchim			1246	Ibid., no. 586.
Wismar	1251/1252			Ibid., 2 (1864), nos. 669 and 670.
Stralsund	1254			M. Wehrmann, "Zur Gründung des Johannisklosters zu Stralsund," *Monatsblätter der Gesellschaft für pommersche Geschichte und Altertumskunde* 15 (1901), 122–124.
Custody of Magdeburg				
Magdeburg	1223			Jordan of Giano, ch. 36.
Halle			1247	Ibid., ch. 75.
Zerbst			1252	*Regesta imperii*, ed. Julius Ficker and Eduard Winkelmann (Innsbruck, 1881–1892), 5, no. 10304.
Wittenberg		1266	1273	Wadding (see above, n. 10), 3:267; *Regesta archiepiscopatus Magdeburgensis*, ed.

Table VII—*Continued*

Convent	Foundation Date	Alleged Foundation Date	First Definite Reference	Source
Custody of Magdeburg				
Wittenberg—*Continued*				Georg Adalbert v. Mülverstedt (Magdeburg, 1886), 3, no. 119.
Barby	1264		1279	Grote, *Lexicon* (see above, Lübeck), 1:32–33; and Georg Adalbert v. Mülverstedt, "Verzeichnis der früher und jetzt noch bestehenden Klöster," *Geschichts-Blätter für Stadt und Land Magdeburg* 2 (1867), 121.
Burg			1303	*Codex diplomaticus Brandenburgensis*, ed. Adolf Friedrich Riedel, 41 vols. (Berlin, 1838–1869), 1. Abteilung, 8, no. 135.
Aschersleben[e]	1290s		1340	Grote, *Lexicon*, 1:23.
Custody of Leipzig				
Altenburg	1228–1238		1242	Grote, *Lexicon*, 1:10; Jordan of Giano, ch. 71.
Leipzig[f]			(1246?) 1259	*Regesta Thuringiae* (see above, Meiningen), 3, no. 2745.
Zwickau	1231		1267	Gustav Hermann Hasse, *Geschichte der sächsischen Klöster in der Mark Meissen und Oberlausitz* (Gotha, 1888), p. 174; *Regesta Thuringiae*, 4, no. 39.
Cheb (Eger)	1260		1270	Greiderer (see above, n. 13), 3:53–54; *Monumenta Erphesfurtensia* (see above, n. 20), p. 682.
Weissenfels			1286	*Regesta Thuringiae*, 4, no. 2558.

Table VII—*Continued*

Convent	Foundation Date	Alleged Foundation Date	First Definite Reference	Source
Custody of Leipzig				
Hof	1292			*Die Regesten der Bischöfe von Eichstätt*, ed. Franz Heidingsfelder, Veröffentlichungen der Gesellschaft für fränkische Geschichte, VI. Reihe (Erlangen, 1938), no. 1171.
Zeitz[g]		before 1242	1340	Felix Scheerer, *Kirchen und Klöster der Franziskaner und Dominikaner in Thüringen*, Beiträge zur Kunstgeschichte Thüringens, 2 (Jena, 1910), p. 32.
Weida[h]		mid-13th	1340	Ibid., p. 97.
Custody of Meissen				
Oschatz		1228	1240	Patricius Schlager, "Inschriften auf Chorstühlen in mittelalterlichen Franziskanerkirchen," *BGSFHK* 1 (1908), 9; Richard Banasch, *Die Niederlassungen der Minoriten zwischen Weser und Elbe* (Breslau, 1891), p. 39.
Torgau			1243	*UB des Hochstifts Meissen*, ed. E.G. Gersdorf, Codex diplomaticus Saxoniae regiae, Zweiter Haupttheil, 1 (Leipzig, 1864), 1, no. 124.
Freiberg		1233	1249	Banasch, *Niederlassungen*, p. 37; *Epitome Lipsiensis* (see above, n. 6), p. 77.
Meissen		1254	1263	Banasch, *Niederlassungen*, p. 43; *UB Meissen*, 1, no. 194.

Table VII–*Continued*

Convent	Founda- tion Date	Alleged Founda- tion Date	First Definite Reference	Source
Custody of Meissen				
Dresden			1265	*Continuatio Saxonica* (see above, n. 5), p. 63.
Seusslitz	1268		1288	Banasch, *Niederlassungen*, p. 49; *Regesta Thuringiae*, 4, no. 2902.
Cottbus[i]	1307		(1266?) 1340	
Custody of Stettin				
Stettin (Szczecin)	1240			*Pommersches UB* (see above, Greifswald), 1, no. 371.
Prenzlau			1253	*Annales et notae Colbaziensis*, ed. Wilhelm Arndt (Hanover, 1866), MGH SS 19:716.
Pyritz (Pyrzyce)			1281	*Regesten der Markgrafen von Brandenburg aus Askanischem Hause*, ed. Hermann Krabbo and Georg Winter, Veröffentlichungen des Vereins für Geschichte der Mark Brandenburg 1 (Leipzig and Berlin, 1910–1955), no. 1271.
Neubrandenburg			1285	*Continuatio Saxonica*, p. 64.
Greifenberg (Gryfice)	1264		1289	Grote, *Lexicon* (see above, Lübeck), 1:190; Hoogeweg, *Stifte Pommern* (see above, Greifswald), 1:584.
Angermünde		before 1292	1299	Grote, *Lexicon*, 1:18; *Continuatio Saxonica*, p. 65.
Arnswalde (Choszczno)			1338	*Codex Brandenburgensis* (see above, Burg), 1. Abteilung, 18, no. 16.
Dramburg[j] (Drawsko)			1340	

Table VII–*Continued*

Convent	Foundation Date	Alleged Foundation Date	First Definite Reference	Source
Custody of Brandenburg				
Berlin		before 1249	1252	Gerhard Bronisch, "Die Franziskaner-Kloster-Kirche in Berlin," *Mitteilungen des Vereins für die Geschichte Berlins* 50 (1933), 141; *Epitome Lipsiensis*, p. 77.
Salzwedel			1261	*Epitome Lipsiensis*, p. 77.
Stendal			1264	*Continuatio Saxonica*, p. 63.
Brandenburg		before 1237	1271	*Codex Brandenburgensis*, 1. Abteilung, 10:41; *Continuatio Saxonica*, p. 63.
Gransee		ca. 1270	1302	Grote, *Lexicon*, 1:189; *Regesten Brandenburg*, no. 1843.
Frankfurt an der Oder		before 1270	1303	Grote, *Lexicon*, 1:154; *Codex Brandenburgensis*, 1. Abteilung, 8, no. 135.
Kyritz			1303	*Codex Brandenburgensis*, 1. Abteilung, 8, no. 135.
Custody of Goldberg				
Görlitz		1234	1245	*Regesten Brandenburg*, no. 627; *UB der Kustodien Goldberg und Breslau*, ed. Chrysogonus Reisch, Monumenta Germaniae Franciscanae, 2. Abteilung, 1 (Düsseldorf, 1917), 1, no. 3.
Bautzen		1240	1248	*Regesten Brandenburg*, no. 667; *UB Goldberg*, 1, no. 4.
Goldberg[k] (Złotoryja)			(1242?) 1258	*UB Goldberg*, 1, no. 26.
Crossen (Krosno Odrzanskie)			1272	Ibid., no. 43.

Table VII—*Continued*

Convent	Foundation Date	Alleged Foundation Date	First Definite Reference	Source
Custody of Goldberg				
Lauban (Lubań)	1273			Ibid., no. 44.
Zittau		1244	1283	*Regesten zur schlesischen Geschichte*, ed. Colmar Grünhagen, 3 vols., Codex diplomaticus Silesiae, 7 (Breslau, 1875–1886), 1:240; *UB Goldberg*, 1, no. 54.
Liegnitz (Legnica)			1284	*UB Goldberg*, 1, no. 66.
Sagan (Żagań)	1284			Ibid., no. 68.
Löwenberg (Lwówek Slaski)		1248	1285	*Regesten zur schlesischen Geschichte*, 1:297–298; *UB Goldberg*, 1, no. 72.
Löbau	1336			*UB Goldberg*, 1, no. 153.
Sorau[1] (Żary)			1340	
Custody of Breslau				
Breslau (Wrocław)		1236	1241	Wadding (see above, n. 10), 2:422; *Chronicon Polono-Silesiacum*, ed. Wilhelm Arndt (Hanover, 1866), MGH SS 19:568.
Schweidnitz (Świdnica)			1249	*UB Goldberg*, 1, no. 6.
Neisse (Nisa)		1257	1284	Greiderer (see above, n. 13), 1:820; *UB Goldberg*, 1, no. 66.
Brieg (Brzeg)			1285	*UB Goldberg*, 1, no. 69.
Namslau (Namysłów)			1285	Ibid.

Table VII—*Continued*

Convent	Foundation Date	Alleged Foundation Date	First Definite Reference	Source
Custody of Breslau				
Strehlen[m] (Strzelin)		1296	1307	Greiderer, 1:847; *UB Goldberg*, 1, no. 117.
Münsterberg[m] (Ziębice)			1307	*UB Goldberg*, 1, no. 117.
Neumarkt[m] (Środa Śląska)			1318	Ibid., no. 129.
Custody of Prussia				
Thorn (Toruń)	1239			*Annales Minorum Prussicorum*, ed. Ernst Strehlke (Leipzig, 1874), Scriptores rerum Prussicarum 5:648.
Culm (Chełmno)	1258			Ibid.
Neuenburg (Nowe)	1282			Ibid.
Braunsberg (Braniewo)	1296			Ibid.

a. The list of convents in Table VII is derived from Schlager, "Verzeichnis" (see above, n. 1).

b. The friars moved from Gotha to Arnstadt in 1250. Jordan of Giano, ch. 42; and *Monumenta Erphesfurtensia*, p. 766.

c. According to the fifteenth-century *Chronicon Holtzatiae auctore presbytero Bremensis dioecesis a. 1172–1428*, ed. Johann Martin Lappenberg (Hanover, 1869), MGH SS 21:266, Count Adolph IV of Holstein entered in 1239 the Franciscan convent in Hamburg, which he had founded in 1227. The thirteenth-century Franciscan chronicler, Albert of Stade, who is the ultimate source of this information, merely states, however, that Count Adolph joined the Hamburg Franciscans; he does not mention that Adolph founded the Hamburg house.

d. According to the *Chronicon Holtzatiae*, Count Adolph IV of Holstein died in 1261 in the convent of Kiel, which he had founded before his entry into the order in 1239. Bartholomew of Pisa, *De conformitate* (see above, n. 1), p. 549, also indicates that Adolph was buried in Kiel. The death date of 1261 appears to be accurate. See *Codex diplomaticus historiae comitum Schauenburgensium*, ed. F.A. von Aspern (Hamburg, 1850), 2, no. 118. The convent is mentioned in a 1271 document. *Kieler Stadtbuch aus den Jahren 1264–1289*, ed. Paul Hasse (Kiel, 1875), no. 91.

Notes-*Continued*

e. The convent is mentioned for the first time in a document in 1377. *UB des Hochstifts Halberstadt und seiner Bischöfe*, ed. Gustav Schmidt, PPrStA 40 (Leipzig, 1889) 4, no. 2886.

f. The *Epitome Lipsiensis* (see above, n. 6), p. 77, states that the 1246 provincial chapter was held in Leipzig. A fifteenth-century inscription in the Franciscan church in Oschatz, which was copied in the eighteenth century, states, however, that the 1246 chapter was celebrated in Oschatz. Patricius Schlager, "Inschriften auf Chorstühlen in mittelalterlichen Franziskanerkirchen," *BGSFHK* 1 (1908), 9. There is no way, as far as I can tell, to reconcile the discrepancy. The convent is mentioned in the 1259 document cited above.

g. I could find no other reference to the convent prior to 1400.

h. The convent was the site of the 1345 Saxon provincial chapter. *Continuatio Saxonica* (see above, n. 5), p. 67. It is mentioned for the first time in a document in 1350. *UB der Vögte von Weida, Gera und Plauen*, ed. Berthold Schmidt, *Thüringische Geschichtsquellen*, NF 2 (Jena, 1885), 1, no. 921.

i. While the *Epitome Lipsiensis*, p. 78, states that the 1266 provincial chapter met in Cottbus, the *Continuatio Saxonica*, p. 63, states that the chapter met in Görlitz. There is no way, as far as I can tell, to reconcile the discrepancy. Grote, *Lexicon* (see above, Lübeck), 1:97, states that the house was founded in 1307. The convent is mentioned for the first time in a document in 1350. *Codex Brandenburgensis* (see above, Burg), 2. Abteilung, 2, no. 933.

j. The convent is mentioned for the first time in a document in 1385. Hoogeweg, *Stifte Pommern*, 1:454.

k. Greiderer (see above, n. 13), 1:840, states that St. Hedwig founded the friary in Goldberg in 1219 or 1220 and several other Silesian houses in the 1220s and that the convent in Goldberg was the site of the 1242 Bohemian provincial chapter. Since Jordan of Giano, ch. 55, indicates that the Franciscans only settled in Poland in the 1230s, Greiderer's early foundation dates are clearly erroneous. It is of course possible that the Bohemian provincial chapter met in Goldberg in 1242. The house is first mentioned in the 1258 document cited above.

l. I could find no other reference to the convent prior to 1400.

m. Since the convents in Münsterberg, Neumarkt, Sorau, and Strehlen were not mentioned in the protracted dispute between Bishop Thomas II of Breslau and Duke Henry IV of Silesia in the 1280s, in which the Franciscans were deeply involved (see above, pp. 75–77), it seems highly unlikely that these Silesian houses were founded before 1290.

TABLE VIII[a]
FRANCISCANS
PROVINCE OF COLOGNE

Convent	Foundation Date	Alleged Foundation Date	First Definite Reference	Source
Custody of Trier				
Trier	1222–1225			*Gesta Treverorum* (see above, n. 26), pp. 399–400.
Koblenz		1233	1236	Bürvenich (see above, n. 11), p. 19; *Mittelrheinische Regesten*, ed. Adam Goerz (Koblenz, 1879), 2, no. 2233.
Andernach		1234?	1246	Bürvenich, p. 22; Franz Jacobi, *Das Franziskanerkloster zu Andernach* (Münster, 1936), p. 117, no. 1.
Oberwesel		1242	1246	Franz Jansen, "Verzeichnis von Klöstern des Franziskanerordens in der Rheinprovinz," *FS* 13 (1926), 25; *UB zur Geschichte der jetzt die preussischen Regierungsbezirke Coblenz und Trier bildenden mittelrheinischen Territorien*, ed. Leopold Eltester and Adam Goerz (Koblenz, 1874), 3, no. 854.
Limburg an der Lahn		1234	1251	Bürvenich, p. 22; *Quellen zur Geschichte der Klöster und Stifte im Gebiet der mittleren Lahn*, ed. Wolf Heino Struck, 4 vols., Veröffentlichungen der historischen Kommission für Nassau 12 (Wiesbaden, 1956–1962), 3, no. 819.
Wetzlar			1260	*Mittelrheinische Regesten*, 3 (1881), no. 1649.

Table VIII—*Continued*

Convent	Foundation Date	Alleged Foundation Date	First Definite Reference	Source
Custody of Trier				
Luxembourg	1255–1257		1262	M. de Villermont, "Les Franciscaines dans le Grand Duché de Luxembourg," *Études Franciscaines* 29 (1913), 155–156; *Urkunden- und Quellenbuch zur Geschichte der altluxemburgischen Territorien*, ed. Camillus Wampach (Luxembourg, 1939), 3, no. 396.
Merl an der Mosel	mid-13th		1294	Patricius Schlager, *Beiträge zur Geschichte der kölnischen Franziskaner-Ordensprovinz im Mittelalter* (Cologne, 1904), p. 55; *Quellen zur Geschichte der Stadt Köln*, ed. Leonard Ennen and Gottfried Eckertz (Cologne, 1867), 3, no. 383.
Custody of Hesse				
Marburg[b]	1235			Bürvenich, p. 23; Wilhelm Maurer, "Zum Verständnis der hl. Elisabeth von Thüringen," *ZKiG* 65 (1953/54), 52–54.
Fritzlar		1229	1236	Konrad Eubel, *Geschichte der kölnischen Minoriten-Ordensprovinz*, Veröffentlichungen des historischen Vereins für den Niederrhein 1 (1906), pp. 250–251.
Fulda	1237			Johann Friedrich Schannat, *Diocesis Fuldensis cum annexa sua hierarchia* (Frankfurt, 1727), no. 54; Michael

Table VIII—*Continued*

Convent	Founda-tion Date	Alleged Founda-tion Date	First Definite Reference	Source
Custody of Hesse				
Fulda—*Continued*				Bihl, "Das Gründungsjahr der ersten Niederlassung der Franziskaner in Fulda," *Fuldaer Geschichtsblätter* 4 (1905), 30—32.
Hofgeismar	1229		1238	Schlager, *Kölnische Ordens-provinz*, p. 22; *Die Urkunden des Bistums Paderborn*, ed. Roger Wilmans and Heinrich Finke, Westfälisches Urkunden-Buch 4 (Münster, 1874—1894), 1, no. 277.
Hersfeld	1229		1269	Julius Battes, "Das Vordringen der Franziskaner in Hessen," *FS* 17 (1931), 323—324; and Schannat, *Diocesis Fuldensis*, no. 73.
Grünberg			1285	*UB der Deutschordens-Ballei Hessen*, ed. Arthur Wyss, PPrStA 73 (Leipzig, 1899), 3 no. 1367.
Göttingen	1246		1308	Bürvenich, p. 32; *UB der Stadt Göttingen*, ed. Gustav Schmidt, UBHistVerNSachs 6 (Hanover, 1863), 1, no. 69.
Custody of Cologne				
Cologne	1222			Jordan of Giano (see above, n. 4), ch. 28.
Neuss		1234	1236	Bürvenich, p. 21; *UB für die Geschichte des Niederrheins*, ed. Theodor Josef Lacom-blet (Düsseldorf, 1846), 2, no. 211.

Table VIII–*Continued*

Convent	Founda-tion Date	Alleged Founda-tion Date	First Definite Reference	Source
Custody of Cologne				
Aachen	1234		1246	Bürvenich, p. 21; *Bullarium Franciscanum*, ed. Giovanni Giacinto Sbaraglia (Rome, 1759), 1, no. 204.
Seligenthal	1231		1247	Eubel, *Kölnische Ordens-provinz*, pp. 129–130; *Bullarium Franciscanum*, 1, no. 204.
Duisburg	1265			Egon Verheyen, *Die Minori-tenkirche zu Duisburg*, Duisburger Forschungen, Beiheft 3 (1959), p. 20.
Bonn	1274			Richard Pick, "Zwei Hand-schriften aus dem ehemaligen Minoritenkloster zu Bonn," *AnnHVNiederrh* 43 (1884), 91–92.
Cleves	1285			Schlager, *Kölnische Ordens-provinz*, p. 47.
Roermond	1307			Bürvenich, pp. 50–51.
Custody of Westphalia				
Paderborn			1238	*Urkunden Paderborn*, 1, no. 279.
Soest		1233	1259	Eubel, *Kölnische Ordens-provinz*, p. 175; *Die Urkun-den des kölnischen Westfalens vom Jahre 1200–1300*, West-fälisches Urkunden-Buch 7 (Münster, 1908–1919), no. 1019.
Höxter		1248	1261	Eubel, *Kölnische Ordens-provinz*, p. 269; *Urkunden Paderborn*, 3, no. 865.

Table VIII—*Continued*

Convent	Founda-tion Date	Alleged Founda-tion Date	First Definite Reference	Source
Custody of Westphalia				
Osnabrück			1263	*Die Papsturkunden Westfalens bis zum Jahre 1378*, ed. Heinrich Finke, Westfälisches Urkunden-Buch 5 (Münster, 1888), 1, no. 632.
Münster	1247		1270	Eubel, *Kölnische Ordensprovinz*, p. 166; *Die Urkunden des Bisthums Münster von 1201–1300*, ed. Roger Wilmans, Westfälisches Urkunden-Buch 3 (Münster, 1871), no. 876.
Dortmund	1244		1278	Schlager, *Kölnische Ordensprovinz*, p. 65; *Urkunden des kölnischen Westfalens*, no. 1640.
Herford	1220s		1286	Schlager, *Kölnische Ordensprovinz*, p. 21; *Urkunden Paderborn*, 3, no. 1879.
Custody of Deventer				
Groningen			1253	*Emonis et Menkonis Werumensium Chronica*, ed. L. Weiland (Hanover, 1874), MGH SS 23:545.
Bolsward	1260s		1281	Michael Schoengen, "Die Klöster des ersten Ordens vom hl. Franziskus im Königreich der Niederlande 1229–1926," *FS* 14 (1927), 9.
Harderwijk			1290	*Oorkondenboek van het Sticht Utrecht tot 1301*, ed. F. Ketner (The Hague, 1954), 4, no. 2421.

Table VIII—*Continued*

Convent	Founda- tion Date	Alleged Founda- tion Date	First Definite Reference	Source
Custody of Deventer				
Kampen			1300	Schoengen, "Klöster," 25.
Deventer			1311	Ibid., 12.
Gross-Faldern (Emden)			1323	Schlager, *Kölnische Ordens-provinz*, p. 73.
Custody of Holland				
Middelburg			1242	Schoengen, "Klöster," 34–35.
Utrecht		1240	1244	Ibid., 42; *Oorkondenboek van Holland en Zeeland*, ed. L.Ph.C. van den Bergh (Amsterdam, 1866), 1, no. 403.
Dordrecht			1248	*Regesta imperii*, ed. Julius Ficker and Eduard Winkelmann (Innsbruck, 1881–1892), 5, no. 4899.
's-Hertogenbosch		1229	1263	Francesco Gonzaga, *De origine seraphicae religionis Franciscanae* (Rome, 1587), pp. 765–766; Schoengen, "Klöster," 23.
Zierikzee			1271	*Oorkondenboek Holland*, Supplement, ed. James de Fremery (The Hague, 1901), no. 163.
Custody of Brabant				
Diest		1228	1232	Gonzaga, *De origine*, p. 998; Stallaert, "Inventaire" (see above, n. 14), 173.
Mechelen		1231	1233	Gonzaga, *De origine*, p. 998; *Diplomatum Belgicorum nova collectio sive supplementum*

Table VIII—*Continued*

Convent	Foundation Date	Alleged Foundation Date	First Definite Reference	Source
Custody of Brabant				
Mechelen—*Continued*				*ad opera diplomatica Auberti Miraei*, ed. Joannes Franciscus Foppens (Brussels, 1748), 4:546—547.
Brussels	1228		1241	Wadding (see above, n. 10), 2:211; André Callebaut, "Lettres franciscaines concernant la Belgique et la France au XIIIe–XVe siècles," *AFH* 7 (1914), no. 2.
Louvain	1228		1252	Gonzaga, *De origine*, p. 991; *Regesta imperii*, 5, no. 10346.
St. Truiden	1231		1258	Bürvenich, p. 19; *Gesta abbatum Trudonensium*, ed. Rudolf Koepke (Hanover, 1852), MGH SS 10:401.
Tienen	1226		1264	Wadding, 2:161; Stallaert, "Inventaire," 185.
Maastricht		1234/1240	1265	Wadding, 3:43; Gonzaga, *De origine*, p. 1000; *Cartulaire de l'abbaye cistercienne du Val-Dieu* (XIIe–XIVe siècle), ed. Joseph Ruwet (Brussels, 1955), no. 147.

a. The list of convents in Table VIII is derived from Bartholomew of Pisa, *De conformitate* (see above, n. 1), pp. 548—549.

b. The text of the indulgence discussed by Maurer may be found in an earlier draft of Adam Bürvenich's *Annales*, the *Annales almae provinciae Coloniae ordinis fratrum Minorum regularis observantiae, nunc recollectorum*, p. 9, written in 1658. This manuscript, like the revised draft of 1665, is located in the Universitätsbibliothek in Düsseldorf.

TABLE IX[a]
FRANCISCANS
PROVINCE OF STRASBOURG

Convent	Founda-tion Date	Alleged Founda-tion Date	First Definite Reference	Source
Custody of the Rhine				
Mainz	1222			Jordan of Giano (see above, n. 4), chs. 27 and 28.
Speyer	1222			Ibid.
Worms	1222			Ibid.
Gelnhausen			1248	*UB zur Geschichte der Herren von Hanau*, ed. Heinrich Reimer, PPrStA 48 (Leipzig, 1891), 1, no. 251.
Frankfurt am Main		ca. 1230	1255	Sigfrid Grän, "Frankfurt am Main: Franziskaner-Konventualen," *AFA* 6 (1960), 121; *UB Frankfurt* (see above, n. 15), 1, no. 201.
Heidelberg	1282			Lemmens, "Chronicon" (see above, n. 7), 678.
Kaisers-lautern	1284			Ibid., 679; Franz Xaver Glas-schröder, *Neue Urkunden zur pfälzischen Kirchengeschichte im Mittelalter*, Veröffentlich-ungen der pfälzischen Gesell-schaft zur Förderung der Wissenschaften 14 (Speyer, 1930), no. 248.
Dieburg		1256	1291	Müller (see above, n. 12), p. 56; Valentin Karst, "Die-burg: Franziskaner-Konven-tualen," *AFA* 4 (1958), 180.
Friedberg		1249	1293	Müller, p. 69; *UB der Stadt Friedberg*, ed. Max Foltz, Veröffentlichungen der his-torischen Kommission für Hessen und Waldeck 3 (Mar-burg, 1904), 1, no. 109.

Table IX—*Continued*

Convent	Foundation Date	Alleged Foundation Date	First Definite Reference	Source
Custody of the Rhine				
Oppenheim		1290	1318	Müller, p. 133; *UB der Stadt Worms*, ed. Heinrich Boos (Berlin, 1890), 2, no. 137.
Custody of Alsace				
Strasbourg[b]	1221–1223			Jordan of Giano, chs. 23 and 32.
Wissembourg			1253	Dambacher, "Urkundenarchiv des Klosters Lichtenthal," *ZGORh* 6 (1855), 457.
Colmar		1230s	1278	Michael Bihl, "Chronique étrangère, 1914–20," *AFH* 16 (1923), 270; *Monuments de l'histoire de l'ancien évêché de Bale*, ed. J. Trouillat (Porrentruy, 1854), 2, no. 227.
Rouffach		1250	1280	Müller, p. 168; *UB der Pfarrei Rufach*, ed. Theobald Walter, Beiträge zur Geschichte der Stadt Rufach 1 (Rouffach, 1900), no. 8.
Offenburg	1280			Bader, "Abdruck und Erläuterung verschiedener Urkunden," *ZGORh* 5 (1854), 243.
Breisach	1285			Lemmens, "Chronicon" (see above, n. 7), 679.
Haguenau		1222	1287	Müller, p. 78; *Regesten Strassburg* (see above, n. 16), 2, no. 2226.

Table IX—*Continued*

Convent	Foundation Date	Alleged Foundation Date	First Definite Reference	Source
Custody of Alsace				
Sélestat		1280	1287	Müller, p. 174; *Regesten Strassburg*, 2, no. 2226.
Sarrebourg		1265	1309	Glassberger (see above, n. 9), p. 78; Lemmens, "Chronicon," 681.
Custody of Basel				
Freiburg im Breisgau		1226	1229	Müller, p. 64; *Freiburger UB*, ed. Friedrich Hefele (Freiburg, 1940), 1, no. 44.
Basel		1231	1238	Müller. p. 35; *UB der Stadt Basel*, ed. Rudolf Wackernagel and Rudolf Thommen (Basel, 1890), 1, no. 148.
Bern	1255			*Cronica de Berno*, ed. G. Studer, Die Berner-Chronik des Conrad Justinger (Bern, 1871), p. 295.
Fribourg	1256			Jean Jacques Joho, "La Naissance de trois couvents de frères Mineurs: Berne, Fribourg, Lausanne," *Revue historique vaudoise* 67 (1959), no. 3.
Burgdorf	1280			Lemmens, "Chronicon," 678.
Solothurn	1280			Ibid.
Mulhouse	1285			Ibid., 679.
Thann	1297			Ibid., 680.
Neuenburg		1294	1320	Müller, p. 126; Lemmens, "Chronicon," 684.
Custody of Swabia				
Würzburg	1222			Jordan of Giano, chs. 27 and 28.

Table IX—*Continued*

Convent	Foundation Date	Alleged Foundation Date	First Definite Reference	Source
Custody of Swabia				
Schwäbisch Hall			1236	*Wirtembergisches UB*, 11 vols. (Stuttgart, 1849–1913), 3, no. 878.
Ulm	1229		1239	Felix Faber, *Tractatus de civitate Ulmensi*, ed. Gustav Veesenmeyer, BLVSt 186 (1889), p. 33; *Ulmisches UB*, ed. Friedrich Pressel (Stuttgart, 1873), 1, no. 45.
Esslingen	1237		1255	Müller, p. 60; *Les Registres d'Alexandre IV*, ed. C. Bourel de la Roncière, Joseph de Loye, Pierre de Cenival, and Auguste Coulon, 3 vols. (Paris, 1902–1953), 1, no. 358.
Reutlingen	1259		1273	Müller, p. 164; *Wirtembergisches UB*, 7, no. 2334.
Heilbronn	1272/ 1275		1278	Müller, p. 85; Greiderer (see above, n. 13), 3:160; Glassberger (see above, n. 9), p. 89; *UB der Stadt Heilbronn*, ed. Eugen Knupfer, WürttGQ 5 (Stuttgart, 1904), 1, no. 27.
Pforzheim	1270		1278	Glassberger, p. 571; *Wirtembergisches UB*, 8, no. 2766.
Schwäbisch Gmünd	1221– 1229		1281	Faber, *Tractatus*, p. 33; Greiderer, 3:212; *Wirtembergisches UB*, 8, no. 3079.
Rothenburg	1281			Hermann Hoffmann, "Franziskanerkloster Rothenburg o. d. T.," *BFA* 3 (1957), p. 523, and nos. 1 and 2.
Tübingen	1272		1293	Müller, p. 209; *Wirtembergisches UB*, 10, no. 4408.

Table IX—*Continued*

Convent	Founda- tion Date	Alleged Founda- tion Date	First Definite Reference	Source
Custody of Lake Constance				
Zürich			1240	*UB der Stadt und Landschaft Zürich*, ed. J. Escher and P. Schweizer (Zürich, 1892), 2, no. 534.
Constance	1240		1247	Müller, p. 52; *Les Registres d'Innocent IV*, ed. Elie Berger, 4 vols. (Paris, 1884–1911), 1, no. 3294.
Lindau[c]		1239/ 1240	1253	Sigismund Keck, "Lindau Franziskaner-Konventualen," *BFA* 5 (1961), p. 594, no. 3.
Schaffhausen			1253	Johannes Gatz, "Schaff- hausen: Franziskaner- Konventualenkloster," *AFA* 1 (1956), 128.
Villingen	1267/ 1268			*Fürstenbergisches UB*, ed. Sigmund Riezler (Tübingen, 1877), 1, nos. 459, 464, 465.
Lucerne			1269	"Belege, bezüglich auf die uranfängliche Gründung des Minoriten Klosters in Lucern," *Der Geschichtsfreund: Mit- theilungen des historischen Vereins der fünf Orte Lu- cern, Uri, Schwyz, Unter- walden und Zug* 3 (1846), pp. 170–172, nos. 1 and 2.
Ueberlingen	1267		1271	Konrad Eubel, *Geschichte der oberdeutschen (strass- burger) Minoriten-Provinz* (Würzburg, 1886), p. 212; *Wirtembergisches UB*, 7, no. 2234.
Königs- felden	1308			Lemmens, "Chronicon" (see above, n. 7), 681.

Table IX—*Continued*

Convent	Foundation Date	Alleged Foundation Date	First Definite Reference	Source
Custody of Bavaria				
Augsburg	1221			Jordan of Giano, ch. 22; Karl Haupt, "Augsburg Franziskaner-Konventualen," *BFA* 5 (1961), 344−350.
Regensburg	1221			Jordan of Giano, ch. 24.
Nördlingen			1243	*Die Urkunden der Stadt Nördlingen*, ed. Karl Puchner (Augsburg, 1952), no. 5.
Nuremberg		1224	1245	Glassberger, p. 29; *Nürnberger UB*, Quellen und Forschungen zur Geschichte der Stadt Nürnberg 1 (Nuremberg, 1959), no. 322.
Munich			1257	Johannes Gatz, "Franziskanerkloster St. Jakob am Anger, München," *BFA* 3 (1957), p. 9, no. 1.
Bamberg		1223	1273	Glassberger, p. 29; Vinzenz Mazet, "Das ehemalige Franziskanerkloster Bamberg," *BFA* 1 (1954), 453.
Ingolstadt		ca. 1270	1281	Bernardin Lins, "Geschichte des früheren (oberen) Franziskaner-Klosters in Ingolstadt," *Sammelblatt des historischen Vereins Ingolstadt* 37 (1917), 1−2; and Glassberger, pp. 94−95.
Landshut		1280	1292	Francesco Gonzaga, *De origine seraphicae religionis Franciscanae* (Rome, 1587), p. 715; *Landshuter UB*, ed. Theo Herzog, Bibliothek familiengeschichtlicher Quellen 13 (Neustadt an der Aisch, 1963), no. 156.

Notes

a. The list of convents in Table IX is derived from Bartholomew of Pisa, *De conformitate* (see above, n. 1), pp. 550–551.

b. Jordan of Giano does not specifically state when the Franciscans settled in Strasbourg. He states in ch. 23 that John of Piancarpino and Barnabas visited in 1221 Würzburg, Mainz, Worms, Speyer, Strasbourg, and Cologne, preaching repentance and preparing dwelling places for the friars who were to follow them. Jordan indicates in ch. 28 that Caesar of Speyer had lodged friars by 1222 "in supradictis civitatibus" and in Cologne. The "supradictis civitatibus" are the towns of Würzburg, Mainz, Worms, and Speyer mentioned in ch. 27. Jordan probably just omitted Strasbourg when he added Cologne. Since Jordan mentions in ch. 32 the appointment in 1223 of a custodian of Alsace, it seems highly likely that the friars had settled by 1223 in Strasbourg, the most important city in Alsace.

c. There has been a great deal of confusion about the foundation date of the convent in Lindau. Gerold Meyer von Knonau, "Deutsche Minoriten im Streit zwischen Kaiser und Papst," *HZ* 29 (1873), 242, n. 1, argued that the house was founded in 1239; Adolf Koch, *Die frühesten Niederlassungen der Minoriten im rechtsrheinischen Bayern* (Heidelberg, 1880), pp. 21–24, offered the date 1224; Konrad Eubel, *Geschichte der oberdeutschen (strassburger) Minoriten-Provinz* (Würzburg, 1886), p. 7, maintained that the house had been founded in 1223 or 1224, but admitted that the Lindau sources seemed to indicate a foundation date of 1239; Ludwig Baur, "Die Ausbreitung der Bettelorden in der Diöcese Konstanz," *Freiburger Diöcesan-Archiv*, NF 1 (1900), 12–14, tried to reconcile the dates 1223 and 1239; Albrecht Schäfer, *Die Orden des h. Franz in Württemberg* (Stuttgart, 1910), p. 7, provided the year 1225; and Keck, "Lindau," 554–558, concluded that the Franciscans had settled in Lindau in 1223.

  The confusion has arisen because no one has bothered to trace the story of the convent's foundation to its original source. The fourteenth-century *Chronica XXIV generalium ordinis Minorum*, AF 3 (Quaracchi, 1897), p. 234, states that brothers from Trent came to Lindau during the generalship of Albert of Pisa, i.e., 1239–1240. Glassberger, pp. 35–36, subsequently transferred the story to the year 1224. Wadding (see above, n. 10), 2:104–105, then placed the events in 1223 during Albert of Pisa's brief tenure as minister of Teutonia. Müller, pp. 99–100, followed Wadding, but added the information that the abbess of Lindau gave the friars in 1240 the land on which to build their convent as well as other facts apparently drawn from the convent archives. It seems highly plausible, therefore, that the convent was in fact founded in 1239–1240 as the *Chronica XXIV generalium*, the oldest source to talk about the foundation of the convent, indicates. The first extant documentary reference to the convent is the 1253 document cited above.

TABLE X[a]
FRANCISCANS
PROVINCE OF AUSTRIA

Convent	Foundation Date	Alleged Foundation Date	First Definite Reference	Source
Custody of Vienna				
Vienna		ca. 1230	1247	Friess, "Geschichte" (see above, n. 3), p. 92 and no. 9.
Wiener-Neustadt		1240	1267	Ibid., pp. 97–98 and no. 37.
Hainburg[b]		1240	1276–1277	Ibid., p. 99.
Valtice (Feldsberg)	ca. 1282			Das "Stiftungen-Buch" des Cistercienser-Klosters Zwettl, ed. Johann von Frast, Fontes rerum Austriacarum, Zweite Abtheilung 3 (Vienna, 1851), p. 608.
Zistersdorf[c]			1400	
Custody of Enns				
Linz		1230s	1231–1254	Friess, "Geschichte," pp. 102–103; Joseph Chmel, "Das Formelbuch K. Albrechts I.," Archiv für Kunde österreichischer Geschichtsquellen 2 (1849), no. 24.
Enns	1276–1277			Das Baumgartenberger Formelbuch, ed. Hermann Baerwald, Fontes rerum Austriacarum, Zweite Abtheilung 25 (Vienna, 1866), Section D, no. 3.
Wels			1283	UB des Landes ob der Enns (Vienna, 1867), 4, no. 17.
Pulkau	1375			Friess, "Geschichte," no. 81.

Table X—*Continued*

Convent	Foundation Date	Alleged Foundation Date	First Definite Reference	Source
Custody of the Danube				
Stein			1253	*Codex diplomaticus et epistolaris Moraviae*, ed. Anton Boczek (Olmütz, 1841), 3, no. 199.
Laa		1237	1260	Friess, "Geschichte," pp. 98−99; *Codex Moraviae*, 3, no. 290.
Tulln[d]		1226	1276−1277	Friess, "Geschichte," p. 96.
Dürnstein	1306			Ibid., pp. 95−96.
Grein[e]			1400	
Custody of Styria				
Graz			1239	Ibid., pp. 107−108.
Wolfsberg	1242			*Monumenta historica ducatus Carinthiae*, ed. August v. Jaksch (Klagenfurt, 1906), 4, no. 2237.
Judenburg			1257	*UB des Herzogthums Steiermark*, ed. J. v. Zahn (Graz, 1903), 3, no. 221.
Bruck an der Mur		1272−1273	1292	Richard Kurt Donin, *Die Bettelordenskirchen in Österreich: Zur Entwicklungsgeschichte der österreichischen Gotik* (Baden bei Wien, 1935), pp. 40−41; Bidermann, "Styriaca aus dem Pestarchiv zu Innsbruck," *Beiträge zur Kunde steiermärkischer Geschichtsquellen* 3 (1866), 105.

Table X—*Continued*

Convent	Foundation Date	Alleged Foundation Date	First Definite Reference	Source
Custody of Villach				
Bolzano[f] (Bozen)	1221?		1237	*Die südtiroler Notariats-Imbreviaturen des dreizehnten Jahrhunderts*, ed. Hans v. Voltelini, Acta Tirolensia 2 (Innsbruck, 1899), 1, no. 680.
Bressanone[f] (Brixen)	1221?		1245	*Die Urkunden zur Geschichte des deutschen Etschlandes und des Vintschgaus*, ed. Franz Huter, Tiroler UB, 1. Abteilung (Innsbruck, 1957), 3, no. 1197.
Villach		1246	1252	Friess, "Geschichte," p. 113; Gottlieb Freiherr von Ankershofen, "Urkunden-Regesten zur Geschichte Kärntens," *Archiv für Kunde österreichischer Geschichtsquellen* 32 (1865), no. 1178.
Custody of Carniola				
Ljubljana (Laibach)		1233	1242	Guido Rant, *Die Franziskaner der österreichischen Provinz: Ihr Wirken in Nieder-Österreich, Steiermark und Krain bis zum Verfalle der Kustodie Krain und ihrer Klöster (1596)* (Stein in Krain, 1908), p. 57 and p. 85, no. 1.
Maribor (Marburg)			1250	Friess, "Geschichte," p. 111.
Ptuj (Pettau)		1239	1324	Ibid., pp. 109–110; Herrgott, *Taphographia* (see above, n. 3), 2, no. 12.
Celje (Cilli)		1241	1324	Friess, "Geschichte," pp. 110–111; Herrgott, *Taphographia*, 2, no. 12.

Table X—*Continued*

Notes

a. The list of convents in Table X is derived from Bartholomew of Pisa, *De conformitate* (see above, n. 1), pp. 552–553.
b. The first definite reference to the convent in Hainburg only occurs in 1291. *Ottokars österreichische Reimchronik*, ed. Joseph Seemüller, MGH, Scriptorum qui vernacula lingua usi sunt, Deutsche Chroniken, 5, Part 1 (Hanover, 1890), lines 43880–43899. Abbot Frederick of Garsten rebuked the Franciscans in 1276 or 1277, however, for establishing a new house in Enns. He complained that the Franciscans already had at least seven convents in the diocese of Passau and consequently needed no additional house. *Das Baumgartenberger Formelbuch*, ed. Hermann Baerwald, Fontes rerum Austriacarum, Zweite Abtheilung 25 (Vienna, 1866), Section D, no. 3. Hainburg appears to have been one of the seven convents to which the abbot referred. The other six were: Vienna, Wiener-Neustadt, Linz, Stein, Laa, and Tulln.
c. Friess, "Geschichte," pp. 100–101, could find no other evidence for the existence of a convent in Zistersdorf. Since the house is not mentioned in the 1324 will of Countess Gutta of Oettingen, the daughter of King Albrecht I, who left bequests to each of the mendicant houses in the Habsburg domains (Marquard Herrgott, *Taphographia principum Austriae*, Monumenta aug. domus Austriacae 4 [Vienna, 1772], 2, no. 12), it appears likely that the convent, if it existed at all, was only founded after 1324.
d. The convent in Tulln is mentioned for the first time in the 1324 will of Countess Gutta. It seems likely, however, that the house had been founded by 1276–1277. See footnote b.
e. Friess, "Geschichte," pp. 106–107, could find no other evidence for the existence of a convent in Grein. Since the house is not mentioned in the will of Countess Gutta, it appears likely that the convent, if it existed at all, was only founded after 1324.
f. Jordan of Giano (see above, n. 4), ch. 21, indicates that the bishop of Trent received the friars in Bolzano and gave them permission to preach in his diocese before they continued on their journey to Germany in 1221. The Franciscans had a similar reception in Bressanone. It is not clear from Jordan's account whether any of the friars stayed behind in either Bolzano or Bressanone to establish permanent convents.

THE FRIARS AND GERMAN SOCIETY

TABLE XI^a
DOMINICANS
PROVINCE OF SAXONY

Convent	Date of Reception
Magdeburg	1224
Bremen	1225
Lübeck	1229
Erfurt	1229
Leipzig	1229
Halberstadt	1232
Hildesheim	1233
Utrecht	1232
Freiberg	1236
Minden	1236
Eisenach	1236
Hamburg	1240
Soest	1241
Riga	1244
Leeuwarden	1245
Neuruppin	1246
Stralsund	1251
Strausberg	1254
Seehausen in der Altmark	1255
Rostock	1256
Norden	1264
Plauen	1266
Halle	1271
Prenzlau	1275
Soldin (Myślibórz	1275
Zierikzee	1279
Winsum	1280
Warburg	1282
Nordhausen	1286
Jena	1286
Röbel	1287
Brandenburg	1287
Treysa	1287
Zutphen	1288
Mühlhausen	1291
Marburg	1292
Luckau	1291
Wesel	1292
Wismar	1293

TABLE XI–*Continued*

Convent	Date of Reception
Göttingen	1296
Osnabrück	1296
Haarlem	1296
Nijmegen	1296
Cheb (Eger)	1296
Dorpat (Tartu)	1300
Berlin	1297
Pirna	1300

[a]The list of convents in Table XI is derived from Loë, *Saxonia* (see above, n. 21), pp. 11–12.

TABLE XII[a]
DOMINICANS
PROVINCE OF TEUTONIA

Convent	Foundation Date	Reception Date	Interpolated Reception Date	First Definite Reference	Source
Friesach	Before 1221				Raymond–J. Loenertz, "La Vie de S. Hyacinthe du lecteur Stanislas, envisagée comme source historique," *AFP* 27 (1957), 22–25 and 31.
Cologne	1221				See above, pp. 81–82.
Strasbourg	1224				*Ellenhardi Argentinensis annales*, ed. Philipp Jaffé (Hanover, 1861), MGH 17:101.
Trier[b]	By 1225				*Gesta Treverorum* (see above, n. 26), pp. 399–400.
Vienna[c]	1225?		1225– 1227	1239	Sebastian Brunner, *Der Prediger-Orden in Wien und Oesterreich* (Vienna, 1867), p. 85; *Quellen Wien* (see above, n. 25), II. Abtheilung, 1, no. 2.
Würzburg		1227?		1231	Meyer, *Chronica* (see above, n. 24), p. 29; *Monumenta episcopatus Wirziburgensis*, Monumenta Boica 45 (Munich 1890), no. 39.

Table XII—*Continued*

Convent	Foundation Date	Reception Date	Interpolated Reception Date	First Definite Reference	Source
Worms	1226	1227?			*Annales Wormatienses* (see above, n. 27), p. 38; Meyer, *Chronica*, p. 29.
Regensburg	1229	1230?			*Codex chronologico-diplomaticus episcopatus Ratisbonensis*, ed. Thomas Ried (Regensburg, 1816), 1, no. 374; Meyer, *Chronica*, p. 29.
Zürich		1230?		1231	Meyer, *Chronica*, p. 29; *UB der Stadt und Landschaft Zürich*, ed. J. Escher and P. Schweizer (Zürich, 1890), 1, no. 466.
Louvain	1228?	1230?		1233	Bernaert de Jonghe, *Belgium Dominicanum* (Brussels, 1719), pp. 126–131; Meyer, *Chronica*, p. 29.
Ptuj (Pettau)	1230–1231				*UB des Herzogthums Steiermark*, ed. J. v. Zahn (Graz, 1879), 2, no. 271; *Salzburger UB*, ed. Willibald Hauthaler and Franz Martin (Salzburg, 1918), 3, no. 865.

Table XII—*Continued*

Convent	Foundation Date	Reception Date	Interpolated Reception Date	First Definite Reference	Source
Koblenz		1230?		1236	Meyer, *Chronica*, p. 29; *Mittelrheinische Regesten*, ed. Adam Goerz (Koblenz, 1879), 2, no. 2233.
Esslingen		1230?		1233	Meyer, *Chronica*, p. 29; *UB der Stadt Esslingen*, ed. Adolf Diehl and K.H.S. Pfaff, *WürttGQ* 4 (Stuttgart, 1899), 1, no. 33.
Constance		1235			*Monumenta Erphesfurtensia* (see above, n. 20), p. 656.
Basel	1233	1233?			*UB der Stadt Basel*, ed. Rudolf Wackernagel and Rudolf Thommen (Basel, 1890), 1, no. 127; Meyer, *Chronica*, p. 29.
Krems	1236?		1236	1246	Brunner, *Prediger-Orden* (see above, Vienna), p. 55; Constantin Höfler, "Albert von Beham und Regesten Papst Innocenz IV.," *BLVSt* 16 (1847), no. 15.
Freiburg im Breisgau	1233	1235?			*Freiburger UB*, ed. Friedrich Hefele (Freiburg, 1940), 1, no. 49; Meyer, *Chronica*, p. 29.

Table XII—*Continued*

Convent	Foundation Date	Reception Date	Interpolated Reception Date	First Definite Reference	Source
Frankfurt am Main	1233?		1235–1243	1243	Heinrich Hubert Koch, *Das Dominikanerkloster zu Frankfurt am Main* (Freiburg im B., 1892), pp. 24–25; *UB Frankfurt* (see above, n. 15), 1, no. 133.
Augsburg[d]	1225?		1235–1244	1241	Polykarp M. Siemer, *Geschichte des Dominikanerklosters Sankt Magdaléna in Augsburg*, QFGDD 33 (1936), pp. 25–29 and p. 26, n. 8.
Antwerp	1243	1244?			Jonghe, *Belgium Dominicanum* (see above, Louvain), pp. 200–201.
Mainz	1257				*Regesten zur Geschichte der mainzer Erzbischöfe*, ed. Johann Friedrich Böhmer and Cornelius Will (Innsbruck, 1886), 2, XXXV, no. 199.
Speyer	1260–1261				Franz Xaver Remling, *Urkundliche Geschichte der ehemaligen Klöster im jetzigen Rheinbayern*, 2nd ed., Pfälzische Bibliothek, ed., Ph. J. Scholler, 2 (Munich, 1913),

Table XII—*Continued*

Convent	Foundation Date	Reception Date	Interpolated Reception Date	First Definite Reference	Source
Speyer—*Continued*					no. 77; *Acta capitulorum generalium ordinis Praedicatorum*, ed. Benedictus Maria Reichert, MOPH 3 (Rome, 1898), 1:112.
Maastricht	1261				*Acta capitulorum generalium*, 1:111–112.
Rottweil		1266			*Monumenta Erphesfurtensia* (see above, n. 20), p. 690.
Bern	1269	1269?			Heinrich Finke, *Ungedruckte Dominikanerbriefe des 13. Jahrhunderts* (Paderborn, 1891), nos. 28, 29, and 31; *Fontes rerum Bernensium* (Bern, 1877), 2, no. 667; *Cronica de Berno*, ed. G. Studer, Die Berner-Chronik des Conrad Justinger (Bern, 1871), p. 296; Meyer, *Chronica*, p. 41.
Wimpfen		1269?		1275	Meyer, *Chronica*, p. 41; *Wirtembergisches UB*, 11 vols. (Stuttgart, 1849–1913), 7, no. 2542.

Table XII—*Continued*

Convent	Foundation Date	Reception Date	Interpolated Reception Date	First Definite Reference	Source
Nuremberg	ca. 1275				Finke, *Dominikan-erbriefe*, nos. 72 and 73; *Nürnberger UB*, Quellen und Forschungen zur Geschichte der Stadt Nürnberg 1 (Nuremberg, 1959), no. 538.
Wiener-Neustadt			1275–1277	1299	*Urkunden der Bene-dictiner-Abtei Unserer Lieben Frau zu den Schotten in Wien*, ed. Ernest Hauswirth, Fontes rerum Austriacarum, Zweite Abtheilung, 18 (Vienna, 1859), no. 81.
Pforzheim[e]			1277–1280	1289	*Wirtembergisches UB*, 10, no. 4531.
Eichstätt	Between 1277 and 1279				*Die Regesten der Bischöfe von Eich-stätt*, ed. Franz Heidingsfelder, Veröffentlichungen der Gesellschaft für fränkische Geschichte, VI. Reihe (Erlangen, 1938), nos. 892a and 919.
Leoben	By 1280				Brunner, *Prediger-Orden* (see above, Vienna), pp. 76–77.

Table XII—*Continued*

Convent	Founda-tion Date	Recep-tion Date	Interpo-lated Reception Date	First Definite Reference	Source
Colmar	1277–1278				*Annales Colmarienses minores*, ed. Philipp Jaffé (Hanover, 1861), MGH SS 17:192; *Annales Colmarienses maiores*, ed. Philipp Jaffé (Hanover, 1861), 17:203; *Monuments de l'histoire de l'ancien évêché de Bale*, ed. J. Trouillat (Porrentruy, 1854), 2, no. 227.
Tulln	1280				Otto Biack and Anton Kerschbaumer, *Geschichte der Stadt Tulln* (Tulln, 1966), p. 454.
Chur	1277	1280?			O. Vasella, *Geschichte des Predigerklosters St. Nicolai in Chur*, DHIHFP 1 (Paris, 1931), Appendix 1, no. 1; Meyer, *Chronica*, p. 40.
Landshut			early 1280s	1289	Finke, *Dominikanerbriefe*, no. 115.
Ulm			early 1280s	1281	*Ulmisches UB*, ed. Friedrich Pressel (Stuttgart, 1873), 1, no. 142.

Table XII—*Continued*

Convent	Foundation Date	Reception Date	Interpolated Reception Date	First Definite Reference	Source
Zofingen	1286				*Die Urkunden des Stiftsarchivs Zofingen*, ed. Georg Boner, Aargauer Urkunden 10 (Aarau, 1945), nos. 21 and 22.
Wissembourg	1288				*Annales Colmarienses maiores*, p. 215; Finke, *Dominikanerbriefe*, no. 133.
Haguenau	1288–1289				*UB der Stadt Strassburg*, ed. Wilhelm Wiegand (Strasbourg, 1886), 2, no. 154; and Finke, *Dominikanerbriefe*, nos. 107, 122, and 131.
Mergentheim	1289				Finke, *Dominikanerbriefe*, no. 143.
Luxembourg	1292–1293				*Urkunden- und Quellenbuch zur Geschichte der altluxemburgischen Territorien*, ed. Camillus Wampach (Luxembourg, 1948), 5, no. 450; *Acta capitulorum generalium*, 1:270.
Schwäbisch Gmünd			1293–1294	1294	*UB Esslingen* (see above, Esslingen), 1, no. 265.

Table XII—*Continued*

Convent	Foundation Date	Reception Date	Interpolated Reception Date	First Definite Reference	Source
Sélestat[f]	1288–1289	1294?			*UB Strassburg*, 2 no. 154; Finke, *Dominikanerbriefe*, nos. 107, 122, and 161; Meyer, *Chronica*, p. 47, n. 19.
Guebwiller	1294	1295?			*Annales Colmarienses maiores*, p. 220; Meyer, *Chronica*, p. 48.
Aachen	1294				*Regesten der Reichsstadt Aachen*, ed. Wilhelm Mummenhoff, PGRhGk 47 (Bonn, 1961), 1, no. 521.
Retz			1295–1301	1295?	Karl Lind, "Die Dominikanerkirche zu Retz," *Berichte und Mitteilungen des Altertums-Vereines zu Wien* 19 (1880), 105.
's-Hertogenbosch[g]		1296?		1301	Bernaert de Jonghe, *Desolata Batavia Dominicana* (Ghent, 1717), pp. 89–90.

a. The list of convents in Table XII is derived from Loë, *Teutonia* (see above, n. 23), p. 7.
b. The chronicler states that the friars arrived in Trier between the election of Henry (VII) in 1220 and the murder of Archbishop Engelbert of Cologne in November 1225.
c. Gregory IX addressed in 1232 a letter to the prior and friars in Austria. MGH Epis. saec. XIII, ed. Carolus Rodenberg, 3 vols. (Berlin, 1883–1894), 1, no. 482. The pope was presumably referring to the house in Vienna, the only Dominican convent located within the duchy in the early 1230s.

Notes—*Continued*

d. The eighteenth-century archivist of the Dominican convent, Antonius Pez, reported that he saw a 1225 document which referred to the Augsburg Dominicans. Siemer, pp. 25–29. Siemer, p. 26, n. 8, indicates that this now lost document has also been ascribed to the years 1255 and 1295. If Pez's information is in fact correct, it would be difficult to explain why more than a decade passed before the house in Augsburg was formally received.

e. There were by 1277 fifty-three Dominican priories in the undivided province of Teutonia. Jacques Quétif and Jacques Echard, *Scriptores ordinis Praedicatorum*, 2 vols. (Paris, 1719–1721), 1:1. Twenty-five of these convents were situated, as Table XI indicates, in the fourteenth-century province of Saxony. The other twenty-eight houses must have belonged to the fourteenth-century province of Teutonia. Since Pforzheim is the twenty-ninth convent on the list, it must have been received after the 1277 general chapter.

f. The long delay between the foundation and the reception of the priory in Sélestat can be attributed to the fact that the convent was originally intended to be only a temporary residence for the exiled Strasbourg Dominicans. See above, pp. 42–43.

g. I could find no reference to the convent in 's-Hertogenbosch before 1301.

TABLE XIII
DOMINICANS
GERMAN CONVENTS IN POLAND

Convent	Foundation Date	Alleged Foundation Date	First Definite Reference	Source
Breslau (Wrocław)	1226			*Regesten zur schlesischen Geschichte*, ed. Colmar Grünhagen, 3 vols., Codex diplomaticus Silesiae 7 (Breslau, 1875–1886), 1, no. 309.
Brieg[a] (Brzeg)			1285?	
Bunzlau (Bolesławiec)		1234	1272	Ibid., 1:203 and 2, no. 1413.
Cammin (Kamień Pomorski)	1228			*Pommersches UB*, ed. Robert Klempin (Stettin, 1868), 1, no. 253.
Crossen[a] (Krosno Odrzanskie)			1285?	
Culm (Chełmno)	1233–1238			Werner Roth, *Die Dominikaner u. Franziskaner im Deutsch-Ordensland Preussen bis zum Jahre 1466* (Königsberg, 1918), pp. 61–64.
Danzig (Gdańsk)	1227			*Preussisches UB*, ed. R. Philippi and August Seraphim (Königsberg, 1882–1909), 1, 1. Abteilung, no. 58.
Dirschau (Tczew)	1289			Ibid., 2. Abteilung, no. 537.
Elbing (Elbląg)	1238			*Codex diplomaticus Warmiensis oder Regesten und Urkunden zur Geschichte Ermlands*, ed. Carl Peter Woelky and Johann Martin Saage, Monumenta historiae Warmiensis, 1. Abtheilung, 1 (Mainz, 1860), 1, Diplomata, no. 1.

Table XIII—*Continued*

Convent	Foundation Date	Alleged Foundation Date	First Definite Reference	Source
Greifswald	1254			H. Hoogeweg, *Die Stifte und Klöster der Provinz Pommern*, 2 vols. (Stettin, 1924–1925), 1:620.
Liegnitz (Legnica)			1278	*Annales Lubenses*, ed. Wilhelm Arndt (Hanover, 1866), MGH SS 19:549.
Oels[a] (Oleśnica)			1285?	
Pasewalk	1272			Hoogeweg, *Stifte Pommern*, 2:229.
Schweidnitz (Świdnica)		1291	1300	*Regesten zur schlesischen Geschichte*, 3:157 and 3, no. 2580.
Stolp (Słupsk)	1278			*Pommersches UB*, ed. Rodgero Prümers (Stettin, 1881), 2, no. 1126.
Thorn (Toruń)	1263			*Preussisches UB*, 1, 2. Abteilung, no. 197.

a. There were eventually eleven Dominican priories in Silesia: Breslau, Brieg, Bunzlau, Crossen, Glogau, Liegnitz, Oels, Oppeln, Ratibor, Schweidnitz, and Teschen. Jacques Quétif and Jacques Echard, *Scriptores ordinis Praedicatorum*, 2 vols. (Paris, 1719–1721), l:xi. A letter of Bishop Thomas II of Breslau indicates that there were by 1285 eight Dominican priories in the diocese of Breslau. *Regesten zur schlesischen Geschichte*, 3, no. 1889. We possess definite information that five of these Silesian houses had been founded before 1285: Breslau, Bunzlau, Glogau (ibid., 2, no. 992), Liegnitz, and Ratibor (ibid., 1, no. 646a). The three houses which were apparently founded after 1285 were: Oppeln (ibid., 1:279), Schweidnitz, and Teschen (ibid., 2:192). The three other Dominican priories in the diocese of Breslau in 1285 were, therefore, Brieg, Crossen, and Oels. The houses in Breslau, Brieg, Bunzlau, Crossen, Liegnitz, Oels, and Schweidnitz would have been considered German under the Franciscan provincial structure.

Appendix II
Individual Friars

This appendix contains the names of the friars whose social origins were analyzed in Table VI in Chapter Four. The friars have been listed according to the social or occupational categories to which they were assigned in Table VI. Where the information is available, this appendix gives the name of the friar, the date he was first mentioned, his official position within the order, the convent to which he belonged, the social status or prior ecclesiastical office of the friar, and the source of the information. An asterisk before a friar's name indicates an individual whose social origin is definitely known. I do not claim that these lists are complete or that all individuals have been correctly identified.

TABLE XIV
DOMINICANS

Nobles

1*, 2.* The sons of two German counts whom Jordan of Saxony converted in Padua in 1223. Berthold Altaner, *Die Briefe Jordans von Sachsen, des zweiten Dominikanergenerals (1222−37): Text und Untersuchungen,* QFGDD 20 (Leipzig, 1925), no. 20.
3.* Count Eberhard of Leiningen, the nephew of Bishop Henry of Worms, ca. 1226, Worms. *Annales Wormatienses,* ed. Georg Pertz (Hanover, 1861), MGH SS 17:38.
4. Dietrich of Regenstein, 1231, Halberstadt, count. *UB der Stadt Halberstadt,* ed. Gustav Schmidt, GQProvSachs 7 (Halle, 1878), 1, no. 27 and index, pp. 497−498. At least two other members of the family joined the mendicant orders. Count Henry of Regenstein referred in 1289 to his brother Ulrich, a Dominican. Ibid., no. 228. A Count Otto of Regenstein was the Franciscan minister provincial of Saxony (1279−1282). *Continuatio Saxonica,* ed. H. Boehmer (Paris, 1908), Collection d'études et de documents sur l'historie religieuse et littéraire du moyen âge 6:63−64. See below, Table XV, no. 15.

5.* Walter of Meissenburg, 1235, prior of Trier, noble. See above, p. 116.
6.* Count Albert of Flankenberg (Blankenburg?), sometime between 1222 and 1237. Thomas of Cantimpré, *Bonum universale de apibus*, ed. Georgius Colvenerius (Douai, 1627), 2.28.11.
7.* Dietrich, the maternal uncle of Count Albert of Flankenberg, who was an archdeacon in Paris. Ibid., 2.28.12.
8.* Count Elger of Hohnstein, 1239–1242, prior of Eisenach, *UB der erfurter Stifte und Klöster*, ed. Alfred Overmann, GQProvSachs, Neue Reihe 5 (Magdeburg, 1926), 1, nos. 259 and 267. In the late fourteenth century Elger's life became the subject of the *Legenda de sanctis patribus conventus Ysenacensis ordinis Praedicatorum*, published by A.L.J. Michelsen, "Legendarium des Dominikanerklosters zu Eisenach," *Z des Vereins für thüringische Geschichte und Altertumskunde* 4 (1861), 361–394. This legend formed the basis of Ludwig Koch's biography, *Graf Elger von Hohnstein: Der Begründer des Dominikanerordens in Thüringen* (Gotha, 1865). Oswald Holder-Egger, "Studien zu thüringische Geschichtsquellen," *Neues Archiv* 20 (1895), 373–421 and 25 (1900), 81–127, demonstrated that the *Legenda* had no value as a historical source.
9.* Conrad of Rastede, former Benedictine abbot and a relative of Archbishop Gerhard of Bremen, before September 1241, Bremen, noble. See above, pp. 116–117.
10.* Walter of Trauchberg, former abbot of Saint Gall, 1244, Constance, noble. *Regesta episcoporum Constantiensum*, ed. Paul Ladewig and Theodor Müller (Innsbruck, 1895), 1, no. 1607 and index, pp. 380 and 389.
11.* Henry of Montfort, bishop of Chur (1252–1272). See above, p. 131.
12.* Otto of Hoya, 1252–1270, Minden, count. *Die Urkunden des Bisthums Minden vom J. 1201–1300*, ed. H. Hoogeweg, Westfälisches Urkunden-Buch 6 (Münster, 1898), nos. 578, 821, 827, 828, 868, 874, 957, and 964. He was not, however, as Jacques Quétif and Jacques Echard, *Scriptores ordinis Praedicatorum*, 2 vols. (Paris, 1719–1721), 1:26, believed, the same person as the Dominican, Bishop Otto of Minden (1267–1270) (see above, p. 132), since Otto of Hoya witnessed a charter of Bishop Otto. *Urkunden Minden*, no. 964.
13.* Count Helger, before 1261, prior of Friesach, Thomas of Cantimpré, *Bonum universale* (see above, no. 6), 2.1.21.
14. Lutold of Regensberg, 1259–1276, Zürich, *Freiherr*. *UB der Stadt und Landschaft Zürich*, ed. J. Escher and P. Schweizer (Zürich, 1895), 3, nos. 1081 and 1166.
15. Berthold of Dassel, 1262, Hildesheim, count. *UB des Hochstifts Hildesheim und seiner Bischöfe*, ed. H. Hoogeweg, QDGNSachs 11 (Hanover, 1903), 3, no. 32 and index, p. 386.
16. Frederick of Esbeke, 1264, Magdeburg, noble. *Regesta archiepiscopatus Magdeburgensis*, ed. Georg Adalbert v. Mülverstedt (Magdeburg, 1881), 2, nos. 1272, 1422–1425, and 1602.

17.* Henry of Hoya, 1265, Minden. *Urkunden Minden* (See above, no. 12), no. 827. See above, no. 12.
18. Conrad of Deggenhausen, 1266, Zürich, *Freiherr*. *UB Zürich* (see above, no. 14), 4 (1896–1898), no. 1323 and index, p. 359.
19. Berthold of Wiesensteig, 1268, Esslingen, noble. *UB der Stadt Esslingen*, ed. Adolf Diehl and K.H.S. Pfaff, *WürttGQ* 4 (Stuttgart, 1899), 1, no. 100 and index, p. 730.
20. Burchard of Eschbach, 1270, *socius* of prior of Freiburg im B., noble. *Freiburger UB*, ed. Friedrich Hefele (Freiburg im B., 1940), 1, nos. 51 and 232.
21.* Count Wolf of Veringen, 1271. *Wirtembergisches UB*, 11 vols. (Stuttgart, 1849–1913), 7, no. 2219.
22. Manigold of Gundelfingen, 1271, noble. Ibid., 3, no. 588 and 7, no. 2240.
23. Dietrich of Kirchberg, 1273, count. Heinrich Finke, *Ungedruckte Dominikanerbriefe des 13. Jahrhunderts* (Paderborn, 1891), no. 61; and *Regesta diplomatica necnon epistolaria historiae Thuringiae*, ed. Otto Dobenecker (Jena, 1939), 4, index, p. 442.

Ministerials

24. Jordan of Saxony, master general (1222–1237), Dassel ministerial. See above, p. 123, n. 47.
25. St. Albertus Magnus, Cologne lector (1248–1254 and 1257–1260), provincial prior (1254–1257), and bishop of Regensburg (1260–1262), Hohenstaufen ministerial in Lauingen. See above, p. 132, n. 92.
26. Henry, brother of Albertus Magnus, 1278, prior of Würzburg. Gabriel M. Löhr, *Beiträge zur Geschichte des kölner Dominikanerklosters im Mittelalter*, QFGDD 15–17 (Leipzig, 1920–1922), 2, no. 58.
27. Frederick of Winnistede, 1231, Halberstadt, Halberstadt ministerial. *UB Halberstadt* (see above, no. 4), 1, nos. 27 and 54.
28. Henry of Westhofen (d. 1252), ca. 1233, first prior of Basel, Alsatian ministerial. See above, p. 123, n. 46.
29. Conrad Tacprot, 1237, Würzburg, Würzburg ministerial. *Urkundenregesten zur Geschichte des Zisterzienserinnenklosters Himmelspforten (1231–1400) (Regesta Herbipolensia IV.)*, ed. Hermann Hoffmann, Quellen und Forschungen zur Geschichte des Bistums und Hochstifts Würzburg 14 (Würzburg, 1962), no. 6; and Johanna Reimann, "Die Ministerialen des Hochstifts Würzburg, in sozial-, rechts- und verfassungsgeschichtliche Sicht," *MfJb* 16 (1964), 231.
30. Conrad of Alvensleben, 1240, Halberstadt, Halberstadt ministerial. *UB Halberstadt* (see above, no. 4), 1, nos. 19 and 42.
31.* Dietrich of Salza, 1242, Erfurt, imperial ministerial. *UB der erfurter Stifte* (see above, no. 8), 1, no. 267; and Karl Bosl, *Die Reichsministerialität der Salier und Staufer*, MGH Schriften 10 (Stuttgart, 1950–1951), pp. 184, 546, 554, and 560–563.

228   THE FRIARS AND GERMAN SOCIETY

32. Hermann Fahner, 1246, chamberlain of the landgraves of Thuringia. *Regesta Thuringiae* (see above, no. 23), 3 (1925), 3, nos. 1270 and 2473 and index, p. 604.

33. H. of Winterthur, 1246, Zürich, Kyburg ministerial. *UB Zürich* (see above, no. 14), 2 (1892), no. 642 and index, p. 423. While H. may only have come from Winterthur, this charter concerned the Dominican nunnery of Töss, which had been founded by the Kyburgs.

34.* Henry of Velturns, 1247, Bressanone ministerial. *Die Urkunden zur Geschichte des deutschen Etschlandes und des Vintschgaus*, ed. Franz Huter, Tiroler UB, 1. Abteilung (Innsbruck, 1957), 3, nos. 955, 1046, 1071, 1212, and 1220.

35.* Henry of Weida, 1248, by 1256 prior of Erfurt, imperial ministerial. *Regesta Thuringiae* (see above, no. 23), 3 (1925), no. 1621; *UB der erfurter Stifte* (see above, no. 8), 1, no. 326; and Bosl, *Reichsministerialität* (see above, no. 31), pp. 528—537.

36.* Frederick of Haguenau, former provost of the Strasbourg cathedral chapter, 1251, Strasbourg. Ch. Wittmer, "L'Obituaire des Dominicains de Strasbourg (1238—1478)," *AFP* 20 (1950), 422. The necrology states that he joined the Dominicans in 1251 and died on March 16, 1251. He was, however, still provost after March 26, 1251. *Regesten der Bischöfe von Strassburg*, ed. Alfred Hessel and Manfred Krebs (Innsbruck, 1928), 2, no. 1359. Frederick was the uncle of Henry of Stahleck, an imperial ministerial, who was bishop of Strasbourg (1245—1260). Ibid., no. 1148; and Bosl, *Reichsministerialität* (see above, no. 31), pp. 320 and 339.

37.* John of Löwenthal, 1257, imperial ministerial. *Wirtembergisches UB* (see above, no. 21), 4, no. 1074, and 5, nos. 1446 and 1449; and Bosl, *Reichsministerialität*, pp. 413—415.

38. John of Hergheim, 1257, subprior of Basel, advocate of Hergheim, Basel ministerial(?). *UB der Stadt Basel*, ed. Rudolf Wackernagel and Rudolf Thommen (Basel, 1890), 1, nos. 225 and 329.

39. Henry of Stekbaron, 1258, Constance, Reichenau ministerial. *UB Zürich* (see above, no. 14), 3, no. 1036, and index, p. 398.

40.* Colo of Lembach, 1259, ministerial of St. Paul's. *UB des Herzogthums Steiermark*, ed. J. v. Zahn (Graz, 1879—1903), 2, no. 112, and 3, no. 283.

41. John of Ravensburg, 1259, imperial ministerial. *Wirtembergisches UB*, 4, no. 1159, and 5, nos. 1518 and 1531; and Bosl, *Reichsministerialität*, pp. 412—417.

42.* Chamberlain of Beatrice of Bohemia, the wife of Margrave Otto III of Brandenburg, after April 1259, Strausberg. *Chronica principum Saxoniae ampliata*, ed. Oswald Holder-Egger (Hanover, 1896), MGH SS 30:34.

43. Henry of Galgennen, 1260, Zürich, Rapperswil ministerial. *UB Zürich*, 3, no. 1132, and index, p. 373.

44, 45. Bernhard and Albert of Staufen, 1260, Esslingen, imperial ministerials. *Wirtembergisches UB*, 5, no. 1571; and Bosl, *Reichsministerialität*, pp. 366—367.

46. Gerhard of Huldenberg, 1261, former prior of Louvain, Brabantine ministerial. *Inventaire des chartes et cartulaires des duchés de Brabant et de Limbourg et des pays d'Outre-Meuse*, ed. Alphonse Verkooren (Brussels, 1910), 1, no. 78; and Paul Bonenfant and G. Despy, "La Noblesse en Brabant aux XIIe et XIIIe siècles: Quelques sondages," *Le Moyen âge* 64 (1958), 50, n. 74.

47. Henry of Herten, 1261, conversus of the Dominican nunnery of Töss, Kyburg ministerial. *UB Zürich*, 3, no. 1158 and index, p. 377. Euphemia of Herten had been an early benefactress of Töss. Hieronymus Wilms, *Das älteste Verzeichnis der deutschen Dominikanerinnenklöster*, QFGDD 24 (Leipzig, 1928), p. 38.

48. Dietrich of Apolda, 1263—1268, Erfurt, butler of the archbishop of Mainz, *Regesta Thuringiae* (see above, no. 23), 3 (1925), no. 3127 and index, p. 580, and 4, no. 232. See below, Table XV, no. 25.

49. Dietrich of Boizenburg, 1265, Hamburg, Hamburg ministerial. *Hamburgisches UB*, ed. Johann Martin Lappenberg (Hamburg, 1842), 1, no. 685 and index, p. 849.

50. Rudolph of Embrach, 1266, Zürich, ministerial of the canons of Sts. Peter and Paul, *UB Zürich*, 4 (1896—1898), no. 1323 and index, p. 361.

51.* Henry of Bigenburg, 1270, imperial chamberlain. *Wirtembergisches UB* (see above, no. 21), 7, no. 2163.

52. Henry of Jerichow, 1271, Magdeburg, steward of the archbishop of Magdeburg. *Regesta Magdeburgensis* (see above, no. 16), 3 (1886), no. 45, and index, p. 158.

53*, 54.* Frederick and Marquard of Nordenberg, 1272, Würzburg, Würzburg ministerials. *Urkundenregesten zur Geschichte der Stadt Würzburg (1201—1401) (Regesta Herbipolensia I.)*, ed. Wilhelm Engel, Quellen und Forschungen zur Geschichte des Bistums und Hochstifts Würzburg 5 (Würzburg, 1952), no. 37; and Reimann, "Ministerialen" (see above, no. 29), 176.

Knights

55.* Henry of Marsberg (d. 1254) joined the Dominicans in about 1220 and became provinical prior of the Holy Land in 1228. Thomas of Cantimpré, *Bonum universale* (see above, no. 6), 2.43.4; Gerard of Frachet, *Vitae fratrum ordinis Praedicatorum*, ed. Benedictus Maria Reichert (Louvain, 1896), MOPH 1:183; and Heribert Christian Scheeben, *Beiträge zur Geschichte Jordans von Sachsen*, QFGDD 35 (Leipzig, 1938), pp. 166—168.

56.* Thomas of Cantimpré, the author of the *Bonum universale de apibus*, joined the Dominicans in 1232 in Louvain and became the lector and subprior of the convent. He was the son of a knight who had accompanied Richard the Lion-Hearted to the Holy Land. Élie Berger, *Thomae Cantipratensis Bonum universale de apibus* (Paris, 1895), pp. 2—6; and Alexander Kaufmann, *Thomas von Chantimpré*, Görres Gesellschaft zur Pflege der Wissenschaften im katholischen Deutschland (Cologne, 1899), pp. 8—14.

57. Louis of Berge, 1238, Trier, knight. *Mittelrheinische Regesten*, ed. Adam Goerz (Koblenz, 1881), 3, nos. 63, 74, and 1072.

58. John of Metrich, 1253, Koblenz, knight. Ibid., nos. 1022, 1026, 1027, and 1085.

59. Frederick of Olvenstede, 1255, lector of Magdeburg, knight, perhaps Magdeburg burgher family. *Regesta Magdeburgensis* (see above, no. 16), 2, nos. 1379, 1514, and 1653.

60. Achilles of Alswilre, 1255–1265, prior of Basel, knight. *UB Basel* (see above, no. 38), 1, nos. 191, 286, and 462. See below, no. 65.

61. Henry of Vetzzenburg, 1257, Frankfurt am Main, knight, *UB der Reichsstadt Frankfurt: Codex diplomaticus Moenofrancofurtanus*, ed. Johann Friedrich Boehmer and Friedrich Lau (Frankfurt, 1901), 1, nos. 215 and 578.

62. Albert Güsse, 1257, Augsburg, knight. *Die Urkunden des Hochstifts Augsburg 769–1420*, ed. Walter E. Vock, Schwäbische Forschungsgemeinschaft bei der Kommission für bayerische Landesgeschichte Reihe 2a, 7 (Augsburg, 1959), nos. 71 and 104.

63. Frederick of Parsberg, 1260, Nuremberg, knight. *Nürnberger UB*, Quellen und Forschungen zur Geschichte der Stadt Nürnberg 1 (Nuremberg, 1959), nos. 386 and 453.

64. John Sapiens, 1265, prior of Minden, knight(?). *Urkunden Minden* (see above, no. 12), nos. 821, 823, and 831.

65. Henry of Alswilre, 1265, Basel, knight. *UB Basel* (see above, no. 38), 1, nos. 191 and 462. See above, no. 60.

66.* Werner Feist, 1265–1273, conversus of Klingental, knight. Ibid., 1, no. 462, and 2 (1893), no. 125.

67.* Dietrich of Hekelingen, former dean of Our Lady in Halberstadt, 1266, Halberstadt, knight. *UB des Hochstifts Halberstadt und seiner Bischöfe*, ed. Gustav Schmidt, PPrStA 21 (Leipzig, 1884), 2, no. 1145 and index, p. 642.

68.* Otto, bishop of Minden (1267–1270). See above, p. 132.

69. William of Alblais, 1272, prior of Utrecht, knight. *Oorkondenboek van Holland en Zeeland*, ed. L.Ph.C. van den Bergh (Amsterdam, 1873), 2, nos. 231 and 405.

70. Gerhard of Gispersleben, 1273, Erfurt, knight. *Regesta Thuringiae* (see above, no. 23), 3 (1925), no. 961, and 4, nos. 909 and 1207.

71. Günther of Wiegeleben, 1273, Erfurt, knight. Ibid., 3, no. 2535 and 4, no. 909.

Patricians

72.* Hugo Ripelin, author of the *Compendium theologicae veritatis*, prior of Zürich between 1232 and 1259, Strasbourg patrician. See above, p. 115.

73. Henry of Basel, 1239, Zürich, Zürich patrician. *UB Zürich* (see above, no. 14), 2 (1892), no. 526 and index, p. 387.

74. Conrad of Aachen, 1239, Zürich, Strasbourg patrician. Ibid., 2, nos. 526 and 539, and 3, no. 990.

75. Albert of Bardowick, 1245, Lübeck, Lübeck patrician. *UB der Stadt Lübeck*, Codex diplomaticus Lubecensis, 1ste Abtheilung (Lübeck, 1843), 1, no. 104 and index, p. 721.

76. Albert of Bolle (Böller, Boller?), 1257, Basel, Basel patrician. *UB Basel* (see above, no. 38), 1, no. 327, and 2 (1893), index, p. 427.

77.* Otto Maness, former provost of the *Grossmünster* in Zürich, 1259—1271, Zürich, Zürich patrician. *UB Zürich*, 3, no. 1129 and index, pp. 384—385.

78. Rudolph of Oerlikon, 1262, Zürich, Zürich patrician. Ibid., no. 1171 and index, p. 388.

79. William Kloton, 1262, conversus of Oetenbach, Kyburg ministerial and Zürich patrician family. Ibid., no. 1175 and index, p. 381.

80. Hildebrand Merz, 1262, conversus of Oetenbach, Zürich patrician. Ibid., no. 1175 and index, p. 386.

81. William Brosma, 1262, conversus of Oetenbach, Zürich patrician. Ibid., no. 1175 and index, p. 365.

82. Conrad of Prato (Preco?), 1270, Soest, Soest patrician. *Die Urkunden des kölnischen Westfalens vom J. 1200—1300*, Westfälisches Urkunden-Buch 7 (Münster, 1908—1919), no. 1373 and index, p. 1540.

83. Rudolph of Vegersheim, 1270, Strasbourg, Strasbourg patrician. *UB der Stadt Strassburg*, ed. Aloys Schulte (Strasbourg, 1884), 3, no. 33 and pp. 412—413.

Burghers

84.* Dietrich, the son of Volmar and Odilia, 1230/31, Cologne, Cologne burgher. Löhr, *Dominikanerkloster* (see above, no. 26), 2, nos. 6 and 16. Dietrich inherited one-fourth of a house and lot and one-fourth of a shop. His brother mended old cloth.

85. Gilbert Anglicus, 1236, Cologne, Cologne burgher. Ibid., no. 14. A Dietrich Anglicus owned a house between 1227 and 1241. Hermann Keussen, *Topographie der Stadt Köln im Mittelalter*, 2 vols. (Bonn, 1910), 1:306, b, 9 and 307, a, 1, 2. A Walter Anglicus owned a house in 1235. Ibid., 2:24, b, b. Before 1246 three brothers named Anglicus sold a lot. Ibid., 2:185, a, c. Finally, a 1267 document refers to a Walter Anglicus, a goldsmith. Ibid., 1:211, b, 13.

86.* Hegelbert, 1247/48, Cologne, Cologne burgher. Löhr, *Dominikanerkloster*, 2, no. 18. He founded a Beguinage for twelve Beguines in a house he owned.

87.* Herman of Petra, the son of Conrad and Petra, 1255, Cologne, Cologne burgher. Ibid., 2, no. 30. He inherited one-sixth of two apartments (*mansio*), one-fifth of a house and its lot, and one-sixth of another house and lot.

88.* Rudolph of Rheinfelden, 1255, Basel?, Basel, Colmar, or Rheinfelden burgher?, *UB Basel* (see above, no. 38), 1, no. 286. The Dominican nunnery in Colmar, Unterlinden, sold property which had belonged to his daughter for twenty marks.

89. Albert Schalle, 1256, Cologne, Cologne burgher. Löhr, *Dominikanerkloster*, 2, no. 30a; and Keussen, *Topographie*, 2:451. The Schalles owned several pieces of property in the city and may have been stone masons.

90.* Wedekind, son of Eilburgis, 1259, Magdeburg, Magdeburg burgher. *Regesta Magdeburgensis* (see above, no. 16), 2, no. 1460. The document refers to the house in which Eilburgis lived. She did not own the land.

Prelates

91.* Henry of Cologne, a canon in Utrecht, joined the Dominicans on February 12, 1220, while he was a student in Paris. He was the prior of Cologne from 1221/22 to 1229. Jordan of Saxony, *Libellus de principiis ord. Praedicatorum*, ed. Heribert Chr. Scheeben, MOPH 16 (Rome, 1935), chs. 67–81. See Josef Kleinermanns, *Der selige Heinrich: Stifter des Dominicanerklosters in Köln* (Cologne, 1900); and Scheeben, *Beiträge* (see above, no. 55), pp. 157–166.

92*, 93.* A canonist who had been a canon in Speyer and rector of the German students in Vercelli and a German master named Gottschalk, a canon in Utrecht, whom Jordan of Saxony converted in Vercelli in 1229. Altaner, *Briefe* (see above, no. 1), no. 49.

94.* Werner, 1231, canon of St. Maurice in Zofingen. *UB Basel* (see above, no. 38), 1, no. 118.

95.* Henry, 1236, former provost of the canons of Osterhofen. *Monumenta Reichersbergensia*, Monumenta Boica 4 (Munich, 1765), 2, Diplomatarium miscellum, pp. 445–446, no. 42.

96.* Kuno, 1237, former provost of the Austin canons of Reichersperg. *Magni presbyteri annales Reicherspergenses*, ed. W. Wattenbach (Hanover, 1861), MGH SS 17:528.

97.* Frederick, 1239, by 1257 prior of Esslingen, former abbot of the monastery of Zwiefalten, which belonged to the congregation of Hirsau. *Annales Zwifaltenses*, ed. Otto Abel (Hanover, 1852), MGH SS 10:59; and *UB Esslingen* (see above, no. 19), 1, no. 75.

98.* Nicholas, 1245, Lübeck, former scholastic of Lübeck. *UB Lübeck* (see above, no. 75), 1, no. 104.

99.* Name unknown, 1249, Augsburg, former scholastic of Augsburg. MGH Epis. saec. XIII, ed. Carolus Rodenberg, 3 vols. (Berlin, 1883–1894), 2, no. 703.

100.* Ulrich of Dellmensingen, died 1252, Strasbourg, precentor and scholastic of Strasbourg (1219–1242) and provost of St. Peter's. Wittmer, "L'Obituaire" (see above, no. 36), 422; and *Regesten Strassburg* (see above, no. 36), 2, no. 845.

101.* Gerhard, 1260, Lübeck, former canon of Ratzeburg. *Meklenburgisches UB* (Schwerin, 1864), 2, no. 859.

102.* Master Solomon, before 1261, Cologne. Thomas of Cantimpré, *Bonum universale* (see above, no. 6), 2.1.20. Thomas described Solomon as an outstanding preacher who had possessed many benefices. Solomon was the name of a Würzburg canon who had served as a crusade preacher in the 1220s. MGH Epis. saec. XIII, 1, no. 244.

TABLE XV
FRANCISCANS

Nobles

1.* Count Bernhard of Poppenburg, a Hildesheim cathedral canon, 1223, Hildesheim. Jordan of Giano, *Chronica*, ed. H. Boehmer, Collection d'études et de documents sur l'histoire religieuse et littéraire du moyen âge 6 (Paris, 1908), ch. 35.
2.* Count Günther of Kevernburg, the nephew of Archbishop Albert of Magdeburg (1205–1235), *Cronica Reinhardsbrunnensis*, ed. Oswald Holder-Egger (Hanover, 1896), MGH SS 30:559.
3. Eilbert of Danneberg, 1237, Hamburg or Stade?, count. Albert of Stade, *Annales Stadenses*, ed. Johann Martin Lappenberg (Hanover, 1859), MGH SS 16:367; and *UB Lübeck* (see above, Table XIV, no. 75), 1, no. 26.
4.* Count Adolph IV of Holstein, 1239–1261, Hamburg. See above, p. 114.
5.* Count Henry of Luxembourg, bishop of Zemgale (1247–1251), bishop of Kurland (1251–1263), and bishop of Chiemsee (1263–1274). See above, pp. 131–132.
6.* Dobisław, 1247–1269, Greifswald, vassal of Warcisław III of Pomerania-Demmin. *Pommersches UB*, ed. Robert Klempin (Stettin, 1868), 1, nos. 403 and 457; and *Meklenburgisches UB* (see above, Table XIV, no. 101), 2, no. 1161.
7. John of Diest, bishop of Sambia (1251/52–1254) and bishop of Lübeck (1254–1259). See above, pp. 132–133.
8. Herman of Solmise, 1255, Andernach?, count. *Mittelrheinische Regesten* (see above, Table XIV, no. 57), 3, nos. 1203, 1427, 1449, and 1515.
9.* Leopold Caupone, 1258, Augsburg, count. *Wirtembergisches UB* (see above, Table XIV, no. 21), 5, no. 1503.
10. Henry of Wengen, 1259, Zürich, *Freiherr*. *UB Zürich* (see above, Table XIV, no. 14), 3, no. 1068 and index, p. 403.
11.* Count of Schwalenburg, before 1261. Thomas of Cantimpré, *Bonum universale* (see above, Table XIV, no. 6), 2. 57.18; and *Die Urkunden des Bistums Paderborn vom J. 1201–1300*, ed. Roger Wilmans and Heinrich Finke, Westfälisches Urkunden-Buch 4 (Münster, 1874–1894), 3, no. 1151.
12.* Rorich of Wernersberg, 1262, Trier, noble. *Mittelrheinische Regesten*, 3, nos. 1758, 1760, 1767, 1781, 1834, 1868, 1875–76, 1910, 1912, 1964, 2526, and 2622.

13. Henry of Rotowe, 1263–1272, Meissen, noble. *UB des Hochstifts Meissen*, ed. E.G. Gersdorf, Codex diplomaticus Saxoniae regiae, Zweiter Haupttheil 1 (Leipzig, 1864), 1, nos. 51, 194, 198, and 214.
14.* Count Henry of Brene, chaplain and envoy of Rudolph of Habsburg. See above, p. 132.
15.* Count Otto of Regenstein, guardian of Hildesheim, custodian of Magdeburg, minister provincial of Saxony (1279–1282). *Continuatio Saxonica* (see above, Table XIV, no. 4), pp. 63–64. See above, Table XIV, no. 4.
16.* Count Albert of Anhalt (d. 1289). *Chronica principum Saxoniae*, ed. Oswald Holder-Egger (Hanover, 1880), MGH SS 25:476; and *Chronica principum Saxoniae ampliata* (see above, Table XIV, no. 42), p. 31.

Ministerials

17. Henry of Rosepe, 1246, Cologne ministerial. *Mittelrheinische Regesten* (see above, Table XIV, no. 57), 3, nos. 514 and 775.
18.* John of Hamme, 1249, Hamburg, Holstein ministerial. *Hamburgisches UB* (see above, Table XIV, no. 49), 1, no. 501 and index, p. 581.
19. Peter of Domburg, 1252, guardian of Middelburg, Middelburg ministerial. *Oorkondenboek Holland* (see above, Table XIV, no. 69), 1 (1866), no. 552; and *Oorkondenboek van het Sticht Utrecht tot 1301*, ed. F. Ketner (The Hague, 1954), 4, no. 1806.
20.* Herman Gnifting of Raderach, 1253, imperial ministerial. *Wirtembergisches UB* (see above, Table XIV, no. 21), 5, no. 1268; and Bosl, *Reichsministerialität* (see above, Table XIV, no. 31), pp. 418–420.
21. Conrad of Hohenburg, 1253, guardian of Basel, imperial ministerial. *Wirtembergisches UB*, 5, no. 1268; and Bosl, *Reichsministerialität*, pp. 204 and 207.
22. Conrad of Rusteberg, 1253, Mühlhausen, Mainz ministerial. *Regesta Thuringiae* (see above, Table XIV, no. 23), 3 (1925), no. 2111 and index, p. 648.
23. Hugo of Lindenberg, 1253, Zürich, by 1265 guardian of Schaffhausen, Saint Gall ministerial. *UB Zürich* (see above, Table XIV, no. 14), 2 (1892), no. 860 and index, p. 404; and Johannes Gatz, "Schaffhausen: Franziskaner-Konventualenkloster," *AFA* 1 (1956), 131.
24. Conrad of Winden, 1253, Ulm, imperial ministerial. *Ulmisches UB*, ed. Friedrich Pressel (Stuttgart, 1873), 1, no. 67; and Bosl, *Reichsministerialität*, p. 393.
25. Dietrich of Apolda, 1254, Erfurt, butler of the archbishop of Mainz. *Regesta Thuringiae*, 3, no. 2297 and index, p. 580. See above, Table XIV, no. 48.
26. Henry of Nawe, 1258, Ulm, Dillingen ministerial. *Ulmisches UB*, 1, nos. 80 and 92.
27. Albert of Seefeld, 1261, Vienna, steward of the duke of Austria. *Urkunden der Benedictiner-Abtei Unserer Lieben Frau zu den Schotten in Wien*, ed. Ernest Hauswirth, Fontes rerum Austriacarum, Zweite Abtheilung 18

(Vienna, 1859), no. 39; and G.E. Friess, "Geschichte der oesterreichischen Minoritenprovinz," *Archiv für österreichische Geschichte* 64 (1882), 100.

28. Henry Fink, 1262, 1265, Schaffhausen, ministerial of the counts of Heiligenberg or Zürich knightly family. *UB Zürich*, 3, no. 1197 and index, p. 372; and Gatz, "Schaffhausen" (see above, no. 23), 131.
29. John of Sumolswalt, 1262, 1265, Bern, Kyburg ministerial family. See above, p. 116.
30. Henry of Alsleben, 1268, Mühlhausen or Nordhausen, steward of the archbishop of Magdeburg. *Regesta Thuringiae*, 4, no. 232 and index, p. 431.
31. Albert of Overvecht, 1272, guardian of Utrecht, Utrecht ministerial. *Oorkondenboek Utrecht* (see above, no. 19), 2 (1940), ed. K. Heeringa, no. 1134, and 4, no. 1286.

Knights

32.* A knight converted by John of Piancarpino in Hildesheim in 1223. Jordan of Giano, *Chronica* (see above, no. 1), ch. 35.
33. Gerhard Lutzelkolb, 1233, companion of Conrad of Marburg, knight. See above, p. 144, n. 40.
34, 35. Two knights named Gykow who joined the Franciscans in Hamburg along with Count Adolph IV of Holstein in 1239. *Chronicon Holtzatiae auctore presbytero Bremensis dioecesis a. 1172–1428*, ed. Johann Martin Lappenberg (Hanover, 1869), MGH SS 21:266. Albert of Stade does not mention them.
36. Rudolph of Aftholderberg, 1250, 1265 in Schaffhausen, knight. *Wirtembergisches UB* (see above, Table XIV, no. 21), 3, no. 718 and 4, no. 1147; and Gatz, "Schaffhausen" (see above, no. 23), 131.
37. Henry of Falkenstein, 1250, knight. *Wirtembergisches UB*, 4, nos. 1147 and 1148.
38. Ulrich Laidolph, 1253, Ulm, knight. *Ulmisches UB* (see above, no. 24), 1, nos. 58, 62, and 67.
39. Dietrich of Sparrewald, 1269, Prenzlau, knight. *Codex diplomaticus Brandenburgensis*, ed. Adolf Friedrich Riedel (Berlin, 1861), Erster Haupttheil, 21, nos. 1 and 4.
40*, 41.* Hartung and Hetzel of Zässingen, 1270, lay brothers in Basel, knights (Pfirt ministerials?). *UB Basel* (see above, Table XIV, no. 38), 1, no. 307, and 2 (1893), no. 41.
42. Dietrich Golin, 1271, Basel, knight. Ibid., 2, no. 69 and index, p. 445.
43. John of Hindenburg, 1271, lector of Stettin, knight. *Pommersches UB*, ed. Rodgero Prümers (Stettin, 1881), 2, nos. 926 and 940.
44. Henry of Gierlichoven, 1273, Ulm?. *Wirtembergisches UB*, 7, no. 2296. No. 2296 was also witnessed by a Liuthold of Gierlichoven, but I have been unable to identify the family. As the charter was issued by the abbot of Reichenau, the Gierlichovens may have been Reichenau ministerials.
45.* Burchard of Leiterberg, 1273, knight. *Wirtembergisches UB*, 7, no. 2342.

236   THE FRIARS AND GERMAN SOCIETY

Patricians

46. Berthold of Regensburg, Franciscan preacher, ca. 1240–1272, Regensburg patrician. Berthold's sister was married to a Merchlin Sachs. Karl Rieder, *Das Leben Bertholds von Regensburg* (Freiburg, 1901), p. 42. A Marquart Sachs was a member of the *Rat* of Regensburg in 1278. *Regensburger UB*, ed. J. Widemann, Monumenta Boica 53 (Munich, 1912), 1, no. 117 and index, p. 897.

47.* Conrad Rufus, 1250, Cologne, Cologne patrician. Hans Planitz and Thea Buyken, *Die kölner Schreinsbücher des 13. und 14. Jahrhundert*, PGRhGk 46 (Weimar, 1937), no. 476; and Friedrich Lau, "Das kölner Patriziat bis zum Jahre 1325," *Mitteilungen aus dem Stadtarchiv von Köln* 9 (1894), 370. (Hereafter the entries from the *Schreinsbücher* which were published by Planitz and Buyken will be cited as Planitz, *Schreinsbücher*; other references to the *Schreinsbücher* are to unpublished entries.)*

48. Gerhard, 1250, Cologne. Planitz, *Schreinsbücher*, no. 476. No. 476 indicates that the nieces of Gerhard became Beguines; their mother was called *Domina* Hadewig. Her title suggests that the family may have been of patrician status though the title was also applied to non-patricians in the *Schreinsbücher*.

49. Herman Episcopus, 1261, Zürich, Basel patrician family. *UB Zürich* (see above, no. 14), 3, no. 1148 and index, p. 354.

50.* Albert, son of Reinhard of the Bulze, 1265, Erfurt, Erfurt patrician. *UB der Stadt Erfurt*, ed. Carl Beyer, GQProvSachs 23 (Halle, 1889), 1, nos. 150 and 199.

51.* Henry Acco, 1265, Hildesheim, Hildesheim patrician. *UB des Hochstifts Hildesheim* (see above, Table XIV, no. 15), 2 (1901), no. 1023 and 3, nos. 32 and 93.

Burghers

52.* Hartmann, the son of Hartmann, 1232, Cologne, Cologne burgher. *Schreinsbuch* 299:7a, II, 183. Hartmann inherited half a house and lot. Gabriel M. Löhr, "Die Mendikanten in den kölner Schreinsbücher," *AnnHVNiederrh* 134 (1939), 1–33, indicates where individual Franciscans, Carmelites, and Austin Friars are mentioned in the *Schreinsbücher*.

53.* Richwin, the son of Conrad Clypelschit and Blithildis, 1234, Cologne, Cologne burgher. *Schreinsbuch* 45n:2, 33. He inherited one-fourth of a house.

54.* Conrad, the son of Wolbero, 1234, Cologne, Cologne burgher. Planitz, *Schreinsbücher* (see above, no. 47), no. 273; and Keussen, *Topographie* (see above, Table XIV, no. 85), 2:9, a, 9. Conrad owned several houses and lots on Blaubach which he gave to the Cistercian nunnery of Mariengarten; he stipulated that the convent pay a total annual census of 24 schillings to various beneficiaries.

55.* Emmundus, the son of Elizabeth, the widow of Heidenreich of Sigen, 1235, Cologne, Cologne burgher. *Schreinsbuch* 4471:5, 37–38. He inherited one-sixth of a house on the fish market and one-fourth of a stall situated among the cloth cutters.

56.* Goswin, the son of Goswin of Acu, 1262, Cologne, Cologne burgher. Planitz, *Schreinsbücher*, no. 189. He inherited one-sixth of a house and lot and one-sixth of an annual rent of 10 schillings.

57.* Christian Coppart, ca.1240, Cologne, Cologne burgher. Planitz, *Schreinsbücher*, no. 662. Christian's mother owned four houses. One of Christian's brothers was named Gerhard. A Gerhard Coppart was called a furrier in 1256. Keussen, *Topographie* 1:16, a, k.

58.* Conrad Probus, 1261, lector in Constance, minister of Strasbourg (1271–1279), bishop of Toul (1279–1296), son of a smith in Isny or Tübingen. See above, p. 133.

59.* John, former husband of Mabilia of Berka, 1263, lay brother in Cologne. *Schreinsbuch* 162:10, 178. Mabilia owned half of two apartments.

60.* Henry of Zeitz, 1268, Breslau, Breslau burgher. *Regesten zur schlesischen Geschichte*, ed. Colmar Grünhagen, 3 vols., Codex diplomaticus Silesiae 7 (Breslau, 1875–1886), 2, nos. 1301 and 1408.

61.* Helerus Bulle, ca. 1271, Kiel, Kiel burgher. *Kieler Stadtbuch aus den Jahren 1264–1289*, ed. Paul Hasse (Kiel, 1875), no. 91. He inherited ten marks.

62.* Henry Knoderer, 1273, lector in Mainz, bishop of Basel (1275–1286), archbishop of Mainz (1286–1288), son of a baker or miller in Isny. See above, p. 133.

Prelates

63.* Albert of Stade, 1240–1261/64, Stade, former Benedictine abbot. See above, p. 114.

64.* Walter of Reutlingen, 1247, Constance(?), scholastic of Chur. *Les Registres d'Innocent IV*, ed. Élie Berger (Paris, 1884), 1, no. 3294.

65.* Louis, 1268, Mainz(?), former dean of the cathedral chapter of Mainz and provost of St. Victor's. *Codex diplomaticus Nassoicus: Nassauisches UB*, ed. W. Sauer (Wiesbaden, 1885–1887), 1, Zweiter Theil, no. 781.

66.* Ulrich, 1271, Schwerin, canon of Schwerin. *Meklenburgisches UB* (see above, Table XIV, no. 101), 2, no. 1221.

Bibliography

Unpublished Sources

Cologne, Stadtarchiv
Schreinsbücher 45n, 92, 156, 162, 299, and 447I.
Düsseldorf, Universitätsbibliothek
Bürvenich, Adam. "Annales almae provinciae Coloniae ordinis fratrum Minorum regularis observantiae, nunc recollectorum." 1658.
――――. "Annales seu chronicon almae provinciae Coloniae fratrum Minorum strictae observantiae regularis seu recollectorum." 1665.

Published Primary Sources

Acta capitulorum generalium ordinis Praedicatorum. Ed. Benedictus Maria Reichert. 1. (MOPH, 3.) Rome, 1898.
Acta imperii inedita saeculi XIII et XIV. Ed. Eduard Winkelmann. 1. Aalen, 1964.
Albert of Stade. *Annales Stadenses.* Ed. Johann Martin Lappenberg. (MGH SS 16:271–379.) Hanover, 1859.
Altaner, Berthold, ed. *Die Briefe Jordans von Sachsen, des zweiten Dominikanergenerals (1222–37): Text und Untersuchungen, Zugleich ein Beitrag zur Geschichte der Frömmigkeit im 13. Jahrhundert.* (QFGDD, 20.) Leipzig, 1925).
Ankershofen, Gottlieb Freiherr von. "Urkunden-Regesten zur Geschichte Kärntens." *Archiv für Kunde österreichischer Geschichtsquellen,* 32 (1865), 157–336.
Annales Basileenses. Ed. Philipp Jaffé. (MGH SS 17:193–202.) Hanover, 1861.
Annales Colmarienses maiores. Ed. Philipp Jaffé. (MGH SS 17:202–232.) Hanover, 1861.
Annales Colmarienses minores. Ed. Philipp Jaffé. (MGH SS 17:189–193.) Hanover, 1861.
Annales Colonienses maximi. Ed. Karl Pertz. (MGH SS 17:723–847.) Hanover, 1861.

Annales Cracovienses compilati. Ed. Richard Röpell and Wilhelm Arndt. (MGH SS 19:582–606.) Hanover, 1866.

Annales Egmundani. Ed. Georg Pertz. (MGH SS 16:442–479.) Hanover, 1859.

Annales et notae Colbazienses. Ed. Wilhelm Arndt. (MGH SS 19:710–720.) Hanover, 1866.

Annales Lubenses. Ed. Wilhelm Arndt. (MGH SS 19:548–549.) Hanover, 1866.

Annales Minorum Prussicorum. Ed. Ernst Strehlke. (Scriptores rerum Prussicarum 5:647–648.) Leipzig, 1874.

Annales Sancti Pantaleonis Coloniensis. Ed. Hermann Cardauns. (MGH SS 22: 529–547.) Hanover, 1872.

Annales Wormatienses. Ed. Georg Pertz. (MGH SS 17:34–73.) Hanover, 1861.

Annales Zwifaltenses. Ed. Otto Abel. (MGH SS 10:51–64.) Hanover, 1852.

Bader. "Abdruck und Erläuterung verschiedener Urkunden." *ZGORh*, 5 (1854), 223–255.

Bartholomew of Pisa. *De conformitate vitae beati Francisci ad vitam Domini Iesu.* (AF, 4.) Quaracchi, 1906.

Das Baumgartenberger Formelbuch. Ed. Hermann Baerwald. (Fontes rerum Austriacarum, Zweite Abtheilung, 25.) Vienna, 1866.

"Belege, bezüglich auf die uranfängliche Gründung des Minoriten-Klosters in Lucern." *Der Geschichtsfreund: Mittheilungen des historischen Vereins der fünf Orte Lucern, Uri, Schwyz, Unterwalden und Zug,* 3 (1846), 170–174.

Bellum Walterum. Ed. Philipp Jaffé. (MGH SS 17:105–114.) Hanover, 1861.

Berthold of Regensburg. *Vollständige Ausgabe seiner Predigten mit Anmerkungen und Wörterbuch.* Ed. Franz Pfeiffer and Joseph Strobl. 2 vols. Vienna, 1862–1880. New edition, ed. Kurt Ruh. Berlin, 1965.

Bidermann. "Styriaca aus dem Pestarchiv zu Innsbruck." *Beiträge zur Kunde steiermärkischer Geschichtsquellen,* 3 (1866), 105–108.

Bihl, Michael. "Statuta generalia ordinis edita in capitulis generalibus celebratis Narbonae an. 1260, Assisii an. 1279, atque Parisiis an. 1292. Editio critica et synoptica." *AFH,* 34 (1941), 13–94, 284–358.

Bonaventure, Saint. *Determinationes quaestionum circa regulam fratrum Minorum.* (Opera omnia, 8:337–374.) Quaracchi, 1898.

Braun, Placidus. "Geschichte der Grafen von Dillingen und Kiburg." *Historische Abhandlungen der königlich-baierischen Akademie der Wissenschaften,* 5 (1823), 373–492.

Bremisches UB. Ed. D.R. Ehmck and W. von Bippen. 1. Bremen, 1873.

Bullarium Franciscanum. Ed. Giovanni Giacinto Sbaraglia. 1. Rome, 1759.

Bullarium ordinis FF. Praedicatorum. Ed. Antonino Bremond. 1 and 2. Rome, 1729–1730.

Burchardi et Cuonradi Urspergensium chronicon. Ed. O. Abel and L. Weiland. (MGH SS 23:333–383.) Hanover, 1874.

Caesarius of Heisterbach. *Dialogus miraculorum*. Ed. Josephus Strange. Cologne, 1851. New edition, Ridgewood, New Jersey, 1966.

———. *Vita, passio et miracula S. Engelberti*. Ed. Albert Poncelet. (Acta sanctorum Novembris, 3:641–681.) Brussels, 1910.

Callebaut, André. "Lettres franciscaines concernant la Belgique et la France au XIIIe–XVe siècles." *AFH*, 7 (1914), 247–263.

Cartulaire de l'abbaye cistercienne du Val-Dieu (XIIe–XIVe siècle). Ed. Joseph Ruwet. (Accadémie royale des sciences, des lettres et des beaux-arts de Belgique, Commission royale d'histoire.) Brussels, 1955.

Cartulaire de l'église Saint-Lambert de Liège. Ed. S. Bormans and E. Schoolmeesters. 1. Brussels, 1893.

Catalogi archiepiscoporum Coloniensium. Ed. Hermann Cardauns. (MGH SS 24:332–367.) Hanover, 1879.

Chmel, Joseph. "Das Formelbuch K. Albrechts I." *Archiv für Kunde österreichischer Geschichtsquellen*, 2 (1849), 211–307.

Chronica principum Saxoniae. Ed. Oswald Holder-Egger. (MGH SS 25:472–480.) Hanover, 1880.

Chronica principum Saxoniae ampliata. Ed. Oswald Holder-Egger. (MGH SS 30:27–34.) Hanover, 1896.

Chronica XXIV generalium ordinis Minorum. (AF, 3.) Quaracchi, 1897.

Chronicon Colmariense. Ed. Philipp Jaffé. (MGH SS 17:240–270.) Hanover, 1861.

Chronicon Holtzatiae auctore presbytero Bremensis dioecesis a. 1172–1428. Ed. Johann Martin Lappenberg. (MGH SS 21:251–306.) Hanover, 1869.

Chronicon Montis Sereni. Ed. E. Ehrenfeuchter. (MGH SS 23:130–226.) Hanover, 1874.

Chronicon Polono-Silesiacum. Ed. Wilhelm Arndt. (MGH SS 19:553–570.) Hanover, 1866.

Codex chronologico-diplomaticus episcopatus Ratisbonensis. Ed. Thomas Ried. 1. Regensburg, 1816.

Codex diplomaticus Anhaltinus. Ed. Otto von Heinemann. 2. Dessau, 1875.

Codex diplomaticus Brandenburgensis: Sammlung der Urkunden, Chroniken und sonstigen Quellenschriften für die Geschichte der Mark Brandenburg und ihrer Regenten. Ed. Adolf Friedrich Riedel. 41 vols. Berlin, 1838–1869.

Codex diplomaticus et epistolaris Moraviae. Ed. Anton Boczek. 3. Olmütz, 1841.

Codex diplomaticus et epistolaris regni Bohemiae. Ed. Gustav Friedrich and Zdeněk Kristen. 3, Part 2. Prague, 1962.

Codex diplomaticus historiae comitum Schauenburgensium: Urkundliches Material zur Geschichte und Genealogie der Grafen von Schauenburg. Ed. F.A. von Aspern. 2. Hamburg, 1850.

Codex diplomaticus Nassoicus: Nassauisches UB. Ed. W. Sauer. 1. Wiesbaden, 1885–1887.

242   THE FRIARS AND GERMAN SOCIETY

Codex diplomaticus Warmiensis oder Regesten und Urkunden zur Geschichte Ermlands. Ed. Carl Peter Woelky and Johann Martin Saage. 1. (Monumenta historiae Warmiensis oder Quellensammlung zur Geschichte Ermlands, 1. Abtheilung, 1.) Mainz, 1860.

Codices traditionum ecclesiae Pataviensis, olim Laureacensis. (Monumenta Boica, 28.) Munich, 1829.

Continuatio Saxonica. Ed. Heinrich Boehmer. (Collection d'études et de documents sur l'histoire religieuse et littéraire du moyen âge, 6:63–67.) Paris, 1908.

Continuatio Vindobonense. Ed. Wilhelm Wattenbach. (MGH SS 9:698–722.) Hanover, 1851.

Corpus documentorum Inquisitionis haereticae pravitatis Neerlandicae. Ed. Paul Fredericq. 1. Ghent, 1889.

Cronica de Berno. Ed. G. Studer. (Die Berner-Chronik des Conrad Justinger, 295–301.) Bern, 1871.

Cronica Reinhardsbrunnensis. Ed. Oswald Holder-Egger. (MGH SS 30:490–656.) Hanover, 1896.

Dambacher. "Urkundenarchiv des Klosters Lichtenthal." *ZGORh*, 6 (1855), 440–466.

De rebus Alsaticis ineuntis saeculi XIII. Ed. Philipp Jaffé. (MGH SS 17:232–238.) Hanover, 1861.

Diplomata imperatorum authentica. (Monumenta Boica, 30.) Munich, 1834.

Diplomatum Belgicorum nova collectio sive supplementum ad opera diplomatica Auberti Miraei. Ed. Joannes Franciscus Foppens. 4. Brussels, 1748.

Ellenhardi Argentinensis annales. Ed. Philipp Jaffé. (MGH SS 17:101–104.) Hanover, 1861.

Elsässische Urkunden vornehmlich des 13. Jahrhunderts. Ed. Alfred Hessel. (Schriften der wissenschaftlichen Gesellschaft in Strassburg, 23.) Strasbourg, 1915.

Emonis et Menkonis Werumensium chronica. Ed. L. Weiland. (MGH SS 23:454–572.) Hanover, 1874.

Epistolae saeculi XIII e regestis Pontificum Romanorum. Ed. Carolus Rodenberg. 3 vols. (MGH.) Berlin, 1883–1894.

Epitome Lipsiensis. Ed. Heinrich Boehmer. (Collection d'études et de documents sur l'histoire religieuse et littéraire du moyen âge, 6:76–81.) Paris, 1908.

Faber, Felix. *Tractatus de civitate Ulmensi.* Ed. Gustav Veesenmeyer. (BLVSt, 186.) Tübingen, 1889.

Finke, Heinrich, ed. *Ungedruckte Dominikanerbriefe des 13. Jahrhunderts.* Paderborn, 1891.

Flores temporum auctore fratre ordinis Minorum. Ed. Oswald Holder-Egger. (MGH SS 24:228–250.) Hanover, 1879.

Fontes rerum Bernensium, Bern's Geschichtsquellen. 2. Bern, 1877.

Freiburger UB. Ed. Friedrich Hefele. 1. Freiburg im Breisgau, 1940.

Fürstenbergisches UB. Ed. Sigmund Riezler. 1. Tübingen, 1877.

Gerard of Frachet. *Vitae fratrum ordinis Praedicatorum.* Ed. Benedictus Maria Reichert. (MOPH, 1.) Louvain, 1896.

Gesta abbatum Trudonensium. Ed. Rudolf Koepke. (MGH SS 10:213−448.) Hanover, 1852.

Gesta Treverorum continuata. Ed. G. Waitz. (MGH SS 24:368−488.) Hanover, 1879.

Glasschröder, Franz Xaver, ed. *Neue Urkunden zur pfälzischen Kirchengeschichte im Mittelalter.* (Veröffentlichungen der pfälzischen Gesellschaft zur Förderung der Wissenschaften, 14.) Speyer, 1930.

Haemmerle, Albert, ed. *Das Necrologium des Ordens der Mindern Brüder zu den Barfüssern in Augsburg.* Munich, 1955.

Hagen, Gotfrid. *Dit is dat boich van der stede Colne.* Ed. Hermann Cardauns and K. Schröder. (Chroniken der deutschen Städte, 12.) Leipzig, 1875.

Hamburgisches UB. Ed. Johann Martin Lappenberg. 1. Hamburg, 1842.

Hermanni Altahensis annales. Ed. Philipp Jaffé. (MGH SS 17:381−407.) Hanover, 1861.

Herrgott, Marquard, ed. *Taphographia principum Austriae.* 2. (Monumenta aug. domus Austriacae, 4.) Vienna, 1772.

Hildegard of Bingen. Epistola 48. (PL 197:243−253.) Paris, 1855.

Historia fratrum Praedicatorum in Dania. Ed. G. Waitz. (MGH SS 29:242−243.) Hanover, 1892.

Historia monasterii Rastedensis. Ed. G. Waitz. (MGH SS 25:495−511.) Hanover, 1880.

Höfler, Constantin. "Albert von Beham und Regesten Papst Innocenz IV." *BLVSt*, 16 (1847), 49−158.

——— . "Analecten zur Geschichte Deutschlands und Italiens." *AbhbayAk*, 4 (Munich, 1846), 1−89.

Huillard-Bréholles, J.-L.-A., ed. *Diplomatica Friderici Secundi.* 5 and 6. Paris, 1857−1860.

Huygens, R. B. C., ed. *Lettres de Jacques de Vitry (1160/1170−1240), évêque de Saint-Jean-d'Acre: Edition critique.* Leiden, 1960.

Inventaire des chartes et cartulaires des duchés de Brabant et de Limbourg et des pays d'Outre-Meuse. Ed. Alphonse Verkooren. Brussels, 1910.

James of Vitry. *Vita b. Mariae Ogniacensis.* (Acta sanctorum Junii, 4:630−684.) Antwerp, 1707.

Jordan of Giano. *Chronica.* (AF, 1.) Quaracchi, 1885.

——— . *Chronica fratris Jordani.* Ed. Heinrich Boehmer. (Collection d'études et de documents sur l'histoire religieuse et littéraire du moyen âge, 6.) Paris, 1908. Translated by E. Gurney Salter in *The Coming of the Friars Minor to England and Germany.* London, 1926.

Jordan of Saxony. *Libellus de principiis ord. Praedicatorum.* Ed. Heribert Chr. Scheeben. (MOPH, 16.) Rome, 1935.

Kieler Stadtbuch aus den Jahren 1264−1289. Ed. Paul Hasse. Kiel, 1875.

Landshuter UB. Ed. Theo Herzog. (Bibliothek familiengeschichtlicher Quellen, 13.) Neustadt an der Aisch, 1963.

Lemmens, Leonhard. "Chronicon provinciae Argentinensis O.F.M. circa an. 1310–27 a quondam fratre Minore Basilieae conscriptum (1206–1325)." *AFH*, 4 (1911), 671–687.

_____. "Continuatio et finis Chronicae fratris Jordani de Yano O.F.M." *AFH*, 3 (1910), 47–54.

Liber anniversariorum fratrum Minorum Ratisbonensium. Ed. Ludovicus Baumann. (MGH Necrologia Germaniae, 3:247–260.) Berlin, 1905.

Liv- Esth- und Curländisches UB. Ed. Friedrich Georg von Bunge. 3. Reval, 1857.

Loë, Paulus von. "Das Necrologium des aachener Dominikanerklosters." *Aus Aachens Vorzeit*, 17 (1904), 1–26.

Löhr, Gabriel M., ed. *Beiträge zur Geschichte des kölner Dominikanerklosters im Mittelalter.* 2 vols. (QFGDD, 15–17.) Leipzig, 1920–1922.

_____. "Das Necrologium des Dominikanerinnenklosters St. Gertrud in Köln." *AnnHVNiederrh*, 110 (1927), 60–179.

Magni presbyteri annales Reicherspergenses. Ed. W. Wattenbach. (MGH SS 17:439–534.) Hanover, 1861.

Matthew of Paris. *Chronica maiora.* Ed. F. Liebermann. (MGH SS 28:107–389.) Hanover, 1888.

Meklenburgisches UB. 1 and 2. Schwerin, 1863–1864.

Meyer, Johannes. *Chronica brevis ordinis Praedicatorum.* Ed. Heribert Chr. Scheeben. (QFGDD, 29), Leipzig, 1933.

_____. *Liber de viris illustribus ordinis Praedicatorum.* Ed. Paulus von Loë. (QFGDD, 12.) Leipzig, 1918.

Michelsen, A.L.J. "Legendarium des Dominikanerklosters zu Eisenach." *Z des Vereins für thüringische Geschichte und Altertumskunde*, 4 (1861), 361–394.

Mittelrheinische Regesten oder chronologische Zusammenstellung des Quellen-Materials für die Geschichte der Territorien der beiden Regierungsbezirke Coblenz und Trier. Ed. Adam Goerz. 2 and 3. Koblenz, 1879–1881.

Monumenta episcopatus Wirziburgensis. (Monumenta Boica, 37 and 45.) Munich, 1864–1890.

Monumenta Erphesfurtensia saec. XII. XIII. XIV. Ed. Oswald Holder-Egger. (MGH SRG 41.) Hanover, 1899.

Monumenta historica ducatus Carinthiae. Ed. August von Jaksch. 4. Klagenfurt, 1906.

Monumenta parthenii Altenhohenau. (Monumenta Boica, 17.) Munich, 1806.

Monumenta Reichersbergensia. (Monumenta Boica, 4.) Munich, 1765.

Monuments de l'histoire de l'ancien évêché de Bale. Ed. J. Trouillat. 2. Porrentruy, 1854.

Necrologium patrum Minorum conventualium ad S. Crucem Vindobonae. Ed. Adalbertus Franciscus Fuchs. (MGH Necrologia Germaniae 5:165–196.) Berlin, 1913.

Nürnberger UB. (Quellen und Forschungen zur Geschichte der Stadt Nürnberg, 1.) Nuremberg, 1959.

Oorkondenboek van het Sticht Utrecht tot 1301. Ed. K. Herringa and F. Ketner. 2, 3, and 4. The Hague, 1940−1954.

Oorkondenboek van Holland en Zeeland. Ed. L. Ph. C. van den Bergh. 1 and 2. Amsterdam, 1866−1873. Supplement. Ed. James de Fremery. The Hague, 1901.

Ottokars österreichische Reimchronik. Ed. Joseph Seemüller. (MGH Scriptorum qui vernacula lingua usi sunt, Deutsche Chroniken, 5, 1. Abteilung.) Hanover, 1890.

Palacky, Franz, ed. *Ueber Formelbücher, zunächst in Bezug auf böhmische Geschichte.* Prague, 1842.

Die Papsturkunden Westfalens bis zum Jahre 1378. Ed. Heinrich Finke. (Westfälisches Urkunden-Buch, 5.) Münster, 1888.

Peter Ferrand. *Chronica ordinis.* Ed. Benedictus Maria Reichert. (MOPH, 1:321−338.) Rome, 1897.

─────. *Legenda Sancti Dominici.* Ed. M.−H. Laurent. (MOPH, 16:195−260.) Rome, 1935.

Planitz, Hans and Thea Buyken, eds. *Die kölner Schreinsbücher des 13. und 14. Jahrhundert.* (PGRhGk, 46.) Weimar, 1937.

Pommersches UB. Ed. Robert Klempin and Rodgero Prümers. 1 and 2. Stettin, 1868−1881.

Preussisches UB. Ed. R. Philippi and August Seraphim. 1. Königsberg, 1882−1909.

Quellen zur Geschichte der Klöster und Stifte im Gebiet der mittleren Lahn bis zum Ausgang des Mittelalters. Ed. Wolf Heino Struck. 4 vols. (Veröffentlichungen der historischen Kommission für Nassau, 12.) Wiesbaden, 1956−1962.

Quellen zur Geschichte der Stadt Köln. Ed. Leonard Ennen and Gottfried Eckertz. 2 and 3. Cologne, 1863−1867.

Quellen zur Geschichte der Stadt Wien. I. Abtheilung. Ed. Anton Mayer. 1. Vienna, 1895. II. Abtheilung. Ed. Karl Uhlirz. 1. Vienna, 1898.

Regensburger UB. Ed. J. Widemann. (Monumenta Boica, 53.) Munich, 1912.

Regesta archiepiscopatus Magdeburgensis: Sammlung von Auszügen aus Urkunden und Annalisten zur Geschichte des Erzstifts und Herzogthums Magdeburg. Ed. Georg Adalbert von Mülverstedt. 2 and 3. Magdeburg, 1881−1886.

Regesta diplomatica necnon epistolaria historiae Thuringiae. Ed. Otto Dobenecker. 3 and 4. Jena, 1925−1939.

Regesta episcoporum Constantiensum: Regesten zur Geschichte der Bischöfe von Constanz von Bubulcus bis Thomas Berlower 517−1496. Ed. Paul Ladewig and Theodor Müller. 1. Innsbruck, 1895.

Regesta imperii. Ed. Julius Ficker, Eduard Winkelmann, and Oswald Redlich. 5 and 6. Innsbruck, 1881−1898.

Die Regesten der Bischöfe von Eichstätt. Ed. Franz Heidingsfelder. (Veröffentlichungen der Gesellschaft für fränkische Geschichte, VI. Reihe.) Erlangen, 1938.

Regesten der Bischöfe von Strassburg. Ed. Alfred Hessel and Manfred Krebs. 2. Innsbruck, 1928.

Die Regesten der Erzbischöfe von Köln im Mittelalter. Ed. Richard Knipping. 3. (PGRhGk, 21.) Bonn, 1909–1913.

Regesten der Markgrafen von Brandenburg aus askanischem Hause. Ed. Hermann Krabbo and Georg Winter. (Veröffentlichungen des Vereins für Geschichte der Mark Brandenburg, 1.) Leipzig and Berlin-Dahlem, 1910–1955.

Regesten der Reichsstadt Aachen. Ed. Wilhelm Mummenhoff. 1. (PGRhGk, 47.) Bonn, 1961.

Regesten zur Geschichte der mainzer Erzbischöfe von Bonifatius bis Uriel von Gemmingen 742?–1514. Ed. Johann Friedrich Böhmer and Cornelius Will. 2. Innsbruck, 1886.

Regesten zur schlesischen Geschichte. Ed. Colmar Grünhagen. 3 vols. (Codex diplomaticus Silesiae, 7.) Breslau, 1875–1886.

Les Registres d'Alexandre IV. Ed. C. Bourel de la Roncière, Joseph de Loye, Pierre de Cenival, and Auguste Coulon. 3 vols. Paris, 1902–1953.

Les Registres de Clément IV. Ed. Edouard Jordan. Paris, 1893–1945.

Les Registres de Grégoire IX. Ed. Lucien Auvray. 4 vols. Paris, 1896–1955.

Les Registres de Grégoire X. Ed. Jean Guiraud and E. Cadier. Paris, 1892–1960.

Les Registres d'Innocent IV. Ed. Élie Berger. 4 vols. Paris, 1884–1911.

Registrum epistolarum fratris Johannis Peckham archiepiscopi Cantuariensis. Ed. Charles Trice Martin. 3. (Rerum Britannicarum medii aevi scriptores, 77.) London, 1885.

Richeri gesta Senoniensis ecclesiae. Ed. G. Waitz. (MGH SS 25:249–345.) Hanover, 1880.

Ryccardi de Sancto Germano notarii chronica. No editor. (MGH SS 19:321–386.) Hanover, 1866.

Salimbene de Adam. *Cronica.* Ed. Ferdinando Bernini. 2 vols. (Scrittori d'Italia, 187–188.) Bari, 1942.

Salzburger UB. Ed. Willibald Hauthaler and Franz Martin. 3. Salzburg, 1918.

Schannat, Johann Friedrich. *Diocesis Fuldensis cum annexa sua hierarchia.* Frankfurt am Main, 1727.

Scheeben, Heribert Chr., ed. *Die Konstitutionen des Predigerordens unter Jordan von Sachsen.* (QFGDD, 38.) Leipzig, 1939.

Siemer, Laurentius. "*Liber obituum et anniversariorum* der Predigerbrüder in Osnabrück." *Archiv der deutschen Dominikaner,* 1 (1937), 15–95.

Stallaert, Ch. "Inventaire analytique des chartes concernant les seigneurs et la ville de Diest." *Compte rendu des séances de la Commission royale d'histoire,* 4th series, 3 (1876), 165–314.

Das "Stiftungen-Buch" des Cistercienser-Klosters Zwettl. Ed. Johann von Frast. (Fontes rerum Austriacarum, Zweite Abtheilung, 3.) Vienna, 1851.

Die südtiroler Notariats-Imbreviaturen des dreizehnten Jahrhunderts. Ed. Hans von Voltelini. 1. (Acta Tirolensia: Urkundliche Quellen zur Geschichte Tirols, 2.) Innsbruck, 1899.

Thomas of Cantimpré. *Bonum universale de apibus.* Ed Georgius Colvenerius. Douai, 1627.

Thomas of Eccleston. *Tractatus fr. Thomae vulgo dicti de Eccleston De adventu fratrum Minorum in Angliam.* Ed. Andrew G. Little. (Collection d'études et de documents sur l'histoire religieuse et littéraire du moyen âge, 7.) Paris, 1909.

Ulmisches UB. Ed. Friedrich Pressel. 1. Stuttgart, 1873.

Urkunden der Benedictiner-Abtei Unserer Lieben Frau zu den Schotten in Wien. Ed. Ernest Hauswirth. (Fontes rerum Austriacarum, Zweite Abtheilung, 18.) Vienna, 1859.

Die Urkunden der Stadt Nördlingen. Ed. Karl Puchner. Augsburg, 1952.

Die Urkunden des Bisthums Minden vom J. 1201—1300. Ed. H. Hoogeweg. (Westfälisches Urkunden-Buch, 6.) Münster, 1898.

Die Urkunden des Bisthums Münster von 1201—1300. Ed Roger Wilmans. (Westfälisches Urkunden-Buch, 3.) Münster, 1871.

Die Urkunden des Bisthums Paderborn vom J. 1201—1300. Ed. Roger Wilmans and Heinrich Finke. (Westfälisches Urkunden-Buch, 4.) Münster, 1874—1894.

Die Urkunden des Hochstifts Augsburg 769—1420. Ed. Walter E. Vock. (Schwäbische Forschungsgemeinschaft bei der Kommission für bayerische Landesgeschichte, Reihe 2a, 7.) Augsburg, 1959.

Die Urkunden des kölnischen Westfalens vom J. 1200—1300. No editor. (Westfälisches Urkunden-Buch, 7.) Münster, 1908—1919.

Die Urkunden des Stiftsarchivs Zofingen. Ed. Georg Boner. (Aargauer Urkunden, 10.) Aarau, 1945.

Urkunden- und Quellenbuch zur Geschichte der altluxemburgischen Territorien bis zur burgundischen Zeit. Ed. Camillus Wampach. 3 and 5. Luxembourg, 1939—1948.

Urkunden zur Geschichte des Bisthums Breslau im Mittelalter. Ed. Gustav Adolf Stenzel. Breslau, 1845.

Die Urkunden zur Geschichte des deutschen Etschlandes und des Vintschgaus. Ed. Franz Huter. 3. (Tiroler UB, Abteilung I.) Innsbruck, 1957.

UB der Deutschordens-Ballei Hessen. Ed. Arthur Wyss. 1 and 3. (PPrStA, 3 and 73.) Leipzig, 1879—1899.

UB der ehemals freien Reichsstadt Mühlhausen in Thüringen. Ed. Karl Herquet. (GQProvSachs, 3.) Halle, 1874.

UB der erfurter Stifte und Klöster. Ed. Alfred Overmann. 1. (GQProvSachs, Neue Reihe, 5.) Magdeburg, 1926.

UB der Kustodien Goldberg und Breslau. Ed. Chrysogonus Reisch. 1. (Monumenta Germaniae Franciscana, 2. Abteilung, 1.) Düsseldorf, 1917.

UB der Pfarrei Rufach. Ed. Theobald Walter. (Beiträge zur Geschichte der Stadt Rufach, 1.) Rouffach, 1900.

UB der Reichsstadt Frankfurt: Codex diplomaticus Moenofrancofurtanus. Ed. Johann Friedrich Boehmer and Friedrich Lau. 1. Frankfurt, 1901.

248   THE FRIARS AND GERMAN SOCIETY

UB der Stadt Basel. Ed. Rudolf Wackernagel and Rudolf Thommen. 1 and 2. Basel, 1890–1893.

UB der Stadt Erfurt. Ed. Carl Beyer. 1. (GQProvSachs, 23.) Halle, 1889.

UB der Stadt Esslingen. Ed. Adolf Diehl and K.H.S. Pfaff. 1. (WürttGQ, 4.) Stuttgart, 1899.

UB der Stadt Friedberg. Ed. Max Foltz. 1. (Veröffentlichungen der historischen Kommission für Hessen und Waldeck, 3.) Marburg, 1904.

UB der Stadt Göttingen bis zum Jahre 1400. Ed. Gustav Schmidt. 1. (UBHistVerNSachs, 6.) Hanover, 1863.

UB der Stadt Goslar. Ed. Georg Bode. 1. (GQProvSachs, 29.) Halle, 1893.

UB der Stadt Halberstadt. Ed. Gustav Schmidt. 1. (GQProvSachs, 7.) Halle, 1878.

UB der Stadt Hannover. Ed. C.L. Grotefend and G.F. Fiedeler. 1. (UBHistVerNSachs, 5.) Hanover, 1860.

UB der Stadt Heilbronn. Ed. Eugen Knupfer. 1. (WürttGQ, 5.) Stuttgart, 1904.

UB der Stadt Lübeck. No editor. 1 and 2. (Codex diplomaticus Lubecensis, 1ste Abtheilung.) Lübeck, 1843–1858.

UB der Stadt Lüneburg bis zum Jahre 1369. Ed. W.F. Volger. (UBHistVerNSachs, 8.) Hanover, 1872.

UB der Stadt Magdeburg. Ed. Gustav Hertel. 1. (GQProvSachs, 26.) Halle, 1892.

UB der Stadt Rottweil. Ed. Heinrich Günter. 1. (WürttGQ, 3.) Stuttgart, 1896.

UB der Stadt Strassburg. Ed. Wilhelm Wiegand and Aloys Schulte. 1, 2, 3, and 4. Strasbourg, 1879–1898.

UB der Stadt und Landschaft Zürich. Ed. J. Escher and P. Schweizer. 1, 2, 3, and 4. Zürich, 1890–1898.

UB der Stadt Worms. Ed. Heinrich Boos. 1 and 2. Berlin, 1886–1890.

UB der Vögte von Weida, Gera und Plauen. Ed. Berthold Schmidt. 1. (Thüringische Geschichtsquellen, NF, 2.) Jena, 1885.

UB des Herzogthums Steiermark. Ed. J. von Zahn. 2 and 3. Graz, 1879–1903.

UB des Hochstifts Halberstadt und seiner Bischöfe. Ed. Gustav Schmidt. 2 and 4. (PPrStA, 21 and 40.) Leipzig, 1884–1889.

UB des Hochstifts Hildesheim und seiner Bischöfe. Ed. H. Hoogeweg. 2 and 3. (QDGNSachs, 6 and 11.) Hanover, 1901–1903.

UB des Hochstifts Meissen. Ed. E.G. Gersdorf. 1. (Codex diplomaticus Saxoniae regiae, Zweiter Haupttheil.) Leipzig, 1864.

Urkunden-Buch des Landes ob der Enns. No editor. 4. Vienna, 1867.

UB für die Geschichte des Niederrheins oder des Erzstifts Cöln, der Fürstenthümer Jülich und Berg, Geldern, Meurs, Cleve und Mark, und der Reichsstifte Elten, Essen und Werden. Ed. Theodor Josef Lacomblet. 2 and 3. Düsseldorf, 1846–1853.

UB zur Geschichte der Herren von Hanau und der ehemaligen Provinz Hanau. Ed. Heinrich Reimer. 1. (PPrStA, 48.) Leipzig, 1891.

UB zur Geschichte der jetzt die preussischen Regierungsbezirke Coblenz und Trier bildenden mittelrheinischen Territorien. 3. Ed. Leopold Eltester and Adam Goerz. Koblenz, 1874.

Urkundenregesten zur Geschichte des Zisterzienserinnenklosters Himmels-pforten 1231–1400, (Regesta Herbipolensia, IV.). Ed. Hermann Hoff-mann. (Quellen und Forschungen zur Geschichte des Bistums und Hochstifts Würzburg, 14.) Würzburg, 1962.

Voigt, Georg. "Die Denkwürdigkeiten (1207–1238) des Minoriten Jordanus von Giano." *Abhandlungen der philologisch-historischen Classe der königlich sächsischen Gesellschaft der Wissenschaften,* 5 (1870), 421–545.

Wakefield, Walter L. and Austin P. Evans, eds. *Heresies of the High Middle Ages.* (Records of Civilization: Sources and Studies, 81.) New York, 1969.

Wilmans, R. "Ergänzungen zu den Regesta Pontificum Romanorum von Jaffé und Potthast." *Archivalische Z,* 3 (1878), 31–60.

Winkelmann, Eduard, ed. *Fratris Arnoldi ord. Praed. De correctione ecclesiae epistola.* Berlin, 1865.

Wirtembergisches UB. No editor. 11 vols. Stuttgart, 1849–1913.

Wittmer, Ch.. "L'Obituaire des Dominicaines des Strasbourg (1238–1478)." *AFP,* 20 (1950), 415–423.

Secondary Sources

Aldinger, P. *Die Neubesetzung der deutschen Bistümer unter Papst Innocenz IV. 1243–1254.* Leipzig, 1900.

Altaner, Berthold. *Die Dominikanermissionen des 13. Jahrhunderts.* (Bres-lauer Studien zur historischen Theologie, 3.) Habelschwerdt, Silesia, 1924.

Arnold, Wilhelm. *Zur Geschichte des Eigentums in den deutschen Städten.* Basel, 1861.

Aubin, Hermann, Ludwig Petry and Herbert Schlenger. *Geschichte Schlesiens.* 1. Stuttgart, 1961.

Auer, Josef. *Studien zu den Reformschriften für das zweite lyoner Konzil.* Freiburg im B., 1910.

Auweiler, Edwin J. *The "Chronica Fratris Jordani a Giano."* Washington, 1917.

Banasch, Richard. *Die Niederlassungen der Minoriten zwischen Weser und Elbe im dreizehnten Jahrhundert.* Breslau, 1891.

Battes, Julius. "Das Vordringen der Franziskaner in Hessen und die Entwick-lung der einzelnen Konvente bis zur Reformation." *FS,* 18 (1931), 309–340.

Baur, Ludwig. "Die Ausbreitung der Bettelorden in der Diöcese Konstanz." *Freiburger Diöcesan-Archiv,* NF, 1 (1900), 1–101; 2 (1901), 1–107.

Bayley, Charles C. *The Formation of the German College of Electors in the Mid-Thirteenth Century.* Toronto, 1949.

Bennett, Ralph Francis. *The Early Dominicans: Studies in Thirteenth-Cen-tury Dominican History.* Cambridge, England, 1937.

Berger, Elie. *Thomae Cantipratensis Bonum universale de apibus.* Paris, 1895.

250   THE FRIARS AND GERMAN SOCIETY

Biack, Otto and Anton Kerschbaumer. *Geschichte der Stadt Tulln.* Tulln, 1966.

Biernacki, Jan Kazimierz. *Speculum Minorum.* Cracow, 1688.

Bihl, Michael. "Chronique étrangère, 1914–1920." *AFH,* 16 (1923), 263–290.

_____. "Das Gründungsjahr der ersten Niederlassung der Franziskaner in Fulda." *Fuldaer Geschichtsblätter,* 4 (1905), 30–32.

Blanke, Fritz. "Die Entscheidungsjahre der Preussenmission (1206–1274)." *Heidenmission und Kreuzzugsgedanke in der deutschen Ostpolitik des Mittelalters,* ed. Helmut Beumann, pp. 389–416. Darmstadt, 1963.

_____. "Die Missionsmethode des Bischofs Christian von Preussen." Ibid., pp. 337–363.

Bligny, Bernard. "Les Premiers Chartreux et la pauvreté." *Le Moyen âge,* 57 (1951), 27–60.

Bonenfant, Paul and G. Despy. "La Noblesse en Brabant aux XIIe et XIIIe siècles: Quelques sondages." *Le Moyen âge,* 64 (1958), 27–66.

Bonenfant, Paul. "L'Origine des villes brabançonnes et la 'route' de Bruges à Cologne." *Revue belge de philologie et d'histoire,* 31 (1953), 399–447.

Boner, Georg. "Das Predigerkloster in Basel von der Gründung bis zur Klosterreform 1233–1429." *Basler Z für Geschichte und Altertumskunde,* 33 (1934), 195–303; 34 (1935), 107–259.

_____. "Ueber den Dominikanertheologen Hugo von Strassburg." *AFP,* 24 (1954), 269–286.

Boos, Heinrich. *Geschichte der rheinischen Städtekultur von ihren Anfängen bis zur Gegenwart mit besonderer Berücksichtigung der Stadt Worms.* 4 vols. Berlin, 1897–1901.

Borst, Arno. *Die Katharer.* (MGH Schriften, 12.) Stuttgart, 1953.

_____. "Das Rittertum im Hochmittelalter: Idee und Wirklichkeit." *Saeculum,* 10 (1959), 213–231.

Bosl, Karl, A. Gieysztor, F. Graus, M. M. Postan, and F. Seibt. *Eastern and Western Europe in the Middle Ages.* Ed. Geoffrey Barraclough. London, 1970.

Bosl, Karl. *Frühformen der Gesellschaft im mittelalterlichen Europa: Ausgewählte Beiträge zu einer Strukturanalyse der mittelalterlichen Welt.* Munich, 1964.

_____. *Die Reichsministerialität der Salier und Staufer: Ein Beitrag zur Geschichte des hochmittelalterlichen deutschen Volkes, Staates und Reiches.* (MGH Schriften, 10.) Stuttgart, 1950–1951.

Braun, Paul. "Der Beichtvater der heiligen Elisabeth und deutsche Inquisitor Konrad von Marburg." *Beiträge zur hessischen Kirchengeschichte,* Ergh. 4 (1911), 248–300, 331–364.

_____. "Der Ketzerprozess des Propstes Minnike von Neuwerk in Goslar." *Z des Vereins für Kirchengeschichte in der Provinz Sachsen,* 6 (1909), 212–218.

Bronisch, Gerhard. "Die Franziskaner-Kloster-Kirche in Berlin." *Mitteilungen des Vereins für die Geschichte Berlins*, 50 (1933), 89–142.

Brooke, C.N.L. "Heresy and Religious Sentiment: 1000–1250." *Bulletin of the Institute of Historical Research*, 41 (1968), 115–131.

———. "The Missionary at Home: The Church in the Towns, 1000–1250." *The Mission of the Church and the Propagation of the Faith*, ed. G.J. Cuming, pp. 59–83. (Papers Read at the Seventh Summer Meeting and the Eighth Winter Meeting of the Ecclesiastical History Society.) Cambridge, England, 1970.

Brooke, Rosalind B. *Early Franciscan Government: Elias to Bonaventure.* Cambridge, England, 1959.

Brunner, Sebastian. *Der Prediger-Orden in Wien und Oesterreich.* Vienna, 1867.

Bumke, Joachim. *Studien zum Ritterbegriff im 12. und 13. Jahrhundert.* (Beihefte zum Euphorion: Z für Literaturgeschichte, 1.) Heidelberg, 1964.

Callebaut, André. "Autour de la rencontre à Florence de S. François et du Cardinal Hugolin (en été 1217)." *AFH*, 19 (1926), 530–558.

———. "Le Chapitre général de 1272 célébré à Lyon." *AFH*, 13 (1920), 305–317.

The Cambridge Economic History of Europe. Ed. M.M. Postan. 1. Cambridge, England, 1966.

The Cambridge History of Poland. Ed. W.F. Reddaway, J.H. Penson, O. Halecki, R. Dyboski. Cambridge, England, 1950.

Cantor, Norman F. "The Crisis of Western Monasticism, 1050–1130." *AHR*, 66 (1960), 47–67.

———. "Medieval Historiography as Modern Political and Social Thought." *The Journal of Contemporary History*, 3 (1968), 55–74.

Cardauns, Hermann. *Konrad von Hostaden: Erzbischof von Köln (1238–61).* Cologne, 1880.

Casutt, Laurentius. *Die Handschriften mit lateinischen Predigten Bertholds von Regensburg O. Min. ca. 1210–1272.* Fribourg, 1961.

Chapotin, Marie-Dominique. *Histoire des Dominicains de la province de France.* Rouen, 1898.

Chenu, M.-D. "Moines, clercs, laics au carrefour de la vie évangélique (XII s.)." *RHE*, 49 (1954), 59–89.

Chronica conventus S. Crucis Coloniensis. (Analecta sacri ordinis fratrum Praedicatorum, 1.) Rome, 1893.

Delorme, Ferdinand. "La Bonne Date de la bulle 'Cum dilecti' d'Honorius III." *AFH*, 12 (1919), 591–593.

Denholm-Young, Noël. *Richard of Cornwall.* Oxford, 1947.

Dereine, Charles. "Les Origines de Prémontré." *RHE*, 42 (1947), 352–378.

Dickinson, Robert, E. "The Development and Distribution of the Medieval German Town." *Geography*, 27 (1942), 9–21, 47–53.

Dondaine, Antoine. "Durand de Huesca et la polémique anti-cathare." *AFP*, 29 (1959), 228–276.

_____. "La Hiérarchie cathare en Italie." *AFP*, 19 (1949), 280–313; 20 (1950), 234–324.

_____. "L'Origine de l'hérésie médiévale." *Rivista di storia della chiesa in Italia*, 6 (1952), 47–78.

_____. "Aux origines du Valdéisme. Une profession de foi de Valdès." *AFP*, 16 (1946). 191–235.

Donin, Richard Kurt. *Die Bettelordenskirchen in Oesterreich: Zur Entwicklungsgeschichte der österreichischen Gotik.* Baden bei Wien, 1935.

Dornfeld, Ernst. *Untersuchungen zu Gottfried Hagens Reimchronik der Stadt Köln nebst Beiträgen zur mittelripuarischen Grammatik.* (Germanistische Abhandlungen, 40.) Breslau, 1912.

Dressler, Fridolin. *Petrus Damiani: Leben und Werk.* (Studia Anselmiana, 34.) Rome, 1954.

Dungern, Otto Freiherr von. *Adelherrschaft im Mittelalter.* Munich, 1927.

Emery, Richard W. *The Friars in Medieval France: A Catalogue of French Mendicant Convents, 1200–1500.* New York, 1962.

_____. "The Second Council of Lyons and the Mendicant Orders." *The Catholic Historical Review*, 39 (1953), 257–271.

Ennen, Leonard. *Geschichte der Stadt Köln.* 5 vols. Cologne, 1863–1880.

Erdmann, Carl. "Der Heidenkrieg in der Liturgie und die Kaiserkrönung Ottos I." *Heidenmission und Kreuzzugsgedanke in der deutschen Ostpolitik des Mittelalters*, ed. Helmut Beumann, pp. 47–64. Darmstadt, 1963.

Eubel, Konrad. *Geschichte der kölnischen Minoriten-Ordensprovinz.* (Veröffentlichungen des historischen Vereins für den Niederrhein, 1.) Cologne, 1906.

_____. *Geschichte der oberdeutschen (strassburger) Minoriten-Provinz.* Würzburg, 1886.

_____. "Der Minorit Heinrich von Lützelburg, Bischof von Semgallen, Curland und Chiemsee." *HJb*, 6 (1885), 92–103.

_____. "Die Minoriten Heinrich Knoderer u. Konrad Probus." *HJb*, 9 (1888), 393–449, 650–673.

Evans, Austin P. "Social Aspects of Medieval Heresy." *Persecution and Liberty: Essays in Honor of George Lincoln Burr*, pp. 93–116. New York, 1931.

Fassbinder, Maria. *Die selige Agnes von Prag, Eine königliche Klarissin.* Werl, 1957.

Fein, Hella. *Die staufischen Städtegründungen im Elsass.* (Schriften des wissenschaftlichen Instituts der Elsass-Lothringer im Reich an der Universität Frankfurt, NF, 25.) Frankfurt am Main, 1939.

Ficker, Julius. "Die gesetzliche Einführung der Todesstrafe für Ketzerei." *MIOG*, 1 (1880), 177–226.

Fischer, Karl. *Die Erbleihe im Köln des 12. bis 14. Jahrhunderts.* Düsseldorf, 1939.

Förg, Ludwig. *Die Ketzerverfolgung in Deutschland unter Gregor IX: Ihre Herkunft, ihre Bedeutung und ihre rechtlichen Grundlagen.* Berlin, 1932.

Freed, John B. "The Friars and the Delineation of State Boundaries in the Thirteenth Century." *Order and Innovation in the Middle Ages: Essays in Honor of Joseph R. Strayer,* ed. William C. Jordan, Bruce McNab, and Teofilo F. Ruiz, pp. 31−40, 425−428. Princeton, 1976.

──────. "The Origins of the European Nobility: The Problem of the Ministerials." *Viator,* 7 (1976), 211−241.

──────. "Urban Development and the *Cura monialium* in Thirteenth-Century Germany." *Viator,* 3 (1972), 311−327.

Friederichs, Heinz F. "Herkunft und ständische Zuordnung des Patriziats der wetterauischen Reichsstädte bis zum Ende des Staufertums." *Hessisches Jahrbuch für Landesgeschichte,* 9 (1959), 37−75.

Friess, G.E. "Geschichte der oesterreichischen Minoritenprovinz." *Archiv für österreichische Geschichte,* 64 (1882), 79−245.

Gatz, Johannes. "Franziskanerkloster St. Jakob am Anger, München." *BFA,* 3 (1957), 7−16.

──────. "Schaffhausen: Franziskaner-Konventualenkloster." *AFA,* 1 (1956), 125−146.

Gidžiunas, Victor. "De missionibus fratrum Minorum in Lituania (saec. XIII et XIV)." *AFH,* 42 (1949), 3−36.

Glassberger, Nicholas. *Chronica.* (AF, 2.) Quaracchi, 1887.

Goll, Jaroslav. "Zu Brunos von Olmütz Bericht an Papst Gregor X (1273)." *MIOG,* 23 (1902), 487−490.

Gonzaga, Francesco. *De origine seraphicae religionis Franciscanae eiusque progressibus de regularis observanciae institutione, forma administrationis ac legibus, admirabilique eius propagatione.* Rome, 1587.

Gottlob, Adolf. "Die Gründung des Dominikanerklosters Warburg." *Z für vaterländische Geschichte und Altertumskunde,* 60 (1902), 109−175.

Graefe, Friedrich. *Die Publizistik in der letzten Epoche Kaiser Friedrichs II.* (Heidelberger Abhandlungen zur mittleren und neueren Geschichte, 24.) Heidelberg, 1909.

Grän, Sigfrid. "Frankfurt am Main: Franziskaner-Konventualen." *AFA,* 6 (1960), 120−170.

Gratien. *Histoire de la fondation et l'évolution de l'ordre des frères Mineurs au XIIIe siècle.* Paris, 1928.

Grau, Engelbert. "Die ersten Brüder des hl. Franziskus." *FS* 40 (1958), 132−144.

Greiderer, Vigilius. *Germania Franciscana seu chronicon geographo-historicum ordinis S.P. Francisci in Germania.* 2 vols. (Innsbruck, 1777−1781). Vol. 3, ed. Gerold Fussenegger, (AFA, 11.) Ulm, 1964.

Greven, Josef. "Engelbert der Heilige und die Bettelorden." *Bonner Z für Theologie und Seelsorge,* 2 (1925), 32−48.

Grote, Otto Freiherr. *Lexicon deutscher Stifter, Klöster und Ordenshäuser.* 1. Osterwieck a. Harz, 1881.

THE FRIARS AND GERMAN SOCIETY

Grünhagen, Colmar. *Geschichte Schlesiens*. 1. Gotha, 1884.

Grundmann, Herbert. "Friedrich II. und das Geistesleben seiner Zeit." *Stupor Mundi: Zur Geschichte Friedrichs II. von Hohenstaufen*, ed. Günther Wolf, pp. 359–364. Darmstadt, 1966.

_____. *Religiöse Bewegungen im Mittelalter: Untersuchungen über die geschichtlichen Zusammenhänge zwischen der Ketzerei, den Bettelorden und der religiösen Frauenbewegung im 12. und 13. Jahrhundert und über die geschichtlichen Grundlagen der deutschen Mystik.* 1st ed. Berlin, 1935. 2nd ed. Darmstadt, 1966.

Guiraud, Jean. *Histoire de l'Inquisition au moyen âge.* 2 vols. Paris, 1935–1938.

Hävernick, Walter. *Der kölner Pfennig im 12. und 13. Jahrhundert.* (Vierteljahrschrift für Sozial- und Wirtschaftsgeschichte, Beiheft 18.) Stuttgart, 1930.

Hamann, Manfred. *Mecklenburgische Geschichte von den Anfängen bis zur landständischen Union von 1523.* Cologne, 1968.

Hampe, Karl. *Geschichte Konradins von Hohenstaufen.* Innsbruck, 1894.

Hasse, Hermann Gustav. *Geschichte der sächsischen Klöster in der Mark Meissen und Oberlausitz.* Gotha, 1888.

Hauck, Albert. "Hugo Ripilin." *ZKiG*, 32 (1911), 378–385.

Haupt, Karl. "Augsburg Franziskaner-Konventualen." *BFA*, 5 (1961), 341–494.

Heins, Walter. "Das ehemalige Franziskanerkloster in Coburg." *BFA*, 1 (1954), 121–138.

Hellmann, Manfred. "Bemerkungen zur sozialgeschichtlichen Erforschung des Deutschen Ordens." *HJb*, 80 (1960), 126–142.

Hinnebusch, William A. *The Early English Friars Preacher.* (DHIHFP, 14.) Rome, 1951.

_____. *The History of the Dominican Order: Origins and Growth to 1500.* 1. Staten Island, New York, 1966.

Hintze, Otto. *Das Königtum Wilhelms von Holland.* Leipzig, 1885.

Hirsch, Hans. "Der mittelalterliche Kaisergedanke in den liturgischen Gebeten." *Heidenmission und Kreuzzugsgedanke in der deutschen Ostpolitik des Mittelalters*, ed. Helmut Beumann, pp. 22–46. Darmstadt, 1963.

Hoffmann, Hermann. "Franziskanerkloster Rothenburg o. d. T." *BFA*, 3 (1957), 517–636.

Holder-Egger, Oswald. "Studien zu thüringischen Geschichtsquellen." *Neues Archiv der Gesellschaft für ältere deutsche Geschichtskunde*, 20 (1895), 373–421, 569–637; 21 (1896), 235–297, 441–546, 685–735; 25 (1900), 81–127.

Hoogeweg, H. "Bischof Konrad II. von Hildesheim als Reichsfürst." *Z des historischen Vereins für Niedersachsen* (1899), 238–265.

_____. *Die Stifte und Klöster der Provinz Pommern.* 2 vols. Stettin, 1924–1925.

Jacobi, Franz. *Das Franziskanerkloster zu Andernach.* Münster, 1936.

Jansen, Franz. "Verzeichnis von Klöstern des Franziskanerordens in der Rheinprovinz." *FS*, 13 (1926), 5–32.

Jörg, Peter Josef. "Albertus Magnus und Würzburg." *MfJb*, 2 (1950), 53–77.

Joho, Jean-Jacques. La Naissance de trois couvents de frères Mineurs: Berne, Fribourg, Lausanne." *Revue historique vaudois*, 67 (1959), 49–75.

Jonghe, Bernaert de. *Belgium Dominicanum sive historia provinciae Germaniae inferioris sacri ordinis FF. Praedicatorum*. Brussels, 1719.

———. *Desolata Batavia Dominicana seu descriptio brevis omnium conventuum et monasteriorum sacri ordinis Praedicatorum quae olim extiterunt in Belgio confoederato*. Ghent, 1717.

Kaeppeli, Thomas. "Heidenricus, Bischof von Kulm (†1263): Verfasser eines Traktates *De amore S. Trinitatis*." *AFP*, 30 (1960), 196–205.

Kahl, Hans-Dietrich. "*Compellere intrare*. Die Wendenpolitik Bruns von Querfurt im Lichte hochmittelalterlichen Missions- und Völkerrechts." *Heidenmission und Kreuzzugsgedanke in der deutschen Ostpolitik des Mittelalters*, ed. Helmut Beumann, pp. 177–274. Darmstadt, 1963.

Kantorowicz, Ernst. *Frederick the Second 1194–1250*. Trans. E.O. Lorimer. New York, 1931.

Karst, Valentin. "Dieburg: Franziskaner-Konventualen." *AFA*, 4 (1958), 178–214.

Kaufmann, Alexander. *Thomas von Chantimpré*. (Görres-Gesellschaft zur Pflege der Wissenschaft im katholischen Deutschland, 1.) Cologne, 1899.

Keck, Sigismund. "Lindau Franziskaner-Konventualen." *BFA*, 5 (1961), 551–604.

Kelleter, Heinrich. "Gottfried Hagen und sein Buch von der Stadt Köln." *WZ*, 13 (1894), 150–218.

Kempf, Johann. *Geschichte des Deutschen Reiches während des grossen Interregnums*. Würzburg, 1893.

Kerling, Nelly Johanna Martina. *Commercial Relations of Holland and Zeeland with England from the Late 13th Century to the Close of the Middle Ages*. Leiden, 1954.

Keussen, Hermann. *Topographie der Stadt Köln im Mittelalter*. 2 vols. Bonn, 1910.

Keyser, Erich. *Deutsches Städtebuch: Handbuch städtischer Geschichte*. 4 vols. Stuttgart and Berlin, 1939–1964.

Kleinermanns, Josef. *Der selige Heinrich: Stifter des Dominicanerklosters in Köln*. Cologne, 1900.

Kleist, Wolfgang. *Der Tod des Erzbischofs Engelbert von Köln*. Münster, 1918.

Klinkenberg, Hans Martin. "Zur Interpretation des Grossen Schied." *Jahrbuch des kölnischen Geschichtsvereins*, 25 (1950), 91–127.

Kluckholm, Paul. *Die Ministerialität in Südostdeutschland vom zehnten bis zum Ende des dreizehnten Jahrhunderts*. (Quellen und Studien zur Verfassungsgeschichte des Deutschen Reiches in Mittelalter und Neuzeit, 4.) Weimar, 1910.

Knowles, David and R. Neville Hadcock. *Medieval Religious Houses: England and Wales.* London, 1953.

Knowles, David. *The Religious Houses of Medieval England.* London, 1940.

Koch, Adolf. *Die frühesten Niederlassungen der Minoriten im rechtsrheinischen Bayern.* Heidelberg, 1880.

Koch, Heinrich Hubert. *Das Dominikanerkloster zu Frankfurt am Main.* Freiburg im Breisgau, 1892.

Koch, Ludwig. *Graf Elger von Hohnstein: Der Begründer des Dominikanerordens in Thüringen.* Gotha, 1865.

Köhler, Hermann. *Die Ketzerpolitik der deutschen Kaiser und Könige in den Jahren 1152–1254.* (Jenaer historische Arbeiten, 6.) Bonn, 1913.

Koehne, Carl. *Der Ursprung der Stadtverfassung in Worms, Speier und Mainz: Ein Beitrag zur Geschichte des Städtewesens im Mittelalter.* (Untersuchungen zur deutschen Staats- und Rechtsgeschichte, 31.) Breslau, 1890.

Köster, Karl. "Die Geschichtsschreibung der kolmarer Dominikaner im 13. Jahrhundert." *Schicksalswege am Oberrhein: Beiträge zur Kultur- und Staatenkunde,* pp. 1–100. (Elsass-lothringisches Jahrbuch, 22.) Heidelberg, 1952.

Kothe, Wilhelm. *Kirchliche Zustände Strassburgs im Vierzehnten Jahrhundert.* Freiburg im Breisgau, 1903.

Koudelka, Vladimir J. "Zur Geschichte der böhmischen Dominikanerprovinz im Mittelalter." *AFP,* 25 (1955), 75–99; 26 (1956), 127–160; 27 (1957), 39–119.

Krautheimer, Richard. *Die Kirchen der Bettelorden in Deutschland.* Cologne, 1925.

Krüger, Emil. "Die Grafen von Werdenberg-Heiligenberg und von Werdenberg-Sargans." *Mitteilungen zur vaterländischen Geschichte herausgegeben vom historischen Verein in St. Gallen,* 22 (1887), 109–398.

Kruse, Ernst. *Kölnische Geldgeschichte bis 1386 nebst Beiträgen zur kurrheinischen Geldgeschichte bis zum Ende des Mittelalters.* (WZ, Ergh. 4.) Trier, 1888.

––––––. "Verfassungsgeschichte der Stadt Strassburg besonders im 12. und 13. Jahrhunderts." *WZ,* Ergh. 1 (1884), 1–64.

Kühnert, Ernst. "Das Dominikanerkloster zu Reval." *Beiträge zur Kunde Estlands,* 12 (1926), 5–46.

Lambert, Malcolm D. *Franciscan Poverty: The Doctrine of the Absolute Poverty of Christ and the Apostles in the Franciscan Order 1210–1323.* London, 1961.

Lampen, Willibrord. "Joannes van Diest, O.F.M." *Bijdragen voor de Geschiedenis van het Bisdom van Haarlem,* 44 (1926), 299–312.

Lau, Friedrich. "Beiträge zur Verfassungsgeschichte der Stadt Köln." *WZ,* 14 (1895), 172–195, 315–343.

––––––. *Die Entwicklung der kommunalen Verfassung und Verwaltung der Stadt Köln bis zum Jahre 1396.* Bonn, 1898.

––––––. "Das kölner Patriziat bis zum Jahre 1325," *Mitteilungen aus dem Stadtarchiv von Köln,* 9 (1894), 65–89, 358–381; 10 (1895), 103–158.

Lea, Henry Charles. *A History of the Inquisition of the Middle Ages.* 3 vols. New York, 1888.

Le Goff, Jacques. "Apostolat mendiant et fait urbain dans la France médiévale: l'implantation des ordres mendiants. Programme-questionnaire pour une enquête." *Annales,* 23 (1968), 335–352.

———. "Ordres mendiants et urbanisation dans la France médiévale: État de l'enquête." *Annales,* 25 (1970), 924–946.

Lemmens, Leonhard. "Annales Minorum Prussicorum." *AFH,* 6 (1913), 702–704.

Lempp, Ed. "David von Augsburg." *ZKiG,* 19 (1899), 15–46, 340–360.

Lerner, Robert E. *The Heresy of the Free Spirit in the Later Middle Ages.* Berkeley, 1972.

Leyser, K. "The German Aristocracy from the Ninth to the Early Twelfth Century: A Historical and Cultural Sketch." *Past and Present,* 41 (1968), 25–53.

Lind, Karl. "Die Dominikanerkirche zu Retz." *Berichte und Mitteilungen des Altertums-Vereines zu Wien,* 19 (1880), 105–112.

Lins, Bernardin. "Geschichte des früheren (oberen) Franziskaner-Klosters in Ingolstadt." *Sammelblatt des historischen Vereins Ingolstadt,* 37 (1917), 1–122.

Lippens, Hugolinus. "Circa divisionem provinciae Rheni disquisito (1246–1264)." *AFH,* 48 (1955), 217–224.

Little, Lester K. "Saint Louis' Involvement with the Friars." *Church History,* 33 (1964), 125–148.

———. "Social Changes and the Vices in Latin Christendom." *AHR,* 76 (1971), 16–49.

Loë, Paulus von. *Statistisches über die Ordensprovinz Saxonia.* (QFGDD, 4.) Leipzig, 1910.

———. *Statistisches über die Ordensprovinz Teutonia.* (QFGDD, 1.) Leipzig, 1907.

Löhr, Gabriel M. "Die Mendikanten in den kölner Schreinsbüchern." *Ann-HVNiederrh,* 134 (1939), 1–33.

Loenertz, Raymond-J. "La Vie de S. Hyacinthe du lecteur Stanislas, envisagée comme source historique." *AFP,* 27 (1957), 5–38.

Lorenz, Ottokar. *Geschichte König Ottokars II. von Böhmen und seiner Zeit.* Vienna, 1866.

Maetschke, Ernst. "Der Kampf um den Grenzwald zwischen den Herzögen und Bischöfen von Breslau im 13. Jahrhundert." *Z des Vereins für Geschichte Schlesiens,* 62 (1928), 65–81.

Manteuffel, Tadeusz. *Naissance d'une hérésie: Les Adeptes de la pauvreté volontaire au moyen âge.* Trans. Anna Posner. Paris, 1970.

Mathis, Burkhard. *Die Privilegien des Franziskanerordens bis zum Konzil von Vienne (1311).* Paderborn, 1928.

Maurer, Wilhelm. "Zum Verständnis der hl. Elisabeth von Thüringen." *ZKiG,* 65 (1953/54), 16–64.

May, Karl Hermann. "Zur Geschichte Konrads von Marburg." *Hessisches Jahrbuch für Landesgeschichte*, 1 (1951), 87−109.

Mazet, Vinzenz. "Das ehemalige Franziskanerkloster Bamberg." *BFA*, 1 (1954), 449−472.

McDonnell, Ernest W. *The Beguines and Beghards in Medieval Culture: With Special Emphasis on the Belgian Scene*. New Brunswick, New Jersey, 1954.

Meersseman, G. "Les Débuts de l'ordre des frères Prêcheurs dans le comté de Flandre (1224−1280)." *AFP*, 17 (1947), 5−40.

Meier, Hermann. "Gertrud Herzogin von Oesterreich und Steiermark." *Z des historischen Vereins für Steiermark*, 23 (1927), 5−38.

Meyer von Knonau, Gerold. "Deutsche Minoriten im Streit zwischen Kaiser und Papst." *HZ*, 29 (1873), 241−253.

Moller, Herbert, "The Social Causation of the Courtly Love Complex." *Comparative Studies in Society and History*, 1 (1958−1959), 137−163.

Moore, R.I. "The Origins of Medieval Heresy." *History*, 55 (1970), 21−36.

Moorman, John. *A History of the Franciscan Order from Its Origins to the Year 1517*. Oxford, 1968.

Morghen, Raffaelo. "Problèmes sur l'origine de l'hérésie au moyen âge." *Revue historique*, 236 (1966), 1−16.

Mortier, R.P. *Histoire des maîtres généraux de l'ordre des frères Prêcheurs*. 2 vols. Paris, 1903−1905.

Müller, Berard and Victor Tschan. *Chronica de ortu et progressu almae provinciae Argentinensis sive superioris Germaniae beatae Elisabethae sacrae fratrum Minorum sancti Francisci conventualium*. Ed. Meinrad Sehi. (AFA, 12.) Ulm, 1964.

Müller, Karl Otto. *Die oberschwäbischen Reichsstädte: Ihre Entstehung und ältere Verfassung*. (Darstellungen aus der württembergischen Geschichte, 8.) Stuttgart, 1912.

Müller, Wolfgang. "Pfarrei und mittelalterliche Stadt im Bereiche Südbadens." *Neue Beiträge zur südwestdeutschen Landesgeschichte: Festschrift für Max Miller*, pp. 69−80. (Veröffentlichungen der Kommission für geschichtliche Landeskunde in Baden-Württemberg, Reihe B, Forschungen, 21.) Stuttgart, 1962.

Mülverstedt, Georg Adalbert von. "Verzeichnis der früher und jetzt noch bestehenden Klöster, Kapellen, Kalande, frommen Brüderschaften und Hospitäler sowie der geistlichen Schutzpatrone der Kirchen." *Geschichts-Blätter für Stadt und Land Magdeburg*, 2 (1867), 49−55, 121, 131−140, 298−306, 449−482, 487; 3 (1868), 283−314; 4 (1869), 541−553; 5 (1870), 522−537; 6 (1871), 250−264; 7 (1872), 172−182.

Nehlsen, Hermann. "Cives et milites de Friburg: Ein Beitrag zur Geschichte des ältesten freiburger Patriziats." *Schau-ins-Land*, 84−85 (1966−1967), 79−124.

Neumann, Eva Gertrud. *Rheinisches Beginen- und Begardenwesen: Ein mainzer Beitrag zur religiösen Bewegung am Rhein*. (Mainzer Abhandlungen zur mittleren und neueren Geschichte, 4.) Meisenheim am Glan, 1960.

Nyhus, Paul L. *The Franciscans in South Germany, 1400–1530: Reform and Revolution.* (Transactions of the American Philosophical Society NS 65, Pt. 8.) Philadelphia, 1975.

Obolensky, Dmitri. *The Bogomils: A Study in Balkan Neo-Manichaeism.* Cambridge, England, 1948.

Oncken, Hermann. "Studien zur Geschichte des Stedingerkreuzzuges." *Jahrbuch für die Geschichte des Herzogtums Oldenburg*, 5 (1896), 27–58.

Oppermann, Otto. "Untersuchungen zur Geschichte des deutschen Bürgertums und der Reichspolitik vornehmlich im 13. Jahrhundert." *Hansische Geschichtsblätter*, 17 (1911), 33–186.

Patschovsky, Alexander. *Der Passauer Anonymus: Ein Sammelwerk über Ketzer, Juden, Antichrist aus der Mitte des 13. Jahrhunderts.* (MGH Schriften, 22.) Stuttgart, 1968.

Patze, Hans. "Der Frieden von Christburg vom Jahre 1249." *Heidenmission und Kreuzzugsgedanke in der deutschen Ostpolitik des Mittelalters*, ed. Helmut Beumann, pp. 417–485. Darmstadt, 1963.

Pick, Richard. "Zwei Handschriften aus dem ehemaligen Minoritenkloster zu Bonn." *AnnHVNiederrh*, 43 (1884), 87–207.

Pipitz, F.E. *Die Grafen von Kyburg.* Leipzig, 1839.

Planitz, Hans. *Die deutsche Stadt im Mittelalter: Von der Römerzeit bis zu den Zunftkämpfen.* Graz, 1954.

Pötter, Wilhelm. *Die Ministerialität der Erzbischöfe von Köln vom Ende des 11. bis zum Ausgang des 13. Jahrhunderts.* (Studien zur kölner Kirchengeschichte, 9.) Düsseldorf, 1967.

Powell, James M. "Frederick II and the Church: A Revisionist View." *The Catholic Historical Review*, 48 (1962–63), 487–497.

Puech, Henri-Charles. "Catharisme médiéval et Bogomilisme." *Oriente ed occidente nel medio evo*, pp. 56–84. (Accademia nazionale dei Lincei, Fondazione Alessandrio Volta, 12.) Rome, 1957.

Puech, Henri-Charles and André Vaillant. *Le Traité contre les Bogomiles de Cosmas le Prêtre.* (Travaux publiés par l'Institut d'études slaves, 21.) Paris, 1945.

Pusch. "Das meininger Franziskanerkloster." *BGSFHK*, 3 (1910), 58–68.

Quadflieg, Eberhard. "Erbnamensitte beim aachener und kölner Patriziats des 13. bis 15. Jahrhunderts." *MWdGFk*, 18 (1957–1958), 169–190.

Quétif, Jacques and Jacques Echard. *Scriptores ordinis Praedicatorum*, 2 vols. Paris, 1719–1721.

Rant, Guido. *Die Franziskaner der österreichischen Provinz: Ihr Wirken in Nieder-Oesterreich, Steiermark und Krain bis zum Verfalle der Kustodie Krain und ihrer Klöster (1569).* Stein in Krain, 1908.

Ratzinger, G. *Forschungen zur bayrischen Geschichte.* Kempten, 1898.

Redlich, Oswald. *Rudolf von Habsburg: Das Deutsche Reich nach dem Untergange des alten Kaisertums.* Innsbruck, 1903.

Reeves, Marjorie. *The Influence of Prophecy in the Later Middle Ages: A Study in Joachimism.* Oxford, 1969.

Reimann, Johanna. "Die Ministerialen des Hochstifts Würzburg in sozial-, rechts- und verfassungsgeschichtliche Sicht." *MfJb*, 16 (1964), 1–266.

Remling, Franz Xaver. *Urkundliche Geschichte der ehemaligen Abteien und Klöster im jetzingen Rheinbayern*. Neustadt a/d Haardt, 1836. 2nd ed. Ed. Ph. J. Scholler. (Pfälzische Bibliothek, Vols. 1 and 2.) Munich, 1913.

Rensing, Theodor. "Die Herkunft des Dominikanergenerals Jordan von Sachsen." *Westfalen: Mitteilungen des Landesmuseums der Provinz Westfalen und des Vereins für Geschichte und Altertumskunde Westfalen*, 17 (1932), 174–175.

Rieder, Karl. *Das Leben Bertholds von Regensburg*. Freiburg im Breisgau, 1901.

Riezler, Sigmund. *Geschichte des fürstlichen Hauses Fürstenberg und seiner Ahnen bis zum Jahre 1509*. Tübingen, 1883.

Rörig, Fritz. *Die europäische Stadt und die Kultur des Bürgertums im Mittelalter*. 4th ed. Ed. Luise Rörig and Ahasver von Brandt. Göttingen, 1964.

Roisin, Simone. "L'Efflorescence cistercienne et le courant féminin de piété au XIIIe siècle." *RHE*, 39 (1943), 342–378.

Rosenwein, Barbara H. and Lester K. Little. "Social Meaning in the Monastic and Mendicant Spiritualities." *Past and Present*, 63 (1974), 4–32.

Roth, Werner. *Die Dominikaner u. Franziskaner im Deutsch-Ordensland Preussen bis zum Jahre 1466*. Königsberg, 1918.

Rothenfelder, Ludwig. "Die Wittelsbacher als Städtegründer in Bayern, von Otto I. dem Grossen bis auf Ludwig IV. den Bayern (1180–1347)." *Verhandlungen des historischen Vereines für Niederbayern*, 47 (1911), 1–106.

Rother, A. "Johannes Teutonicus (v. Wildeshausen)." *Römische Quartalschrift für christliche Altertumskunde und für Kirchengeschichte*, 9 (1895), 139–170.

Russell, Jeffrey Burton. *Dissent and Reform in the Early Middle Ages*. Berkeley, 1965.

_____. "Interpretations of the Origins of Medieval Heresy." *Mediaeval Studies*, 25 (1963), 26–53.

Russell, Josiah Cox. *Medieval Regions and their Cities*. Bloomington, Indiana, 1972.

Schäfer, Albrecht. *Die Orden des h. Franz in Württemberg bis zum Ausgang Ludwigs des Bayern*. Stuttgart, 1910.

Scheeben, Heribert Christian. *Albert der Grosse: Zur Chronologie seines Leben*. (QFGDD, 27.) Leipzig, 1931.

_____. *Albertus Magnus*. Bonn, 1932.

_____. *Beiträge zur Geschichte Jordans von Sachsen*. (QFGDD, 35.) Leipzig, 1938.

_____. *Jordan der Sachse*. Vechta in Oldenburg, 1937.

Scheerer, Felix. *Kirchen und Klöster der Franziskaner und Dominikaner in Thüringen*. (Beiträge zur Kunstgeschichte Thüringens, 2.) Jena, 1910.

Schieckel, Harald. *Herrschaftsbereich und Ministerialität der Markgrafen von Meissen im 12. und 13. Jahrhundert: Untersuchungen über Stand und*

Stammort der Zeugen markgräflicher Urkunden. (Mitteldeutsche Forschungen, 7.) Cologne, 1956.

Schlager, Patricius. *Beiträge zur Geschichte der kölnischen Franziskaner-Ordensprovinz im Mittelalter.* Cologne, 1904.

———. "Geschichte des Franziskanerkloster in Bremen." *BGSFHK*, 4—5 (1911—1912), 1—42.

———. "Inschriften auf Chorstühlen in mittelalterlichen Franziskanerkirchen." *BGSFHK*, 1 (1908), 1—15.

———. "Verzeichnis der Klöster der sächsischen Franziskanerprovinzen." *FS*, 1 (1914), 230—242.

Schmidt, C. "Notice sur le couvent et l'église des Dominicaines de Strasbourg jusqu'au seizième siècle." *Bulletin de la Société pour la conservation des monuments historique d'Alsace*, IIe série, 9 (1876), 161—224.

Schönbach, Anton E. "Studien zur Erzählungsliteratur des Mittelalters. Vierter Theil. Ueber Caesarius von Heisterbach. I." *Sitzungsberichte der kaiserlichen Akademie der Wissenschaften in Wien, Philosophisch-historische Klasse*, 144 (1902), no. 9.

———. "Studien zur Geschichte der altdeutschen Predigt." Ibid., 142 (1900), no. 7; 147 (1904), no. 5; 151 (1905), no. 2; 152 (1906), no. 7; 153 (1906), no. 4; 154 (1907), no. 1; 155 (1908), no. 5.

Schoengen, Michael. "Die Klöster des ersten Ordens vom hl. Franziskus im Königreich der Niederlande 1229—1926." *FS*, 14 (1927), 1—51.

Schomburg, Dietrich. *Die Dominikaner im Erzbistum Bremen während des dreizehnten Jahrhunderts: Mit einer einleitenden Uebersicht über die Ausbreitung des Ordens in Deutschlands bis 1250.* Brunswick, 1910.

Schulte, Aloys. *Der Adel und die deutsche Kirche im Mittelalter: Studien zur Sozial-, Rechts- und Kirchengeschichte.* 3rd ed. Darmstadt, 1958.

Schulte, Wilhelm. "Das Ende des Kirchenstreits zwischen dem breslauer Bischof Thomas II. und dem Herzog Heinrich IV." *Z des Vereins für Geschichte und Altertums Schlesiens*, 39 (1905), 199—225.

Schultze, Johannes. *Die Mark Brandenburg.* Vol. 1. *Entstehung und Entwicklung unter den askanischen Markgrafen (bis 1319).* Berlin, 1961.

Schulz, Knut. "Die Ministerialität als Problem der Stadtgeschichte: Einige allgemeine Bemerkungen, erläutert am Beispiel der Stadt Worms." *Rheinische Vierteljahrsblätter*, 32 (1968), 184—219.

———. *Ministerialität und Bürgertum in Trier: Untersuchungen zur rechtlichen und sozialen Gliederung der trierer Bürgerschaft vom ausgehenden 11. bis zum Ende des 14. Jahrhunderts.* (Rheinisches Archiv, 66.) Bonn, 1968.

Schumacher, H. A. *Die Stedinger: Beitrag zur Geschichte der Weser-Marschen.* Bremen, 1865.

Schwesinger, H. "Das Franziskanerkloster in Saalfeld a. S." *FS*, 10 (1923), 246—266.

Seitz, Anton Michael. "Die Grafen von Dillingen und ihre Klosterstiftungen."

Jahrbuch des historischen Vereins Dillingen an der Donau, 64–65 (1962–1963), 39–60.

Selge, Kurt-Victor. *Die ersten Waldenser mit Edition des Liber antiheresis des Durandus von Osca*. 2 vols. Berlin, 1967.

Showalter, Dennis E. "The Business of Salvation: Authority and Representation in the Thirteenth-Century Dominican Order." *The Catholic Historical Review*, 58 (1973), 556–574.

Siemer, Polykarp M. *Geschichte des Dominikanerklosters Sankt Magdalena in Augsburg (1225–1808)*. (QFGDD, 33.) Leipzig, 1936.

Simon, André. *L'Ordre des Pénitentes de Ste. Marie-Madeleine en Allemagne au XIIIme siècle*. Fribourg, 1918.

Southern, Richard W. *Western Society and the Church in the Middle Ages*. Harmondsworth, England, 1970.

Stein, Friedrich. *Geschichte Frankens*. 1. 2nd ed. Aalen, 1966.

Stimming, Manfred. "Kaiser Friedrich II. und der Abfall der deutschen Fürsten." *HZ*, 120 (1919), 210–249.

Stöckerl, Dagobert. *Bruder David von Augsburg: Ein deutscher Mystiker aus dem Franziskanerorden*. (Veröffentlichungen aus dem kirchenhistorischen Seminar München, IV. Reihe, 4.) Munich, 1914.

Strait, Paul. *Cologne in the Twelfth Century*. Gainesville, Florida, 1974.

Stüdeli, Bernhard E.J. *Minoritenniederlassungen und mittelalterliche Stadt: Beiträge zur Bedeutung von Minoriten- und anderen Mendikantenanlagen im öffentlichen Leben der mittelalterlichen Stadtgemeinde insbesondere der deutschen Schweiz*. (Franziskanische Forschungen, 21.) Werl, Westphalia, 1969.

Tellenbach, Gerd. *Church, State and Christian Society at the Time of the Investiture Contest*. Trans. R.F. Bennett. Oxford, 1940.

―――― . *Studien und Vorarbeiten zur Geschichte des grossfränkischen und frühdeutschen Adels*. (Forschungen zur oberrheinischen Landesgeschichte, 4.) Freiburg, 1957.

―――― . "Vom karolingischen Reichsadel zum deutschen Reichsfürstenstand." *Adel und Bauern im deutschen Staat des Mittelalters*, ed. Theodor Mayer, 2nd ed., pp. 23–73. Darmstadt, 1967.

Thouzellier, Christine. *Catharisme et Valdéisme en Languedoc à la fin du XIIe et au début du XIIIe siècle*. 2nd ed. Louvain, 1969.

Tumler, Marian. *Der Deutsche Orden im Werden, Wachsen und Wirken bis 1400*. Vienna, 1955.

Van Cleve, Thomas Curtis. *The Emperor Frederick II of Hohenstaufen: Immutator Mundi*. Oxford, 1972.

―――― . *Markward of Anweiler and the Sicilian Regency: A Study of Hohenstaufen Policy During the Minority of Frederick II*. Princeton, 1937.

Vasella, Oskar. *Geschichte des Predigerklosters St. Nicolai in Chur von seinen Anfängen bis zur I. Aufhebung (1280–1538)*. (DHIHFP, 1.) Paris, 1931.

Vauchez, André. "La Pauvreté volontaire au moyen âge." *Annales*, 25 (1970), 1566–1573.

Verheyen, Egon. *Die Minoritenkirche zu Duisburg: Neue Untersuchungen zu ihrer Geschichte.* (Duisburger Forschungen, Beiheft 3.) Duisburg-Ruhrort, 1959.

Villermont, M. de. "Les Franciscaines dans le Grand Duché de Luxembourg." *Études franciscaines*, 29 (1913), 154–170; 288–304.

Wadding, Luke, *Annales Minorum.* 2nd ed. 26 vols. Rome and Quaracchi, 1731–1933.

Walter, Johannes von. *Die ersten Wanderprediger Frankreichs: Studien zur Geschichte des Mönchtums.* Theil I. *Robert von Arbrissel.* (Studien zur Geschichte der Theologie und der Kirche, 9.) Leipzig, 1903. Neue Folge. Leipzig, 1906.

Walter-Wittenheim, G. von. *Die Dominikaner in Livland im Mittelalter.* (DHIHFP, 9.) Rome, 1938.

Wand, Karl. "Die Englandpolitik der Stadt Köln und ihrer Erzbischöfe im 12. und 13. Jahrhundert." *Aus Mittelalter und Neuzeit: Gerhard Kallen zum 70. Geburtstag*, ed. Josef Engel and Hans Martin Klinkenberg, pp. 77–96. Bonn, 1957.

Wehrmann, M. "Zur Gründung des Johannisklosters zu Stralsund." *Monatsblätter der Gesellschaft für pommersche Geschichte und Altertumskunde*, 15 (1901), 122–124.

Weise, Erich. *Die Amtsgewalt von Papst und Kaiser und die Ostmission besonders in der 1. Hälfte des 13. Jahrhunderts.* (Marburger Ostforschungen, 31.) Marburg, 1971.

Weller, Karl. "Gottfried und Konrad von Hohenlohe im Dienste Kaiser Friedrichs II. und seiner Söhne, der Könige Heinrich (VII.) und Konrad IV." *Württembergische Vierteljahrshefte für Landesgeschichte*, NF, 5 (1896), 209–233.

————. "Die staufische Städtegründung in Schwaben." *Ibid.*, 36 (1930), 145–268.

Werner, Ernst. *Pauperes Christi: Studien zur sozial-religiösen Bewegungen im Zeitalter des Reformpapstums.* Leipzig, 1956.

Werner, Ernst and Martin Erbstösser. "Sozial-religiöse Bewegungen im Mittelalter." *Wissenschaftliche Z der Karl-Marx-Universität Leipzig, Gesellschafts- und sprachwissenschaftliche Reihe*, 7 (1957/58), 257–282.

White, Hayden V. "The Gregorian Ideal and Saint Bernard of Clairvaux." *Journal of the History of Ideas*, 21 (1960), 321–348.

Wiesehoff, Josef. *Die Stellung der Bettelorden in den deutschen freien Reichsstädten im Mittelalter.* Borna-Leipzig, 1905.

Wilms, Hieronymus. *Das älteste Verzeichnis der deutschen Dominikanerinnenklöster.* (QFGDD, 24.) Leipzig, 1928.

Winkelmann, Eduard. *Kaiser Friedrich II.* 2 vols. Leipzig, 1889–1897.

Winter, Georg. *Die Ministerialität in Brandenburg: Untersuchungen zur Geschichte der Ministerialität und zum Sachsenspiegel.* (Veröffentlichungen des Vereins für Geschichte der Mark Brandenburg, 19.) Munich, 1922.

Winterfeld, Luise von. *Handel, Kapital und Patriziat in Köln bis 1400.* (Pfingstblätter des hansischen Geschichtsvereins, 16.) Lübeck, 1925.

Wunder, Gerd. "Zu den Anfängen der kölner Overstolz." *MWdGFk*, 18 (1957–58), 385–388.

Index